Praise for

UNITED STATES OF JIHAD

A *New York Times* Editors' Choice

"Mr. Bergen writes with authority and range. . . . His profiles of jihadists . . . leave the reader with a harrowing appreciation of the banality of evil and an unnerving sense of missteps made by the authorities. . . . Mr. Bergen's detailed accounts of terror plots (both executed, foiled, or failed) make for chilling reading."

—Michiko Kakutani, *New York Times*

"Excellent . . . Bergen's book is the best one-volume treatment available on the current state of jihad in America."

—Janet Napolitano, *New York Times Book Review*

"Peter Bergen is a skilled and sensitive reporter with unparalleled access to the law enforcement and intelligence communities. . . . He has written what in effect are two books about terrorism. Both are valuable. One is a riveting, thoroughly researched account of the evolving state of the threat as a growing number of American citizens join the ranks of foreign terrorist movements—and of how U.S. intelligence and law enforcement agencies are addressing the constantly shifting threat. The other is a skilled defense of . . . the Obama administration's anti-terror effort: one that attempts to steer between the perceived extremes of panicky overreaction and a failure to acknowledge how politically and socially devastating terror attacks can be."

—Walter Russell Mead, *Wall Street Journal*

"Peter Bergen . . . one of America's most prominent terrorism experts, makes a compelling and often unsettling case that, in the years since September 11, 2001, Islamist terrorism in the United States has metamorphosed. . . . The transformation of domestic jihadism has not only dispersed the Islamist terrorist threat but, in a perverse process of cultural intermingling, has partly Americanized jihad itself. The 'soft power' appeal of American culture is often considered to be one of this country's most enduring assets, but the new admixture of jihadi terror and pop culture savoir faire potentially turns this idea on its head. . . . Bergen takes a generally skeptical view of the growth of the post-9/11 national security state and of the fear-mongering about Islam that has increasingly transfixed the darker crannies of American politics. This skepticism, I think, is not only strategically and morally sound but also borne out by the facts."

—*Los Angeles Times*

"There's drama in the cases Bergen relates. . . . He makes a highly reliable guide on the road to the present day."

—Karl Vick, *Time*

"A crisply methodical detailing of the types of people and attacks involved in Islam-inspired terrorism here and abroad . . . Bergen knows his topic extremely well."

—*USA Today*

"Disturbing and topical . . . [*United States of Jihad*] is an engrossing and edifying book. . . . It is to Bergen's immense credit that, without downplaying the threat of Islamist terrorism—homegrown or directed at America by groups abroad—he refrains from overstating it and attempts to maintain perspective. . . . The author deserves kudos for simultaneously recognizing the potential of secular Muslims—who are too often ignored—to change people's attitudes."

—*Boston Globe*

"Bergen pulls you in with snappy, conversational writing . . . exploding some of the easy assumptions about jihadists in the United States."

—*Washington Post*

"Bergen, who has interviewed convicted terrorists, their families and friends, and people working across the counterterrorism profession, is the most sober guide to the subject one could hope for. . . . But Bergen also has an eye for the human factor, which makes this book, for all its horror, humane. 'Jihadization' is usually a great blow to the families of the person involved, and Bergen presents poignant family portraits."

—*Globe and Mail*

"Gripping . . . There is much to commend in Mr. Bergen's important book. Readers will benefit from his astute observations, based on numerous case studies. . . . [Mr. Bergen] offers a sobering assessment that should not be overlooked."

—*Washington Times*

"Bergen's book provides sobering reading in a feverish U.S. political climate."

—*Al Jazeera America*

"Bergen has been at the forefront of reporting on terrorism for more than twenty years. In this innovative and illuminating work . . . Bergen explores nearly every aspect of terrorist activity, from ISIS's use of social media to the FBI's development of behavioral profiles that identify potential terror activists. Both balanced and galvanizing, Bergen's meticulous portrait of violent extremism is required reading for anyone who truly wants to understand the nature of the evolving threats from within and without."

—*Booklist* (starred review)

"Bergen calmly and lucidly examines the diverse stories of the more than three hundred people in the United States who have been charged with jihadist terrorist crimes since September 11, 2001. His nuanced insights, couched within a series of gripping narratives, offer readers a solid foundation to knowledgeably face the barrage of political opinions being flung about by many Americans this election year. . . . Highly recommended for all readers seeking an informed view of current events."

—*Library Journal*

"There are a number of fine scholars of jihad, but no one matches Peter

Bergen in clarity and wisdom, qualities abundantly on display in this valuable book."

—Lawrence Wright, author of *The Looming Tower* and *Going Clear*

"Nobody burrows deeper into the horrifying world of organized terror, uncovering harrowing stories of near-misses and fatal attacks, than Peter Bergen. And nobody analyzes this fraught subject with such calm, careful rigor. His portrait of the terrorists next door and the agents who hunt them is worthy of *Homeland*—except that it's all too real."

—Franklin Foer, author of *How Soccer Explains the World*

"Peter Bergen has become one of America's most important analysts of Islamist militancy and terrorism. Here he again provides a timely, sober study of the diverse and fragmentary character of homegrown violent jihadists. He places the scale of the threat into accurate perspective without minimizing its dangers. Every American should read this book."

—Steve Coll, author of *Ghost Wars* and *Private Empire*

"A fascinating and vitally important look at the rise of American jihadists. Brilliantly reported and researched, this is an essential book for anyone who wants to understand why hundreds of Americans have turned to radical Islam."

—Anderson Cooper

"It is hard to imagine a timelier book than this one. Peter Bergen does what he does best—telling mesmerizing stories that weave together exhaustive research to illuminate a critically important subject. He shows us that the Americans among us who turn to jihad are not who we imagine them to be, suggesting ways in which we can be simultaneously more humane and more secure."

—Anne-Marie Slaughter, author of *The Idea That Is America;* president and CEO of New America

"With his latest book, Peter Bergen shows once again that he has become the premier chronicler of jihadism in the twenty-first century.

Read it and come away with a new understanding of America and of terrorism."

"In this incisive book Peter Bergen answers many questions about terrorism that preoccupy Americans today. Why does extremism appeal to some young Muslims in America? What is the nature and scope of the threat? Rich in detail and eminently readable, this unique book explains both the challenge of terrorism and the turmoil in the Muslim heartland that fuels it."

ALSO BY PETER BERGEN

MANHUNT

THE LONGEST WAR

THE OSAMA BIN LADEN I KNOW

HOLY WAR, INC.

DRONE WARS (COEDITOR)

TALIBANISTAN (COEDITOR)

الدولة الإسلامية بالعراق والشام

UNITED

STATES OF

AMERICA

JEHAD

PETER

Who Are America's Homegrown
Terrorists, and How Do We Stop Them?

BERGEN

B\D\W\Y
BROADWAY BOOKS
NEW YORK

Broadway Books and its logo, B \ D \ W \ Y, are
trademarks of Penguin Random House LLC.

Originally published in hardcover in the United States by
Crown, an imprint of the Crown Publishing Group, a division
of Penguin Random House LLC, New York, in 2016.

Library of Congress Cataloging-in-Publication Data
is available upon request.

ISBN 978-0-8041-3956-4
Ebook ISBN 978-0-8041-3955-7

Printed in the United States of America

Book design by Barbara Sturman
Cover design by Darren Haggar
Cover photograph: Steve Bronstein/Photodisc/Getty Images

10 9 8 7 6 5 4 3 2 1

First Paperback Edition

For

Sarah Elizabeth Lampert Bergen
April 24, 1936–September 10, 2015

and for

Grace Donovan Bergen,
born January 21, 2014,
and her mother,
Tresha Marie Mabile

WHOEVER FIGHTS MONSTERS SHOULD SEE TO IT THAT

IN THE PROCESS HE DOES NOT BECOME A MONSTER.

AND IF YOU GAZE LONG ENOUGH INTO AN ABYSS, THE

ABYSS WILL GAZE BACK INTO YOU.

—FRIEDRICH NIETZSCHE, *BEYOND GOOD AND EVIL*

CONTENTS

CHAPTER 1

AMERICANS FOR ISIS

AGAINST THEM MAKE READY YOUR STRENGTH TO THE UTMOST OF YOUR
POWER, INCLUDING STEEDS OF WAR, TO STRIKE TERROR INTO [THE
HEARTS OF] THE ENEMIES OF ALLAH.

—The Koran

On the thirteenth anniversary of 9/11, nineteen-year-old Mohammed Hamzah Khan sent an e-mail to the U.S. State Department inquiring about the application he had made for a passport, which had "still not arrived." Two weeks later Khan paid $2,679 for flights from Chicago to Vienna and then on to Istanbul for himself and his two younger siblings. He had planned meticulously, saving up the money for the tickets while working at a local big-box home supply store, assembling tourist visas for Turkey, and packing sleeping bags and clothes for the trip. Khan had met someone online who had provided him with the number of a contact in Istanbul who would help to get him and his siblings to the Turkish-Syrian border, and from there on to the region occupied by the Islamic State of Iraq and Syria (ISIS).

Accompanying Khan would be his seventeen-year-old sister, Mina, and his sixteen-year-old brother, Khalid, all three excited to make their pilgrimage to the Promised Land. Mina planned to marry an ISIS fighter, while Khan himself planned to serve in a combat role perhaps, or with the group's police force. As he contemplated the trip, Khan doodled in his notebook a picture of a fighter with the legend "Come to Jihad" in Arabic behind him, as well as the distinctive ISIS flag: white

Arabic letters on a black background. Meanwhile, Mina watched *Saleel Sawarim* (The Clanking of the Swords), one of a series of one-hour videos showing summary executions of ISIS's enemies. She later tweeted that she had watched it, including emoticons of a smiley face and a heart.

Earlier that month, on September 2, 2014, American journalist Steven Sotloff had been executed by ISIS following a brutal imprisonment. The beheadings of both Sotloff and his fellow hostage, James Foley (also an American journalist), were videotaped, carried out off-camera while a black-clad terrorist demanded that U.S. air strikes against ISIS cease. In an unmistakable London accent, the terrorist addressed President Barack Obama, promising that "just as your missiles continue to strike our people, our knife will continue to strike the necks of your people."

According to a *Wall Street Journal*/NBC poll, the executions were the most widely followed news story of the past five years in the United States, provoking widespread outrage. Yet even as the story developed, the three American teenagers living in suburban Chicago were finalizing their plans to join what they saw as the perfect Islamic state. Hamzah Khan and his siblings saw the soldiers of ISIS not as fanatical, Taliban-style murderers, but as the creators of a utopia.

Khan, who had been six at the time of the 9/11 attacks, wrote a three-page letter to his parents explaining why he was leaving Chicago. He told them that an Islamic utopia had been established by ISIS and that he felt obligated to "migrate" there, grandly extending "an invitation to my family" to join him. He couldn't bear that his American tax dollars would be used to kill "my Muslim brothers and sisters," and wrote that he was upset by the depravity of the West, which he described as "getting more immoral day by day." He didn't want his own children "to be exposed to filth like this." Writing in capital letters, Khan instructed his parents to "FIRST AND FOREMOST, PLEASE MAKE SURE NOT TO TELL THE AUTHORITIES."

Khan's siblings also wrote letters. His brother wrote that the "evil of this country makes me sick," citing the deaths of innocent Afghan children in attacks by American drones. His sister wrote of her longing for death and the afterlife. Both begged their parents not to call the police, seeming to understand that joining ISIS was viewed as a crime by American authorities.

The infatuation the Khan teenagers felt for ISIS was hard to square with their upbringing. Their father, Shafi, and mother, Zarine, had come to the United States from India as college students, and both readily embraced life in America, which they viewed as a "paradise." Even now, Zarine says, "Everything is so organized. The people are so nice. You know everything is by the rules." Her husband, Shafi, explains, "There's a lot of opportunities. You can do anything you want. You can be a lawyer. You can be a doctor. You can be a businessman. You can study whatever you like." While he earned a degree in environmental science from Northeastern Illinois University, Shafi worked as a gift store supervisor at Chicago's O'Hare Airport before going on to work for an Islamic charity. Zarine stayed at home with their five children. They became U.S. citizens.

The household in which the Khan children grew up was observant but not extreme. The Khan parents went out of their way to shield their children from elements of American culture they deemed too permissive, such as television shows that featured profanity. When the kids were young the TV broke, and it was never replaced. Zarine wore a veil, and all the Khan children attended Islamic schools; this was partly because the education there was better than in the local public schools—in India, Zarine and Shafi had attended Catholic schools for the same reason—but also because the Khan parents wanted their children to grow up as practicing Muslims. When Hamzah turned thirteen he spent more than two years learning to recite the Koran from memory, a feat that entails memorizing some six thousand Arabic verses.

Yet even as Zarine and Shafi respected Muslim traditions, they raised their children to be Americans. The children grew up playing basketball and reading Marvel comics and Tintin books. They shopped at Walmart and went on a vacation to Niagara Falls. The whole family pitched in to do yard work. During high school Hamzah volunteered at the local mosque but also read Japanese manga. He was a fan of TV shows such as *The Walking Dead* and *CSI* and had a girlfriend. When

Kim Kardashian was visiting Chicago, Hamzah took a selfie with her. Like many Chicagoans, he was a big fan of the Bulls and the Bears.

After high school Hamzah started studying engineering at Benedictine University. The Khans were then homeschooling Mina, who planned to be a doctor. As for so many other Muslim American families, the American Dream seemed to be working its magic for the Khans.

On October 4, 2014, Hamzah Khan rose before dawn to say the first of the five daily prayers with his father. When they returned from the local mosque at around 6:00 a.m., Shafi returned to bed and Hamzah and his brother and sister launched their plan. They folded up comforters in their beds to make it appear that they were still sleeping there, gathered their freshly issued U.S. passports and tickets to Vienna and Istanbul, and took a taxi to O'Hare Airport. Their contact in Turkey was a shadowy ISIS recruiter they had met online, Abu Qa'qa, with whom they had arranged—communicating anonymously via the smartphone messaging applications Kik and WhatsApp—to travel to Raqqa, Syria, completing a five-thousand-mile journey from the heart of the Midwest to ISIS headquarters. At last their dream of jihad was becoming a reality.

They didn't make it. U.S. Customs and Border Protection officials stopped the Khans at O'Hare. Around noon, FBI agents arrived at the Khan house, where Shafi opened the door. One of the agents asked, "Do you know where your kids are?" Shafi replied, "They are upstairs sleeping." The agent said, "No, they're at the airport. They were trying to board a plane." The Khans were in shock: Hamzah always told them where he was going, even if it was just to the nearby Walmart. The only untoward behavior the Khans had lately seen in their three teenagers was their inordinate attachment to their phones, which the parents didn't monitor with the same vigilance as they did their home computers.

At first Hamzah told FBI agents that he and his siblings were going on vacation to Istanbul to see the famous Blue Mosque, but over the course of a marathon eleven hours of interviews he revealed their plan to meet with members of ISIS. A search of the Khan household soon turned up the incriminating letters the Khan children had written to their parents. Hamzah faced up to fifteen years in prison for trying to provide "material support" to ISIS in the form of his own services. At seventeen years old, Mina faced the possibility of being charged as an adult.

The Khan kids had never been in trouble with the law; nor did federal prosecutors allege that they planned any acts of violence. Hamzah seemed motivated more by the desire to join ISIS's "perfect" Islamic state than by the prospect of fighting in ISIS's overseas campaign; Mina told FBI agents that "none of us will ever hurt anybody." But to federal prosecutors, the Khan siblings were knowingly trying to join an anti-American death cult recently designated a Foreign Terrorist Organization by the Obama administration.

Three months after the Khan teenagers were arrested, some three hundred supporters gathered in a suburban mosque on a frigid Chicago night to raise money for their defense. It was a representative cross section of the Muslim American community: computer engineers from India, doctors from Pakistan, South Asian cabdrivers, Albanian businessmen, and a sprinkling of more fundamentalist students wearing black turbans in the style of the Taliban.

The Khan family had retained Thomas Durkin to defend their oldest son. Durkin, a professorial sixty-eight-year-old lawyer and a former federal prosecutor, had represented a range of clients few would defend, including neo-Nazis and one of the key plotters of the 9/11 attacks. He greeted the congregation with a rousing *Salaam Alaikum* ("Peace be upon you") and, in a strong Chicago accent, warmed up the crowd with jokes about his Irish-Catholic background. Durkin then turned serious, saying that if Hamzah Khan had been an Irish Catholic instead of a Muslim American, the FBI would have contacted his parents about the online activity of their son.

This was close to what had happened in the case of Shannon Conley of Denver, exactly the same age as Hamzah Khan, whom FBI agents met with repeatedly beginning in late 2013 to talk her out of her plan to join ISIS. The agents suggested that she work for a humanitarian organization instead. These interventions failed; Conley was arrested at Denver International Airport in April 2014 while trying to board a flight for her trip to Syria and was sentenced to four years in prison the following year. With the Khan children, no attempts were made by the FBI to intervene or alert their parents. Instead, the FBI had mounted an investigation that could put Hamzah away for a crime he had not actually succeeded in committing.

Durkin described his client as a true believer who thought he was going to join the perfect society. In that sense, Hamzah was similar to an earlier generation of idealistic Americans who flocked to Spain in the 1930s to show their solidarity with the antifascists fighting Franco. In the absence of social media, Durkin said, Hamzah would never have been persuaded by ISIS's message. He was, in short, a misguided kid who needed to be defended against both the U.S. government, with its unlimited resources and scant respect for the rights of Muslim Americans, and the siren call of ISIS's slick propaganda. The congregation applauded loudly.

Next up was Fisal Hammouda, an Egyptian-American cleric sporting a well-trimmed short beard and a smart gray suit. Hammouda's task was to drum up money for Hamzah Khan's defense. Financing an effective defense of an alleged terrorist in federal court, where terrorism cases have a conviction rate of 99 percent, is no small matter. The cleric first made the point that America "is our home," but then segued into claims that 9/11 had been an "internal demolition job" calculated to justify a war in Afghanistan in which a million people were killed. The cleric also said that mosques across the country were riddled with government "infiltrators." Durkin and the other members of his legal team looked uncomfortable.

After shouting, "Hamzah Khan is our son!" the cleric said that one hundred thousand dollars was needed to fund Hamzah's defense. He began by asking for a ten-thousand-dollar donation, which was met with a long silence. No one in the mosque had that kind of money to give. When he lowered the ask to five thousand, a couple of hands went up, greeted by loud cries of *"Takbir!"* and *"Allahu Akbar!"*—Arabic phrases signifying the greatness of God. Smaller donations trickled in, and by the end of the evening many tens of thousands of dollars had been promised.

On January 12, 2015, Hamzah pleaded not guilty at the federal courthouse in Chicago. Outside the courthouse Zarine said, "We condemn the brutal tactics of ISIS and groups like them. And we condemn the brainwashing and the recruiting of children." Fighting back tears, her husband standing beside her, Zarine addressed herself to the leader of ISIS, Abu Bakr al-Baghdadi: "We have a message for ISIS, Mr. Baghdadi and his fellow social media recruiters: Leave our children alone!"

In 2014, ISIS made alarming strides toward becoming the "Islamic State of Iraq and Syria" it claimed to be, having seized large regions of both countries, including population centers such as Mosul, the second-largest city in Iraq. The group assumed some of the conventional trappings of a state, implementing its own police force and ambulances in the cities it controlled, and even issuing its own license plates. It also imposed Taliban-style rule (a draconian implementation of sharia, or Koranic, law that has involved throwing homosexuals to their deaths from tall buildings, lopping off the hands of thieves, beheading women accused of "sorcery," and enslaving and raping minority women) over some eight million Syrians and Iraqis. Within several months of conquering Mosul, ISIS had drawn to its banners a dozen or so affiliated terrorist groups around the Muslim world, stretching from the coast of North Africa to the mountains of the Hindu Kush.

Al-Qaeda, ISIS's rival for the leadership of the global jihadist movement, could only dream of such success. Originally an al-Qaeda off-shoot, ISIS had splintered from the group in early 2014 over a number of tactical differences. Al-Qaeda leader Osama bin Laden saw the establishment of the caliphate (the sharia-ruled Promised Land to which the Khan siblings thought they were traveling) as a distant goal, whereas ISIS had a more aggressive timetable, claiming its leader, Abu Bakr al-Baghdadi, to be the successor of the Prophet Muhammad as leader of the Islamic world. And while al-Qaeda believed that killing Muslims, at least, was generally to be avoided, an integral part of ISIS's bid for dominance was the mass murder of anyone and everyone who didn't follow its precepts to the letter.

Whenever ISIS carried out a new atrocity, whether executing hundreds of Iraqi Shia soldiers in one day, murdering more than a hundred civilian Kurds, or burning its Muslim victims alive, analysts asked why, against all strategic sense, the group seemed bent on accruing enemies. ISIS's ferocious campaign against the Shia, Kurds, Yazidis, and Christians had united every ethnic and religious group in Syria and Iraq against it. The group's beheading of the journalist James Foley galvanized much of the Western world and led to an intensified U.S.-led air campaign against its army. And when, in early 2015, ISIS burned to death a captured Jordanian pilot, most of the Arab world united in revulsion.

ISIS cemented its leadership of the global jihadist movement during the fall of 2015 with a quick succession of devastating attacks. On October 31, a local branch of ISIS brought down a Russian Metrojet airliner with a bomb shortly after it had departed Sharm el-Sheikh Airport in South Sinai, Egypt, killing all 224 people on board. This was the worst assault on commercial aviation since 9/11. On November 12, ISIS dispatched suicide bombers to a Shiite neighborhood in Beirut, killing 43; it was the most lethal attack in the city since the end of the Lebanese civil war in 1990. A day later, the organization launched the deadliest terrorist attack in the West in more than a decade. Using suicide bombings and assaults by multiple gunmen, ISIS terrorists killed 130 people at locations around Paris. Their targets were not government buildings or military facilities but rather a concert hall where an American rock band was playing, a soccer stadium, a popular restaurant—places where young Parisians typically gather on a Friday night, selected because of their very ordinariness. The message was clear: The terrorists could attack at anytime, anywhere.

Despite its dominance in the present field of global jihad, ISIS's strategic rationale is anything but modern. The group's ideology is that of a millenarian cult, certain that the End Times are approaching and that it is the vanguard in an ultimate religious war Allah has determined it will win. After seizing Mosul, Baghdadi named himself caliph, which meant that in his own mind and in the eyes of his followers he was the leader not only of ISIS but also of Muslims everywhere. ISIS's distinctive black flags are a reference to a *hadith*, a saying of the Prophet Muhammad: "If you see the black banners coming from the direction of Khorasan, then go to them, even if you have to crawl, because among them will be Allah's Caliph the Mahdi." In other words, from Khorasan (an ancient term for the region that now encompasses Afghanistan, where al-Qaeda first went into battle) will come an army bearing black flags and including the Mahdi, the Islamic savior of the world. Even the name of ISIS's English-language webzine, *Dabiq,* is an allusion to ancient prophecy; some believe the Prophet Muhammad predicted the Syrian town of Dabiq to be the site of the final battle between the armies of Islam and "Rome," which will occasion the end of time and the triumph of true Islam.

This combination of fatalism and righteousness has empowered ISIS members to kill anyone they perceive to be standing in their way, even when this threatens their position. When American aid worker Peter Kassig was murdered in November 2014, "Jihadi John," the masked British terrorist who has appeared in many ISIS videos, said of Kassig, "We bury the first crusader in Dabiq, eagerly waiting for the rest of your armies to arrive." In other words, ISIS wanted a Western ground force to invade Syria, as that would confirm the prophecy about Dabiq.

ISIS's deadly intolerance extends even to other Muslims. The group practices *takfir,* the excommunication of any Muslim who doesn't follow its particular teachings and who is therefore deemed an enemy of true Islam—guilty of apostasy, the faith's gravest crime. The highly sectarian *Dabiq* has repeatedly published images of Shia shrines and tombs (which ISIS believes to be idolatrous) that have been bombed. Iraqi Army soldiers, generally Shia, are referred to as "apostates," and photos of their executions have been a staple of the magazine. For its supporters, the rhetoric and the graphic images are further evidence that ISIS is waging a righteous war. They are part of its appeal to new recruits—proof that ISIS is enacting its promise to restore the caliphate as it purportedly existed at the time of the Prophet Muhammad.

The Khan teenagers were not alone in their infatuation with this supposed new world order. Muslims who believe that ISIS has indeed established a true caliphate consider it a religious obligation to join it, and by the end of 2016 some forty thousand "foreign fighters" had traveled to Syria. This number included a few dozen Americans. Two hundred other Americans had tried to travel to Syria, and the FBI investigated supporters of ISIS in all fifty states during 2015. By the fall of that year, more than eighty extremists had been charged with some kind of jihadist crime, ranging from planning travel to Syria to plotting an attack in the States, almost all of them inspired by ISIS. It was the peak year for such cases since 2001.

ISIS is one on a long list of terrorist groups that have inspired American Islamist militants, starting with al-Qaeda and encompassing similar organizations, including al-Shabaab and the Taliban. The term *jihadist* will be used to describe all those who have espoused the militant beliefs of these groups, because that is how these radical Muslims describe themselves. *Jihad* has an alternative, nonviolent meaning within Islam, as the internal struggle Muslims wage against un-Islamic behavior, but today's Islamist militants explicitly reject this understanding of jihad and embrace its interpretation as a literal "holy war." All Muslims recognize five "pillars" as integral to the practice of their religion (the profession of faith, praying to Allah five times a day, giving alms to the poor, fasting during Ramadan, and performing the Haj pilgrimage), but many militant extremists feel that these are not enough to make one a "true" Muslim. Jihad, to them, is a "forgotten" pillar.

Since the attacks of September 11, 2001, more than 360 people in the United States have been charged with some kind of jihadist terrorist crime ranging in seriousness from murder to sending small sums of money to a terrorist group. An astonishing four out of five of them are U.S. citizens or legal permanent residents. This finding flies in the face of the conventional belief (largely attributable to the fact that the 9/11 attacks were carried out by nineteen foreign-born Arab hijackers) that those involved in terrorist activity in the United States are foreigners. In fact, the overwhelming number of those engaged in jihadist crimes in the States have been Americans. Moreover, more than one hundred American citizens or residents have been charged after traveling overseas to join a terrorist group, and a further seventy-four were arrested in the States while planning to do so.

In its simplest terms, this is a form of treason: to join a group or accept an ideology whose goal is to kill Americans. This book is an attempt to discern why these Americans made that choice, how U.S. institutions and the Muslim community in the United States have responded, and how the threat of terrorism on American soil has changed us.

The American jihadists we will meet in this book adopted "Binladenism," the dogma laid out by Osama bin Laden in a series of interviews and statements made before his death in 2011. Binladenism is an ideology: a set of ideas that claim to explain the world and, even, history itself. Marxist-Leninism contended that history should be understood as a class struggle between the capitalists and the workers; Nazism asserted that the German/Aryan race's rightful dominance could be attained only by the enslavement or elimination of lesser races, particularly Jews. Ideologies, by their nature, are not susceptible to challenges posed by countervailing evidence. Whether secular or religious, they are fundamentally theological, in the sense that they are not open to question or scientific inquiry. You either believe or you don't.

Common to many ideologies is the belief that history has a direction and a purpose, and that the end point is some form of utopia. In the case of Marxist-Leninism, this utopia was conceived of as a classless society of perfect communism; for Nazism, it was to be the Thousand-Year Reich. In the minds of true believers, those purportedly blocking the creation of this utopia are seen as irredeemably evil. This belief explains both Stalin's campaign to murder millions of supposed counter-revolutionaries and Hitler's Holocaust.

Binladenism holds that the world will finally be made perfect after the restoration of a Taliban-style caliphate that will stretch across the Muslim world from Indonesia to Morocco. Evil people and nations stand in the way of this dream: the Jews, Israel, the United States, and any Middle Eastern regime that doesn't follow Taliban-style rule. Bin Laden himself, and core al-Qaeda, saw this restoration as the product of generations of holy war, while ISIS, as we've seen, views it as a present-day strategic imperative—but the underlying ideology is the same.

Bin Laden spoke of a global conspiracy against true Islam involving the whole West and its puppet allies in the Muslim world and led by the United States. America's support for Israel and for authoritarian

Arab governments was central to bin Laden's charge. In turn, moral outrage about U.S. foreign policy in the Muslim world is a recurring theme in the radicalization of American militants. Queens-born Samir Khan told his high school classmates that U.S. policy was to blame for 9/11. He would later join al-Qaeda in Yemen. Tennessee native Carlos Bledsoe, who railed against the U.S.-led wars in Afghanistan and Iraq, would go on to kill an American soldier in Arkansas. For Najibullah Zazi the trigger was the American-led war in his native Afghanistan, a regular topic of discussion in the New York Afghan community where he lived as a teenager. He would be recruited by al-Qaeda to launch a bombing in Manhattan. Another would-be Manhattan bomber, Faisal Shahzad of Connecticut, said at his sentencing hearing that it was the covert CIA drone campaign in his birthplace, Pakistan, that triggered his rage. Sometimes it was a jihad in a distant, ancestral homeland that incited American Binladenists; a trigger for Boston Marathon bomber Tamerlan Tsarnaev's militancy was the conflict in his native Caucasus region, where Islamist militants have battled their Russian overlords on and off for centuries.

Binladenism is one of the last violent revolutionary ideologies left standing. The American political scientist David Rapoport pointed out shortly after the 9/11 attacks that there have been four "waves" of global revolutionary terrorism in the past century or so, each of which burned itself out after several decades. The first was the anarchist wave, whose many victims included U.S. president William McKinley (assassinated in 1901). The next was the anticolonial wave, which began in the 1920s and was typified by the campaign to oust the French from Algeria and by the Jewish militants who forced the British out of Palestine. The "New Left" wave began in the late sixties and included antiestablishment terrorist groups such as the Weather Underground.

Finally, the religious wave. This began in 1979 with the overthrow of the Shah of Iran by Ayatollah Khomeini and his followers—a revolution that made a great impression on bin Laden and other Islamist revolutionaries, as it demonstrated that religious zealots could topple Western-backed despots. We are still caught up in this wave of religious revolutionary violence, which has shown scant signs of burning itself out and whose newest incarnation, ISIS, is inspiring and radicalizing more Americans than any other jihadist group before it.

That bin Laden's ideology has found any purchase among Americans is somewhat surprising. There have been Muslims in the United States since the Colonial era, and their right to practice their faith has been enshrined since 1786, with the passage of the Virginia Act for Establishing Religious Freedom. Thomas Jefferson, the law's principal author, wrote that it was "meant to comprehend, within the mantle of its protection, the Jew, the Gentile, the Christian and the Mahometan [Muslim], the Hindoo and Infidel of every denomination." The act became the basis for the First Amendment protections of freedom of religion.

Many Muslims have observed how open America is to Islam's many strains and sects compared to their home countries. Imam Mohamed Magid, a Sudanese American cleric who presides over one of the country's largest mosques, in the suburbs of northern Virginia, says, "Every time I come from overseas, including coming from the most religious countries, when I arrive in the airport, always I say: 'May God bless America.' I see the difference. There's no place on the face of the earth, including Europe, to live as a Muslim, to be really expressing yourself as a Muslim, more than the United States."

In a number of Muslim nations, membership in the Muslim Brotherhood, a nonviolent Islamist movement with many millions of supporters, is discouraged or banned; in others, worshipping as a Shia Muslim is difficult or even deadly. Ahmadis, a minority sect who hold controversial beliefs, are officially considered non-Muslims in their native Pakistan. In the United States, where Muslims currently number around five million, anyone can practice whatever brand of Islam he or she wishes. There are African American imams, Muslim feminists, Ismaili followers of the Aga Khan, hard-core Salafists, secular Shias, and Christian converts to Islam. Islam is, in fact, one of the fastest-growing religions in the United States.

The American Muslim experience also contrasts favorably with the ghettoized living and racial discrimination that is the daily lot of many European Muslims. Consider that only around 7 percent of the

French population is Muslim, but an astonishing 70 percent of its prison population is Muslim. For many, there is little in the way of legitimate opportunity: Muslim citizens in France are two and a half times less likely to be called for a job interview than a similar Christian candidate, and many French Muslims live in grim *banlieues*, the suburbs of large French cities (not dissimilar to public housing projects in the United States), where they find themselves largely divorced from mainstream French society. According to the Renseignements Généraux, a police agency that monitors militants in France, half the neighborhoods with a high Muslim population are isolated from French social and political life. The French term for these neighborhoods is equivalent to "sensitive urban zones," where youth unemployment averages 45 percent.

For French Muslims, in short, there is no "French Dream," nor, by extension, any "EU Dream." It's perhaps small wonder that France has supplied more foreign fighters to the war in Syria (more than fifteen hundred) than any other Western nation. It's also not surprising that it is the European country that has suffered the most severe "blowback" from the Syrian war. Some of the ISIS militants who launched the November 2015 attacks in Paris had grown up in the city's grim ghettos before their time training and fighting in Syria.

The American Dream, by contrast, has worked pretty well for the majority of American Muslims, who are both as wealthy and educated as the average American.

Jihadists are, of course, a tiny minority of the American Muslim population. Yet Americans have played a key role in al-Qaeda ever since the group was founded. Only a dozen men attended its first meeting, convened in Pakistan by bin Laden in late August 1988. One of these was Mohammed Loay Bayazid, who grew up in Kansas City and was studying engineering in Arizona at the time. Al-Qaeda's most important military trainer was Ali Mohamed, a sergeant in the U.S. Army posted to Fort Bragg, North Carolina, in the late 1980s. Mohamed traveled the world training al-Qaeda members and scoping out targets for the terrorist group. Wadi el-Hage, who attended college in Louisiana and married an American, was bin Laden's personal secretary during the early 1990s. New Mexico–born Anwar al-Awlaki directed al-Qaeda's Yemeni affiliate's operations to attack his home country, and would also become the most influential militant cleric in the English-speaking world. Floridian Adnan Shukrijumah was in charge of al-Qaeda's operations to attack the United States until his death in Pakistan in 2014. Californian Adam Gadahn was the group's spokesman and media adviser until he was killed in a CIA drone strike in early 2015. Among al-Qaeda affiliates, Alabama native Omar Hammami played a leadership role in al-Shabaab, the brutal Somali group, and the Pakistani organization Lashkar-e-Taiba recruited Chicagoan David Headley in planning the 2008 Mumbai attacks that killed 166 people. Since 9/11 a number of Americans have also become radicalized on their own, inspired by Binladenism but without a connection to al-Qaeda or any of its affiliates. Major Nidal Hasan, who grew up in Virginia and killed thirteen fellow Americans at Fort Hood, Texas, in 2009, was a classic "lone wolf," operating without a group of coconspirators or direction from any organization. The Tsarnaev brothers, who carried out the Boston Marathon bombings in 2013, similarly had no connections to any terrorist organization.

As we will see, many of the easiest assumptions about jihadists in the States are not borne out in the lives of most American militants. It is tempting to assume that the decision to turn to terrorism must be rooted in some traumatic life experience; that these men must be young hotheads without family obligations; that they are pathologically disturbed, or career criminals, or, at the very least, not very bright. Among the 360 militants examined for this book, none of these generalizations hold. Their average age is twenty-nine; more than a third are married and a similar proportion have children; 12 percent have served time in prison, compared to 11 percent of the American male population, while around 10 percent had mental health issues, a lower incidence than in the general population. They are, on average, as well educated and emotionally stable as the typical citizen.

They are ordinary Americans.

How, then, did these ordinary Americans become terrorists? The science of criminal behavior is not chemistry, where there is a predictable, replicable set of causes for any given reaction. As Immanuel Kant observed, "Out of the crooked timber of humanity, no straight thing was ever made." But based on the collective work of psychiatrists, terrorism experts, and police officials, we do know considerably more about Islamist terrorists than we did a decade and a half ago, when flying bombs killed almost three thousand Americans.

For many of these recruits, their turn to militancy was prompted, at least in part, by a desire for recognition or belonging, often both. Jihad offered them the opportunity to be "somebody," and at the same time to be part of something bigger than they were. Zachary Chesser, who grew up in Virginia and became a notorious militant Islamist ideologue on the Internet, reveled in the "enormous influence" he wielded in the English-speaking world of militant Islam. Charlotte-based Samir Khan was so excited by the romance of holy war that, driving toward his first meeting with members of al-Qaeda in a remote part of Yemen, he enthused that it was "enthralling." There is, after all, something exciting, even heroic, about casting yourself as a holy warrior fighting in a glorious, Allah-sanctioned war against the enemies of Islam—especially when you might otherwise be just another suburban office worker, as Samir Khan was, or, like Tamerlan Tsarnaev, unemployed. These ordinary men wanted to be heroes in their own story, fighting against "infidels." Through jihad they could play out their heroic fantasies with the added comfort of believing that Allah was on their side. In the 1970s, idealistic American recruits to jihadist groups might have joined other organizations that promised a revolution to install a utopia here in the United States, such as the Weather Underground or Black Panthers. Just as it was for these 1970s revolutionaries, there was something glamorous and exciting for American militants such as Khan and Tsarnaev about leaving behind their otherwise humdrum lives to join the jihad.

One way of looking at why some Americans chose jihad is to find out why people with comparable experiences chose a different path. Nader Hasan, the first cousin of Fort Hood shooter Nidal Hasan, grew up treating Nidal almost as if he were a brother, yet Nader founded and runs a foundation dedicated to speaking out against violence perpetrated in the name of Islam. Bernie Culveyhouse grew up in the same small town in Alabama as Omar Hammami and undertook with him a multiyear journey of radicalization, even living overseas with his friend as an ultrafundamentalist—yet right at the point when Hammami decided to join al-Shabaab, Culveyhouse turned back, deciding to return to a normal life of family and work in the States.

Beyond attempting to plumb the psyches of American jihadists, this book will also explore how the government has grappled with a threat that, while real, is far from existential. Since 2001 ninety-four Americans have been killed by jihadist terrorists in the United States. In that same period, by contrast, forty-eight Americans have been killed in acts of political violence by far-right extremists. Yet, in the name of defeating Islamist terrorism, since 9/11 the FBI has instigated more jihadist terrorist "plots" in the States than al-Qaeda or any of its affiliated groups— thirty versus ten. Undercover FBI informants act as agents provocateurs, finding potential terrorists and goading them to mount plots that are in reality controlled by law enforcement. The FBI has put a number of Americans in prison for plotting crimes they would likely never have become involved in had they not had the misfortune of encountering an informant on the FBI's payroll. "Entrapment," however, has never succeeded as a legal defense in such cases.

While the FBI deployed thousands of informants across the country, the New York City Police Department (NYPD) was conducting surveillance on mosques and other public places in the New York area where Muslims gather—years of surveillance that netted little. The National Security Agency (NSA) has swept up vast amounts of American phone data. Despite government claims that such measures have averted multiple serious terrorist plots, there is, in fact, little to show for them.

This is not to say that the job of law enforcement and intelligence agencies has been easy. After all, if a bomb were to blow up in Manhattan, killing dozens, it is the NYPD that would be the first to deal with the consequences, and the FBI and the intelligence community would be tarred with failing to stop such an attack wherever it occurred. We will hear from key FBI, NYPD, and intelligence officials who have had to make difficult decisions in striking the balance between security and liberty.

September 11 remains a scar on the national psyche. A large majority of Americans consider it the most memorable event of their lives, just as an earlier generation was haunted by the assassination of President John F. Kennedy. Polls taken every year since 9/11 have found that four out of ten Americans worry that they or a family member will be the victim of an act of terrorism. The public is not alone in this fear. Between 2006 and 2008, *Foreign Policy* magazine regularly surveyed one hundred of the country's top foreign policy experts; a quarter of them consistently believed that a catastrophic act of jihadist terrorism was likely within six months, while two-thirds or more believed that such an assault was likely within five years.

This widespread fear of another 9/11, one of the hinge events in American history, helps to explain the hysteria that has grown up around Muslims in the United States in the years since. In a 2012 poll, about 60 percent of Republicans had negative views of Muslim Americans. Indeed, Muslim Americans polled less favorably than Americans of every other faith, among respondents of all political persuasions—an especially notable finding given how relatively well integrated into American society Muslims have long been. Another poll, also from 2012, found that nearly a third of Americans, including 43 percent of Republicans, believed President Obama to be a Muslim, despite all evidence to the contrary. Outside of the mainstream, a virulent minority believed that Obama was seeking to populate his administration with members of the Muslim Brotherhood as part of a secret plan to bring sharia law to the United States.

These views are ironic given that, as commander in chief, President Obama presided over or launched more military operations in Muslim countries (Afghanistan, Iraq, Libya, Pakistan, Somalia, Syria, and Yemen) than any previous president. The most conservative estimate of drone strike fatalities under Obama comes to more than three thousand, and that figure includes much of the leadership of al-Qaeda. Obama was the first American president since the Civil War to authorize the assassination of a fellow American, the Muslim cleric and al-Qaeda leader Anwar al-Awlaki, who was killed by a U.S. drone strike in Yemen in

2011. This is not the record of a president with any secret proclivities for sharia law.

The long, sometimes reality-distorting shadow of September 11 aside, the fact remains that American jihadist terrorism has proved to be a real and enduring threat—one that has challenged our government's approach to national security on every level, and that forces us to consider: How could it happen in the United States? The most deadly jihadist attacks in the United States since 9/11, and the most threatening plots, have been carried out by or instigated by Americans. By the end of 2016, more than two hundred and fifty people had been charged with jihadist terrorism crimes in the United States during Obama's presidency alone.

A sobering reminder of the threat came on the morning of December 2, 2015, when Syed Rizwan Farook and his wife, Tashfeen Malik, opened fire at office workers attending a training session in San Bernardino, California, killing fourteen. Inspired by ISIS, Farook and Malik were "homegrown" militants who had become increasingly radicalized while living comfortably in the California suburbs.

In 2010, Anwar al-Awlaki gloated that "Jihad is becoming as American as apple pie." That absurd claim has, it turns out, some merit.

CHAPTER 2

ALL AMERICAN AL-QAEDA

"I HAVE ALWAYS DREAMED," HE MOUTHED FIERCELY, "OF A BAND
OF MEN ABSOLUTE IN THEIR RESOLVE TO DISCARD ALL SCRUPLES
IN THE CHOICE OF MEANS, STRONG ENOUGH TO GIVE THEMSELVES
FRANKLY THE NAME OF DESTROYERS, AND FREE FROM THE TAINT OF
THAT RESIGNED PESSIMISM WHICH ROTS THE WORLD. NO PITY FOR
ANYTHING ON EARTH, INCLUDING THEMSELVES, AND DEATH ENLISTED
FOR GOOD AND ALL IN THE SERVICE OF HUMANITY."

—Joseph Conrad, *The Secret Agent*

In the tense months following the 9/11 attacks, Anwar al-Awlaki was
feeling particularly horny. About once every two weeks he made his
way to a variety of upscale hotels in downtown Washington, DC, for assignations with "escorts," whose sexual services cost him three hundred
to four hundred dollars per session.

One of the women found Awlaki especially memorable because of
his strong resemblance to Osama bin Laden, whose aquiline features
then filled every TV screen. Awlaki used his real name but told the
women he was a computer engineer originally from India, now living
in California. To one, he mentioned that he occasionally traveled to
Florida, where he found the escort services to be quite good.

In his day-to-day life, Awlaki was a respected, married cleric from
the nearby Dar al-Hijrah mosque in Falls Church, Virginia. His lax
efforts at concealment—when the prostitutes asked him to verify his

identity by providing his home address, he sometimes gave the actual street address of his mosque—reflected an easy confidence in his double life. Despite having spent his entire professional life as a cleric, Awlaki had been visiting prostitutes for years, a habit he seems to have first developed while working as an imam at the Arribat al-Islami mosque in San Diego in the mid- and late nineties. Arribat al-Islami is in a neighborhood just a few blocks from San Diego's El Cajon Boulevard, an area notorious for prostitution. In 1996 and 1997 Awlaki was arrested for soliciting prostitutes there, for which he paid fines of $400 and $240 and was ordered to attend an HIV/AIDS awareness seminar and to perform community service. (Years later, when news of his San Diego arrests became public, Awlaki claimed that he had been set up in a government sting operation.)

Awlaki lived a double life in other ways. Being a U.S. citizen, raised in New Mexico and Minnesota, he was easily able to flit back and forth between the carefully cultivated persona of an all-American, moderate Islamic cleric and the al-Qaeda sympathizer he had been for much of his adult life. It was the moderate cleric who, just a few weeks before 9/11, preached in a meeting room inside the U.S. Capitol—one of the intended targets of the hijackers. Indeed, Awlaki's familiarity with Washington and his unaccented English made him a go-to figure for both the media and the U.S. government.

On 9/11, Awlaki was on an early morning flight home from a conference in California. He first heard the news of the attacks in the cab leaving Reagan National Airport; he told the driver to take him immediately to the Dar al-Hijrah mosque. Awlaki and other leaders decided to close the mosque for the day—a sensible precaution, as that night a man drove up to the building and screamed threats for half an hour.

On September 12, Awlaki posed at the mosque for some arty stills by Andrea Bruce, a top photographer at the *Washington Post*. An interfaith prayer meeting was in progress when Bruce visited. She shot Awlaki from above, showing his hands clasped and his head lowered in prayer.

Awlaki condemned the attacks in multiple interviews during the subsequent weeks. Speaking to two reporters from *National Geographic*, the cleric said that he hadn't owned a TV before the attacks but had rushed out to purchase one and had since been "glued" to the set. He also said that the attacks on New York City and Washington were a double burden for Muslims: "We're suffering as Muslims and as human beings because of the tragic loss for everyone. And then in addition, we suffer the consequences of what will happen to us as an American Muslim community since the perpetrators are, so far, identified as Arabs or Muslims." *So far.*

When asked what had motivated the attacks, Awlaki said, "What really ticked off Osama bin Laden was [the presence of thousands of] US soldiers in the Holy Land" of Saudi Arabia, the site of the two holiest places in Islam. In the *National Geographic* interview, Awlaki came across as reasonable, balanced, and serious. He even said that bin Laden "was considered to be an extremist," although he was careful not to tell the reporters his own opinion. He allowed himself slightly more leeway during a subsequent interview, with the website IslamOnline.net, in which he conspiratorially suggested that the timing of the attacks could have had something to do with Israel "going through a serious PR crisis" because of a lawsuit recently filed against its then prime minister, Ariel Sharon. No doubt he was confident that few Americans would read his comments there.

A week after Awlaki spoke to *National Geographic,* the American war against the Taliban began in Afghanistan. A few days later Awlaki participated in an extensive question-and-answer session for the *Washington Post's* website. Much of it focused on anodyne questions such as the role of fasting during the Muslim holy month of Ramadan, but occasionally a glimmer of the real Awlaki came through. He said the Taliban had repeatedly asked that any evidence of bin Laden's role in the 9/11 attacks be handed over to them, but that this had never happened. He opined that "the US should have given them the benefit of the doubt. Also our government could have dealt with the terrorist attacks as a crime against America rather than a war against America."

Although Awlaki rarely showed his radical colors in the mainstream media, the FBI had long been suspicious of him. He first attracted its attention in 1999, while studying at San Diego State, because of his purported acquaintance with Ziyad Khaleel, who did odd jobs for bin Laden in the States. Then, in early 2000, Awlaki was visited in San Diego by a close associate of the "Blind Sheikh," or Omar Abdel Rahman, an Egyptian cleric then serving a life term in a U.S. prison for his role in sanctioning terrorist plots in New York in the early nineties. The Blind Sheikh was in many ways al-Qaeda's foremost spiritual guide; he had religious credentials that bin Laden and other al-Qaeda leaders did not have. The FBI became interested in understanding the nature of Awlaki's connection to him.

This interest quickly intensified following the attacks on New York City and Washington, particularly when it became clear that Awlaki had spent time with two of the 9/11 hijackers, Khalid al-Mihdhar and Nawaf al-Hazmi, when they were living in San Diego during the previous year. Within the first eight days after 9/11, FBI agents met with Awlaki four times, and they followed his white Dodge Caravan for many months afterward, dutifully recording his every move—from shopping at Safeway, to eating pizza, to appearing on the popular NPR show *Talk of the Nation,* to consorting with prostitutes.

Awlaki assured the agents who interviewed him that although he had met the hijacker al-Hazmi on numerous occasions, they had discussed only trivial matters. He also said that al-Hazmi, five foot five and scrawny, could not possibly have been involved in the attacks, as he could not have offered much in the way of protection to the hijackers. "Al-Hazmi was so slight of build," Awlaki told the FBI agents, that he "might have trouble slaughtering a chicken."

The FBI could not determine if Awlaki had just happened to regularly encounter a number of nefarious individuals in the years before 9/11 or if he was acting as some sort of ringleader. Soon, however, in internal documents, FBI agents began referring to Awlaki as the "spiritual leader" of the hijackers on the flight that crashed into the Pentagon. On October 25, 2001, the FBI circulated a notice to be on the lookout for any travel bookings for Awlaki in airline reservation systems.

The FBI's suspicions, however, were not public, and in January 2002 Awlaki's visibility in the media garnered him an invitation from an unlikely quarter: the Pentagon. An official in the Pentagon's Office of Legal Counsel had heard him speak and e-mailed her colleagues to suggest that they invite Awlaki to brief them. She "particularly liked how he addressed how the average Middle Eastern person perceives the United States." The official planned a lunchtime event featuring turkey and bacon sandwiches, which indicated that her knowledge of Islam was not especially deep.

FBI agents were still trailing Awlaki on February 5, 2002, the day he was the featured speaker at the luncheon at the Pentagon—a sign, perhaps, that interagency communication was poor. According to the FBI surveillance log from that day, they followed him on the Metro train but stopped surveillance soon after he went inside the Pentagon. One wonders what they made of his destination.

Jihad was already being waged in America many years before 9/11. Most Americans just weren't aware of it. The World Trade Center was attacked for the first time on February 26, 1993, when a truck bomb detonated in a basement parking garage, killing six people. The attack, intended to bring down both towers, was masterminded by Ramzi Yousef, who had trained in an al-Qaeda camp on the Afghan-Pakistani border, but five American citizens also played active roles in the plot. Three years earlier, El Sayyid Nosair, an American citizen born in Egypt, had shot and killed Meir Kahane, a militant Zionist rabbi, at a Manhattan hotel. Nosair's circle included a number of the 1993 Trade Center conspirators.

These plots notwithstanding, it came as a great shock to most Americans when CNN ran an interview with twenty-year-old Californian John Walker Lindh two months after the 9/11 attacks. Lindh lay on a stretcher caked in mud as he recovered from wounds he had sustained during a battle in northern Afghanistan between U.S. forces and the Taliban. Speaking in a strange, foreign-sounding accent, he explained, "I was a student in Pakistan, studying Islam. . . . The people there in general have a great love for the Taliban. So I started to read some of the literature of the scholars and my heart became attached to it. I wanted to help them one way or another." For an American citizen to say that his heart had become attached to the Taliban, the same group that had harbored al-Qaeda for years, caused outrage in the States. In a poll taken a few weeks after Lindh was captured, 60 percent of Americans disagreed with the Justice Department's decision not to charge Lindh with treason, which carries the death penalty.

Lindh was born in Washington, DC, in 1981 and grew up in Marin County, California. When he was sixteen he converted to Islam, which led him to travel to Yemen to study Arabic, and then to Pakistan. He joined the Taliban in June 2001 and trained at an al-Qaeda camp, where he attended three lectures by bin Laden. In November 2001, Lindh was imprisoned in a northern Afghanistan fortress along with some one thousand other captured Taliban fighters. The prisoners staged an escape during which they killed CIA officer Johnny Spann, who had been interrogating Lindh at the time. Lindh and the other Taliban fighters hid out in the cellars of the fortress, but Afghans allied to the United States pumped in diesel fuel and water to flood them out of their refuge. Lindh was shot in the leg and was one of fewer than eighty-five survivors who finally surrendered on December 1.

Lindh's plea agreement stated that he had provided his "services" to the Taliban, contravening President Bill Clinton's executive order that had slapped sanctions on the Taliban in 1999. What services had Lindh provided to the Taliban? Himself, it turned out. Lindh had refused offers by al-Qaeda leaders to take part in operations against Americans, and there was no proof that he was involved in any militant activity other than training at a Taliban training camp, but that was enough to convict him of the charge.

Lindh's case set an important precedent of providing "material support" to a terrorist group in the form of his own "services" and would be used against more than one hundred American citizens and residents of the States in the years after 9/11. These ranged from Hamzah Khan, who didn't make it past the airport in his quest to join ISIS, to those who, like Lindh, actually joined militant organizations.

Just as Lindh's enrollment in the Taliban stunned many Americans, they were surprised when, around the fourth anniversary of the 9/11 attacks, ABC News broadcast a video from al-Qaeda featuring an American, his face partially concealed, who predicted future attacks in Los Angeles. He was identified by U.S. intelligence officials as Adam Gadahn. Like Lindh, Gadahn was a California convert to Islam. He had grown up on a small farm and as a teenager had developed an intense interest in death metal music, which gave way to an equally intense immersion in militant Islam.

At the time of the 9/11 attacks, Gadahn was living in Afghanistan and helping al-Qaeda translate its training manuals into English. Like anyone else at the training camps in the weeks before 9/11, Gadahn had heard rumors that al-Qaeda was about to launch a big attack on American interests, though he thought the attack was likely to take place in the Middle East, maybe Saudi Arabia. Gadahn's reaction to the attacks on the World Trade Center and Pentagon is unrecorded, but he could not have missed the jubilation in al-Qaeda's training camps, where some militants fell to the ground and wept with joy.

From 2004 on, Gadahn would be a regular presence in al-Qaeda videos, a heavily bearded man in his twenties wearing a white robe and turban, using his jihad handle of "Azzam al-Amriki" (Azzam the American) and delivering finger-wagging lectures about the perfidious United States. Typical of those appearances was a video in which Gadahn said, "Fighting and defeating America is our first priority. . . . The streets of America shall run red with blood." In 2006, Gadahn became, in absentia, the first American to be charged with treason in more than five decades.

While Gadahn and Lindh were the first American jihadis on the public's radar, they were not the only ones active at the time; nor would they prove to be the most influential. That distinction belonged to Awlaki. A proponent of "leaderless jihad," the great strategic innovation of post-9/11 militant Islamists, he would become an early and singularly adept user of the Internet to recruit militants and an important cultural translator for Arab-led al-Qaeda once the group started producing colloquial English-language propaganda. He would also help develop Yemen into the crucial "field of jihad" it has become. And he would, finally, provoke the U.S. government to take the unprecedented measure of targeting an American citizen, him, for death in the war against al-Qaeda and its allied groups.

The FBI's characterization of Awlaki, in the months after 9/11, as a "spiritual leader" to some of the hijackers raises an important question: What did the attacks on the Trade Center and Pentagon, and jihadist terrorism since then, have to do with Islam? The hijackers certainly saw themselves as taking part in a heroic religious war to defend Islam. They awarded themselves *kunyas,* Islamic nicknames that referred to heroic figures from Islam's early history; the lead hijacker, the dour Egyptian Mohamed Atta, was known as Abu Abdul Rahman, after an Egyptian who was told by the Prophet that he would go to Paradise. In luggage Atta left in a car at Boston's Logan Airport on the morning of 9/11, authorities discovered an Arabic document titled "Manual for a Raid," which used the Koranic word *ghazwah* for "raid," demonstrating his belief that the attack would be in the great religious tradition of the battles fought by the Prophet. In the manual, the hijackers were urged to invoke God as they entered the aircraft and were told you "will be with your heavenly brides soon." The manual mentioned the "martyrs'" ascension into heaven twelve times.

Islamist terrorism does have some kind of a relationship to the religion of Islam, something that cannot be wished away by claims that Islam is simply a religion of peace, or by the desire not to offend, or because it is too easy to underestimate the strength of others' religious beliefs in our increasingly secular world. The worldview of jihadist militants is informed by a certain reading of Islamic texts, and there is more than sufficient ammunition in the Koran (which, for believers, is the literal Word of God) to buttress their assertions that jihad is necessary against the perceived enemies of Islam. One well-known verse commands Muslims to "fight and slay the nonbelievers wherever you find them, seize them, beleaguer them, and lie in wait for them in every stratagem [of war]." The same verse adds that if the nonbelievers "repent" and donate money to the poor or, in some translations, pay a tax to their Muslim overlords, they can be spared. When bin Laden made his formal declaration of war against "the Jews and the Crusaders" in 1998, he cited this Koranic verse as the religious rationale for the 9/11 attacks.

Assertions that Islamist terrorism has nothing to do with Islam are as nonsensical as claims that the Crusades had nothing to do with Christian beliefs about the sanctity of Jerusalem, or that the exponential growth of Israeli settlements on Palestinian lands is not rooted in the beliefs of certain Jewish fundamentalists about the God-given rights of Jews to live in their God-given homeland.

Of course, only a tiny minority of Muslims are willing to do violence in the name of Allah, and Muslims as a group are certainly no more violent than the adherents of any other religion. Christians, for example, have invoked Christ's name to justify any number of crusades, pogroms, wars, and imperial adventures. Nor is this to make the claim that religion itself causes violence, but rather that ideologies of any form, including those that are avowedly secular, that claim to have discovered "the Truth" often end up leaving a great trail of dead bodies in their wake. The monstrous political religions of Nazism and Stalinism, in their relatively brief tenancies, created more human misery than any of the creeds that preceded them.

Islam is a very big tent, and the one and a half billion Muslims in the world run the gamut from mystical, pacifist Sufis to Salafists. Almost all the militants described in these pages follow Salafism, an ultrafundamentalist branch of Sunni Islam particularly prevalent in Saudi Arabia. Salafism is intolerant of what its adherents consider to be Islamic deviancy, such as Shia Islam, and of other religions. Salafism is not a gateway to violence for the tens of millions of its peaceful adherents around the world, but Sunni jihadist terrorists generally are Salafists. A similar point could also be made about Christian fundamentalists in the United States; while very few kill doctors at abortion clinics, anyone who does is generally a Christian fundamentalist.

If there is an analogue in the United States to the violent beliefs of the Salafi jihadists it is the Christian Identity movement. Members of the sect, which is based on a highly idiosyncratic reading of the Book of Genesis, believe that whites are superior to all other races because they are the true "lost tribe" of Israel. They also believe that they are warring to the death with other, supposedly lesser races such as blacks and Jews, whom they term "mud people." The Christian Identity movement began in the 1940s and informed the beliefs of the Ku Klux Klan and later those of The Order, a white supremacist group whose members assassinated Jewish talk show host Alan Berg in Denver in 1984. Eric Rudolph, who bombed a park in Atlanta during the 1996 Olympics and two abortion clinics in 1998, subscribed to Christian Identity beliefs. In late November 2014, police in Austin, Texas, shot to death another believer, Larry McQuilliams, who was carrying multiple weapons and hundreds of rounds of ammunition and had tried to burn down the Mexican consulate there.

For the American militants portrayed in this book, their Salafism became increasingly politicized. In their minds, the only answer to the purported American-led assaults on Islam was revenge, a point of view intimately connected to their Islamic beliefs. Their opposition to American foreign policy in the Muslim world was rooted in their religious beliefs about the sanctity of Islamic lands and the necessity to wage jihad to defend the *umma,* the worldwide community of Muslim believers, from the infidels. Their political objections to American foreign policy were channeled through an ultrafundamentalist view of the world. Indeed, for these militants the distinction that the West has long drawn between politics and religion is a mirage. For them, politics and theology merge with the caliphate.

A s the FBI had suspected, Awlaki's march to militancy began long before the 9/11 attacks. He was born in Las Cruces, New Mexico, in 1971, where his father was studying agricultural economics at New Mexico State University as a Fulbright Scholar. When Awlaki's father took a job at the University of Minnesota, the family moved to St. Paul; when Awlaki was six years old, his family returned to Yemen. By the time Awlaki was in high school in the Yemeni capital of Sana'a during the 1980s, the brutal Soviet occupation of Afghanistan was in full swing. For Awlaki and his classmates, the Afghan mujahideen were true "holy warriors," fighting the infidel Soviets. Families gathered in Aw-laki's neighborhood to watch videotapes featuring the heroic exploits of the mujahideen.

One of the top students in the country, Awlaki was apparently not excited by the thought of going to university in Yemen, the poorest na-tion in the Arab world. He instead returned to the country of his birth, to attend Colorado State, studying engineering at the behest of his fa-ther. Around this time, Awlaki began to develop a private hatred for the United States. This was sparked by the first Gulf War. Six months after Saddam Hussein's invasion of Kuwait in August 1990, a massive Ameri-can army based in Saudi Arabia went on the offensive. After Saddam's armies were ignominiously pushed out of Kuwait, a large-scale U.S. mil-itary presence in Saudi Arabia continued for many years. For politicized, fundamentalist Muslims such as Awlaki, the presence of thousands of "infidel" American troops on the holy soil of Saudi Arabia was a deep irritant—just as it was for bin Laden.

The Gulf War also pushed Awlaki to become more religious, and his newfound zealotry impelled him to take action. During a winter break from college, age twenty, he traveled to Afghanistan to witness "the muj" in action. It was 1991; by then the Soviets had withdrawn from Afghanistan, but the muj continued to battle the Communist govern-ment that remained after the Soviet withdrawal. The Afghan holy war had made a lasting impression on Awlaki, who sometimes wore a dis-tinctive Afghan hat on the campus of Colorado State and would quote the words of Abdullah Azzam, the Palestinian cleric who led the Arabs against the Soviets in Afghanistan and was bin Laden's most important mentor.

In 1994, while living in Colorado, Awlaki married his first wife, a cousin from Yemen. The next year, his first son, Abdulrahman, was born, and the following year Awlaki, age twenty-five, moved to San Diego to take a job as a cleric at the Arribat mosque. Arribat had been founded by conservative Muslim students from the Gulf who found the teachings of the more mainstream San Diego Islamic Center not to their taste. Awlaki also started attending San Diego State, where he earned a master's degree in education.

It was in San Diego, five years later, that Awlaki encountered the two men who, together with seventeen coconspirators, would transform American history. The CIA began tracking Khalid al-Mihdhar and Nawaf al-Hazmi when they attended an al-Qaeda summit in Malaysia on January 5, 2000. Ten days after the meeting in Malaysia, they flew to Los Angeles. The CIA did not alert the FBI to the identities of the suspected terrorists, so the Bureau did not know to look for them once they were inside the United States. Under their real names, Mihdhar and Hazmi rented an apartment in San Diego, obtained driver's licenses, opened bank accounts, purchased a car, and took flight lessons at a local school. They also began spending time with Awlaki. Awlaki even wrote a check to Hazmi for $281.50 just three months before the 9/11 attacks.

If it was a strange coincidence that Awlaki met with two of the hijackers when they were living in San Diego, it was an even greater coincidence that he met with another hijacker in Virginia in the months immediately before the attacks. Hani Hanjour, the pilot of the flight that crashed into the Pentagon, worshipped at the Virginia mosque where Awlaki served as a cleric. An informant told FBI agents that Hazmi, Hanjour, and Awlaki all met at the mosque in March 2001. After the 9/11 attacks, the telephone number of the mosque was found in the Hamburg apartment of Ramzi Binalshibh, who had played a critical role in coordinating the attacks.

The precise nature of Awlaki's' relationship with the hijackers remains mysterious, but a neighbor, Lincoln Higgie, who was fond of the big-bearded Awlaki for his habit of giving him some of his catch after he had gone deep-sea fishing, recalls a strange conversation with the cleric shortly before he left San Diego. Awlaki told Higgie he was leaving town because "something very big is going to happen."

Something very big, of course, did happen. The slogan of the Bush administration immediately became "Never Again," which on the domestic front translated into an overhaul of law enforcement—for better and sometimes for worse. The FBI and other key law enforcement agencies, such as the New York City Police Department, were reconfigured from crime-solving organizations into entities whose primary mission was to prevent terrorist attacks.

In the weeks following 9/11, the FBI came in for a great deal of scrutiny from Bush administration officials and in the media for its handling of the Zacarias Moussaoui case. If the FBI had done a better job of investigating Moussaoui, critics asserted, the 9/11 plot could have been detected. Moussaoui, a French citizen of Moroccan descent, was attending flight school in Minnesota in the summer of 2001 when he attracted attention from instructors because he had little knowledge of flying but wanted to learn how to "take off and land" a Boeing 747. The flight school contacted the FBI and on August 16, Moussaoui was arrested and charged with overstaying his visa. Although Moussaoui was not "the twentieth hijacker," as was later widely reported, he had received funding from Ramzi Binalshibh, one of the 9/11 coordinators, and by his own account was going to take part in a second wave of al-Qaeda attacks sponsored by Binalshibh.

The FBI agent in Minneapolis who handled Moussaoui's case believed that he might have been planning to hijack a plane. He was also concerned that Moussaoui had traveled to Pakistan, as militants had often used the country as a transit point on the way to terrorist training camps in Afghanistan. On August 23, CIA director George Tenet was told about the case in a briefing titled "Islamic Extremist Learns to Fly." But FBI headquarters determined that there was not sufficient "probable cause" of a crime for the Minneapolis office to conduct a search of Moussaoui's computer hard drive and belongings. Such a search could have turned up Binalshibh's phone number.

The failure to prevent 9/11 and the fear that there would be a second wave of attacks help account for the roundup of thousands of young Muslim men in the States in the weeks after the attacks. In the end, these detentions yielded only one terrorist actually linked to al-Qaeda: Ali Saleh Kahlah al-Marri, arrested in Peoria, Illinois, in December 2001. At the time of his arrest, Marri had set up multiple fake credit card accounts; he was jailed on charges of credit card fraud and lying to federal investigators. The FBI then searched Marri's laptop and found that he had conducted extensive research on chemical weapons, and had gathered technical information that, investigators concluded, "far exceeds the interests of a merely curious individual." In the 1990s, Marri had trained at al-Qaeda camps in Afghanistan and later met with Mustafa al-Hawsawi, the Dubai-based paymaster for much of the 9/11 operation, who gave him ten thousand dollars to conduct an operation in the States. After denying the charges against him for years, Marri finally entered a plea agreement in 2009 in which he admitted his deep ties to al-Qaeda.

The roundup of Muslim men was the opening salvo of the post-9/11 FBI, which now had preventing terrorism as its top priority. FBI director Robert Mueller III had been on the job for only one week before the attacks. Three days later he was in the Oval Office to deliver his first briefing to President George W. Bush. Mueller had prepared to describe what the FBI was doing at the crime scenes where the hijacked planes had crashed, to outline the steps the Bureau had taken to identify the hijackers, and to make the criminal case that al-Qaeda was behind the attacks. He'd spent a few minutes describing these measures when Bush interrupted him, saying, "Stop it! Bob, what you're telling me the Bureau is doing is what you've been doing for a hundred years. My question for you today is: What is the Bureau doing today to prevent the next terrorist attack?" Bush told Mueller to adopt a wartime mentality, to disrupt attacks before they happened rather than investigating them after they had taken place.

Given this crystal-clear directive, Mueller set about transforming the Bureau into more of an intelligence-driven organization, to operate not only as the nation's top law enforcement organization but also as a bulwark against terrorist attacks. The new post-9/11 FBI would catch terrorists *before* they could strike. Mueller quickly shifted two thousand agents from working criminal cases to counterterrorism, and in doing so doubled the personnel focusing on terrorism to four thousand out of the eleven thousand agents then working at the Bureau.

One of those agents was Art Cummings, who would play a key role in the evolution of the Bureau's counterterrorism strategies. Cummings, a former Navy SEAL who spoke Mandarin, had spent much of his career in counterterrorism (CT). Before 9/11, CT had been seen as something of a backwater; the Bureau's high flyers investigated organized crime. But when the first Trade Center attack happened in 1993, Cummings saw it as a watershed event—it blew up the prevailing wisdom that terrorists would not attack the States, given that it often served as a fund-raising base for organizations such as Hezbollah and the IRA. "Holy shit!" Cummings told one of his fellow agents. "They brought it here! Whatever happened to the philosophy that they would never do it here?" Following the 1993 attack, Cummings investigated the West Coast support network of the "Blind Sheikh," which familiarized him with the world of militant jihadists long before they became a central national security concern.

Seen as an agent with a very promising career ahead of him, Cummings was moved out of CT and into the investigation of violent crimes in the years before the 9/11 attacks. On the morning of 9/11, Cummings was attending a management training session at the FBI academy in Quantico, Virginia. After seeing the second plane hit the South Tower on television, Cummings rushed to his room and grabbed his go-bag. Dale Watson, a senior FBI counterterrorism official, called Cummings and told him to get to headquarters in downtown DC "ASAP."

A few hours later Cummings arrived at the FBI's Strategic Information and Operations Center (SIOC), where senior FBI officials quickly put together three teams. One team was tasked with coordinating the investigation. This was in the FBI's wheelhouse; the Pentagon crash site and the smoking ruins of the Trade Center were now massive crime scenes. Hundreds of agents from all over the country were sent there. The second team was a smaller group, working with the intelligence community to establish who was responsible for the attacks. This determination needed to be made quickly because the Bush administration was planning a military response, but it had to be solid.

Within forty-eight hours the FBI had a definitive case against al-Qaeda. FBI agents reviewed the list of passengers on the hijacked planes with airline officials to find out if family members had asked about each of them. Of all the passengers, there were only nineteen that no one had inquired about. Those were the hijackers.

Watson assigned Cummings to help run the third group, which was in charge of disrupting a possible second wave of attacks. Intelligence officials were greatly concerned that another attack was imminent, says Cummings. "We don't know where it's coming from, but it's probably in the planning stages, and if we're down on our knees now, that would be the coup de grâce." Cummings asked himself, "So what do we do? How do we keep them from executing an operation that we don't even know exists?" One answer was to look through FBI files and find anyone who had overstayed his visa and might have an association with terrorism. As a result, U.S. immigration authorities sent hundreds of "overstays" back to their home countries.

The FBI also deployed a small army of informants to ferret out suspected Islamist terrorists in sting operations. Not only could such operations foil actual plots, Bureau officials reasoned, but they could have the ancillary benefit of making militants wary of dealing with other radicals out of fear that they were informants. This kind of disruption strategy became the central focus of the FBI. Mueller recalls that every day for several years after 9/11 the president would ask him, "What is the Bureau doing to prevent the next terrorist attack?" That was the right question, but as we will see, given the federal government's vast resources and intense focus, this laudable mission could shade into over-kill, pursuing suspects who were hardly real terrorists.

In the months after the attacks, Cummings was living on a twenty-three-foot boat moored in Annapolis, Maryland, and commuting to FBI headquarters in DC, where he worked sixteen hours a day, six days a week. Cummings's family was understanding. "My wife married a Navy SEAL. When 9/11 happened, they were a thousand times go. 'Go do this.'" Cummings went home to see his family in Richmond, Virginia, once a month.

T he FBI wasn't the only law enforcement organization that immediately ramped up its counterterrorism operations after 9/11. So, of course, did the New York City Police Department. New York City continued to be an iconic target for jihadist terrorists long after 9/11; five years after the attacks on the Trade Center, New York City mayor Michael Bloomberg pointed out, "When you catch a terrorist and look at the map in his or her pockets, it is always a map of New York; it's not a map of some other place." If a bomb went off in downtown Manhattan, not only would the NYPD be the first responders at the scene, but the department would also take as much, if not more, heat than the federal government for not preventing the attack.

Recognizing this, after 9/11 New York City police commissioner Ray Kelly recruited David Cohen, a three-decade veteran of the CIA, to turn the NYPD into an organization that aimed to prevent terrorist attacks before they happened. Cohen was unusual at the CIA because he had run both the operations and intelligence divisions of the Agency, meaning both the spies and the analysts. He was uniquely well qualified to run an intelligence unit looking for how and when New York City could be struck next.

Cohen hadn't been one of the typical WASPy CIA recruits of the mid-1960s. His father was a truck driver, and David was raised Jewish in the working-class Dorchester neighborhood of Boston. After grad school, Cohen saw an ad for the CIA in a newspaper and decided to apply. He rose fast at the Agency, first working as an analyst on Africa and economic issues and then taking on ever-more-senior jobs. He earned a reputation as a demanding, hardworking officer.

In the fall of 1995, Winston Wiley, the head of the CIA's Counterterrorist Center, went to see Cohen, who was by that point the deputy director of operations, overseeing the Agency's spies. Wiley said, "David, there is a man named Osama bin Laden who is living in Sudan. You know he's got a lot of money; we think he's behind a lot. His capacities are growing. His network is getting larger and more and more dangerous. We need to understand this guy a lot better; he's getting more powerful." Wiley suggested setting up a CIA unit to monitor bin Laden. Cohen told Wiley that they should think bigger and make the unit a "station" similar to the CIA's overseas stations, and put it outside CIA headquarters so that those working on the bin Laden file wouldn't have their days consumed by unrelated meetings.

Wiley suggested Michael Scheuer to run the station. Scheuer, an intense workaholic with a PhD in history, would typically arrive at four o'clock in the morning to prepare a "rack and stack" of what had gone on overnight across the globe in the world of terrorism so that CIA counterterrorism officials could hit the ground running when their days began around 7:00 a.m. Cohen approved the proposal, marking it the first time the CIA had created a unit targeting a particular individual. The bin Laden unit, which became known as Alec Station, was, along with the New York City field office of the FBI, the only place in the government during the half decade before the 9/11 attacks that developed real expertise on bin Laden and al-Qaeda. It was a prescient decision by Cohen.

In December 2001, Cohen, recently retired from the CIA, received a call at his office on 70 Pine Street, a short walk from the World Trade Center. Commissioner Kelly, a former U.S. Marine officer, didn't ask Cohen to join the New York City Police Department; it was more like an order. Kelly said, "I want you to run the intelligence division in the NYPD. It has a lot of problems. I want you to figure out what to do about it, and let me know in two weeks." Cohen remembers that he still could smell the acrid odor of burnt rubber, burnt wires, and burnt people from the nearby Trade Center site. The only possible answer to this job offer was yes.

When Cohen took over the NYPD's Intelligence Division two months later, it was a moribund outfit largely known for driving visiting dignitaries around town. Cohen aimed to make it into the NYPD's CIA. As Cohen familiarized himself with the story of jihadist terrorism in New York City, he realized with something akin to shock that militant Islam had first planted its flag in America more than a decade earlier, with the assassination of Meir Kahane and the 1993 World Trade Center bombing. In the early 1990s there was what was effectively a branch office of bin Laden's Pakistan-based group on Atlantic Avenue in Brooklyn. And in 1997 a Palestinian had plotted to blow up a subway station in Brooklyn. Cohen concluded that "New York has been tar-geted more times than we recognize," and, going further, that "they're coming back if they can, because of what we represent in New York City: the financial and media heart of America."

Kelly had been police commissioner when the Trade Center was first attacked in 1993. He and Cohen shared the conviction that there would be more plots against New York City. They also agreed that terrorists are innovative. Cohen recalls thinking, "If someone told me that some guys with box cutters were going to change America forever, I would say, 'You're out of your fucking mind.'" Kelly told Cohen, "Our job is to every day move the odds a little bit more in our favor. Every single day."

How best to move the odds in the NYPD's favor? Cohen decided that the NYPD needed an intelligence-gathering program that would systematically dig into the methods and materials terrorists had used in preparing their operations. One way to understand those methods and materials was to understand better how terrorist operations were being carried out around the world.

With the aim of learning from the experiences of other countries with terrorism problems, Cohen sent NYPD detectives and analysts across the globe to dig into terrorist plots from Madrid to Melbourne. Cohen was far more interested in what had happened during a plot—how exactly it was carried out—than about who had done it. That was someone else's problem. Cohen wanted to learn the modus operandi of each plot and use that information to strengthen New York against similar attacks.

Armed with the knowledge of a given type of plot, the NYPD could then figure out where in the New York City area materials that could be used in such an operation were sold or distributed. These could be any-thing from pipes useful for pipe bombs to the explosive "black powder" found in fireworks. Detectives could then go to individual stores and explain to the owners how their products might be used in a terrorist plot. Each store owner would be told, "If you see an anomaly in a pur-chase, let us know." The program, known as Operation Nexus, would mushroom into tens of thousands of store visits by the NYPD.

Cohen and other top NYPD officials had an ulterior motive for gathering intel outside U.S. borders: they didn't want to rely solely on the intelligence they were getting from the CIA or FBI. After all, the intelligence the CIA was getting in the summer of 2001 about some kind of large-scale anti-American attack by al-Qaeda hadn't filtered down to the NYPD. And, as Cohen explained following the Madrid bombings in 2004, the deadliest terrorist attack in European history, "We got a report from the FBI on the Madrid bombing which was terrific, it was great. It was fucking eighteen months later!" Cohen wasn't going to rely on anyone but the NYPD to provide the kind of timely intelligence that might help protect New York City.

To address this issue of inadequately shared information, the bipartisan commission that investigated the 9/11 attacks recommended that a new center be created that would gather under one roof intelligence analysts from agencies such as the Department of Homeland Security, the CIA, and the FBI. The 9/11 commissioners concluded that the U.S. government had had enough information during the summer of 2001 to predict that al-Qaeda was planning a major attack, and even that a jihadist militant was training at a flight school in Minnesota, but that that information was not sufficiently widely shared among the various intelligence and law enforcement agencies; nor was it analyzed deeply enough—a failure to "connect the dots." The National Counterterrorism Center (NCTC) was founded in 2004 to connect those dots.

One of the first directors of the NCTC was Michael Leiter. Leiter, who exudes considerable nervous energy and intelligence, edited the *Harvard Law Review* (a role that Obama had held a decade before him) before serving in the Navy as a pilot for six years. On September 11, 2001, Leiter was clerking for Supreme Court justice Stephen Breyer. At the time, there was no Internet connection at the court; the only information source was a five-inch black-and-white TV in one of the justices' chambers. The Supreme Court was ordered evacuated. Justice Breyer later told Leiter, "All the time you just spent in the navy, that's going to be very important and relevant." His words would seem prescient when Bush appointed Leiter to run the NCTC in 2007. Leiter was suddenly in charge of setting U.S. government strategy against al-Qaeda and its allied groups.

One of Leiter's first major insights at the NCTC was the importance of Yemen, which would become more and more prominent as a hotbed of militant training and recruitment over the coming years. It would also prove to be the origin point for the most threatening anti-American plots after 9/11, displacing Pakistan, the birthplace of al-Qaeda, as the country that most worried U.S. counterterrorism officials. Leiter's interest in Yemen centered first on al-Qaeda's long history there, of which the 2000 bombing of the USS *Cole* in the port city of Aden was emblematic. There was also gathering intelligence that "Al-Qaeda in the Arabian Peninsula" had relocated to Yemen from Saudi Arabia following an aggressive crackdown by the Saudi government, which had killed and imprisoned many of the group's members over the previous several years.

Leiter's interest was also piqued by Anwar al-Awlaki. A year into Leiter's stint as director of the NCTC, Awlaki started a personal website on which could be found many of his sermons in English, which were, by this point, not only fundamentalist but openly militant. The site started attracting attention from Islamists around the English-speaking world. The NCTC was trying to better understand the process that led some American Islamists to radicalize into militants, and Awlaki's name kept cropping up in investigations of those who had become radicalized. As far as Leiter was concerned, some English speakers who possessed Awlaki's sermons and writings were clearly becoming radicalized.

B ack in the early spring of 2002, Awlaki had become sufficiently concerned about recent FBI raids on a number of Muslim institutions in Northern Virginia that he told Johari Abdul-Malik, also an imam at the Dar al-Hijrah mosque, that he was going to leave the States for Yemen. "The climate here, you can't really do your work, because it's always anti-terrorism," Awlaki said. "The FBI wants to talk to you. That's not what I signed up for. I would rather go somewhere where I can preach. I can teach. I can have a discourse that's not about 9/11 every day." Abdul-Malik found Awlaki's desire to leave the States a little puzzling, protesting, "You speak English, dude. You're an American. You're going to do more for Islam in Yemen?" Abdul-Malik later suspected something else was at play. "I didn't know then that he'd been busted for soliciting. When I found out, I thought, 'Okay, he's afraid of being exposed.' He was afraid the FBI was going to expose him."

Federal prosecutors were, in fact, already starting to cast around for ways to prosecute Awlaki. One idea was to charge him under the obscure turn-of-the-century Mann Act, which prohibits bringing women across state lines for immoral purposes, since Awlaki had sometimes traveled between DC and Virginia in the company of prostitutes. In 2002, prosecutors instead charged Awlaki with fraud, for falsely claiming in a 1990 U.S. visa application that he was born in Yemen. Awlaki seems to have made this false claim in order to obtain a twenty-thousand-dollar scholarship for foreign students at Colorado State.

Not a man of small ambitions, Awlaki told Abdul-Malik that once he was out of the States he was thinking of running for parliament in Yemen. This was not as presumptuous as it might sound. Awlaki's father was a government minister in Yemen, and the Awlaki tribe from which his family hails is one of the largest in the country, with some 750,000 members. Awlaki was also smart; at the time that he left the United States, he was studying in a doctoral program at George Washington University.

Awlaki arrived in London in March 2002 and found a more congenial environment than in the States. The city was sometimes referred to in the media as "Londonistan" because of the relatively large number of Islamist militants living there and for the permissive British laws regarding free speech. In London, Awlaki could be more freely himself, and he began experimenting with a more strident, fundamentalist public persona. In a videotaped 2002 sermon, he told his young followers that they should never trust non-Muslims.

After a couple of years in London, Awlaki returned to his family's ancestral home in Yemen, where he shed his longtime persona of a moderate American cleric for good. In 2006 he was thrown into a Yemeni jail. Awlaki characterized this as the result of his intervention in one of Yemen's numerous, and often deadly, tribal disputes. The U.S. government asserted that his imprisonment, in fact, happened after Awlaki became involved in an al-Qaeda plot to kidnap a U.S. official.

Awlaki spent much of his prison sentence in solitary confinement, during which time he read the Koran and the Egyptian writer Sayyid Qutb, whose eloquent 1960s writings on the necessity of holy war against the enemies of Islam are deeply influential on Islamist militants. The FBI's interest in Awlaki remained high during this period; agents went to the Yemeni prison where he was being held to interrogate him.

In December 2007, Awlaki was released, perhaps because of the prominent role his father had once played in the Yemeni government. Those who knew Awlaki found him to have emerged hardened after his time in jail. This is a trope among jihadists: Qutb wrote his most militant works while serving time in an Egyptian prison in the 1960s. Al-Qaeda leader Ayman al-Zawahiri's three years in an Egyptian prison during the early 1980s turned him into a lifelong radical. And it was Abu Musab al-Zarqawi's years in a Jordanian jail in the late 1990s that turned him from an ordinary militant into the man who would go on to become the brutal leader of Al-Qaeda in Iraq—someone who thought nothing of personally beheading his hostages and videotaping their murders.

Awlaki's profile rose quickly after his release from jail, as he became the cleric that more and more English-speaking Muslims inquisitive about militant Islam turned to for answers. Bin Laden was still the overall inspirational head of the al-Qaeda network, but he remained inaccessible in his hideout in Pakistan, whereas militants in the West could chat with Awlaki through his blog at www.alawlaki.com, and in colloquial English to boot. The blog had a vibrant comments section, where the cleric engaged with some of his thousands of followers around the world. And unlike a number of leaders of al-Qaeda, bin Laden included, Awlaki was a genuine cleric, so he could present himself as a leading religious figure. Awlaki's many sermons were now also becoming widely available on YouTube, which had launched a year before Awlaki's imprisonment in Yemen.

Awlaki's journey from obscure American cleric to foremost religious advocate of jihad in the English-speaking world would span the decade after 9/11, during which he would also undergo a further transformation: into the operational leader of an ascendant branch of al-Qaeda.

His meteoric rise, while owing something to his personal charisma, had everything to do with the changing face of jihad, as militant Islam expanded from a top-down enterprise masterminded by a few core groups to a decentralized system of recruitment and inspiration that took advantage of new technologies to propagandize far beyond the Middle East. To follow the trail of Awlaki's influence is to trace the post-9/11 evolution of jihad involving Americans. Of the more than 360 Americans charged with or convicted of involvement in jihadist terrorist activity since the 9/11 attacks, more than 90 were found to have Awlaki's writings or sermons in their possession or cited him as an influence, and a further 7 had corresponded with him or traveled to Yemen to meet him.

As the threat from jihadist terrorists evolved, so did the U.S. response. In the years after al-Qaeda's attacks at the Trade Center and the Pentagon, the American terrorist hunters and the hunted American militants were to play a perpetual game of cat-and-mouse.

CHAPTER 3

WHO ARE THE TERRORISTS?

FOR MEN TO PLUNGE HEADLONG INTO AN UNDERTAKING OF VAST
CHANGE, THEY MUST BE INTENSELY DISCONTENTED YET NOT DESTITUTE,
AND THEY MUST HAVE THE FEELING THAT BY THE POSSESSION OF SOME
POTENT DOCTRINE, INFALLIBLE LEADER OR SOME NEW TECHNIQUE
THEY HAVE ACCESS TO A SOURCE OF IRRESISTIBLE POWER. THEY
MUST ALSO HAVE AN EXTRAVAGANT CONCEPTION OF THE PROSPECTS
AND POTENTIALITIES OF THE FUTURE. FINALLY, THEY MUST BE
WHOLLY IGNORANT OF THE DIFFICULTIES INVOLVED IN THEIR VAST
UNDERTAKING.

—Eric Hoffer, *The True Believer* (1951)

I t was the strangest job interview Mitchell Silber had ever experienced. After traveling to NYPD headquarters at the southern tip of Manhattan, he was put in a dark, unmarked car and driven around. The police lieutenant driving the car at one point wisecracked, "We heard you're smart. If you're so smart, tell us where bin Laden is." Silber was driven to Chelsea, where the NYPD Intelligence Division was based, and dropped off at a coffee shop. Sitting at a table was David Cohen, who had a proposition: Silber should come work for him as a special assistant at NYPD Intel.

It wasn't a tough decision. Silber would be joining what was effectively a start-up intelligence agency, based, almost literally, at Ground Zero. And Cohen was a legend in the intelligence community—profane, tough, demanding, and results-oriented. Cohen had discovered Silber a little over a year earlier, in December 2003, when Silber led a group of fellow Columbia graduate students in analyzing Saudi Arabia's laws and regulations on terrorism finance for the Council on Foreign Relations, a project on which Cohen advised.

Silber was one of a wave of thousands of Americans who felt compelled by the events of 9/11 to work in law enforcement, the intelligence community, or academia to try to understand and contain the jihadist threat. He had been a successful financial analyst in Manhattan but read books about the Middle East to relax, and had followed the news about al-Qaeda for years. As Silber watched the second tower fall on the walk home from his evacuated office building, he guessed that bin Laden was responsible. In the wake of the attacks, he applied to Columbia University to pursue a master's degree in international affairs with a concentration in Middle East studies, with the thought that these academic credentials would help him to get into the fight against terrorists. He had read that during World War II some attorneys and investment bankers gave up their jobs to join the Office of Strategic Services, the forerunner of the CIA, and he thought this fight was analogous.

At Columbia, Silber had used his background in corporate finance to study the mechanisms of terrorism financing. He brought the same analytical mentality to the NYPD's internal think tank, where he soon took a lead role. One of his first actions was a trip to Amsterdam, where in November 2004 filmmaker Theo van Gogh had been assassinated because of a film he had directed in which verses of the Koran were projected onto the bodies of naked women. Mohammed Bouyeri, a twenty-six-year-old Moroccan Dutchman who had recently embraced a militant form of Islam, calmly shot van Gogh as the filmmaker was bicycling through the streets. Then he slashed the filmmaker's throat with a machete. Bouyeri had no links to formal terror organizations. Van Gogh's assassination would prove an early warning sign of more "homegrown" attacks to come in the West.

Silber met with Dutch police and intelligence officials and toured the neighborhoods where Bouyeri had lived, trying to understand the process of how he had become a homegrown militant. According to the

Dutch officials to whom Silber spoke, Bouyeri and the other second-generation Moroccan immigrants he associated with were not assimilating well. They felt alienated, neither Dutch nor Moroccan, and were in search of a new, stable identity. There was therefore an appeal in trying to understand their religious heritage better, which put some on a trajectory that exposed them to fundamentalist and even violent interpretations of Islam.

Silber's next stop was West Yorkshire, in the north of England, where the group that carried out the July 2005 suicide bombings in London had grown up. Silber found that the radicalization process for these individuals looked a lot like that of Bouyeri and his circle. Like Bouyeri, the London bombers were second-generation immigrants; three of the four were of Pakistani heritage. Silber was also struck that both Bouyeri and the London bombers had eventually rejected the mosques they attended because they weren't radical enough for them. Instead, the London bombers gathered, and became increasingly radicalized, at an Islamic bookstore in Leeds and a nearby gym where they worked out together.

Silber also studied the 2004 Madrid bombings, in which a group of mostly first-generation immigrants to Spain set off bombs that killed 191 people. He found that the plotters had few links to formal terrorist organizations. Finally, he traveled to Canada to examine the case of the "Toronto 18," a group of mostly second-generation Canadian Muslims who'd plotted to attack the Canadian Parliament in the spring of 2006. They had experimented with homemade bombs and planned to detonate truck bombs outside their targets, but were arrested before they could carry out the plot. They had no links to overseas militants.

Silber kept on finding similarities among jihadist plots: The perpetrators were often second-generation immigrants who didn't start out as observant Muslims. As they became more devout, they often left the mosque they had once attended, finding it insufficiently militant, sometimes breaking away as a group. Together they would watch jihadi videos and engage in bonding activities such as playing paintball. Silber started thinking about creating a model to describe the process by which some young men became fundamentalists, then militants, and, finally, full-fledged terrorists.

He decided to compare eleven jihadist plots that had taken place in Europe, Australia, Canada, and the States after 9/11 in order to identify the commonalities among the plotters. Increasingly convinced that homegrown militants with few or no connections to groups such as al-Qaeda represented the future of the terrorist threat, he believed these comparisons would have an important influence on NYPD policy. At that time, the prevailing wisdom was that the United States was better at integrating immigrants than other Western countries, and the government's focus was on al-Qaeda. Few were worried about the homegrown threat.

Silber's research was originally intended only for internal NYPD consumption, but department officials encouraged him to go public with his findings. Published in August 2007, his report, *Radicalization in the West: The Homegrown Threat,* coauthored with another intelligence analyst at the NYPD, Arvin Bhatt, featured the stamp of approval of police commissioner Raymond Kelly, who wrote the introduction. The report lays out a taxonomy of jihadist terrorists in the West: "unremarkable" male Muslims between the ages of fifteen and thirty-five, generally well educated and middle class, many of whom grew up as nonobservant Muslims or were converts to Islam. Many of the plotters had no links to formal terrorist organizations.

Some kind of personal crisis (the loss of a job, the experience of racism, moral outrage caused by the way Muslims were being treated in international conflicts, or the death of a close family member) provided a "cognitive opening" for a turn to Salafi beliefs, demonstrated by wearing traditional Islamic clothing and growing beards. This was not in itself alarming; these were simply fundamentalist practices. In the next stage of their radicalization, however, as their views became more politicized, they separated themselves from society, spending more and more time only with similar, radicalized individuals.

The report describes the final stage before the men turn to terrorism as "Jihadization": the point at which a militant decides to perform jihad.

This often takes the form of travel abroad for training or, if overseas training is not an option, bonding activities with other radicalized men. (Even paintball is not always innocuous: in early 2001 a group of aspiring jihadists in Northern Virginia played paintball explicitly to simulate combat.) The report explains that there is no perfect linear progression toward jihadization, but it concludes that individuals who pass through all these stages are "quite likely to be involved in the planning or implementation of a terrorist act."

Following the 9/11 attacks, TV screens were filled with arresting scenes of rows of young boys at madrassas learning to recite the Koran by rote. It was common wisdom that these religious schools were a breeding ground for terrorism. In October 2003, Secretary of Defense Donald Rumsfeld wondered, "Are we capturing, killing or deterring and dissuading more terrorists every day than the madrassas and the radical clerics are recruiting, training and deploying against us?" But this assessment was wrong, at least as it related to terrorism in the West; the majority of conspirators in the eleven terrorist plots Silber had examined came from secular backgrounds, and none was the product of a madrassa. For Silber this was a key finding. It also made a great deal of intuitive sense: After all, learning the Koran by heart in Arabic was hardly going to serve someone well in preparing to launch an attack in the States. For that, one would need a decent command of English and a real understanding of the West—linguistic and cultural skills not taught at madrassas.

In a 2006 study, Swati Pandey, a researcher at the New America Foundation, and I examined the educational backgrounds of seventy-nine terrorists responsible for five of the worst anti-Western jihadist attacks in recent memory—the World Trade Center bombing in 1993, the bombings of two U.S. embassies in Africa in 1998, the September 11 attacks, the Bali nightclub bombings in 2002, and the London bombings on July 7, 2005. We found that more than half of the terrorists had attended college, making them as well educated as the average American. Two in our sample had doctoral degrees, and two others had begun working toward their doctorates. The data also showed a strong correlation between technical education and terrorism. Of those who attended college or graduate school, more than half attained scientific or technical degrees, with engineering and medicine as the most popular majors.

All those credited with masterminding the five terrorist attacks had university degrees, and none had attended a madrassa. Three of the four pilots who led the September 11 attacks spent time at universities in Germany; they began plotting the attacks while completing their degrees. The lead hijacker, Mohamed Atta, was studying for a doctorate in, of all things, urban preservation at the University of Hamburg-Harburg in Germany. The fifteen "muscle hijackers" varied in educational background, but six of them had completed some university studies.

Another mainstream assumption at the time of our study was that poverty fed terrorism. "We fight against poverty because hope is an answer to terror," President George W. Bush explained in 2002. Almost two years later, Democratic presidential candidate Howard Dean declared, "Today, billions of people live on the knife's edge of survival, trapped in a struggle against ignorance, poverty, and disease. Their misery is a breeding ground for the hatred peddled by bin Laden and other merchants of death." A couple of months after 9/11 the United Nations General Assembly held a meeting involving forty-one heads of state, who issued a statement that "terrorism could only be eliminated if conditions creating a fertile breeding ground for terrorism, such as poverty and marginalization, were removed."

In fact, the poor are generally too busy making ends meet to be the vanguard of any revolution. History shows that terrorism is a largely bourgeois endeavor, from the Russian anarchists of the late nineteenth century to the German Marxists of the Baader-Meinhof Gang of the 1970s, to the apocalyptic Japanese terror cult Aum Shinrikyo of the 1990s. Islamist terrorists, it turns out, are no different.

Silber's 2007 report and Pandey's and my 2006 study helped to counter the then prevalent notions that jihadist terrorists were poor or uneducated or madrassa graduates, and did so by examining a number of prominent terrorist attacks and plots that hitherto hadn't been the subject of much comparative research. An important feature of both reports, however, was that they weren't breaking entirely new ground. Though largely ignored outside the academy, theories about terrorism had been proposed before 9/11, and the new studies accorded with previous scholarship. In 1999 the Library of Congress issued a study that asked the question "Who becomes a terrorist and why?" and concluded, following a survey of all the published literature, that there were only a few "major exceptions to the middle- and upper-class origins of terrorist groups" and that terrorists generally "have more than average education." In other words, the U.S. counterterrorism establishment was slowly realizing that asking "Who becomes a terrorist?" turns out, in many cases, to be much like asking "Who owns a Volvo?"

Arguably the most influential, and controversial, post-9/11 theorist of jihad in the West was Dr. Marc Sageman, who introduced to America the specter of "leaderless jihad." He was in many ways uniquely qualified to delve into these questions. The son of Polish Holocaust survivors, Sageman studied sociology at Harvard and later became a psychiatrist. After medical school he became intrigued by the CIA, where he trained to be a case officer. He worked in Pakistan during the 1980s, helping to arm the Afghan mujahideen fighting the Soviets.

Following the Afghan War, Sageman practiced psychiatry, specializing in the study of murderers. He interviewed many as they faced a possible death penalty. He also taught at the University of Pennsylvania, where one of his courses examined how the dynamic of group loyalty helped ordinary German soldiers kill Jews even though many found the task personally distasteful.

Like so many other Americans, Sageman was riveted to the television on September 11, 2001, and over the days that followed. He knew that much of what the talking heads were saying about the motivations and backgrounds of the perpetrators of the attacks—"they hate our freedoms," etc.—was likely total nonsense, and he decided to do something about it. This would launch him down an entirely new career path; he would end his psychiatry practice in Philadelphia and apply himself instead to understanding who becomes a jihadist terrorist and why.

Sageman was haunted by the possibility that CIA aid to the Afghan mujahideen had ended up in the wrong hands: "I didn't know that there were no Afghans in al-Qaeda at that time, but people conflated the

Taliban and al-Qaeda. I was like, 'Holy shit, those are guys I trained.' That's really what drove me at first. It was really kind of this sense of guilt." Sageman eventually concluded that al-Qaeda had not recruited Afghans, and he knew from his work in Pakistan that bin Laden and his men had never received CIA aid or training, but he was still fascinated by the question of who joined al-Qaeda and why. He started assembling a database of men associated with al-Qaeda. The sample grew from 25 militants to 45 and then to 172 documented members and associates of al-Qaeda from around the world.

Based on court records and media accounts about these men, Sageman wrote the 2004 book *Understanding Terror Networks*. His analysis of who joined terrorist organizations squared with some of the findings of the 1999 Library of Congress study and presaged the work of Silber and Pandey: the men who joined were middle-class, relatively well educated, mentally stable, and often married with children. It was a far cry from the brainwashed, freedom-hating thugs of popular imagination.

The key new insight of *Understanding Terror Networks,* though, which went on to have an impact on policy and law enforcement, was the importance of group dynamics. Drawing on network analysis and social movement theory, and also on his work as a psychiatrist, Sageman concluded that "social bonds" formed by friendships (and sometimes kinship) played a more important role than ideology in creating jihadist groups. Friends decided to join the jihad together, Sageman wrote, motivated as much by "in-group love" as by "out-group hate." The paintball trips and jihadi video sessions that Silber would later observe weren't just solidarity measures among a group of already like-minded people; they were the instigating factors, a mechanism of mutual reinforcement that drove potential jihadists further along the path toward terrorism than they likely would have gone alone. Sageman's Exhibit A was the 9/11 plot. The planners and pilots had been a close-knit fraternity, studying and living together in Hamburg for years. They ate together, prayed together, and plotted jihad together.

Typical of such a "bunch of guys," as Sageman called them, was the group that plotted in 2005 to attack U.S. military installations in California. While jailed in California's New Folsom Prison, Kevin Lamar

James, an African American convert to Islam, formed a group dedicated to holy war that he conceived of as "Al-Qaeda in America." James recruited five others to help with his plans, one of whom had a job at Los Angeles Airport (LAX). In a list of potential targets James named LAX, the Israeli consulate in Los Angeles, and a U.S. Army base in Manhattan Beach. James's crew decided to attack a U.S. military recruiting station in Los Angeles on the fourth anniversary of 9/11. They financed their activities by sticking up gas stations; their plans only came to light during a routine investigation of a gas station robbery in Torrance, California, during which police found documents laying out the group's plans for jihadist mayhem.

A year later a similar "bunch of guys," this time a group of largely Albanian immigrants angered by the Iraq War, plotted to attack the Fort Dix army base in southern New Jersey. The Fort Dix plotters assembled a number of rifles and pistols and regularly conducted firearms training in the Pocono Mountains of Pennsylvania. In August 2006 the ringleader surveilled the Fort Dix base and told a government informant, "[T]his is exactly what we are looking for. You hit four, five, or six Humvees and light the whole place [up] and retreat completely without any losses." All the Fort Dix plotters were convicted and given lengthy prison sentences.

The same year that Sageman published his groundbreaking study, across the world in Pakistan, a Syrian militant, Abu Musab al-Suri, was publishing his magnum opus about the theory and practice of "leaderless jihad," which would prove prescient. This form of radicalization, in which lone fundamentalists forged their own paths toward militancy, would soon attract much notice among U.S. terrorism analysts. Its first herald, however, was a man fomenting jihad, not studying it. An intense intellectual, Suri had fought in the Afghan War in the 1980s, after which he married a Spanish woman and settled in London. There he was part of a circle of militants close to bin Laden, but in the late 1990s he moved back to Afghanistan to run a jihadist training camp independent of al-Qaeda. In 2004 he released to the Internet a sixteen-hundred-page book, *The Call for Global Islamic Resistance.* It was the culmination of a life devoted to thinking about and teaching jihad.

Suri's work was an extensive critique of bin Laden's al-Qaeda organization as it had existed on 9/11. At the time of the attacks, al-Qaeda was a top-down bureaucracy of committees presided over by bin Laden, who exercised dictatorial authority. A videotape recovered in Afghanistan after the fall of the Taliban showed Suri in front of a whiteboard, drawing a diagram to indicate how easy it is to cripple a conventional top-down organization once one of their number has been arrested (a matter of interrogating the arrestee about other members). Suri instead recommended a model for jihad as "spontaneous operations performed by individuals and cells all over the whole world without connection between them." This system would confuse intelligence agencies, he reasoned, and any militants who were arrested would give up less information because they wouldn't know who else was part of the movement. Suri advised each of his followers in Afghanistan to form a "brigade" that "doesn't exceed ten members," an ideal that sounded much like Sageman's "bunch of guys," but he also exhorted individuals to take jihad into their own hands. "If a man living in Sweden spots a Jewish security target, he attacks it." He formalized his concept of leaderless jihad into the Arabic slogan *nizam la tanzim,* "a system, not an organization."

In the decade and a half after 9/11, as the number of such attacks proliferated in the West, Suri became perhaps the most visionary strategic thinker in militant jihadi circles. The direct influence of his writing— reprinted at length and regularly in al-Qaeda's English-language magazine, *Inspire*—is difficult to measure, however, because his call for a leaderless jihad was a self-fulfilling prophecy. As Suri himself pointed out in his 2004 manifesto, following bin Laden's foolhardy decision to attack the Trade Center and Pentagon, U.S. forces destroyed the safe haven that al-Qaeda had once enjoyed in Taliban-controlled Afghanistan: "The jihad movement rose to glory in the 1960s, and continued through the '70s and '80s, but was destroyed after 9/11." Once al-Qaeda had lost its Afghan training camps and safe haven, there wasn't much option of rebasing the group somewhere else as a top-down organization with training camps that could be easily destroyed all over again. The head of the hydra had been cut off; if a worldwide jihadist movement were to thrive, it would have to rely, at least to some extent, on personal initiative.

In early 2008, Marc Sageman published a second book, *Leaderless Jihad*. The book made the case that Suri's vision was becoming a reality—that a movement of individual militants guided by al-Qaeda's ideology was the new frontier of jihadist terrorism. He argued that "the present threat has evolved from a structured group of al-Qaeda masterminds controlling vast resources and issuing commands, to . . . 'homegrown' wannabes." This was due in large part, he said, to the increasing penetration of the Internet around the world; Web forums and chatrooms could provide the encouragement necessary for a lone fundamentalist to turn militant. It was in many ways a natural extension of Sageman's bunch-of-guys paradigm—the ultimate in DIY radicalization. In the summer of 2008, Sageman doubled down on his expanded vision of the radicalization process in the pages of the *Washington Post,* where he declared that homegrown militants, whether bunches of guys or individual "lone wolves," "must now be seen as the main terrorist threat to the United States"—more threatening than al-Qaeda.

This was a departure from the contemporary focus of U.S. intelligence, which in the first years after 9/11 was on purported al-Qaeda "sleeper cells," or militants trained by al-Qaeda and sent to the States to await orders to attack. In 2001, FBI director Robert Mueller had declared that "our greatest threat is from al-Qaeda cells in the United States that we have not yet been able to identify," and Larry Johnson, a former CIA operative who later became a counterterrorism official at the State Department, told UPI in 2002 that there were likely as many as two thousand al-Qaeda cell members in the States. In 2004 the *Washington Times* warned readers that hundreds of individuals trained abroad by al-Qaeda had been sent back to the States to act as sleeper agents. Two years later Walid Phares, a TV "terrorism expert," claimed on CNN that there were two hundred sleeper cell members in the States. All these assertions turned out to be false.

As well-publicized plots such as those targeting military installations in California and Fort Dix began to bear out Sageman's conclusions about the risks posed by independent militants, the establishment began to take notice. In 2008, David Cohen invited Sageman to be the first scholar in residence at NYPD, where he taught terrorism workshops to detectives and worked with Silber's team of intelligence analysts. The theory of leaderless jihad would now be injected directly into the thinking of the largest police force in the nation.

The idea of a leaderless revolutionary movement was not new. In the 1980s, Louis Beam, a prominent white supremacist, advocated "leaderless resistance" as a way for his fellow racists to combat the government without fear of being discovered by law enforcement agencies. Beam explained: "Utilizing the Leaderless Resistance concept, all individuals and groups operate independently of each other, and never report to a central headquarters or single leader for direction or instruction, as would those who belong to a typical pyramid organization." Timothy McVeigh, who masterminded the 1995 bombing of the Alfred P. Murrah Federal Building in Oklahoma City, killing 168 people, carried out his attack with no support from any organization, demonstrating that the "leaderless resistance" model could be lethal.

Still, in 2008 it was a seismic shift in perspective for the U.S. counterterrorism establishment, for which the specter of a vast overseas bureaucracy of terror, and the memory of its destructive power, still loomed large. But as the Bush presidency drew to a close, leaving a legacy of two overseas wars, a number of Americans began wondering whether the most threatening front of the "war on terror" was the home front.

Mitch Silber, by this point recognized as an influential counterterrorism analyst, agreed with Sageman's theories. As Sageman served his term as NYPD scholar in residence, the two men taught a class at Columbia University together that emphasized leaderless jihad and homegrown militants over groups such as al-Qaeda.

The very next year, two tragedies would make Silber and Sageman's case more indelibly than any classroom lecture could.

CHAPTER 4

LONE WOLVES

THE LESS JUSTIFIED A MAN IS IN CLAIMING EXCELLENCE FOR HIS OWN
SELF, THE MORE READY HE IS TO CLAIM ALL EXCELLENCE FOR HIS
NATION, HIS RELIGION, HIS RACE OR HIS HOLY CAUSE.

—Eric Hoffer, *The True Believer*

M elvin Bledsoe is a charismatic, blues-loving entrepreneur who owns
Blues City Tours, a tour bus company that shuttles tourists to Beale
Street, a string of honky-tonk bars and clubs in downtown Memphis.
Bledsoe's buses also roll over to Graceland, Elvis Presley's opulent home,
and to the legendary Sun Studio, where Elvis and his collaborators invented rock 'n' roll. It was while working as a tour guide at Graceland in
the early 1980s that Melvin developed a taste for the business, and soon
catering to the tourists of Memphis became his life's work.

In late April 2009, Melvin dispatched his twenty-three-year-old son,
Carlos, to Little Rock, Arkansas, to open up a branch of the family
tour company. He hoped the experience would do Carlos some good;
frankly, Melvin and his wife, Linda, were worried about their only son.
Both mother and father were serious Baptists who had been utterly per-
plexed by Carlos's conversion to Islam at the age of nineteen. Even more
confounding was a mysterious sixteen-month trip he had just made to
Yemen, where he had ended up in jail. But now that Carlos was back in
the United States, the Bledsoes hoped this phase would come to an end.
And putting him to work in the family business seemed an ideal way to
help that along. After all, Carlos had grown up around the business, and

his parents had keen memories of him standing at his father's side during tours, decked out in a little conductor's uniform.

But by the end of May, Melvin and Linda began worrying about Carlos all over again. "From Friday to Monday we hadn't heard one drop of word out of him," Melvin says. Melvin called the other employees in Little Rock, but none of them had seen or heard from his son. An employee checked his apartment. Carlos had vanished.

On the morning of June 1, 2009, Melvin and Linda jumped in their car for the two-hour drive from Memphis to Little Rock, which they took very fast. Just before they arrived, Melvin's cell phone rang. It was an FBI agent. "Mr. Bledsoe, we need to talk to you. Something has happened. Somebody got shot. Somebody's dead, and we think your son is involved. We want you to come to the Little Rock field office."

"My heart dropped to my shoes," says Melvin. He looked over at his wife of three decades, who was listening to his end of the conversation, not knowing what the FBI agent had just said. Telling her was the most painful thing Melvin had ever done.

At the field office, agents told the Bledsoes that Carlos had fired shots at a local U.S. military recruiting center. He had killed Private William "Andy" Long, twenty-three, as he stepped out of the center for a smoke. He had also wounded Private Quinton Ezeagwula, eighteen. Both were shot at close range with a semiautomatic rifle from the window of a black Ford Explorer. Private Long fell to the ground immediately, mortally wounded, while Private Ezeagwula crawled to the safety of the recruiting station. Private Long's mother, Janet, was waiting for her son in the parking lot and heard the gunshots. Bledsoe kept firing; several rounds entered the station but did not strike any of the fifteen people inside. Then, just as abruptly as he had started firing, Bledsoe drove off. Going to prison was not part of his plan.

During the Obama administration, "lone wolves" such as Bledsoe, motivated by al-Qaeda's ideology but with no connections to a formal terrorist organization, became the face of jihad in America. These self-radicalized terrorists proved far harder to detect than either al-Qaeda operatives or independent groups, as they did not generally communicate with other militants, which meant there were no phone calls or e-mails to intercept and no meetings to monitor. Lone wolves have not, however, proved capable of pulling off operations anywhere near the scale of 9/11, which required extensive training, many plotters, and hundreds of thousands of dollars. Still, they could come from anywhere, at any time—and they could also be deadly. Since 9/11 every act of jihadist terrorism resulting in a fatality on American soil has been carried out by lone wolves.

The transformation of Carlos Bledsoe of Memphis into Abdulhakim Mujahid ("Holy Warrior") Muhammad offers a prime example of how difficult it is to predict self-radicalization, even when it follows known patterns, and the law enforcement failures that can result. Bledsoe would chart an unlikely course from the Deep South to Yemen and back, and although FBI agents became aware of his militant views along the way, they did not foresee what happened in Little Rock.

The Bledsoes, a large African American family from rural Tennessee, have served in America's wars since the Civil War. Melvin's father was a laborer, his mother a housekeeper and nanny, and their six boys and two girls were put to work at an early age. "We learned the value of a dollar early," Melvin says. Melvin sought to instill the same values of hard work and discipline in his own son. As a teenager, Carlos worked at a Chuck E. Cheese's in addition to helping out with the family tour business.

Carlos's upbringing was also infused with fundamentalist Christianity. Melvin's Southern Baptist beliefs put a premium on abstinence from smoking, drinking, and swearing. As a member of the Church of God in Christ, Carlos's mother, Linda, practiced an even more austere version of Christianity. That meant that the Bledsoes often went to church twice on Sundays, for morning and evening services. At their church, congregants shouted, danced, and praised the Lord at the top of their lungs. Some fell to the ground, seized by the Holy Ghost.

Along with jobs and churchgoing, young Carlos also played basketball. And the tight-knit Bledsoe family went on vacations to New

Orleans, Biloxi, and even, once, the Bahamas. But as he grew older, Carlos got into trouble. There were the typical teen dabblings with marijuana, but there were also rumblings at high school that Carlos had joined a gang. In August 2002 he was involved in a brawl during which one participant pulled a knife. A year later Carlos threatened the driver of a Chevy Cavalier, hitting the vehicle with brass knuckles and shouting, "I'm gonna kill you! Get out! I'm going to kill you!"

Melvin felt Carlos's schoolmates were pressuring him. "The climate in Memphis was really growing, with gangs and kids wanting to join a gang. The West Coast influence was now pushing toward the South, the rap music and the TV and the videos, and all this glamorous stuff, and these kids didn't know what to think. They just thought they'd like to try some of this. So that was beginning to be a problem, and we saw that and of course we tried to make sure that he stayed away from that as much as possible."

Carlos graduated from high school in 2003. For Melvin, Carlos's graduation was both a proud day and a relief. Now, he thought, Carlos would escape the bad influence of his peers and apply to college. Carlos began studying business administration at Tennessee State University—a prelude, his father hoped, to joining the family business. But in February 2004, Carlos ran into serious trouble with the law. A police officer arrested him in Knoxville, Tennessee, after a car he was riding in was pulled over. In the car, the officer found a loaded SKS assault rifle, two shotguns, and marijuana. Carlos was looking at as many as fourteen years in prison. He took a plea deal that gave him a year's probation; the deal specified that any further criminal offense would net him fourteen years.

Carlos was, in the words of his father, "scared out of his shoes," and began casting around for a religious anchor that might provide him with self-discipline. He visited a synagogue but came away feeling that Judaism did not embrace blacks. He then became interested in the ideas of the Nation of Islam, which combine elements of Islam with black nationalism and a philosophy of self-help. One day he dropped into a mosque in Nashville, where he saw more than fifty men bowing and prostrating themselves to Allah. It made a strong impression. He tried to join in, and one of the worshippers asked him, "When did you become a Muslim?" Carlos explained that he had only recently become interested in Islam, at which point all the worshippers shouted "Allahu Akbar!" and embraced him as if he were a long-lost relative.

Carlos made his formal declaration of faith in December 2004, at a Memphis mosque. He was nineteen. His older sister, Monica, thought this might turn out to be all for the good; all the Muslims she knew stayed out of trouble. His parents were less accepting. Monica explains, "There's no religion better than theirs. So it was a hard pill for them to swallow."

Carlos's conversion soon began to exert a major force in his life. He stopped smoking marijuana and listening to hip-hop in favor of reading the Koran. His high school girlfriend began to drift away as his requests that she, too, convert grew more insistent. When he began rolling his jeans above his ankles (in imitation of the way the Prophet Muhammad is said to have worn his pants), Monica noticed and wondered about it. The Muslims she knew did not dress like that; they were more Americanized.

She and her brother debated religion. "I'm trying to save you all from going to hell," Carlos told her. "Carlos, that's the religion you chose," Monica replied. "This is my religion. I'm not forcing my religion on you, so you don't force your religion on me." Carlos warned her, "Y'all going to learn."

Soon came a symbolic break with his family. One night, when he was staying at his parents' house, Carlos found a picture of Dr. Martin Luther King Jr. hanging on the wall of his bedroom. He took it down. When his father confronted him, he explained that, according to his religion, hanging images of people on the wall signified worshipping something other than Allah, which was forbidden.

"What kind of religion do you really have?" said Melvin. "This is foolish. This is crazy. All your life, Dr. King fought for the rights of the race of people who we are. And you have no respect for that." On a regular basis the Bledsoe tour buses stopped at the Memphis motel where Dr. King had been assassinated. The next time Carlos visited his parents, he left the King picture on the wall but covered it whenever he was in the room.

Carlos started avoiding his parents entirely. He had a pit bull puppy but gave it away because some Muslims consider dogs to be "unclean." He began wearing a *thobe,* the white ankle-length robe worn by men in Saudi Arabia. Perhaps his most decisive step away from his old life was to marry a Muslim "sister" with no connection to anyone he had known before his conversion. He followed this, to his family's consternation, by dropping out of school during the fall of 2005. Melvin was especially upset. He had not gone to college because his parents couldn't afford it; his dream was that his own son would. Feeling that they were losing their son, Melvin and Linda drove the three hours to Nashville to drop in on him. His house, they found, was almost empty save for a couch and a picture of Mecca on the wall.

Carlos was now spending all his time with a small group of strict Salafists, and on April 23, 2006, he legally changed his name to Abdulhakim Mujahid Muhammad. As far as Muhammad was concerned, Carlos Bledsoe was dead.

In the late summer of 2007, Carlos surprised his parents by telling them that he was planning to move to Yemen to learn Arabic. "You aren't a really true Muslim until you can speak the language," he explained. Carlos said he would support himself by teaching English. Melvin told his son that he and Linda loved him and didn't want him to "get into any crap over there."

"I love you guys, too," Carlos said. His sister was wary of the rumors of terrorism in Yemen, but he reassured her: "That's not what I'm going over there to do. I'll be careful. I'm going over there to teach."

Carlos Bledsoe arrived in Yemen on September 11, 2007. It was a revelation to him. Yemenis were hospitable and treated him with great respect, and the cost of living was low in the poorest country in the Arab world. Bledsoe found a job teaching English for three hundred dollars a month in the southern Yemeni port of Aden—the city where, seven years earlier, al-Qaeda suicide attackers had blown up a bomb-filled skiff, nearly sinking the USS *Cole* and killing seventeen American sailors.

Though Bledsoe might appear to be an unlikely candidate for radicalization, his path to jihad largely followed the template identified by Silber, Sageman, and other terrorism researchers: a middle-class background; the "cognitive opening" to embrace fundamentalist Islam—provided, in Bledsoe's case, by his 2004 arrest and probation; and the isolation Bledsoe fostered by quitting school and marrying a woman who shared his rigid beliefs. Bledsoe's journey abroad also fit the paradigm. Traveling to a "field of jihad" such as Yemen was a critical marker of what Silber's NYPD report termed "Jihadization," the final stage of radicalization before a militant might launch a terrorist attack.

On November 18, 2008, Bledsoe was arrested in Yemen for possessing a fake Somali identification card. The card was part of an ill-conceived plan to travel to Somalia to wage jihad against Jews and Americans there. (Bledsoe seemed to have been unaware that Somalia is 99 percent Muslim and that there are hardly any Jews or Americans in the country.) When he was arrested, Bledsoe was found to possess literature from Anwar al-Awlaki and manuals about how to make bombs and gun silencers. On his cell phone was contact information for several militants wanted in Saudi Arabia. Haphazard though his efforts were, they revealed a dark truth: Bledsoe had made the transition from fundamentalist to militant bent on violence.

Bledsoe was incarcerated in a prison run by Yemen's feared Political Security Organization, which handles the country's internal security. There he mixed with hardened jihadists, some of whom may have been members of al-Qaeda. It was here that Bledsoe began hatching a plan to bring holy war to America.

Some weeks into Bledsoe's imprisonment, Nashville-based FBI special agent Greg Thomason traveled to Yemen to interrogate him. The FBI had opened an "assessment" of Bledsoe, which, while not a full-scale investigation, showed that he had caught its attention.

Though Bledsoe insisted to Thomason that he had gone to Yemen only to teach English and learn Arabic, Thomason informed him that he would be deported to the States. When Bledsoe said he didn't want to go back, the agent told him he had no choice in the matter. Thomason thought that maybe Bledsoe could be turned into a confidential informant for the Bureau, perhaps able to shed some light on the circle of Islamists in Nashville who had provided him with his initial contacts in Yemen.

On January 29, 2009, after sixteen months in Yemen, Bledsoe was deported. Waiting for him at Memphis International Airport were his parents, who hugged and kissed him, then whisked him home for a celebratory dinner. At the house a banner proclaimed "Welcome Home, Carlos."

To his family, Carlos seemed not unlike his old self, though he would occasionally flare up, declaring, for example, that Arab women were being "raped by infidels." When he watched news reports about the wars in Iraq and Afghanistan, he fumed sullenly.

Following instructions to report to the FBI, Bledsoe met again with Thomason, who tried to recruit him as an informant. When Bledsoe refused, the FBI stopped tracking him. This decision is hard to reconcile with the information the Bureau had at the time. After all, Bledsoe had been arrested in Yemen with a fake Somali identification card, jihadist literature, and manuals on bomb making and guns. Perhaps this information was not properly communicated by the Yemeni intelligence service, but even so, Bledsoe's long stay in Yemen and his arrest should have been enough to raise concerns about what he might do next. Michael Leiter, director of the NCTC, believes that the FBI committed an unequivocal error by not apprising the rest of the intelligence community of its information on Bledsoe. "There should have been broad dissemination on this," he later said.

On the other hand, the signal-to-noise ratio in the counterterrorism system was extremely high, with about ten thousand FBI investigations going on simultaneously, and the Bureau had determined that there was, in official terms, no "derogatory" information about Bledsoe that merited opening a full-scale investigation. Under U.S. law, merely being a radical is not sufficient cause to detain a suspect or to continue an open-ended investigation.

By now Bledsoe was privately nurturing a great hatred for the United States, particularly the U.S. military. He believed that American soldiers regularly urinated on the Koran and used it for target practice, and that U.S. servicemen were raping Muslim women and children in the Middle East—common talking points in jihadist propaganda. He was also angry at CNN for not showing what was "really going on" in the Arab world.

It was around this time that Melvin decided that setting Carlos up in Little Rock, where he could open a branch of the family business, would be the best way to "Westernize" him. But the program of Westernization didn't take. Bledsoe instead began to develop plans for a holy war targeting army recruiting centers and Jewish organizations. He searched the Internet for potential targets in Little Rock, Memphis, Nashville, Kentucky, Baltimore, Philadelphia, and Washington, DC. Conscious of the fact that he might die in his jihad, he made out a will, leaving his few possessions to mosques. In the will he asked for "a complete Islamic funeral . . . No church. No crosses. No singing."

Bledsoe also started buying weapons and stockpiling ammunition. Because he was on a budget, he made the purchases over time. He also paid in cash, since, like many other fundamentalists, he believed that paying interest was anti-Islamic. Following his interview with agent Thomason, Bledsoe expected the FBI to be tracking him and wanted to avoid any scrutiny that might arise from a gun store purchase. Instead, he bought one semiautomatic rifle from an acquaintance and bought a semiautomatic pistol on the street. All these actions made his purchases much harder to trace.

Finally, to test whether he was under FBI surveillance, Bledsoe bought a .22 semiautomatic rifle over the counter at a Walmart. Walking through the parking lot with his new gun, he thought, "I'm not under surveillance. It's on." Bledsoe then went to an empty construction site to practice shooting and, in his own mind, to practice shooting people.

On the final weekend in May 2009, Bledsoe began his holy war. The plan was to assassinate three rabbis. After midnight on May 30, he fired ten rounds from a .22 rifle at the home of Little Rock rabbi Eugene

Levy. The shots missed the house. Bledsoe then drove several hours to a Jewish community center in Nashville, but he aborted the mission when he found there were too many children around. He then drove several more hours to his next target, an army recruiting center in Florence, Kentucky. This had looked promising because it was near an interstate and bordered Ohio, allowing Bledsoe to make a quick getaway, but the office was closed for the weekend. At about 2:00 a.m. on June 1, Bledsoe arrived at the Nashville home of an Orthodox rabbi and threw a Molotov cocktail at the house, but it bounced off a window and failed to detonate.

Dejected and frustrated, Bledsoe returned to Little Rock. So far his plan for a glorious jihad had been an inglorious failure. Buying firearms and ammunition had drained his meager finances, as had the long drives across Arkansas, Tennessee, and Kentucky; gasoline cost close to four dollars a gallon.

Back at his apartment, unable to sleep, Bledsoe watched jihadist propaganda online that purported to show Muslim women being raped. Enraged anew by the abuses heaped on Muslims, Bledsoe was determined to retaliate. Later that morning, he drove through Little Rock until he noticed two men in army fatigues smoking outside what he knew to be a recruiting center. Driving around the corner so they couldn't see him, he picked up his SKS rifle, the most powerful weapon he had, and positioned it out the window of his vehicle. Then he cruised slowly past the recruiting center and began shooting, killing one soldier and wounding the other. When he was done he drove toward Memphis, hoping to change vehicles there to avoid getting caught.

In his haste, Bledsoe left his SUV's tailgate down, which made it easy to identify. He was soon arrested. Police officers found three firearms, hundreds of rounds of ammunition, and a number of Molotov cocktails in the vehicle. Bledsoe told the arresting officer that he "wanted to kill as many people in the army as possible because of what they had done to Muslims." Days after the shooting, Bledsoe made a collect call from jail to a reporter at the Associated Press to explain that he wasn't guilty of murder because "murder is when a person kills another without justified reason."

While awaiting trial, Bledsoe continued to wage his own private jihad. On April 12, 2010, he stabbed a prison guard with a shank fashioned from the earpiece of his glasses, shouting, "I got ya white boy, you gonna die, Allah, Allah, Allah. You gonna die white boy. I got your ass." The injury to the guard was relatively minor. Bledsoe later claimed that the officer he stabbed had just returned from Iraq and had bragged about killing "sandniggers" in the Middle East.

At Bledsoe's trial the jury was shown a video of police detectives interrogating him shortly after his assault on the military recruiting center. Asked how he felt about the fact that an American soldier was dead, he said, "I don't really feel nothing, you know. I don't feel nothing." His lawyer argued that he was suffering from delusions, but this line of defense was rendered moot by a letter Bledsoe had sent the judge. The handwritten letter stated:

> I'm writing this because I wish to plead guilty. To all charges I'm facing. Without deals without respite. I wrote the prosecutor and Federal Bureau of Investigations and TBI [Tennessee Bureau of Investigation]. Informing them of all of the acts I was involved in around or about May 29–June 1 2009. I do not wish to receive funds for my defense. I don't wish to have a trial. I'm affiliated with Al-Qaeda in the Arabian Peninsula. Member of the Abu Basir's Army. [Abu Basir was then the leader of al-Qaeda in Yemen.] This was a Jihadi Attack on infidel forces. That didn't go as plan. Flat out truth. I plead to capital Murder, Attempt capital Murder and The other 10 counts without compulsion without deals . . . my lawyer has no defense. I wasn't insane or post traumatic nor was I forced to do this act. Which I believe it is justified according to Islamic Laws and the Islamic Religion Jihad to fight those who wage war on Islam and Muslims. At the next hearing I look forward to pleading guilty and await sentencing.

By pleading guilty in midtrial, Bledsoe avoided a possible death sentence. On July 25, 2010, the judge sentenced Bledsoe to twelve life sentences, plus an additional 180 years.

Despite his grandiose claim that he was part of the "army" led by al-Qaeda's leader in Yemen, and although he might have met members of al-Qaeda while in prison there, there is no evidence that Bledsoe was part of al-Qaeda in any formal sense. Rather, he was a classic example of leaderless jihad—exactly what al-Qaeda wanted. Using ever-more-sophisticated propaganda, the group would seek to nurture other Bledsoes in a systematic way.

The Bledsoe family was bitter that the FBI hadn't done more to stop their son before his rampage. Melvin asks, "How the hell did Carlos go and get a gun in Walmart with his own name with his own ID in ten minutes?" Melvin also says he never would have set his son up in Little Rock if he had had any inkling of the radicalization he had gone through in Yemen. "My family has paid a heavy price. I lost my only son. We love our son. Somebody else stole my son." He hopes that what happened to Carlos will serve as a warning to families whose sons might be going through a similar process. "I hope that I can talk enough that I can save someone's family from this ever happening to them. Because the pain we go through is unbearable."

The parents of Private Andy Long also live with the loss of their son. Andy's father, Daris, grew up in Afghanistan, a Muslim country, and served in the U.S. Marines for decades. In their common grief, Melvin Bledsoe and Daris Long have found a common link. They have toured the country together, decrying the ideology that destroyed the lives of both Carlos and Andy. Daris Long reflects: "Mr. Bledsoe the father and the family are as much victims in this as we are. At 10:56 on the first of June 2009, I became a father of a dead soldier. Nothing changes that. At that same time, between 10:19 that morning and 10:56 that morning, when Abdul Mujahid Abdulhakim Muhammad was arrested, Mr. Bledsoe lost his son. My heart hurts for them, and I know he's said his heart hurts for us. But his pain is going to be longer and is going to get worse."

B y the time President Obama took office in early 2009, jihadist groups—such as the one formed by Kevin Lamar James to carry out attacks in California in 2005—were on the wane. This was no accident. The massive increase in law enforcement efforts and intelligence gathering following 9/11 made working as a group far more risky for militants. The Internet was also key to this shift. An individual who once might have radicalized alongside a cluster of like-minded acquaintances could now deepen his militant views within a virtual extremist community, supplemented by a growing online trove of lectures, videos, and instructional resources.

The deadliest lone wolf of all was Major Nidal Hasan—in some ways an even more unlikely convert to jihadism than Carlos Bledsoe. Major Hasan grew up middle class in Virginia, surrounded by examples of moderate, non-militant Muslims, not least a first cousin who was like a brother to him. At the time he staged his attack, he was employed by the army. Still, the government remained oblivious to his plotting—disturbing evidence of the difficulty of tracking lone wolves.

The story of the Hasans begins in Ramallah, a Palestinian city in the West Bank, where Nidal Hasan's parents owned land and grew olives, figs, grapes, and almonds. In the mid-1960s Malik Hasan decided to leave to seek his fortune in the States. He and his wife, both in their early twenties, had met at the wedding of their respective brother and sister. Their siblings also decided to immigrate to the States, so the two Hasan brothers and the sisters they had married settled in Arlington, Virginia, just across the Potomac River from Washington, DC.

The children born to the Hasans in the States were double first cousins, genetically similar to brothers and sisters. Nidal Hasan was born in Arlington on September 8, 1970, a year after his cousin Nader. Their families lived just blocks apart, and the two cousins grew up playing together often.

Like any number of Muslim American families, the Hasans were not especially observant—no one prayed five times a day. They did fast during the holy month of Ramadan every year, and alcohol wasn't allowed at home; nor was there bacon for breakfast. Otherwise, the Hasan children had a typical American upbringing. While their mothers shopped at the mall, Nader and Nidal played hide-and-seek among the racks of women's clothing. Santa visited at Christmas and left presents for the kids. They played soccer and caught fireflies together and rode their bikes farther away from home than their parents allowed. Nader got Nidal his first job, at a Pizza Hut.

Their fathers worked at diners and as cab drivers, providing enough financial stability for their sons to aspire to even more comfortable lives. Nader would become a sought-after lawyer in Northern Virginia, his office featuring a conference room with a fireplace and photos of him posing with President George W. Bush. He would remain Muslim but grow more secularized, not averse to keeping a few beers in the refrigerator. Nidal would qualify as both a doctor and a U.S. army officer and would practice as a psychiatrist at Walter Reed Army Medical Center in Washington, DC, the nation's leading hospital for wounded soldiers. He would also become a Sunni fundamentalist bent on violence.

Yet that was all a long way in the future when, during his fourth-grade year, Nader's parents divorced. He and his four siblings were raised by their mother, Nawal, who worked her way up from a mailroom job to a position as teller and finally vice president for wealth management at a Wachovia bank. She loved America and taught her children that there was no conflict between America and Allah; good Muslims could also be good Americans. Nader joined the Boy Scouts, played football, and wrestled on his high school team.

Nidal's parents remained together, but his adolescence was marked by a different disruption. When he was fourteen his family moved to Roanoke, deep in southwestern Virginia. Roanoke has a markedly more southern culture than Arlington, which, though south of the Mason-Dixon Line, feels more like the Northeast. In Roanoke the Hasans started the Capitol Restaurant, in a seedy downtown neighborhood. They served one-dollar Buds and cheap all-you-can-eat meals to a clientele of lower-income African Americans and college students. Nidal's mother was known for her ability to keep the rowdier customers out of trouble and for her generous handouts to those who might otherwise have gone hungry. Later the Hasans opened the more upscale Mount Olive Grill and Bar and a local convenience store. When Nidal wasn't in high school, he worked with his parents at their businesses.

Unlike Nader, Nidal passed through high school like a ghost, making few friends or lasting impressions. As he was about to graduate, Nidal told his parents he wanted to enter the military. His father and mother didn't share his enthusiasm for this plan, but Nidal pushed back, saying, "I was born and raised here, I'm going to do my duty to the country." He enlisted in the army and, in 1995, after graduating from Virginia Tech with a degree in biochemistry, he entered an officer-training program in Texas.

Two years later he transferred to medical school at the Uniformed Services University of Health Sciences, in Bethesda, Maryland. At the time, this seemed like a safe career choice; Nidal's tuition was paid for in full by the army, and with the Cold War long over, he had no reason to anticipate being ordered to deploy to a war zone.

In 1998, a year into his medical training, Nidal's father died. Not having grown up religiously observant, Nidal did not know how to recite the proper prayers at his father's funeral. Three years later, his mother also died. As she was declining, she told him to "get to know God," and he took the request seriously, beginning to attend mosque. Nidal's parents had died at relatively young ages (his father at fifty-two and his mother at forty-nine), and he seemed never to get over the loss. The deaths of his parents provided his "cognitive opening," the life events that precipitated his turn to fundamentalist Islam.

The memorial service for Hasan's mother was held at none other than the Dar al-Hijrah mosque, Anwar al-Awlaki's home congregation, on May 31, 2001. By this point Awlaki was already an imam at the mosque, and the dynamic young preacher enthralled Hasan.

Then came the 9/11 attacks. While still in law school, Nader had opened a restaurant in Washington, DC, the Foggy Dogg, which catered to graduate students from nearby George Washington University. Nader lived above the restaurant, and on the morning of 9/11 he watched from his window as black smoke billowed up from the Pentagon. He worried that if the attackers were revealed to be Muslims it would create problems for Arab Americans, even relatively secular ones.

A friend of Nader's who worked at the Bush White House reached out to him shortly after 9/11, asking if he would be willing to attend some public events with the president. It would be good for the public to see that Arab Americans supported the president, she explained, particularly since any future military action against al-Qaeda should not be construed as a war against Islam. Nader readily agreed. He felt that Bush had done some of the right things in the days after 9/11, such as visiting a mosque in Washington, and the president had also talked about recognizing a Palestinian state, so it was important for Arab Americans to show their solidarity. Six weeks after 9/11, Nader traveled to New York with the presidential press corps to attend a Yankees game, where Bush threw out the ceremonial first pitch. He volunteered at presidential events in Washington and attended a Christmas party at the White House.

At the same time, Nidal became steadily more pious. He began asking Nader whenever he saw him, "When was the last time you read the Koran? Aren't you afraid of burning in hell?" Nader eventually pushed back, saying, "I don't enjoy seeing you. Every time I come I feel like I have to defend myself. You're pushing me further away from ever reading that book." But Nidal's views became even more rigid. By 2005 he worried about there possibly being lard made from pig fat in the bread he was eating, and when Nader brought his Iranian girlfriend to dinner, Nidal coldly asked, "Who's she here with?" making clear that he disapproved of a woman socializing without a male relative as her escort.

At the Silver Spring, Maryland, mosque where he worshipped, Nidal was regarded as devout. Issa Ndour, a local real estate agent, frequently saw Nidal at the 4:30 a.m. prayer service, recalling that he "used to score all the points in Islam: He did the prayers. He read the Koran. He listened to lectures. He was one of those perfect guys who did everything right."

Not all his fellow worshippers thought Nidal was a perfect guy. Golam Akhter, a Bangladeshi American civil engineer in his late sixties, often got into fierce theological debates with Nidal. One such argument was about how to interpret the concept of jihad. Nidal said, "Jihad means holy war. When your religion isn't safe, you have to fight for it." Akhter responded, "Jihad means an inner struggle, fighting against corruption and injustice." Nidal shot back, "Then you are not a Muslim." Akhter said, "Only Allah can say who is good."

Hasan's conversion to fundamentalism differed from Bledsoe's in that he was already Muslim, but the progress of their radicalization had many features in common: their gradual isolation from their families, their preoccupation with piety and with what constituted a "real" Muslim, and their embrace of Salafist ideas and practices. Both were firm opponents of the American wars in Afghanistan and Iraq, and both became increasingly obsessed with the idea of jihad to defend Islam.

Nidal, who had never had a girlfriend, now wanted to find a like-minded wife. He asked his relatives to help him meet potential spouses; they introduced him to several women, but Nidal found them all wanting. He asked one marital candidate what would happen if he hit her; she didn't pursue the relationship further. He also asked around his Maryland mosque for a suitable marriage prospect—someone who prayed five times a day and wore a burqa that covered her entire body—but though a few women liked the fact that he had a steady job, he didn't find any of them pious enough.

In 2003, having graduated from medical school, Nidal was commissioned as a captain. He did his internship and residency in psychiatry at Walter Reed and then a two-year fellowship at the hospital as well. At a time of continuous warfare in both Afghanistan and Iraq, these commitments kept him far away from the war zones.

Nidal's religious fervor soon began spilling over into his work. At Walter Reed he became embroiled in arguments about the wars in Iraq and Afghanistan. During an environmental health seminar, while other students focused on topics such as air quality and water contamination, Nidal gave a presentation titled "Is the War on Terror a War on Islam: An Islamic Perspective." The instructor had to stop the presentation (which included a defense of Osama bin Laden and contained no discussion of health care issues) after the class erupted in protest.

During a PowerPoint presentation titled "The Koranic World View as It Relates to Muslims in the US Military," Hasan told fellow students at Walter Reed that "the Department of Defense should allow Muslim soldiers the option of being released as conscientious objectors to increase the morale of non-Muslim soldiers in the military as well as decrease adverse events." Hasan explained that military service was difficult for Muslim soldiers because they owed more allegiance to Allah than to America, saying, "We always talk about God and country, but here [what] we're really about is God versus country." He went on to claim that former American soldiers were joining the Taliban and al-Qaeda, "so you have to ask yourself, there's something out there with these groups that's really resonating." When someone in the class asked him about the number of virgins in Paradise, Hasan stammered in a high-pitched voice, "There's a lot of virgins. It's heaven. You know, it's heaven. That's all I can say," inspiring nervous laughter.

Hasan went so far as to tell classmates that his religious beliefs took precedence over the U.S. Constitution. He submitted a proposal for a research study about whether Muslims in the U.S. military had religious conflicts that interfered with their ability to do their jobs properly, proposing to give Muslim American soldiers a survey that asked if their beliefs raised the possibility of fratricide against non-Muslim soldiers. In a class about human behavior, Hasan gave a presentation that seemed to justify suicide bombing. A number of the wounded soldiers at Walter Reed were victims of suicide bombings in Iraq or Afghanistan. One of Hasan's fellow students approached members of the faculty after class to call Hasan a "ticking time bomb."

Adding to his dissatisfaction with military service, Hasan was upset by the battlefield injuries of the patients at Walter Reed. One patient he saw had been burned so intensely that his face had melted. Hasan also complained to his family about harassment from fellow soldiers. He told relatives that someone had drawn a camel on his car and written under it, "Camel Jockey, Get Out!" Hasan also divulged that patients had told him of alleged war crimes by U.S. soldiers, such as the rape of civilians.

During the third year of his residency, one of Hasan's supervisors tried to persuade him to leave the military, saying it didn't seem like a good "fit." Hasan and the supervisor explored the possibility of his applying for conscientious objector status, but it was the height of the wars in Iraq and Afghanistan, a time when there was a great need for army psychiatrists, and this was not a realistic option.

In the last month of his residency, Hasan chose to fulfill an academic requirement by submitting a draft presentation that consisted almost entirely of references to the Koran. It also suggested that violence by Muslims against non-Muslims was permissible. His supervisors warned Hasan that the presentation was neither scientific nor scholarly and that he wouldn't graduate if he didn't revise it. Hasan's program director, who thought Hasan both lazy and a religious fanatic, doubted he was fit to graduate at all. Hasan revised his presentation slightly and was allowed to graduate.

While Hasan was finishing his residency, his admiration for Awlaki and his ideas deepened into something akin to worship. Having been released from jail in Yemen, Awlaki had launched his website in 2008, and Hasan became one of the thousands of Muslims hanging on the religious insights of "Sheikh" Awlaki. However, as a serving officer in the U.S. military, Hasan could not suddenly disappear to Yemen as Bledsoe had done; his trip to the Yemeni "field of jihad" would have to be a virtual one.

Through the Contact section of Awlaki's blog, Hasan sent the cleric an e-mail on December 17, 2008, asking his advice about "Muslims in the US military." In particular, he was interested in the question of whether a Muslim American soldier who turned his gun on fellow U.S. soldiers "in the name of Islam" would be fighting a "true jihad." And if he died in such an assault, would he be considered a *shaheed,* a martyr for Islam?

Two weeks later Hasan sent another query, asking if Awlaki thought it would be better if Muslims didn't identify themselves by sect names, such as Sunni and Shia. His next question was whether it was religiously permissible for Hamas to fire rockets into Israel that might kill civilians, followed by another lengthy query about Hamas, prefaced with the note "I know your [sic] busy but please comment if the logics of this piece is accurate." Awlaki responded to none of these messages.

On February 16, 2009, Hasan wrote to Awlaki that their paths had crossed "briefly a very long time ago when you were the Imam at the Dar al Hijra [in Northern Virginia]." Hasan went on to explain that he had set up a five-thousand-dollar scholarship prize for the best essay on "Why Anwar Al Awlaki is a great activist and leader," and said that "we would be honored if you would award the prize." This offer, at last, got a response out of Awlaki, who e-mailed that he wouldn't be able to travel to award the prize and, in any event, was too "embarrassed" to award it. But Hasan wouldn't take no for an answer. Referring to the essay contest, he wrote, "Unfortunately, when I sent the email to you everyone was giving me the green light," inventing a story about how the winning essay was already scheduled to run in a Muslim magazine.

Hasan asked if Awlaki could help him find a wife, saying that he would "strongly consider" any recommendation. He also offered to contribute money to the cleric suggesting some kind of "privacy" arrangement for this donation. Hasan was earning about ninety thousand dollars a year at this point and donating as much as a third of his income to Islamic charities. Awlaki sent his thanks, saying there was much need for financial assistance, given the "poor people, orphans, widows" in Yemen. He also asked Hasan to tell him more about himself, assuring him that he would "keep an eye for a sister" suitable for marriage.

Hasan continued to pepper Awlaki with e-mails, sending him a news article about a Muslim cleric living in Maryland; telling Awlaki that he would send money to him via PayPal; asking Awlaki to phone him (collect). In a lengthy e-mail on May 31, 2009, Hasan suggested that suicide attacks might be "permissible" particularly in cases where the aim was "to kill enemy soldiers," even in instances where there was collateral damage to innocent bystanders. Hasan ended that e-mail "P.S we miss hearing from you." Awlaki ignored Hasan's continued overtures; by now the officer's one-sided correspondence had assumed the tone of an unrequited lover.

Taken together, the eighteen e-mails Major Hasan exchanged with Awlaki reveal a chillingly persistent line of inquiry: Hasan was seeking an Islamic justification for the killing of fellow American soldiers in a suicide mission that might also kill civilians. Awlaki never gave him one.

Astonishingly, the entire correspondence was known to the FBI. After Hasan sent his first message to Awlaki, a member of the Joint Terrorism Task Force in the San Diego office of the FBI reviewed it and wrote an e-mail to colleagues: "Here's another e-mail sent to Aulaqi by a guy who appears to be interested in the military. The header information suggests that his name is 'Nidal Hasan,' but that might not be true.

The IP address resolves to Reston, VA. Can we check to see if this guy is a military member?"

After some digging around, the agent in San Diego found a Nidal Hasan assigned to Walter Reed in Washington, DC. Concerned by this discovery, in FBI parlance he "set a lead" to the FBI's Washington Field Office (WFO), which has handled many prominent terrorism cases. The WFO did its own investigation and responded, "Given the context of his military/medical research and the content of his, to date, unanswered messages, WFO does not currently assess Hasan to be involved in terrorist activities."

Agents in the FBI San Diego field office found the response puzzling. The Washington office had examined only Hasan's personnel files, which were completely innocuous. A far more useful approach would have been to talk to some of Hasan's superiors, or even to Hasan himself, which they did not do. The San Diego agents, confused, e-mailed back, asking if perhaps Hasan was a "friend," or informant, for the WFO. They wrote: "The response looks a little slim, i.e. limited probing into this individual's background, no contact w/ command and no interview of Hasan. We were wondering if we were missing something, i.e. we need to read between the lines (Hasan is a friend of WFO)?"

The WFO wrote back that Hasan was not "'a friend of WFO.' If you have additional information regarding HASAN's links to terrorism or request any specific action, please share and we will re-assess."

One of the San Diego agents called the FBI office in Washington to explore the issue further and was told, "This is not San Diego, it's DC and we don't go out and interview every Muslim guy who visits extremist websites. Besides, this guy has legitimate work-related reasons to be going to these sites and engaging these extremists in dialogue." After this, all FBI investigation of Hasan was dropped. It was, in the words of a senior FBI official, "a screwup." It is true that during this period there were hundreds of Americans reaching out to Awlaki through his website, most of them seeking perfectly legitimate religious advice; to investigate them all would not have been feasible. Still, it remains astonishing that the FBI's Washington Field Office elected to dismiss Hasan as a serious threat. After all, a militant Islamist with constant access to U.S. military bases was in a position to do considerable damage. And there was no shortage of red flags in the e-mails themselves.

Michael Leiter and his number two, Andy Liepman, who together oversaw the National Counterterrorism Center, were surprised not to have been brought in when the FBI's San Diego office first flagged Hasan. "Mike and I were pretty furious that the NCTC didn't even get to be involved, because it was not yet at that point considered terrorism and it was protected," Liepman said. "In hindsight, looking at the eighteen pieces of communication with Awlaki, they were sufficiently squirrely that I think we might have said, 'Who is this guy?'"

Despite Hasan's unconventional views and the fact that he was a sub-par psychiatrist, ranked in the bottom quarter of his peer group, his officer evaluation reports were always glowing. The evaluations even spun his public discussions of Islamist extremism as useful to U.S. counterterrorism efforts. Hasan's evaluation report for 2008 described him as "among the better disaster and psychiatry fellows . . . at the Uniformed Services University." The report said that Hasan had "focused his efforts on illuminating the role of culture and Islamic faith within the Global War on Terrorism" and that his "work in this area has extraordinary potential to inform national policy and military strategy." It went on: "His unique interests have captured the interest and attention of peers and mentors alike."

This was certainly true, but not in the way the report painted it. Two of Hasan's peers were so concerned about his militant views that they had complained about him to the faculty, and Hasan's program director at Walter Reed continued to distrust him, regarding him as a fanatic. Yet Hasan sailed through his six years at Walter Reed as an intern, resident, and fellow without any serious scrutiny of either his beliefs or his shortcomings. (He often didn't even show up for work.) The free pass that Hasan received seems to have come from those who felt they were respecting his religious beliefs. Academic freedom also worked in Hasan's favor; his views about the U.S. wars overseas, which would have been intolerable at an ordinary army base, were less worrisome in an environment of academic inquiry. An element of political correctness may also have helped Hasan, who was both a Muslim army officer and a Muslim doctor in an institution with very few of either.

In May 2009, during the same period when Hasan was e-mailing Awlaki, he received a routine promotion to major and was transferred to Fort Hood, in Texas, arriving there on July 15. It was now certain that Major Hasan would be ordered to the war zone in Afghanistan. He was to provide psychiatric support to an Army Reserve unit, a deployment scheduled to begin in the fall of 2009. This was the realization of Hasan's greatest fear. His cousin Nader says, "Nidal was afraid of war. He was afraid of combat. He did everything he could to wiggle out of it." Hasan had hoped that the newly elected president would wind down both wars, in Iraq and Afghanistan. Instead, Obama had rapidly ramped up the number of soldiers deployed to Afghanistan.

Despite Major Hasan's history of questioning America's wars and his pronounced Islamist stance at Walter Reed, he was ordered to deploy to a combat zone where the U.S. military was battling Islamist extremists. The officer at Walter Reed who selected Hasan for deployment told a Fort Hood officer, "You're getting our worst."

It was six weeks after Carlos Bledsoe had attacked the recruiting center in Little Rock that Hasan arrived at Fort Hood. The Arkansas attack had made a deep impression on Hasan. "This is what Muslims should do," he told fellow officers. "They should stand up to the aggressor."

Hasan began formulating his own plan of action. He was about to turn forty, with no prospects of marriage and no children. His parents were both dead; he had few, if any, real friends; and he was about to be sent to a war zone where Americans were killing Muslims. Suicide was against his religion, but what if he went out in a blaze of glory as a martyr for his religion, a true Soldier of Allah? Two weeks after his arrival, Hasan, who had never been much for guns, purchased a Belgian FN Herstal 5.7-millimeter pistol, a weapon favored by SWAT teams.

At the same time, Hasan began attending the Islamic Community of Greater Killeen mosque. One of the mosque's founders was Osman Danquah, a retired U.S. Army sergeant who had served in the first Gulf

War. Hasan asked Danquah what advice he should give to Muslim soldiers who might have objections to the Iraq and Afghan wars, saying, "What if a person gets in [the military] and feels it's just not right?" Danquah told Hasan that there wasn't much advice he could give on that score; in an all-volunteer army, he reasoned, Muslim soldiers owed as much to their commitments as any other enlistees. (He also pointed out that Muslims were fighting *one another* in countries such as Afghanistan.) Danquah felt that something was not right about the army major, who seemed almost incoherent during a second conversation about the matter.

On October 14, Hasan learned that his deployment to Afghanistan was imminent. Two weeks later he e-mailed one of his brothers, Anas, "If I happen to die obviously split it according to the Islamic inheritance law and give the maximum allowable amount to a charity. . . . I think its 1/3 of my wealth. I am not aware of any psychiatrist that have [*sic*] died in Iraq/Afghanistan by enemy fire however it's always good to be prepared."

The next day, the 467th Combat Stress Control Detachment to which Hasan was assigned was due to report at the Soldier Readiness Processing Center at Fort Hood—the last stop before the unit shipped out to Afghanistan. This was the day that Hasan selected to conduct his jihad.

November 5, 2009, began, as it always did for Hasan, with early morning prayers at his local mosque. On his way home, he stopped, as usual, at a 7-Eleven for coffee and hash browns. The surveillance camera at the store caught him on tape—a big man wearing a white skullcap and a capacious white robe.

Hasan believed the day to be sacred: he would finally fulfill Allah's will by killing as many American soldiers as possible. He had printed up business cards identifying himself as a "Soldier of Allah." Today he would be that person. Today he would die a martyr, ascending to heaven to enjoy the carnal attentions of seventy-two virgins.

After his trip to the 7-Eleven, Hasan returned to Casa del Norte, the rundown apartment complex where he rented a spartan one-bedroom for three hundred dollars a month. He used a paper shredder to destroy his birth certificate and medical school degree; he wouldn't need them anymore. He then returned to the mosque to perform his noon prayers. He told acquaintances there, "I'm going traveling. I won't be here tomorrow." Hasan then drove to Fort Hood dressed in his battle fatigues.

He entered Fort Hood's medical processing facility, also known as Building 42003, at 1:15 p.m., knowing that the building would be crowded with hundreds of soldiers waiting to be processed for deployment. Pretending to chat with someone on his cell phone, he scanned the room for military policemen. There were none. Near the front entrance he saw a receptionist working at a desk. Hasan didn't want to kill civilians if he could avoid it, so he told the receptionist, "Major Parish has an emergency and needs to see you." Major Parish ran the medical processing facility, and Hasan knew that her office was at the opposite end of the large building.

With the civilian out of the way, Hasan drew his semiautomatic pistol from the waistband of his pants. He had prepared for this moment with great care. He carried some twenty magazines of ammunition, each containing twenty bullets—more than enough to do the job he had in mind. He had considered using magazine extensions, each containing a further ten bullets, but had discarded the idea because of the tendency of extensions to jam. He wore earplugs so that his hearing wouldn't be damaged by the repeated loud reports of his weapon.

"Allahu Akbar! Allahu Akbar!" he shouted as he fired a hail of bullets at a group of soldiers waiting in line for vaccinations. Turning on the laser sight on his gun, Hasan then started firing into the area of the facility with the greatest density of soldiers. After a couple of minutes he ducked behind a desk, only to emerge minutes later to hunt more soldiers. Twenty-one-year-old private Francheska Velez, from Chicago, had recently returned from Iraq, where she had learned that she was pregnant with her first child. Ignoring her pleas, Hasan shot and killed her. Specialist Jason Hunt, twenty-two, took three bullets, which pierced his lungs, liver, spinal cord, spleen, and stomach. He died within seconds.

A big, white-bearded, sixty-two-year-old physician's assistant, Michael Cahill, jumped out from behind a cubicle holding a chair above his head and charged toward the shooter, hoping to hit him with it. Hasan pivoted in Cahill's direction and fired a burst of shots, hitting him six times. Cahill crumpled to the ground. Specialist Frederick Greene also charged Hasan, who riddled his body with a dozen bullets.

And so it went for the nine other soldiers Hasan killed. He fired more than two hundred rounds at the panicked, unarmed servicemen and servicewomen. There was so much gun smoke in Building 42003 that the air turned dark and people could taste the bitter cordite. As the floor became slick with blood, Major Hasan shot Specialist Matthew Cooke, thirty, in the back. Corporal Nathan Hewitt, twenty-seven, thought it was only a training exercise when he first heard the gun shots. He realized it wasn't a drill when he felt the first bullet hit his thigh. During a break in the shooting Hewitt crawled forward on his belly, but the pause was only Hasan reloading; Hewitt was shot again, in the calf.

Looking for more targets, Hasan exited the building and made his way over to a graduation ceremony for soldiers, but he abandoned that plan when he couldn't easily distinguish soldiers out of uniform from civilians attending the ceremony. He headed back toward the medical facility.

The first two police officers to arrive at Building 42003 found Major Hasan chasing down a wounded soldier. Because of his earplugs, Hasan didn't hear the officers approach. Sergeant Mark Todd yelled, "Stop! Drop your weapon!" Hasan pivoted and fired two shots at Todd, who quickly fired back five shots that hit Hasan. The police officer's bullets left Hasan paralyzed. He blacked out. It was 1:27 p.m.

In just over ten minutes, Major Hasan had killed twelve soldiers and one civilian and wounded thirty-two others. Brett Mills, a firearms expert for the FBI with more than two decades' experience, recalls, "When I walked in there, it was probably the worst scene I have ever seen." He found more than 270 bullet holes. Another FBI agent recovered 146 shell casings and 6 magazines.

When Hasan regained consciousness hours later he was paralyzed from the waist down. There were no virgins; there were only medical personnel working to save his life at the intensive care unit of the Brooke Army Medical Center in San Antonio.

Nader was finishing a round of golf when his mother called to say that his cousin Nidal was mixed up in some kind of shooting in Texas. Nader rushed home. He initially assumed his cousin was a victim, but he soon learned the truth. Even as he stared at the TV, seeing images of the shooting and of his cousin, Nader did not believe it could be Nidal. His cousin wasn't prone to violence; he wouldn't kill a bug found in the house. Reached for comment by Fox News, Nader said that deploying to Afghanistan was his cousin's "worst nightmare." He continued: "We're blown away. The guy was born and raised here, my cousin, a good American." By this, Nader meant that his cousin had never been arrested and was, reluctantly or not, serving his country; the comment would cause Nader a good deal of consternation in coming days.

When the news of the Fort Hood attack flashed across American TV screens, the San Diego FBI agent who had been pushing for further investigation of Hasan told a colleague, "You know who that is? That's our boy!"

The following day, Nader and his family spent many hours telling FBI agents what they knew of Nidal, which had become less and less over time. Nidal hadn't told anyone in his family that he had been promoted to major, and very few knew that he was deploying to Afghanistan. Meanwhile, TV satellite trucks had lined up on Nader's street and enraged Fox News viewers were phoning his law office to berate him for calling his cousin "a good American." Nader quickly distanced himself from his off-the-cuff comment, issuing a statement the next day: "Our family is filled with grief for the victims and their families involved in yesterday's tragedy. We are mortified with what has unfolded, and there is no justification, whatsoever, for what happened. We are all asking why this happened, and the answer is we simply do not know." Still, Nader received hostile e-mails, and business at his law office slowed for a couple of months. He felt as though his family now had a terrorist label on their foreheads.

Months after the attack, Nidal Hasan told a psychiatric panel that he wished he had died during his assault because then Allah would have chosen him as a martyr. He said that the attack had been justified because U.S. soldiers were fighting "against the Islamic Empire," and that he felt no remorse for killing thirteen men and women. He even expressed hope that the government would execute him: "If I died by lethal injection, I would still be a martyr." During jury selection, Hasan told one of the potential jurors that he identified with Carlos Bledsoe, calling the Little Rock jihadist "my brother and my friend."

On October 18, 2012, as he awaited the beginning of his court martial, Hasan wrote a note that was released to Fox News in which he renounced his U.S. citizenship, saying he was "compelled to renounce any oaths of allegiances that require me to support/defend man made constitution (like the constitution of the United States) over the commandments mandated in Islam." In a second note, Hasan described Anwar al-Awlaki as my "teacher, mentor and friend."

Acting as his own lawyer, Hasan claimed that the Fort Hood attack was justified under the legal doctrine of the "defense of others," asserting that he was defending the Taliban and its leader, Mullah Omar, from the attacks of American soldiers. This is consistent with Harvard political scientist Louise Richardson's important observation that terrorists see themselves as "altruists defending others." In her 2006 study, *What Terrorists Want,* she explains, "The two biggest gaps in how terrorists see themselves and how they are seen by others are precisely on the points of being altruistic versus being self-serving, and being defenders versus aggressors. Terrorists see themselves as working heroically for others, not for themselves. In this way they see themselves as morally distinguishable from criminals out for their own selfish gain." Richardson based her study, in part, on the IRA, but many American jihadist militants have felt similarly.

A legal "defense of others" plea, however, requires proof that the aggressor was compelled to use force to protect someone in immediate danger from an unlawful use of force. Unarmed soldiers at Fort Hood did not qualify as either "immediate" or "unlawful" wielders of force— members of the Taliban were thousands of miles away in the battlefields of Afghanistan, and they had been sanctioned targets of the use of American military force since a UN resolution just days after 9/11, a vote in the U.S. Congress that authorized the use of force against al-Qaeda and its allies, and the participation of some forty other coalition countries in the Afghanistan war, including the whole of NATO. The judge rejected Hasan's plea.

For Nader Hasan, the explanation for his cousin's rampage was far more simple. He says Nidal had nothing to live for: no wife, no children, no parents, no friends, and a deployment he dreaded into a war against other Muslims. "He went postal. And he called it Islam. He sucked every Muslim into his suicidal plan."

With his attack at Fort Hood, the frightened and lonely serviceman made himself internationally notorious—a hero to jihadist militants. The attack even garnered comment from Awlaki, who said in an interview with a jihadist website, "I am proud that there are people like Nidal Hasan among my students. What he did was a heroic act, a wonderful operation. I ask Allah to make him steadfast, to protect him, and to free him. I support what he did, and I call upon anyone who calls himself a Muslim, and serves in the U.S. army, to follow in the footsteps of Nidal Hasan." Hasan had finally captured the attention of his hero.

Since it was a capital case, the judge did not allow Hasan to plead guilty, but the trial moved quickly, since there was no doubt that Hasan had carried out the attacks. He was found guilty and sentenced to death.

The families of Hasan's victims were generally satisfied with the sentence, but they were disturbed by the military prosecutors' decision not to prosecute Hasan as a terrorist. If the victims had been determined to have been killed or wounded as the result of a terrorist act, the Pentagon would have given them or their families medical and other benefits similar to those received by soldiers killed or wounded in Iraq and Afghanistan. Prosecutors had made the calculation that trying Hasan for murder was preferable because it would not open up complex discussions about whether the attack was truly an act of terrorism, which typically targets civilians rather than soldiers. In addition, the Uniform Code of Military Justice does not have a category for terrorism offenses.

The last time the army carried out an execution was more than half a century ago, so Hasan will likely remain on death row for many years, or until he dies of natural causes. His most fervent wish, to die a martyr for Allah's cause, is unlikely to be granted.

CHAPTER 5

PRE-CRIME

U.S. Justice Department official: BUT LET'S NOT KID OURSELVES, WE'RE
ARRESTING INDIVIDUALS WHO'VE BROKEN NO LAW.
Washington, DC, police official: BUT THEY WILL. . . .
Justice Department official: BUT IT'S NOT THE FUTURE IF YOU STOP IT.
ISN'T THAT A FUNDAMENTAL PARADOX?

—An exchange in Steven Spielberg's *Minority Report* (2002)

The tragedies at Little Rock and Fort Hood in 2009 were the most visible proof yet that homegrown militants were likely to be the most persistent terrorism threat of the new century. But if law enforcement and the intelligence establishment had finally acknowledged the homegrown threat, they still struggled to respond effectively. We have already seen how they could sometimes make too little of the signs of self-radicalization, but under the continuing aegis of the "war on terror," they were also susceptible to doing too much.

Mitch Silber's 2007 NYPD report on the radicalization process had been immediately welcomed by New York City police officials, but not everyone celebrated its conclusions. It had landed with a loud thud in the Muslim American community, prominent members of which thought it fueled already widespread and unfair suspicions of Islam in the United States. Critics said the report had painted with a broad brush the kind of places that Islamist militants might be lurking, including mosques,

cafés, cabdriver hangouts, flophouses, student associations, nongovern-
mental organizations, hookah bars, butcher shops, and bookstores. They
also protested that the radicalization "indicators" Silber had identified,
such as "wearing traditional Islamic clothing, growing a beard," and
"becoming involved in social activism and community issues," could be
true of just about any observant Muslim.

Silber had also asserted that radicalization was "indiscriminate," attracting "New York City citizens from all walks of life, ranging from
university students, engineers, business owners, teachers, lawyers, cab
drivers to construction workers." The Council on American-Islamic
Relations (CAIR), the nation's largest Muslim advocacy organization,
stated that the report's "sweeping generalizations and mixing of unrelated elements may serve to cast a pall of suspicion over the entire
American Muslim community." Kareem Shora, legal adviser for the
American-Arab Anti-Discrimination Committee, told NBC News, "It
plays right into the extremists' plans because it's going to end up anger-
ing the community."

A variety of Muslim groups joined forces to deliver a dense, twenty-
two-page rebuttal to the NYPD report, saying that it had blurred "lines
between mainstream Muslims and fringe elements by focusing on religious beliefs rather than indicia of violent acts of terrorism," and accus-
ing the NYPD of conflating "extremist speech with imminent security
threats." The rebuttal also pointed out that the wide range of locations
identified as havens for nascent radicals raised "First Amendment freedom of association concerns." The rebuttal concluded: "If taken in its
entirety the NYPD Report calls for increased police surveillance of the
American Muslim community."

Unbeknownst to the writers of the rebuttal, the NYPD was already
doing exactly that. Over the previous four years, David Cohen had masterminded an aggressive campaign to root out any Muslim extremists
who might be living in the New York City area. Since 2003 a secretive
section of Cohen's Intelligence Division known as the Demographics
Unit had been deploying its plainclothes officers and informants to New
York City mosques, to take the temperature of their clerics' sermons. By
2006 the unit had identified fifty-three "mosques of concern."

The unit also identified twenty-eight "ancestries of interest" (all Muslim) and developed information about where these various diaspora communities gathered. The unit documented in minute detail, for instance, which mosques Albanian Americans gathered at and the "level of rhetoric" at each mosque. Police officers also mapped "Locations of Concern" where Albanian Americans congregated in each of the five boroughs of New York City, including cafés, grocery stores, athletic clubs, barber shops, pizza joints, bakeries, travel agencies, and video shops. And that was just for the Albanians!

They did the same thing for the Egyptians, for the Pakistanis, and for some two dozen other identified Muslim ethnic groups. The unit even documented locations on Long Island and in New Jersey, both of which were outside the NYPD's jurisdiction, and also monitored Muslim student associations at a variety of colleges around the city. Officers noted that some Muslim students at Brooklyn College were going on "militant paintball trips."

The NYPD's extensive monitoring of Muslim life finally became public in 2011, through the reporting of Adam Goldman and Matt Apuzzo of the Associated Press. Despite the protests of American Muslim groups, none of it was proved illegal; the NYPD was monitoring places or events that were open to the public. In his 2008 book, *Crush the Cell,* Michael Sheehan, who two years earlier had served as the NYPD's top counterterrorism official, says as much—that the NYPD was looking on "college campuses, in coffeehouses, and in bookstores" for those who might be militants—but the Associated Press stories made clear the full scope of this effort.

As with many fishing expeditions, this one didn't yield much of anything. Instead, the NYPD treated as a potential terrorist the likes of Imam Hamid Raza, a Brooklyn-based cleric and American citizen who first came under surveillance in 2008. Imam Raza became sufficiently concerned about the visits from strangers that he spent $2,400 on a video camera and three hard drives in order to record his sermons, so that they could not be taken out of context if an NYPD informant were listening in. The cleric stopped discussing current events in his sermons and ceased any discussion of jihad—a word he had used in its larger sense as the struggle to behave in accordance with Islam—and encouraged his congregants to follow suit for fear such discussions might be misinterpreted. Raza also became fearful of new worshippers, worrying they might be informants, which cast a pall of distrust over his congregation. This was not the way freedom of religion was supposed to work in the United States, he thought.

In early 2012 the cleric was beginning to close up his mosque late one evening when a strange man appeared who seemed nervous. The stranger said he wanted to become a Muslim and then asked Imam Raza what he thought about the wars in Afghanistan and Iraq, taking out his phone to record the cleric's answers. Imam Raza said he was more concerned with what was going on in New York City than what was going on in other countries. The man then suddenly asked to become a Muslim by reciting the *shahada,* the declaration of Islamic faith. This was not how people usually converted to Islam; Raza believed the man was an informant.

With the help of the American Civil Liberties Union, Imam Raza eventually sued the NYPD for intruding on his work as a cleric. As the case unfolded, the NYPD defended its surveillance of Raza's mosque on the grounds that an al-Qaeda recruit, Najibullah Zazi, had once attended a lecture there. By this logic, NYPD surveillance of a church in Little Italy would be justified because a Mafia member once attended mass there. The case was settled in the summer of 2015, with a confidentiality order barring all sides from discussing it. Three years earlier a similar case of alleged unconstitutional surveillance was filed on behalf of eleven plaintiffs in New Jersey; this was dismissed in 2014 by Judge William Martini, who found that the plaintiffs had not demonstrated any discriminatory intent behind the NYPD's actions. On October 13, 2015, the Third Circuit Court of Appeals reversed that decision, ruling that the plaintiffs did have grounds to sue.

To the NYPD's critics, its surveillance program was a domestic spying operation unprecedented in its scope. To the department's supporters, the fact that there had been no successful terrorist attack in New York City since 9/11 spoke for itself. Supporters also pointed to a multitude of interrupted plots, with officials claiming a decade after 9/11 that there had been a total of sixteen serious plots targeting New York City. They neglected to mention, however, that many of those plots were sting operations initiated by the FBI or the NYPD, and that a number of them had never gotten past the drawing board stage.

In 2003, for example, Iyman Faris, a Pakistani American truck driver and secret al-Qaeda operative, developed a cockamamie plan to bring down the Brooklyn Bridge by using a gas torch to burn through its steel cables. This idea was improbably inspired by the movie *Godzilla,* a favorite of one of al-Qaeda's leaders. Cutting through the massive steel cables of the bridge with a gas torch would be akin to demolishing the Empire State Building with firecrackers, and a Pakistani man clambering around the Brooklyn Bridge wielding a gas torch in the post-9/11 era would surely have attracted considerable attention from commuters, not to mention the police officers who guard the bridge. Faris never went through with any element of his plan, but the NYPD counted it among the sixteen averted attacks.

Another such case was that of Long Island native Bryant Neal Vinas, who managed to link up with some al-Qaeda members in Pakistan. They discussed a possible attack on the Long Island Rail Road, but Vinas was arrested in Pakistan in September 2009 and deported to the United States, his "plot" never more than a vague idea.

As it turned out, the two most threatening plots targeting Manhattan after 9/11 were not homegrown, but rather orchestrated by al-Qaeda and the Pakistani Taliban, who trained American citizens to plant bombs in New York City in 2009 and 2010, respectively, as we'll see in the next chapter. Both plots fizzled, but neither the NYPD nor the intelligence community was aware of the al-Qaeda plot until a last-minute tip-off from British intelligence officials, and the Taliban recruit was not on the radar screen of any U.S. agency, including the NYPD.

The NYPD was not the only branch of American law enforcement developing controversial and sometimes ineffective responses to the threat of homegrown jihadists. The FBI could be, if anything, more heavy-handed in investigating suspected terrorists.

In March 2011, computer consultant Steve Llaneza was working at home in a quiet suburb of San Jose, a hub of Silicon Valley in Northern California, when he heard someone knock on the front door. Looking out the window, Steve saw a man who looked like a homeless Arab, but when he opened the door he realized it was his son, Matthew, whom he hadn't seen in more than six years. The man in front of him looked nothing like his son; he had grown a full beard, wore loose-fitting robes, and was emaciated.

"Hey, how you doing?" Steve said, trying to disguise his shock.

"Sorry for all the things that happened, you know, six, seven years ago," Matthew said.

"Okay. That's good. I mean at least that's a start. Come on in. You need a place to stay? What are you doing in your life? What's happening?"

Matthew stepped into the house his father had thrown him out of more than half a decade earlier.

Steve estimated that his five-foot-eight son now weighed 115 pounds. He fed him and they bought new clothes, although Matthew was adamant that he wanted only Arab-style robes. But it soon became apparent that Matthew needed far more than clothing and food. Steve was alarmed by his son's mental condition. Matthew had always been a bit different; as a child, he had been overly apprehensive, prone to manic fits of laughter, even paranoid. When he was in the fourth grade he complained that his head "felt funny." He had always yearned to be accepted by other kids his age, but he found it hard to make friends and was regularly bullied. More than once, his mother enrolled him in a new school, but the results were always the same. Matthew just didn't fit in.

The last time Matthew had lived in Steve's house it hadn't gone well. When Matthew was eighteen, after he had graduated from high school in Arizona, his mother and grandparents shipped him to California to live with Steve. Steve and Matthew's mother had separated when Matthew was young, so Steve saw his son infrequently, but now Matthew was going to be living with him for an extended period. Steve soon noticed that his son struggled to follow even the simplest directions.

When Steve asked him to rake leaves in the yard and Matthew said, "I'm done," it looked like he had hardly started.

While attending a nearby community college, Matthew fell in with a group of Muslim American students. Suddenly Matthew was always out with these new friends, who treated him like their taxi driver. Steve felt that they had hijacked his son: "Why are you following these people? You don't even know them—all of a sudden they're correct about everything?" In 2004, Matthew converted to Islam at a mosque in San Francisco and adopted the name Tariq Khan.

By this point Steve was remarried and beginning a new family. After he and his new wife, a Filipina Catholic, baptized their first son, they had a small party for relatives and friends at their home, which was decorated with ornate statues of saints. Matthew arrived at the party with one of his Muslim friends and began preaching about Islam to the partygoers. Steve cornered him, saying, "This is a party for your brother. We're Catholic. Why are you doing this?"

Matthew began casting about for a job and was childishly suggestible about his future career path. Someone told him that the military was a great option and that the Marines were "awesome." His father disliked the idea, given Matthew's difficulty with instructions and discipline, but his son was convinced it was the right choice. In his imagination, Matthew saw himself making friends with the Islamic people the Marines were then fighting in Iraq. Instead, he washed out of the Marines after one month due to chronic asthma.

Steve gave his son an ultimatum: get a real job or get serious about college. After a year, when neither of these things had happened, Steve threw him out of his house. Then followed the six and a half years when they had no contact.

After Matthew showed up on his doorstep, it took Steve a while to piece together what his son had been doing during that time. Without any real skills, Matthew had drifted from job to job and had not worked in nearly a year. His last job had been as a window washer. He was taking Zyprexa and Remeron, medications for schizophrenia, bipolar depression, and anxiety disorders.

At twenty-seven, Matthew had become far stranger than the teen-ager Steve remembered. The young man believed that the "secret po-lice" were trying to follow him; when a helicopter flew overhead, he assumed the fetal position until it had passed. He blabbered nonsensi-cally, telling his father he had gone to get a DNA test to see if he was of Middle Eastern heritage; as soon as the test results came back that "proved" he was of Arab descent, he said, "Tons of Muslim people came up to me and said I was part of their tribe. I mean from everywhere." (In fact, Matthew's heritage was Filipino, Anglo-Irish, and Hispanic.) He couldn't handle money or remember to feed himself. He was clearly not just "different" but disturbed.

Steve began thinking of Matthew as a child trapped inside a man's body. Matthew entertained delusions, talking about a girl in California whom he wanted to marry and take with him to go live in Afghanistan. There they would raise goats. He boasted that he could make remote-controlled submarines; that he could withstand torture by "erasing" his memory; that he had training in guerrilla warfare; and that he wanted to negotiate with the Taliban to release Bowe Bergdahl, an American soldier who had been taken hostage by the group in 2009. Steve tried to convince Matthew to see a psychologist or a doctor, but Matthew resisted.

A month after his son's return, Steve hosted a party. At first Mat-thew seemed to be doing all right, talking to others and acting jovial. But when he started drinking (which he did despite his conversion to Islam), he quickly became delusional. A helicopter clattered overhead, and Matthew cowered, shouting, "Don't hurt me! Don't hurt me! Don't kill me!" He began spitting out a series of numbers, saying, "This is my Social Security number." Certain that it would be obvious to any doc-tor that there was a problem, and that Matthew would get the help he needed, Steve called 911.

It would turn out to be the biggest mistake he had ever made. By the time the ambulance arrived, Mathew was worse, shouting, "They're going to kill me!" and "Allahu Akbar! God is Great!" Alarmed, the emergency responders called the police. Matthew was about to enter a rabbit hole of post-9/11 government paranoia, where a man with a serious mental illness could be portrayed as a dangerous terrorist.

Matthew was taken to the hospital and given a number of tests. San Jose police officers interviewed him as he lay on a gurney in the emergency room. He told them that he suffered from depression and a posttraumatic stress disorder that stemmed from people trying to recruit him into an Arizona drug cartel, saying, "Someday you are going to find me dead in the desert." He said he had binged on vodka and wine that night in an effort to kill himself. He repeatedly banged his head against the wall and tried to choke himself by pressing his neck down on the gurney. The medical staff had to restrain him.

Matthew also told the police officers that he was an "armorist," able to assemble a gun from scratch, a skill he claimed to have learned by reading magazines. The idea that Matthew, who found raking leaves challenging, could build a gun from scratch was clearly ludicrous. Observing that he was likely psychotic, potentially a danger to himself or others, the police officers recommended involuntary psychiatric detainment.

The following day, officers from the San Jose Police Department interviewed Steve. The conversation did not go well. "Everything I told them, they turned it around and turned Matthew into a terrorist. It didn't take long for me to realize that I should just keep my mouth shut. Everything I said just made it worse," says Steve. Following up on Matthew's claim that he built guns, the cops asked Steve to give up any kind of weapon Matthew might possess. Steve searched his son's Winnebago and found an AK-47 assault rifle in a safe. Matthew had purchased the weapon legally in Arizona, where gun ownership is common; he even possessed a valid concealed weapon permit. Steve gave the cops his son's gun and thought about calling a lawyer.

Gun laws in California are far stricter than in Arizona, and Matthew was charged with possessing an illegal weapon. Steve went to Matthew's court date and listened to the case against his son. He was stunned by the portrayal of Matthew; he felt prosecutors were making it look as though Matthew were bin Laden's right-hand man. "They're going to put him away for the rest of his life," he thought. "They're going to send him to Guantanamo Bay, just because I tried to get him a doctor." Matthew was sentenced for the illegal possession of the assault rifle and spent the next six months in county jail. When he was released, in November 2011, Steve effectively became his home caregiver, feeding and nursing his son and accompanying him on regular visits to Dr. Farhan Matin, a psychiatrist recommended by Matthew's probation officer.

Dr. Matin diagnosed Matthew with bipolar disorder and paranoid schizophrenia and began tinkering with his medications. Matthew's mental condition slowly improved, but after many months of treatment, he was still unable to fend for himself, which was both disheartening and problematic. Steve ran his computer consulting business out of his home, which enabled him to give his son his almost full-time attention, but legal bills and his son's fragile state were exhausting his financial and emotional resources. Steve's wife, the mother of three young children, had already taken a job to help make ends meet, and tensions at home were rising.

Adding to his anxiety was Steve's belief that the feds were now watching Matthew's every move, and that the family phone was tapped. Steve wasn't being paranoid. From the moment Matthew was released from jail, the FBI was tracking him. The probation officer to whom Matthew reported had an "assistant" who was in fact an FBI agent.

As his mental condition stabilized, Matthew began looking for work, a search that proved fruitless until a contact from his probation officer secured him a job at a plumbing company. An FBI informant at the plumbing company told his handlers that "Matthew has the mind of a little child" and that he was "slow" and he "drooled, while his body often shook uncontrollably." The informant observed that Matthew's level of competence was "barely above that of a manual laborer" and that he was "unable to operate complex machinery." He also told the FBI's case agent that Matthew didn't "really talk much. If [I] didn't start a conversation [Matthew] would just sit in the truck and not say anything." Matthew had boasted that he knew how to build a bomb "from scratch," according to the informant, but had promptly added that he wanted to stay away from weapons and explosives so that he didn't violate the terms of his probation. The informant repeatedly pressured Matthew to go to a shooting range, but Matthew always said he didn't want to go because it would violate his probation. The informant believed it was highly likely that Matthew would convert back to Christianity, as per his family's wishes.

The informant's assessment was that Matthew was "harmless" and that his main preoccupation was staying out of jail. He also observed that Matthew was responding well to his medication, was looking into taking courses at a local community college, and was acquiring the skills to "build a career for himself." He noted approvingly that Matthew never called in sick for work and was "very responsible" about checking in with his probation officer. He even told handlers that, after the FBI had completed its investigation, he would like to hire Matthew himself.

Despite the informant's positive reports, FBI officials then arranged for an undercover agent to introduce to Matthew the notion of a terrorist plot. The agent led Matthew to believe he was connected to the Taliban in Afghanistan, which, with someone as credulous as Matthew, was easy to do. They soon began discussing the idea of doing jihad in the States. Matthew proved a recalcitrant plotter, however, telling the undercover agent that he would like to carry out only some kind of "failed" terrorist attack. A defense filing in Matthew's case noted his belief that his "friend" had promised him a "field of weed" to sweeten the deal. (Matthew's felony conviction prevented him from obtaining the medical marijuana he found useful for managing his mood swings.)

Steve was happy that Matthew was working and attending a vocational school to learn plumbing. But he also noticed that Matthew was hanging out more and more with his one and only "best friend," whom Matthew described vaguely as "from some Middle Eastern country" and as "just a guy who kind of helps out once in a while." Steve warned Matthew that "he's not your friend," and that he had to understand that anyone he met might be surveilling him. Nevertheless, Matthew soon stopped going to school and often came home late with the excuse that he had taken on a second job.

Over the next ten weeks, Matthew and his new best friend, the FBI officer, met several times to map out a plan to carry out a holy war in the

United States. At first, Matthew suggested conducting an attack that would make it appear as if antigovernment militias were involved, triggering a U.S government response, militia retaliation, and eventually a civil war. Matthew identified the Federal Reserve Bank in San Francisco as a potential target, but he decided it would have too much security and suggested bombing the Bank of America in Oakland, California, instead. His new best friend thought that was a good idea. After discussing how they would proceed, Matthew told the undercover agent, "I will dance with joy when the bomb explodes," but quickly added that he wanted to stage the attack between the hours of 2:00 a.m. and 4:00 a.m., in order to "avoid unintended casualties."

FBI officials rented a storage facility where the "bomb" could be built and provided an SUV to be the delivery vehicle for the device. In January 2013 the friends met again to discuss their plan. Matthew offered to travel to Afghanistan to train Taliban fighters, telling the agent that he would go to Afghanistan as soon as possible after the attack on the bank. The two men agreed that after the attack Matthew would travel to Pakistan by ship and from there to Afghanistan. For the second time, Matthew suggested timing the bombing for early in the morning, between 2:00 and 4:00 a.m., in order to avoid killing people unnecessarily. Matthew then laughed and hugged the agent. Throughout his life, Matthew had struggled to fit in. Now he had a real friend and an important and exciting purpose in life.

In late January, the two conspirators started building the "bomb." They loaded twelve-gallon drums filled with purportedly explosive chemicals—the chemicals were inert—into a Mazda SUV with tinted windows. The agent told Matthew that he needed two cell phones in order to trigger the bomb from a distance, which Matthew purchased. A few days later, as the men conducted reconnaissance of the bank, Matthew told his friend, "I have jihad in my heart, consider jihad mandatory, and am willing to lay down my life for it."

On the evening of February 7, 2013, Matthew drove to meet his friend at the storage facility about twenty minutes from their target. The undercover officer asked him if he still wanted to proceed with the bombing. Matthew assured him that he did. In the early morning hours of February 8, Matthew drove the bomb-laden SUV to the four-story Bank of America office and parked it under the overhang of the building. He walked to meet his waiting friend nearby. Once they met, Matthew attempted to detonate the bomb twice, but it didn't work. Instead he was arrested by FBI agents.

Matthew's case underlines a surprising fact: since 9/11 the FBI has organized more jihadist terrorist plots in the United States than any other organization. Al-Qaeda's core group in Pakistan has mounted six terrorist plots (of varying degrees of sophistication); al-Qaeda's branch in Yemen has mounted two; the Pakistani Taliban and al-Qaeda's Syrian affiliate have each mounted one. Three other plots were engineered by the NYPD. The FBI has been responsible for thirty.

As we have seen, in the aftermath of 9/11, the FBI came in for a great deal of criticism for its mishandling of the case of al-Qaeda member Zacarias Moussaoui. Following that embarrassing failure, in the weeks after 9/11 more than a thousand Muslim men were detained, many hundreds of visitors from the Middle East who had overstayed their visas were deported, and hundreds of new names were added to the "no-fly" list. At the same time, the FBI sought to emulate Britain's domestic spying outfit, MI5, developing a sizable network of fifteen thousand informants in the States. (Since counterterrorism was the primary mission of the FBI after 9/11, it's reasonable to assume that the number of these informants connected to terrorism investigations was significant.)

As the years went on, the disruption strategy that Art Cummings had helped spearhead, to disrupt a terrorist plot before it could take place, became a core part of the FBI's mission. Cummings remembers an event in 2003 that spurred him to consider how to take the disruption strategy to the next level. He was running the FBI's International Terrorism Operations Section when an agent mentioned that a man on the no-fly list had shown up at the Canadian border and had consequently been "sent home." That had been the protocol because, as Cummings explains, the FBI had "been afraid that we didn't know what these guys were up to and that we just didn't have the intelligence to allow us to make a really good informed judgment." Better to err on the side of removing the threat, the thinking went. Cummings realized an opportunity had been missed and told the agent to let such suspects into the country in the future. Cummings wanted to let suspected terrorists into the States in order understand their intent, follow them, and track whom they were in contact with.

The original rationale for this kind of disruption was to smoke out al-Qaeda sleeper cells, but by 2005 a secret internal FBI report had concluded that "US Government efforts to date also have not revealed evidence of concealed cells or networks acting in the homeland as sleepers." Like the NYPD, the FBI was reorienting its focus toward self-radicalized militants not allied to any formal terrorist organization, who were often harder to detect.

As controversial as some elements of the FBI's counterterrorism strategy had been from the beginning, the government's pivot toward tracking homegrown militants would lead to even more controversial tactics. One such tactic was the FBI's focus on sting operations, using the network of informants it had established several years previously. The modus operandi was for an informant to find a suspicious individual or group and present the idea of a terrorist operation; if the subject(s) took the bait and developed the plot, it would be a way of luring militants out into the open and establishing evidence with which to prosecute them.

The informants were not, generally speaking, a savory bunch. In 2011 alone, informants committed almost six thousand crimes, according to FBI statistics. Shahed Hussain, a Pakistani-born con artist who faced criminal charges for running a scam to help DMV test takers cheat on their driving exams, became one of the FBI's go-to terrorism informants and a sting participant. All too often, however, the hapless "militants" whom Hussain and his FBI handlers found were coaxed to execute "plots" that would never have happened without these interventions.

After a sting operation in Albany, New York, in 2004, in which Hussain led two men to believe they were laundering money from the sale of a missile to be used in a terrorist attack, he was relocated to the town of Newburgh. Despite its small size and bucolic Hudson River setting, Newburgh was a blight-ridden place, with a rate of violence worse than that of the Bronx. Hussain drove around town in flashy cars (alternating among a Hummer, a Mercedes, and a BMW) and became a notable figure at the local mosque. There he befriended James Cromitie, a virulently anti-Semitic African American former drug addict. Cromitie was a blowhard who claimed to have visited Afghanistan, stolen guns while on the job at Walmart, and thrown bombs at police stations—none of which was true.

Hussain lured Cromitie, along with three other small-time criminals, into a preposterous plot: they would bomb two synagogues in the Bronx and then shoot down U.S. military planes flying from a base in New York State with a Stinger surface-to-air missile. The "bombs," obtained with the help of the informant, were inert, and the "missile" could not actually be fired. The "terrorists," meanwhile, were inept organizers and seemed entirely motivated by Hussain's blandishments of material rewards. Hussain at one point promised Cromitie, who was homeless, $250,000, and at other times offered him a new BMW, a vacation in Puerto Rico, and help starting his own business.

On May 20, 2009, the "Newburgh Four" left bags filled with what they thought were explosives in vehicles outside two synagogues in the Bronx and were soon arrested. At Cromitie's sentencing, the judge said, "Only the government could have made a 'terrorist' out of Mr. Cromitie, whose buffoonery is positively Shakespearean in scope. . . . I believe beyond a shadow of a doubt that there would have been no crime here except the government instigated it, planned it and brought it to fruition." Nonetheless, all the plotters were sentenced to twenty-five years in prison, and the informant walked away with almost one hundred thousand dollars for his services and expenses.

An appeals judge wrote that there was "something decidedly troubling about the government's behavior. . . . Hussain was the prime mover and instigator of all the criminal activity that occurred, right up until the last moments of the conspiracy, when he had to stop the car he was driving and 'arm' the 'explosive device' because the utterly inept Cromitie could not figure out how to do it. . . . Finally, it took quite a while for Cromitie to take the bait that was offered to him; it was fully nine months between the time Hussain met the defendant and the early April 2009 date when Cromitie finally became a committed and enthusiastic participant in the mission. . . . This court is not familiar with a case in which so many different tactics were used on a single individual." The judge acknowledged, however, that while "Cromitie is not a particularly intelligent man . . . it defies reason to think that he was unaware" that his plotting involved terrorism.

A number of the FBI stings undeniably netted hapless deadbeats like James Cromitie rather than dangerous terrorists. One of the FBI's most notorious misfires was the case of the "Liberty City Seven," a group of mostly Haitian immigrants who imagined they had sworn allegiance to al-Qaeda in 2006 in Liberty City, one of Miami's poorest and most dangerous neighborhoods. The impoverished group of men, arrested for plotting to blow up the Sears Tower in Chicago, spent most of their time smoking marijuana and subscribed to the obscure beliefs of an outfit called the Moorish Science Temple. So nascent were their terrorist plans that they never even bothered to travel to Chicago. Upon their arrests, Attorney General Alberto Gonzales commented, "Homegrown terrorists may prove to be as dangerous as groups like al-Qaeda"—but the Liberty City Seven were hardly strong evidence of this. The FBI had to put them on trial three times before a jury would convict five of the men. Two of the accused were acquitted, two of only four acquittals in any post-9/11 jihadist terrorism case.

This is not to say that the informant program was without successes. An informant played an important role in the case of the "homegrown" North Carolina group led by Daniel Patrick Boyd, who had lived in Pakistan during the Afghan jihad against the Soviets. Members of the group did weapons training in rural North Carolina in 2010 and traveled to Gaza, Jordan, and Kosovo in the hope of waging jihad in those locations. Boyd was convicted of conspiring to murder, kidnap, and injure persons overseas, and others in his circle of followers pled guilty to similar charges, for which they were all given lengthy sentences. This was the kind of well-publicized case that dissuaded militants from forming cells in the United States by demonstrating how easy it was to get caught as part of a group. (It was this realization that also spurred the appearance of a larger number of lone-wolf terrorists.)

The Council on American-Islamic Relations (CAIR), which had protested the NYPD's surveillance, also railed against the FBI's use of informants, releasing a report in 2009 that asserted, "The FBI has used informants and agents provocateurs to infiltrate mosques, befriend and provoke worshippers into making incriminating statements, or induce vulnerable Muslims into discussing illicit activity. Informants are both Muslims hired to spy within mosques and community organizations, as well as people with criminal backgrounds posing as Muslims." The CAIR report pointed to the FBI's remuneration system for its informants as evidence of encouragement for entrapment: "They are paid and/or rewarded based on the amount of information they produce; therefore, these informants are inclined to exaggerate, instigate and fabricate cases of a 'terrorist' nature." It was, CAIR concluded, yet another example of unfair law enforcement scrutiny of Muslims.

Among leading counterterrorism officials, there was considerable frustration about this backlash. Some felt the Muslim community was turning a blind eye to the radicalization problem in its midst. In 2005, Art Cummings met with Muslim American leaders and became irritated when one of them asked, "Why do you guys just concentrate on Muslims?" "Tell me you're joking, dude. I mean tell me you're joking," Cummings responded. "I tell you what I'm going to do. I'm going to get a map of the United States. And I'm going to plot for you every terrorism case that we have worked in the last year in the United States. Homegrown cases, where they were actually planning to do something. Do you want to see that they are one hundred percent Islamic, or do you want to take my word for it? When the Japanese start killing Americans in acts of terrorism, we'll start investigating the Japanese, but today it's Muslims, so that's where we are."

Cummings's exasperation was shared by the powerful chairman of the House Committee on Homeland Security, Representative Peter King, R–New York, who in 2011 held congressional hearings to investigate the issue of radicalization of Muslim American communities. The problem, he asserted, was compounded by the community's lack of cooperation with law enforcement. In fact, contrary to King's assertion, tips from the local community or from family members played a role in more than a quarter of the cases of the 360 militants examined for this book. It was someone in the Muslim community, for instance, who tipped off authorities to the danger posed by Daniel Boyd, after which an FBI informant infiltrated his circle of followers. And it was family members who raised the alarm about five young Muslim American men from Virginia who traveled to Pakistan in 2009 to fight with the Taliban against U.S. soldiers in Afghanistan. Their families contacted a Muslim rights group that in turn alerted the FBI that the men had disappeared. They were arrested in Pakistan.

The night Matthew Llaneza was arrested by the FBI, he didn't come home. Steve called his son's cell phone repeatedly, but there was no answer. The following morning, Steve was woken by loud banging on his front door and he sprang out of bed to find a group of officers outside his house and police cars everywhere. Steve's young children were now awake, too. As an officer yelled, "Open this door before we bust it down," Steve shouted at the children to get back in their rooms and not move. Steve opened the door. An officer pushed his way in and pointed his gun at Steve. "What do you want?" Steve asked. "Why are you guys doing this, scaring my family and my children? What are you going to do? Shoot me?" The cop told him to "back down."

The day Steve found out that Matthew had been arrested was the same day he learned that his son had finally qualified for disability payments. Steve had planned to manage his son's disability money and to place him in a community home for people who shared his condition. Now that hope was over. It seemed all but certain that Matthew was headed to prison for a very long time.

Even with the best lawyers in the world Matthew would have faced almost insurmountable odds. In the 360 jihadist terrorism cases since 9/11, no defendant has successfully argued an entrapment defense, though by any reasonable standard the FBI had gone out of its way to ensnare Matthew Llaneza. As his defense lawyer, Jerome Matthews, put it in a memo to the judge, "Matthew was not a radicalized jihadist but rather a delusional, severely mentally disturbed young man; he had no technical skills to speak of. He had no training or background that would have helped him to accomplish an actual bombing; he was preternaturally suggestible and desirous of being accepted; and, not least, he had no desire to inflict mass casualties." Nevertheless, Matthew's chance of being acquitted—whether on the grounds of entrapment or using some other defense—was close to zero. As we have seen since 9/11, four jihadist defendants have been acquitted, less than 2 percent of the total number prosecuted. A plea bargain for a reduced sentence is almost always the sensible plan.

On February 27, 2014, Steve traveled to Oakland to attend the sentencing hearing of his son. At the hearing, Judge Yvonne Gonzalez Rogers acknowledged that Matthew's involvement in the bombing plot was as much as anything else an effort to fit in and to "belong," and said, "This case, like many others we all read about, seems to indicate there are individuals who have been rejected time and time again who are looking to belong and to be accepted. This was a most unfortunate way of going about it." She went on to say, "One of my concerns is how mental illness is manifesting itself. Our failure to deal with mental illness is having serious repercussions."

The U.S. Attorney's Office argued in a presentencing memo to the judge that while Matthew certainly had mental problems, "Defendant's conduct here was very serious. He knowingly and willfully participated in a plan to blow up a bank building. . . . Had the bomb been real, it would have destroyed at least a portion of the building and easily could have killed or seriously injured innocent bystanders."

Matthew pleaded guilty to attempting to use a weapon of mass destruction. Steve was the only family member who was able to attend his son's sentencing. He sat toward the back of the courtroom, which was filled with law enforcement officials, lawyers, and members of the public waiting to hear about the disposition of other cases. When Matthew's case came up, his defense lawyer spoke, telling the packed courtroom that Matthew's father was present. Steve stood up, and all eyes turned toward him. He waved at Matthew, who turned to look at him. Steve thought his son seemed glad he was there.

The judge expressed disappointment that things had happened the way they had, and speculated that there was probably a better way to handle cases like this. She finished with the bland hope that society might learn from Matthew's unfortunate example. In handcuffs, Matthew glanced back at his dad as the sentence was read: fifteen years. If his case had gone to trial and he had been convicted, he would have faced thirty years to life. As it is, Matthew will be in his early to mid-forties when he is released.

"If nine-eleven hadn't happened, I don't think any of this would have happened," says Matthew's father. "I feel like my country's turning into one that you must be afraid of. I hate my life now. I hate that America's turned into this. This is my country. I love it. But why do we do this to people?"

CHAPTER 6

LEADER-LED JIHAD

THE TIME IS VERY NEAR WHEN OUR SOLDIERS WILL ATTACK THE
AMERICAN STATES IN THEIR MAJOR CITIES.

—Hakimullah Mehsud, leader of the Pakistani Taliban,
in a propaganda video released in early 2010

Even as the threat of homegrown jihadists loomed larger during the
first years of the Obama administration, a countervailing school of
thought was developing. It was spearheaded by academic Bruce Hoffman, who pointed out that the harm of even the worst lone-wolf attack
paled in comparison to the threat posed by a large-scale al-Qaeda attack. More significantly, Hoffman asserted that analysts such as Marc
Sageman had wrongfully dismissed the true scope of the continuing
threat from al-Qaeda and its affiliated groups.

Hoffman was already a formidable force in the world of American
national security. He directed the top-tier Security Studies Program at
Georgetown University, and had previously run the Washington, DC,
office of RAND, a think tank often commissioned by the Pentagon. He
had worked as a scholar in residence at the CIA and an adviser to the
U.S. military in Iraq, and he was also editor in chief of *Studies in Conflict and Terrorism,* the key scholarly journal in the field.

In May 2008, Hoffman took to the pages of *Foreign Affairs,* the
in-flight magazine of America's foreign policy elite, to launch a blistering critique of Sageman's claim that "leaderless" militants unconnected

to a formal terror group were now the main threat to American security. Hoffman wrote that this was "a fundamental misreading of the al-Qaeda threat." In the genteel world of terrorism research, these were fighting words; the *New York Times* even ran a story about the debate. Sageman, who had previously worked for the Secret Service and was then with the NYPD, fired back at Hoffman in an interview with the *Times*, saying, "Maybe he's mad that I'm the go-to guy now." Sageman's personal style tended toward abrasive and dismissive, and this was a bit of hyperbole. Though Sageman had done the most innovative post-9/11 theorizing about radicalization, Hoffman still had deep connections to many of the leading scholars and practitioners in the world of counterterrorism.

Henry Kissinger is said to have quipped, "The reason why academic quarrels are so nasty is that the stakes are so small." But in the case of the Sageman-Hoffman spat, the stakes were enormously high. If Sageman was correct that the West was threatened largely by homegrown militants, then why spend hundreds of billions of dollars on a global "war on terror" in countries such as Afghanistan, Pakistan, and Yemen? If Hoffman was correct, the course that both the Bush and Obama administrations had followed in taking the war to wherever al-Qaeda and its allies had found sanctuary made a great deal of sense.

As it turned out, Sageman and Hoffman were both correct. As previously noted, while lone wolves have been the source of all deadly jihadist attacks in the States since 9/11, the deadliest terrorist attack in British history, the July 7, 2005, bombings that killed fifty-two commuters on London's transportation system, was directed by al-Qaeda leaders living in Pakistan. So, too, was the abortive plan a year later to bring down seven American and Canadian passenger jets leaving Heathrow Airport; if that plot had succeeded, the carnage could have been on the scale of 9/11. All these plotters were following orders handed down to them by the leaders of al-Qaeda, precisely the opposite of leaderless jihad.

The Sageman-Hoffman debate unfurled over the course of the summer of 2008, and it was only a year later that the most significant real-world proofs for each side emerged. That was the year of Nidal Hasan's and Carlos Bledsoe's attacks, but it was also the year of a sophisticated plot that, while it failed, emphatically demonstrated that al-Qaeda was far from done with jihad in America.

The plot to bring down Northwest Flight 253 over Detroit on Christmas Day 2009, otherwise known as the "underwear bomb" plot, was masterminded by the Yemeni branch of al-Qaeda. If the attack had succeeded, 290 passengers and crew would have been killed, along with residents of Detroit on the ground. This was a prime example of "leader-led jihad," in which a terrorist organization with long experience and a wealth of resources orchestrates an attack of a scale and sophistication well beyond any lone gunman.

The underwear bombing was also, in its own way, more proof of how dangerous the homegrown threat could be, as its mastermind was an American citizen: Anwar al-Awlaki. Though Awlaki was anything but a lone wolf, his American background had proved a deadly asset, as he had attracted and trained a recruit to infiltrate his home country. While independent militants perpetrated the most deadly jihadist attacks in the United States after 9/11, the American leaders and key operatives of jihadist groups from Yemen to Pakistan played a more important role in the overall global jihad—men such as Awlaki, who not only inspired but also planned multiple attacks in the West, or Alabama-born Omar Hammami, who, as we shall see, became a key recruiter for the Somali terror group al-Shabaab, or Floridian Adnan Shukrijumah, who oversaw from Pakistan al-Qaeda's operations to attack Western targets.

The "Underwear Bomber" was Umar Farouk Abdulmutallab, the son of Alhaji Umaru Mutallab, a Muslim banker in the northern Nigerian city of Kaduna and one of the richest men in Africa. Abdulmutallab, privileged and pious, was a solemn loner in his teens. While his peers were going to parties, he spent hours reading the Koran or worshipping at the mosque that was built by his father, across the street from the family home.

In 2005, Abdulmutallab was accepted to study engineering at the academically rigorous University College, London. This was also the year he started listening to Awlaki's online lectures, an important factor in his starting to think seriously about "accepting martyrdom as a possibility." Living alone in a three-bedroom apartment in the heart of west London, Abdulmutallab fell in with a "Londonistan" crowd. As the president of the Islamic Society at his university, he presided over a "War on Terror Week" in 2007, in which members of the society, wearing Guantanamo-style orange jumpsuits, applauded a lecture by a former Guantanamo inmate.

After his undergraduate years, Abdulmutallab enrolled in a master's program at a college in Dubai, but during a summer break he felt called by Allah to seek out Awlaki in the mountains and deserts of Yemen—and perhaps, finally, to realize his long-held dream of waging jihad. In August 2009, Abdulmutallab arrived in Yemen, purportedly to study Arabic (a language he already spoke). He went from mosque to mosque in the Yemeni capital of Sana'a looking for his hero, and eventually obtained a cell number through which he sent the cleric a text message. Awlaki later called his young acolyte, assigning him the task of writing an essay about "why he wanted to become involved in jihad." Abdulmutallab found it an easy task.

After reading Abdulmutallab's essay, Awlaki summoned him to his desert hideout, where for three days they discussed the necessity of holy wars against the enemies of Islam. The young man told Awlaki that he was willing to carry out any mission the cleric asked of him.

In October 2009, Abdulmutallab sent a text message to his family: "Oh mother don't despair or worry and never lose hope in the mercy of Allah. . . . May Allah take care of you wherever you are like you took care of me all of my life." He sent a text also to his father: "Please forgive me, I will no longer be in touch with you." Around the same time, Awlaki posted to his blog a provocative piece titled "Could Yemen Be the Next Surprise of the Season?" arguing that Yemen could become "the single most important jihad front in the world."

Alarmed by the text from his son, on November 18, 2009, Abdulmutallab's father went to the U.S. embassy in Abuja, Nigeria, and told State Department officials there that he believed his son was meeting with extremists in Yemen. He told the officials, "Look at the texts he is sending. He's a security threat." At the time, Abdulmutallab had a multiple-entry visa for the States. On November 20 the U.S. embassy in Nigeria issued a warning to the National Counterterrorism Center, but Abdulmutallab was not put on the four-thousand-person "no-fly" list or on the "selectees" list of around fifteen thousand people who had to go through a rigorous screening before they could board a flight—he appeared only on a much larger list of more than a half million suspected militants known as the "TIDE" list. (Short for Terrorist Identities Datamart Environment, it's the sort of name that only officials in the counterterrorism-industrial complex could come up with.) NCTC analysts made no effort to see if Abdulmutallab possessed a valid U.S. visa.

Abdulmutallab was dispatched by Awlaki to meet Ibrahim al-Asiri, al-Qaeda's master bomb maker in Yemen. An unsentimental killer, Asiri had recently sent his younger brother on a suicide mission to assassinate the Saudi official in charge of counterterrorism, Prince Mohammed bin Nayef. The younger Asiri had concealed the bomb, made of PETN, in his underwear. PETN, a plastic explosive, was not picked up by the metal detectors through which the would-be assassin had to pass to meet with the prince. Though the attack failed—when the bomb went off, it killed the assassin, but the prince sustained only minor injuries—PETN's versatility was proved.

With the knowledge that his underwear bomb could pass through metal detectors, a technical feat well beyond the capabilities of most lone wolves, al-Qaeda's master bomb maker was determined to launch his most spectacular operation yet. The bomb maker suggested a suicide bombing targeting an American plane, a plan Awlaki approved. Asiri showed Abdulmutallab how to use the chemical syringe that would detonate the bomb, and they practiced the operation together.

In early December, al-Qaeda's leaders decided it was time to videotape Abdulmutallab's "martyrdom" statement, which Awlaki worked with him to polish. Abdulmutallab recited a script about the need for Muslims to avenge the wrongs done to them. Behind him was propped a black al-Qaeda flag with white Arabic lettering (the Islamic profession of faith) and an AK-47, the standard accoutrements of such videos.

Abdulmutallab saw himself now as an instrument of jihad, fulfilling the orders of his "sheikh," Awlaki. The young Nigerian didn't have any role in deciding that an American plane should be the target of his attack; that was Awlaki's decision alone. The cleric told his acolyte that he should "wait until the airplane was over the United States and then take it down." (It was left up to Abdulmutallab to choose which airline and which date.) Awlaki was now a deadly enemy of his country of birth.

On December 16, Abdulmutallab bought a round-trip ticket from Lagos to Detroit via Amsterdam for $2,800 in cash. He chose Detroit because he had only enough money to fly round-trip to one of two American cities, Houston or Detroit, and he was savvy enough to know that a one-way ticket might attract the attention of intelligence agencies. Secreted on his person was a slip of paper bearing an encryption code that al-Qaeda in Yemen used to communicate secretly over the Internet.

Eight days after purchasing the ticket, Abdulmutallab flew from Lagos and transferred in Amsterdam, where he passed through the usual security checks, including a metal detector. He boarded Northwest Flight 253 for Detroit on December 25. There were 290 passengers and crew on the plane. Abdulmutallab was in seat 19A, near the fuel tank, an ideal place for his concealed bomb to cause maximum damage. The bomb, stitched into a pocket in his underwear, consisted of two hundred grams (seven ounces) of highly explosive PETN.

During the flight, Abdulmutallab was fasting; he didn't eat or drink as he prepared himself for his holy mission. Somewhere over the U.S.-Canadian border he went to the bathroom to perform a purification ritual. He spent around twenty minutes washing his face, brushing his teeth, and dabbing on cologne before returning to his seat. Telling his seatmates that his stomach was upset, Abdulmutallab pulled a blanket over himself. After making his final prayers, he pushed the plunger of the detonator syringe.

Passengers heard a popping sound, like a very loud firecracker. The bomb did not detonate properly—likely in part because Abdulmutallab had been wearing the bomb in his underwear for three weeks, to get used to it—but Abdulmutallab's clothing and the blanket that covered him were set ablaze. One of the passengers sitting next to him shouted, "Your pants are on fire! Hey, dude. Your pants are on fire!" Smoke poured from his seat. Abdulmutallab remained motionless and expressionless throughout this ordeal. Whatever happened next was for Allah to decide.

The passengers around Abdulmutallab tried to smother the flames, but it was a chemical fire, not easy to put out. The aircrew used blankets and fire extinguishers. A flight attendant asked Abdulmutallab what he had been hiding in his pants, and he explained: an "explosive device." Passengers and members of the flight crew escorted Abdulmutallab to the front of the plane, where they could easily observe him. They took his pants completely off—all that was left was a bit of the underwear that contained the bomb, which looked like a mangled piece of diaper. He was given a blanket to cover himself. The smell of Abdulmutallab's burned flesh permeated the cabin.

Customs and Border Protection agents detained Abdulmutallab when the plane arrived at the Detroit airport. He told them that he was with al-Qaeda and had been given the bomb in Yemen and that he had "tried to bring down the airplane."

Christmas dinner was in the oven at Art Cummings's home in Richmond, Virginia, when Andy Arena, the special agent in charge of the Detroit FBI office, called to say, "We got a problem. We got a guy who tried to blow himself up on a plane." Cummings told his family he had to leave. They were used to this kind of thing. He picked up his "go bag" and jumped in his car, turning on the lights and siren as he drove north to DC.

The U.S. intelligence community's growing nervousness about the al-Qaeda franchise in Yemen had intensified in the weeks before the attempted bombing. The group's leaders appeared to be meeting frequently, and SIGINT, or signals intelligence, suggested something was going on, though it wasn't clear exactly what. There was sufficient anxiety that for the first time in seven years the CIA had launched a drone strike in Yemen, which on December 17 had killed at least a dozen members of al-Qaeda—and some forty civilians. Another drone strike on the day before Christmas had killed an estimated thirty militants.

At 3:30 in the afternoon, Mike Leiter was painting his basement steps in Washington, DC—"because that's what Jews do on Christmas Day"—when he received a call from Cummings. He drove for the fifteen-minute trip to the NCTC, in Northern Virginia, a short drive from CIA headquarters. At the nondescript complex of modern buildings hidden behind groves of thick trees, NCTC officials determined that Abdulmutallab was on the TIDE list and also, worrisomely, that the National Security Agency had recently picked up SIGINT about a "Nigerian" working with al-Qaeda in Yemen. These two dots had not previously been connected. A couple of hours after Abdulmutallab's botched attack, Leiter was on a video teleconference with Obama's top White House counterterrorism adviser, John Brennan, and told him, "John, based on everything we have, our assessment is this is an al-Qaeda-associated terrorist attack."

Cummings was worried that Abdulmutallab—currently being treated for serious burns at the University of Michigan hospital—would be formally arrested and, exercising his right to remain silent, would stop giving up important intelligence information. Cummings called the Detroit office of the FBI, saying, "I don't want to hear you guys arrested him. Goddamn if they Mirandize him and it shuts him down before they get intelligence out of him."

Two of the FBI agents who had escorted Abdulmutallab to the hospital made the determination that, given the possibility of other attacks being in progress, as there were on 9/11, they should not immediately read Abdulmutallab his Miranda rights, as would have been standard practice, and should instead place a premium on finding out the exact dimensions of his plot. Abdulmutallab repeated to them that al-Qaeda in Yemen had given him the explosive device, but he also said he did not think he was part of a larger wave of attacks. Abdulmutallab was lucid and answered the agents' questions without hesitation, but after an hour of discussion, the agents felt he had started to mislead them. They read him his rights.

On December 28, al-Qaeda in Yemen released a two-page written claim of responsibility for the failed attack that featured a photograph of Abdulmutallab standing in front of an al-Qaeda flag and smiling. Despite the plot's failure, al-Qaeda's leaders had reason for celebration. They had manufactured bombs that could pass metal detectors and had vetted a recruit capable of smuggling the bomb onto a U.S.-bound flight who was willing to sacrifice his own life in the attack. More immediately, they had reawakened Americans' fears about the safety of their aviation system and had caused a political crisis for the relatively new U.S. president. If Carlos Bledsoe and Major Nidal Hasan epitomized the real threat posed by American citizens who self-radicalized, al-Qaeda's attempt to bring down Northwest Flight 253 over Detroit was a reminder to the Obama administration that organized terrorist groups with large-scale resources and ambitions to wreak destruction on the United States still posed a far deadlier potential threat. This realization was to lead, in the coming years, to a covert new chapter in the war against al-Qaeda and allied groups.

In addition to Abdulmutallab's botched jihad, the two most threatening plots targeting New York City after 9/11 further bolstered Bruce Hoffman's case. Both plots occurred relatively early in the Obama administration and, along with the Underwear Bomber, added to the government's awareness that a large-scale attack by al-Qaeda or a likeminded group remained a distinct possibility—and that American citizens could well be instrumental in such attacks.

The skinny, bearded man wearing a baseball cap and pushing a shopping cart down the aisles of the Beauty Supply Warehouse in suburban Denver on July 25, 2009, looked like just another suburbanite. Of course, not too many suburban guys buy six bottles of Clairoxide hair bleach or return a few weeks later to buy a dozen bottles of Ms. Kay Liquid hair bleach. Conscious that these were hardly the typical purchases of an Afghan American male in his mid-twenties, Najibullah Zazi joked with the checkout staff that he "had a lot of girlfriends." But the hair bleach wasn't for Zazi's girlfriends. It was the key ingredient for the bombs he had learned to make the previous year at an al-Qaeda training camp in the tribal regions of Pakistan.

For the past half decade, al-Qaeda's trainers in Waziristan, a region along Pakistan's border with Afghanistan, had been teaching their Western recruits to build effective bombs from commonly available household items, the kind of ingredients that could be purchased in bulk in stores in the United States without triggering the suspicions of law enforcement. Their star pupils had been the British suicide bombers who carried out the "7/7" London bombings on July 7, 2005, who had used their training to heat up and distill ordinary hair bleach (combining it with other ingredients, such as black pepper) into powerful explosives.

In an apartment the London plotters had rented to serve as their bomb factory, they mixed the chemicals. As they brewed up batches they wore disposable masks because of the high toxicity of the materials, which bleached their dark hair a noticeably lighter color. They installed a commercial-grade refrigerator in the apartment to keep the highly unstable bomb ingredients cold. They built four devices.

Fifty-two commuters were killed when the bombs detonated on three Underground trains and a double-decker bus. The skill in making such highly lethal bombs was getting the hair bleach to the right high level of concentration, a process that took many hours of careful preparation. It was not expertise that could be picked up by reading recipes on the Internet, and without training, aspiring bomb makers could meet a bad end. Three years before Zazi was making his bulk purchases of hair bleach in Denver, Matthew Rugo and Curtis Jetton, twenty-one-year-old roommates in Texas City, near Houston, were making explosives from concentrated bleach when the concoction blew up, killing Rugo and injuring Jetton. The pair had no political motives; they had just wanted to blow up a van for fun.

Zazi's aims were far more malevolent. He wanted to blow up as many commuters as possible, and himself, on the New York City subway system.

What had brought him to this point? After all, New York City was Zazi's adopted hometown. Five years after his birth in a small village in the Pashtun-dominated province of Paktia, in eastern Afghanistan, his father had moved to New York City, working long days and nights as a cabdriver and remitting money to his family, who had fled to Pakistan to escape the Soviet war then raging in Afghanistan. In 1996, Zazi's father was granted asylum in the States, and three years later Zazi arrived in New York and enrolled as a freshman at Flushing High School, in

Queens. Zazi did typical American teen stuff: playing basketball, hanging out with friends, and playing video games and pool.

Then came 9/11. In the weeks after the attacks, furious arguments broke out at the Hazrati Abu Bakr mosque in Flushing, where Najibullah Zazi and his father worshipped. One contingent of mosquegoers supported the Taliban and did not believe that bin Laden had masterminded 9/11. They started saying their prayers in the parking lot. The Zazi family, including sixteen-year-old Najibullah, prayed with this more radical contingent, although the reason for their protest was more that they supported the Pashtun-led Taliban than for any love of al-Qaeda.

Najibullah Zazi dropped out of high school at age sixteen to work stocking shelves at a Korean-owned grocery. By the time he was twenty he had graduated to manning his own coffee cart in downtown Manhattan, a few blocks from Wall Street. Zazi was "the doughnut guy"; his customers fondly remembered the "God Bless America" sign on his cart and his ability cheerfully to recall all the coffee orders of his regulars.

Now that he had a steady job, Zazi married one of his cousins, as is typical for many Pashtuns. The wedding took place in Peshawar, Pakistan, in 2006. Zazi's wife stayed in Pakistan to raise their kids. It was following a trip to Pakistan to visit his family that Zazi stopped wearing jeans and started wearing traditional Pakistani-style clothing. Zazi also grew a bushy beard, and when he picked up his coffee cart at a depot in Brooklyn in the early morning hours, he would now be listening to religious chants. He told another Afghan cart operator whose musical tastes ran to dance music that such tunes were "dishonest" to Islam. Zazi was also becoming increasingly angered by the U.S.-led war in Afghanistan, which he believed was indiscriminately killing Afghan women and children. He began listening obsessively to the lectures of Awlaki.

Zazi started racking up tens of thousand of dollars in purchases on multiple credit cards, charges he had no intention of paying back. He was using the credit to finance his plans for holy war. In August 2008, he and two high school friends, Zarein Ahmedzay, an Afghan American, and Adis Medunjanin, a cabdriver of Bosnian descent, flew from

Newark to Peshawar, where they hoped to join the Taliban. Medunjanin harbored a vision that he would be appointed a Taliban general.

In Peshawar, where Zazi could use the cover story that he was visiting his wife and kids, the trio met with "Ahmad," an al-Qaeda operative who put them in touch with two al-Qaeda leaders. When those leaders asked the trio to participate in attacks against the United States, Zazi refused. He wanted to fight the U.S. military in the fields and mountains of his homeland, not to kill American civilians in the streets of his adopted country. So al-Qaeda's leaders brought in someone more persuasive: someone who could speak to Zazi in his own language, someone who had also grown up on the streets of New York City in the 1990s, a man whose meteoric rise through the ranks of al-Qaeda had taken him, over the past decade, from camp dishwasher to the leader of the group's operations in the West.

Adnan Shukrijumah was born in Saudi Arabia in 1975, but his family had moved to Trinidad in the 1980s and then to Brooklyn in the early '90s, where his father had taken a job as a cleric at a mosque on Atlantic Avenue. In 1995, Shukrijumah's family left New York City for the Fort Lauderdale area in Florida, where Shukrijumah sold used cars to pay for his studies at a local community college. After Muslim acquaintances gave him books and videotapes about the holy wars in Kashmir and Afghanistan, he became so moved by these stories that in late 1999 he traveled to Afghanistan to attend an al-Qaeda training camp. Upon his return, Shukrijumah told his mother that he was opposed to the excesses of the West (alcohol, drug abuse, revealing clothing), and in May 2001 he left Florida again. Shortly after the 9/11 attacks, he called his mother from Afghanistan, saying, "Did you hear what happened? They are putting it on the Muslims." His mother advised him not to come back to the States, and her son never contacted her again.

It was Shukrijumah who now made the pitch to Zazi and his friends from Queens that instead of fighting alongside the Taliban's tens of thousands of fighters, they could help the cause of holy war best by going back to the States and launching attacks there. It was the last six months of Bush's second term, and the administration had significantly amped up the CIA drone program in the tribal regions of Pakistan.

Angered by the drone program and persuaded by his fellow American, Zazi agreed to return to the States to conduct his jihad. He also volunteered to be a suicide bomber, as did his two friends. They discussed with Shukrijumah potential targets, including the New York Stock Exchange, Times Square, and a Walmart.

Al-Qaeda trainers gave Zazi five days of training on building hydrogen peroxide–based bombs. Zazi took careful notes, which he e-mailed to himself before leaving Pakistan, so he wouldn't have them on him when he went through immigration in the States. When he returned to New York in mid-January 2009, he had been living on the Afghan-Pakistani border for five months, during which time he had been in almost continuous contact with members of al-Qaeda. He was now ready to launch what al-Qaeda's leadership hoped would be the most lethal terrorist attack in the States since 9/11.

Al-Qaeda's leaders had earlier pinned similar high hopes on Bryant Neal Vinas, a Hispanic American convert to Islam who was also from Long Island. Vinas had traveled to Pakistan's tribal areas during the summer of 2008, where he attended al-Qaeda training courses on explosives and other weapons. As an American recruit, Vinas enjoyed a quasi-celebrity status in the group's training camps. He took part in a Taliban rocket attack on a U.S. base in Afghanistan and discussed with members of al-Qaeda the idea of attacking the Long Island Rail Road, but by November 2008 Vinas had been captured in Pakistan and turned over to the FBI.

Don Borelli was the top FBI counterterrorism official in New York. Borelli had been working al-Qaeda cases for more than a decade, beginning when the group bombed two U.S. embassies in Africa in 1998, killing more than two hundred people. The Vinas case worried Borelli. Vinas was emblematic of what law enforcement termed "the foreign fighter pipeline," through which Western recruits to al-Qaeda and its allied groups were ending up in the tribal regions of Pakistan, receiving training designed to make them lethal terrorists when they returned home to the West. The foreign fighter pipeline wasn't linear—more of an ad hoc affair: Westerners who spent enough time in jihadist circles in Pakistan eventually wound up making the right connections to meet someone in al-Qaeda. Vinas had bounced around in Pakistan for months before he finally got his shot at joining the group. It was unnerving for FBI officials such as Borelli to realize that even seven years after 9/11, an American citizen could end up in an al-Qaeda training camp.

With the arrest of Vinas, al-Qaeda's hopes for another successful attack on the United States now rested with Zazi and his friends. It was an unprecedented number of American recruits for a terrorist operation: three men, all of whom were from New York City, and all of whom were willing to commit suicide in the operation. Al-Qaeda's leaders hoped that the attacks launched by Zazi's crew would be on the scale of the London 7/7 bombings.

Following their trip to Pakistan, the three al-Qaeda recruits met on a basketball court in Queens where they could discreetly discuss their attack plans. They would make bleach-based bombs and pack them into backpacks and would then board three separate subway trains and blow themselves up. The plan was virtually identical to what the London bombers had done four years earlier. The three agreed to conduct the coordinated suicide bombings during the holy month of Ramadan, in September 2009, which also happened to coincide with the eighth anniversary of 9/11. According to Zazi, the purpose of the attacks was "to make America weak." The plotters planned to attack trains leaving Grand Central Terminal at rush hour, so "people would have a lot of fear."

Just like the London bombers, Zazi set up a bomb factory. During early September 2009, he checked into the HomeStead Studio Suites motel in Aurora, Colorado, on the outskirts of Denver, where he mixed and cooked batches of hair bleach in his kitchenette. On the night of September 6, as he labored over the stove, Zazi sent several e-mails to the al-Qaeda operative "Ahmad." The e-mails contained a well-known al-Qaeda code for a terrorist operation being imminent—"the marriage is ready"—and also asked for specific instructions "right away, please" about flour and oil. Zazi had mastered the manufacture of the hair bleach–based bombs but had forgotten the precise proportions of flour and ghee (a clarified butter used in South Asian cooking) needed to ignite the mixture.

If Zazi had sent these e-mails to an ordinary e-mail account in Pakistan, anyone monitoring it would have assumed the query was about making a wedding cake. But Zazi sent the e-mail to an account that, in the parlance of intelligence professionals, was "covered," meaning that it was monitored by the NSA. They knew the account was being used by a big player in al-Qaeda, though it wasn't clear exactly who. The leaders of al-Qaeda typically used dozens of different e-mail accounts, often dispatching couriers to work each account on their behalf. NSA cyber experts could sometimes figure out who was using a given account based on the way the user communicated, or his log-in times, or the location he had logged in from.

The e-mail address Zazi used to touch base with "Ahmad" was sana _pakhtana@yahoo.com, an account that was being monitored by British intelligence because someone using it had also been in touch with al-Qaeda recruits in the United Kingdom. Sometime before April 2009 (when they arrested an al-Qaeda-linked group they had been tracking), the Brits tipped off American officials that the e-mail account belonged to an al-Qaeda operative living in Pakistan.

This point deserves underscoring: The NYPD, and indeed the whole U.S. intelligence community, was unaware of the most serious al-Qaeda plot in the States in almost a decade until Zazi's e-mail alerted them just days before he was planning to carry out the attacks. And the only reason the NSA was monitoring this e-mail was because of a tip-off from the British. The NYPD monitoring of locations in New York City where Muslims gathered, which included the mosque in Queens where Zazi worshipped and a number of the restaurants in the Queens neighborhood where he and his two coconspirators lived, had yielded nothing of value in uncovering their plans.

Had the increased focus on leaderless jihadis distorted the priorities of law enforcement, leaving the United States more open to a terrorist spectacular mounted by al-Qaeda or a like-minded organization, as Bruce Hoffman continued to warn? It's not a question that can be readily answered, but it is a fact that the three most threatening plots to attack the States after 9/11 were the work of Al-Qaeda in the Arabian Peninsula, core al-Qaeda, and the Pakistani Taliban, and in all those cases, the perpetrators were largely or completely unknown to U.S. law enforcement and the American intelligence community. Although, for that matter, these entities didn't see Major Hasan and Carlos Bledsoe (or the Tsarnaevs) coming, either.

On September 6, as Zazi repeatedly pinged his al-Qaeda contact in Pakistan, the NSA investigated the IP address of the mysterious e-mail sender in the States. It resolved to an address in suburban Denver, hitherto not known as a hotbed of Islamist terrorism. The FBI found that a number of people were living at the address, but the Bureau quickly focused on Zazi because of his recent travels to Pakistan. FBI techs went to the motel room where Zazi had been preparing his bombs and swabbed for explosives. The tests came back positive.

The FBI initiated "Operation High Rise" and started twenty-four-hour surveillance of Zazi. Cummings called the FBI special agent in charge in Denver to say, "Don't make any mistakes here. This guy is operational right now." The worst thing that could happen was that Zazi got spooked too early in the investigation and the FBI couldn't scope out the exact dimensions of his plot, or who his confederates were. For the Zazi case, Cummings wanted to dismantle the entire conspiracy.

On September 9, as Zazi began driving a rental car the two thousand miles from Colorado to New York City, the FBI began tailing him. Zazi had elected not to fly back to New York, with good reason. In the trunk of his car he had secreted his explosive materials and detonators, and the laptop onto which he had downloaded his bomb-making instructions. By now President Obama was receiving daily briefings about Zazi, although what the militant was planning to do as he approached Manhattan was still not clear. Philip Mudd, second in charge of the National Security Branch at the FBI, remembers thinking, "Serious case. You're eight years after 9/11 and you still have a significant threat directed by the al-Qaeda core organization that's gotten its ass kicked. To me that was like: Sit up." Adding to the worries of FBI officials was that in only two weeks the annual United Nations General Assembly was scheduled in Manhattan, which was to be attended by Obama and more than 150 other heads of state. A terrorist event in the run-up to the assembly would be a disaster.

Relations between the FBI and the NYPD were often tense. NYPD officials believed that the Bureau needed to share more information about threats to the city they were sworn to protect, while the FBI was leery of what it considered to be the NYPD's overzealous investigative techniques. In this case, FBI agents told NYPD officials what they knew about Zazi and asked the department if they could find out anything more about him. New York City was, after all, his hometown.

David Cohen was particularly worried about Zazi because of the approaching UN General Assembly, a target-rich environment for any terrorist. NYPD officers went to one of their informants in the Afghan community in Queens, a cleric named Ahmad Afzali, on September 10. They showed Afzali a photo of Zazi and asked if he knew him. The cleric said, "Yes, I know the family very well."

Mudd, a two-decade veteran of the CIA who had then been working at the FBI for four years, observed that while the FBI often was at fault in its dealings with the NYPD, reaching out to Afzali was a serious breach of investigative procedure: "I thought the Bureau was regularly on the wrong side with NYPD, but that's a no-no. You don't do that." Such a procedural misstep ran the risk of tipping off the subject of the investigation that he was being watched, which is exactly what happened in Zazi's case. After the interview, Afzali called Zazi's father, and Zazi's father soon called his son to tell him that the police were asking questions about him.

FBI officials at the New York City Joint Terrorism Task Force, who had wiretapped Zazi, went ballistic when they found out that their investigation might have been blown. Cohen tried to soothe one of the FBI officials, saying, "We did what we were asked to do. We were doing good work, and as you know in this business, stuff happens. This is in the 'stuff happens' category. I'm sorry it happened, but I can't apologize for what we did. We didn't do anything wrong."

A senior FBI official involved in the case described it as a "colossal screwup"; this was not some suspected plot of uncertain origin, but rather a well-developed plot by al-Qaeda to attack New York City. With no coordination with the FBI, and despite knowing the seriousness of this threat, NYPD officers had gone to an informant of questionable loyalties who had then tipped off the family of the lead terrorist. The FBI official says, "We got lucky that it didn't completely ruin the case, but it came close. Just think for a second if their plan was much more advanced and they already had a device built and in a backpack and they were ready to put it on a train. That would have been it: successful attack; not thwarted despite the fact that we really were ahead of this one."

Meanwhile, the FBI had made a mistake of its own. As a way to continue surveillance as long as possible while ensuring that Zazi would be kept out of New York City if he was transporting a bomb, officials came up with a plan to perform "random" searches on the roads into Manhattan around the time Zazi would be approaching the city. They were not sure which bridge or tunnel he would take into the city, and the search would have to be performed by the Port Authority, which controls the bridges and tunnels in New York. Without providing specifics on the case, FBI agents gave Port Authority officials a description of Zazi and the car he was driving and instructed them to search his car in a seemingly random fashion.

The maneuver was a disaster. Zazi unexpectedly took the George Washington Bridge from New Jersey toward Manhattan. Caught off guard, the Port Authority police officers who performed the search of his car looked like they were targeting Zazi rather than performing a random search. Worse, the officers' bomb-sniffing dog didn't reveal the explosive materials in Zazi's trunk. Suddenly Zazi was in New York City with his bomb materials and detonators.

Cummings was furious about the inept search, asking, "Who authorized that?" He was told that there had been a container of mysterious liquid on the floor of the passenger side of Zazi's car. Cummings, who had been a bomb tech earlier in his career, knew that this could be hydrogen peroxide or some other explosive precursor. He made finding the container his team's number one priority.

The car search had made Zazi suspicious, and he learned from his father that law enforcement officers were asking questions about him. Zazi sent a text message to his buddy and coconspirator Medunjanin, saying, "We are done." He drove to a mosque in Queens, where he threw away the liquid chemicals and other bomb-building items. He spent the night of September 10 at a nearby apartment, which agents searched when he was out. They found an electronic scale of a type helpful for building a bomb. They also found multiple brand-new backpacks—not hard evidence in itself, but anyone who had followed the 2005 London bombings recalled the parallel modus operandi.

Sensing that the jig was up, Zazi flew back to Colorado on September 12. He was arrested there a week later.

Before Medunjanin was arrested he called 911, telling the operator, "We love death more than you love life," a common slogan of jihadist militants, and repeatedly screaming, "There is no God but Allah, and Muhammad is his messenger." After hanging up he crashed his car into a randomly selected vehicle on the Whitestone Bridge, which connects Queens with the Bronx. It proved to be a failed suicide attack. The trio of al-Qaeda recruits from Queens were all given long prison sentences.

The case of Faisal Shahzad was an even closer call. Shahzad had been trained in bomb making by the Pakistani Taliban, yet he was not on the radar screen of any U.S. intelligence or law enforcement agency, including the NYPD, until after he had driven a bomb-loaded vehicle into Times Square on the evening of May 1, 2010.

In the years after 9/11 the Pakistani Taliban was not seen as a threat to the American homeland. Conventional wisdom in the U.S. intelligence community was that members of the Taliban were focused exclusively on attacks in and around their Pashtun homeland, which straddles the Afghan-Pakistani border. This belief should have been dented when the then leader of the Pakistani Taliban, Baitullah Mehsud, dispatched suicide bombers on a botched mission to the Spanish port city of Barcelona in January 2008. A Pakistani Taliban spokesman confirmed this during a videotaped interview a few months later in which he said that those bombers "were under pledge to Baitullah Mehsud," but because the attack had failed, not many recognized this for what it was: the Taliban's expansion to Western targets. In March 2009, Mehsud also threatened an attack in the United States, telling the Associated Press by phone, "Soon we will launch an attack in Washington that will amaze everyone in the world." This was largely discounted as bloviation, but by the end of the year the Taliban was indeed training an American recruit to attack in the States.

By 2009 the Pakistani Taliban was increasingly influenced by al-Qaeda, a fact that could be seen in the suicide bombing that killed seven CIA officers and contractors in the American base at Khost, in eastern Afghanistan, on December 30, 2009. The suicide bomber, Humam Khalil Abu-Mulal al-Balawi, a Jordanian doctor, released a lengthy interview with al-Qaeda's production arm. Videotaped sometime before he died, the interview laid out how Balawi planned to attack the group of Agency officials using a bomb made from C-4. The chief of the Pakistani Taliban, Hakimullah Mehsud, also appeared alongside Balawi in a prerecorded video saying the attack was revenge for the drone strike that had killed Hakimullah's predecessor, Baitullah Mehsud, six months earlier.

If more attention had been paid to the growing anti-American ambitions of the Pakistani Taliban, perhaps more attention might also have been paid to Faisal Shahzad.

For the Taliban, the fact that Shahzad was a so-called clean skin, with no criminal record and no profile among the tiny community of Islamist militants in the States, made him the perfect recruit. He was far from one of their typical foot soldiers, who were generally recruited from the goat-herding class in Pakistan's tribal belt bordering Afghanistan. Shahzad was the youngest of four children of Baharul Haq, who rose to become vice air marshal in the Pakistani air force. As the son of a senior Pakistani military officer, Shahzad grew up in a privileged world of servants and drivers.

In 1999, Shahzad went to college in the States, a prerogative of the Pakistani elite, first to the now-defunct Southeastern University and then to the University of Bridgeport in Connecticut, where he earned a BA in computer science. His student adviser, William Greenspan, remembers him as "personable, a nice guy, but unremarkable." On weekends, Shahzad hung out at South Asian nightclubs in New York, drank, and chased women. He was, in sum, a not untypical American student.

What set him apart from his peers was his reaction to 9/11. A class-mate remembers walking into Shahzad's apartment after the attacks and hearing him saying, "They had it coming." Shahzad became intrigued by bin Laden's ideology. He started contemplating all the humiliation Muslim countries were going through, always in need of Western pow-ers to give them money, and soon accepted the central claim of Binlad-enism: that there was an American-led conspiracy to oppress Islam and that the only appropriate response was holy war.

At the same time that Shahzad was privately radicalizing he was pub-licly embracing the American Dream. By 2002 he was working for the cosmetics giant Elizabeth Arden in Stamford, Connecticut, while also pursuing an MBA at the University of Bridgeport. By age twenty-five he had bought a snazzy black Mercedes and a condo. Two years later, in 2004, he traded up for a three-bedroom house when he married Huma Mian, a glamorous Pakistani American conversant in four languages. An aspiring accountant, Huma was wholly Americanized. Her online profile trumpeted *Friends* and *Everybody Loves Raymond* as her favorite TV shows and her passions as "fashion, shoes, bags, SHOPPING!!" She also wrote on her Facebook page, "Im a Muslim & Im Proud!" and "I LOVE ALLAH."

Faisal and Huma Shahzad soon had two children, and Faisal was granted a green card in early 2006. He was earning seventy thousand dollars a year at a new job as a financial analyst. Despite all this suc-cess, Shahzad was still stewing with anger at the United States. Around the time that he received his green card, he wrote a lengthy e-mail to a group of friends decrying the wars in Iraq and Afghanistan and the publication in Denmark a year earlier of cartoons depicting the Prophet Muhammad, concluding, "Everyone knows the kind of humiliation we are faced with around the globe." By now Shahzad was listening to lectures by militant clerics, including Awlaki. The onetime party boy stopped drinking and started praying five times a day. On visits back to Pakistan he started clashing with his more liberal father, disapproving of his purportedly lax faith and denouncing the Pakistani government for not doing anything to stop CIA drone strikes.

In the Pakistani capital of Islamabad, Shahzad fell in with a group of like-minded militants, many of whom gathered at the Red Mosque, notorious for attracting jihadists. It was there that Shahzad met a man who put him directly in touch with the Pakistani Taliban. Shahzad asked permission from his father to travel to Afghanistan to fight alongside the Taliban, a request his father denied. (In traditional Islamic jurisprudence, those who go on jihad are supposed to secure the permission of their parents.) In early 2009, Shahzad sent an e-mail to friends observing that his "sheikhs are in the field," meaning that his spiritual guides were waging holy war rather than simply preaching in a mosque.

On April 17, 2009, Shahzad finally obtained his U.S. citizenship, but by now he was entirely disenchanted with life in the States and was having financial problems to boot. Over the past three years he had tried to sell off his house, but the real estate bubble had burst. He took out a $65,000 equity loan on his house and began selling off furnishings, and in June he abruptly quit his job and stopped paying his mortgage.

As Shahzad became more religious his five-year marriage soured. He began to pressure his wife to wear the head and chest covering, the hijab; yet her sartorial tastes ran to designer handbags and black leather coats. In this attempt to impose his beliefs on his family, Shazhad was typical of many militants in the West. Nidal Hasan pushed his cousin to be more religious, telling him he would burn in the "hell fire" if he didn't read the Koran. The Underwear Bomber, Umar Abdulmutallab, tried to persuade his father to leave the banking industry because it was an un-Islamic occupation. Carlos Bledsoe took down the picture of Martin Luther King Jr. in his parents' house, likening it to idol worship, and so on. Also, as with these others, Shahzad's attempt to impose his hard-line beliefs was unsuccessful. On June 2 he telephoned his wife from JFK Airport in New York to inform her that he was leaving for Peshawar, Pakistan, and that it was up to her to decide whether to follow him. She refused.

Once in Peshawar, Shahzad met with Hakimullah Mehsud, during the fall of 2009, and Mehsud urged Shahzad to attend a training camp. In the first week of December, Shahzad told his family in Peshawar that he was going on a several-day trip. Instead, he lived for about six weeks with members of the Taliban in North Waziristan. He was given a crash course in bomb making, spending five days building and detonating different types of devices. Because of the ever-present threat of CIA drone strikes, training happened at a different location each day. Shahzad was given a bomb-making manual for reference, and he met with a Taliban leader who gave him five thousand dollars in cash for his impending mission.

All that was left for Shahzad to do was record his "martyrdom" video, standard operating procedure for the aspiring Western suicide bomber. The Taliban planned to release the video sometime after the spectacular attack, milking additional media coverage long after Shahzad's bombs had gone off.

On the video, Shahzad delivered a by turns halting, scripted, and rambling forty-minute indictment of American foreign policy: "And . . . uh . . . jihad . . . the importance that it has, I'm just going to explain that to you." After reciting that jihad was "one of the pillars on which [Islam] stands," he continued: "This attack on the United States will . . . be a revenge attack from all, for all the mujahideen people of Muslims. . . . The intention of making this video is not to show off or gain fame. But the reason I am making this video is . . . uh . . . to grab the attention of people. . . . If you have drones to target us in our homes, we also have human drones to target you in your homes, and our attack will not end until we completely stop your aggression and completely defeat your evil forces and free our lands. We are planning to wage an attack on your side in Manhattan."

On February 3, 2010, after eight months in Pakistan, Shahzad returned to the States. During his stint overseas the bank had foreclosed on his house, so he moved into an apartment in a shabby part of Bridgeport. He began accumulating the supplies for his bomb (fertilizer, propane, gasoline) from stores across Connecticut, and he traveled as far away as Pennsylvania to pick up fireworks, which would set off the massive car bomb he planned to detonate. Meanwhile, the Taliban kept sending him chunks of cash. He received five thousand dollars through a *hawala* broker in Massachusetts and two months later picked up another seven thousand from a broker in Long Island.

He used some of this money to pay for a 1993 Nissan Pathfinder found through Craigslist, which would be the bomb-delivery vehicle. On the afternoon of May 1, 2010, Shahzad loaded the bomb into the SUV and folded a 9-millimeter Kel-Tec semiautomatic rifle he had recently purchased into a laptop computer bag. The rifle might come in handy if someone tried to stop him. Shahzad had taken the precaution of practicing his shooting at a gun range in Connecticut. He drove the SUV the hour commute into Manhattan. He had spent the past three months on the Internet looking at real-time video feeds of Times Square and had concluded that the thickest concentration of foot traffic was on a Saturday at 6:00 p.m. With the sidewalks swarming with tourists and theatergoers, it would be the perfect time and location to kill as many people as possible. Shahzad estimated that if all went to plan, his bomb would kill around forty people.

Shahzad parked the SUV at the corner of Forty-Fifth Street and Seventh Avenue and initiated the timer that would detonate the bomb in two to five minutes. The SUV was filled with bags of fertilizer, three propane gas tanks, two large gasoline canisters, and a stack of more than 150 firecrackers. Shahzad left the engine of the SUV idling as he sauntered away from the vehicle. He didn't plan to commit suicide in this attack; if it worked, he planned to do another bombing in two weeks.

Street vendor Alioune Niass soon noticed smoke coming out of the SUV and told a police officer. The officer began evacuating the area. The bomb squad arrived and blew open the locked doors of the SUV, finding it littered inside with propane canisters and gasoline containers. The SUV was a giant bomb, but a very flawed one. This may have been, in part, because Shahzad had received only five days of bomb-making training—a likely consequence of the fact that Waziristan was the leading target for CIA drone strikes, which made it harder for the Taliban to run their training camps there. Also the M-88 firecrackers Shahzad had bought contained only tiny amounts of explosive powder. Illegal fireworks could have been up to one thousand times more powerful. It's not clear why Shahzad didn't purchase more powerful firecrackers, but he may have wanted not to draw undue attention to himself. Similarly, likely because of well-publicized efforts by the NYPD and other government agencies to crack down on the sale of the type of fertilizer most suitable for bomb making, Shahzad bought fertilizer of the kind that wouldn't trigger a suspicious activity report, but that was also (by definition) not as incendiary. All these factors conspired to make the bomb a dud. FBI agent Don Borelli recalls, "That plot was only thwarted through chemistry and physics."

Shahzad walked to Grand Central Terminal to catch a train back to Connecticut, carrying the rifle in his bag. En route he listened for the blast of the bomb detonating but heard only the regular buzz of New York City traffic. When he got home he sent a message to his Taliban contact explaining the failed attempt and began watching media coverage.

That night, NYPD intelligence officials began taking a hard look at an audio message that the leader of the Pakistani Taliban, Hakimullah Mehsud, had released on the Internet a few days earlier promising to launch an attack in the United States. There was reason to be skeptical. A year earlier, a Pakistani Taliban leader had taken credit when a disturbed Vietnamese American shot up a post office in upstate New York, killing more than a dozen people—a claim that was clearly nonsensical. But there was also reason to take Mehsud seriously, given the 2008 Barcelona plot. Within a day or so, NYPD officials determined that the Pakistani Taliban threat to carry out an attack in the States was credible.

Meanwhile, the bomb squad examined Shahzad's vehicle and found its unique vehicle identification number (VIN). No current owner was registered, but the VIN did resolve back to the previous owner of the SUV. Agents asked her to whom she had sold the SUV; she told them, "I don't know, but he called me back the next day because there was something wrong." This meant that one of Shahzad's numbers was on her telephone. The number turned up a hit: when Shahzad had flown back from Pakistan to the States in February, a savvy Customs and Border Protection agent had decided to put him into a secondary screening (likely because of the length of his stay in Pakistan, eight months) and had taken down his phone number. It matched the number used to call the SUV's previous owner.

Within twenty-four hours of the botched bombing, the feds now had a plausible suspect. They went to Shahzad's apartment in Connecticut, but he was gone. Worried by TV coverage that implied that the cops were closing in on him, he had left for JFK Airport. He made a last-minute reservation for a flight on Emirates airline to the Pakistani capital, Islamabad, via Dubai, paying for the ticket in cash at the airport. This should have triggered an alarm at Emirates but didn't. Shahzad had just been added to the no-fly list, but the information was not processed in Emirates' computer system; Customs and Border Protection agents discovered that Shahzad was on the Emirates flight only when they checked the passenger manifest. Agents ran to the Emirates gate only to find the jet's doors closed and the pilots about to taxi to the runway. The agents got the crew to open the doors. When Customs agents boarded the plane and found Shahzad, he said, "I was expecting you. Are you NYPD or FBI?"

The botched Times Square bombing remains among the most serious indictments of post-9/11 counterterrorism efforts. Shahzad was trained in bomb making by the Taliban, yet no U.S. intelligence or law enforcement agency was aware of him. That said, the offensive and defensive measures that the U.S. government had put in place after 9/11 likely saved the lives of many Americans that Saturday evening. The aggressive CIA drone campaign in the Pakistani tribal regions meant that Shahzad received only five days of training there, while the publicized effort by law enforcement agencies to reach out to fertilizer sellers in the States meant that Shahzad downgraded the type of fertilizer he used for the bomb. Not least, the careful work of a single Customs agent was critical, capturing as it did the phone number later linked to the purchase of the SUV that carried the bomb.

David Cohen is confident that, had he not been found, Shahzad would have tried to attack again, most likely in a suicide bombing. At his sentencing, Shahzad was unrepentant, telling the judge, "I'm going to plead guilty one hundred times forward."

CHAPTER 7

JIHADINAMERICA.COM

YOU TOOK JUST A SHOCKING LEAP FROM A HIGH-SCHOOL ATHLETE TO A
HIGHLY ENERGIZED TRAITOR TO YOUR COUNTRY. IT'S STARTLING.

—U.S. district judge Liam O'Grady, sentencing Zachary
Chesser to twenty-five years in prison on February 24, 2011

At the age of nine Zachary Chesser could name every major battle
of the American Civil War, which generals participated, how many
soldiers had died, and which side had won. When he was a kid, Zac's
greatest desire was to be a U.S. Army general. His grandfather was career army; he had gone to West Point and then fought in Vietnam, retiring as a colonel. Zac's mother, Barbara, says that her father inculcated an
atmosphere of intense patriotism in her household: "Loyal, loyal, loyal
American."

David Chesser met his future wife in the mid-1980s, when both were
working part-time at the Pierce Street Annex bar in downtown Washington, DC. David was studying for his master's in economics at nearby
George Washington University; Barbara worked in human resources.
After they were married they moved down to Charlottesville, Virginia,
so that David could pursue his PhD at the University of Virginia. Their
first son, Zachary, was born three days before Christmas 1989, and another son followed three years later.

The Chessers moved to Missouri, where David taught at the University of Missouri and Barbara obtained a law degree, but eight years
later they headed back east. Fairfax County, an affluent suburb of DC,

is the kind of place that puts the white in white bread, where comfortably middle-class subdivisions sprawl for miles in every direction, home to hosts of civil servants and government contractors. David worked as an economist for the Department of Transportation, and Barbara was a prosecutor for the DC government in Washington.

By the time of their move back east, David and Barbara's marriage was unraveling. When Zac's parents divorced, his mother moved in with her partner, Stacy Anderson, also a government lawyer.

Zac was eleven on September 11, 2001. He and his school friends made up songs about torturing and killing Osama bin Laden. A teacher who overheard them singing these songs didn't discourage them; after all, their school was only a dozen or so miles away from the still-smoldering Pentagon. Zac wrote a poem about the attacks:

> America will stand proud and tall
> No matter how hard she's shaken she will not fall,
> America's the finest out of every country,
> No matter how hard she's shaken she'll always be free,
> Everyone's love combines into one giant heart,
> But no matter how hard she's shaken she won't fall apart.

Zac was a clever boy, reading at a sixth-grade level by age six and thriving in the "gifted and talented" program in elementary and middle school. Like many clever boys, he acquired a number of obsessional interests. At age eight he refused to wear leather shoes because he worried about cruelty to animals. A year later he was boycotting Nike products because the company ran sweatshops. By his early teens he was a long-haired, vocal pacifist and a vegetarian in protest of the slaughterhouse system. He dabbled in Buddhism and had discussions with his father about how best to end poverty. He learned to draw well and played the guitar. He studied Latin, and then Japanese for four years.

His mother says, "He had a tendency to find something he felt like he was really good at and then dig his teeth in and go full force. He might not have been the best at it, but when he thought of himself as one of the best at it, he kept with it." Zac devoured books about history, particularly the Civil War, but like any other teen boy, he also played video games and watched TV; a favorite was the animated series *South Park,* of which he was a "ginormous" fan.

Standing six foot one by his mid-teens, Zac was also something of a jock. He played youth basketball and soccer, rowed crew, and in eleventh grade even began break-dancing with a group of Korean American students. He was well-rounded, finding sports and calculus equally manageable, and he largely stayed out of trouble.

In twelfth grade Zac fell hard for a Muslim girl, Fatimah, the daughter of Somali immigrants. He was dating Fatimah behind her father's back—he didn't approve of his daughter dating—so they had to sneak out to the prom together. Never one to do anything by half measures, Zac threw himself into learning everything he could about Islam. "I became Muslim after reading the first four chapters of a translation of the Koran," he says. He started playing on a football team organized by a member of Hizb ut-Tahrir, a fundamentalist but nonviolent organization that aims to install sharia law around the Muslim world. In the summer of 2008, Zac formally converted to Islam. He was eighteen.

Zac immediately set out to be the best Muslim he could be: "I had very little exposure to religious knowledge growing up, so when I learned anything about Islam, I immediately adopted it and tried to practice completely. I did not do a lot of critical thinking about what I learned. I just felt like I had to do everything to the fullest extent, whether it was how I dressed, who I spoke to, or how I prayed." After three months of practicing Islam, Zac was given a copy of some lectures by Anwar al-Awlaki. "They had an element of radicalism to them which served as a gateway for me to other more extreme beliefs," says Zac.

Zac soon told Fatimah that he wanted to travel to Yemen or to her native Somalia to study Islam. Fatimah had no nostalgia for Somalia, telling him, "I've been there, and I know what it's like and I'm not going back." The relationship ended shortly afterward, when Zac announced that "Islam does not allow paramours."

Now Zac started ranting to his family that the Koran demanded that he not use toilet paper. Though he had recently signed up to help with the Obama presidential campaign, he suddenly said he couldn't even vote because it was supposedly against Islam. He told his mother that his religious beliefs prevented him from having health insurance. When his mother checked this with a local imam and he assured her it was nonsense, Zac scoffed: "That imam, he doesn't know what he's talking about."

One day Zac came home wearing the full-length robes worn by men in the Gulf States. Soon he was wearing them all the time, as well as a *kufi*, or Islamic cap, and he kept his pant legs well above his shoes. He grew a beard, started adopting an odd, slightly foreign accent, and soon quit his job at Blockbuster Video, refusing to work at a place that rented out videotapes showing women in stages of undress. He stopped going out to dance clubs and made it clear that he didn't want to take part in any family Christmas festivities or gift giving when the holiday season came around. He told his mother that he could no longer be around her partner, Stacy, as she was an unmarried female outside his family. To Stacy he said flatly, "My religion precludes me from being in the same room with you."

Zac spent more and more time in his room watching jihadist propaganda online. He would stare at his computer screen for hours, seemingly frozen in place. Zac's stepmother, Meg, thought that some of the lectures sounded like rants delivered by Hitler. She and Zac's father were now in a bit of a panic, particularly because Zac would soon be living by himself in a dorm room at George Mason University. They explored intervention options but learned there wasn't much they could do now that Zac was eighteen. Increasingly worried, Zac's father tried to sound out his son about his views on the 9/11 attacks. Zac assured his father, "I don't believe in violence."

As a freshman at George Mason, Zac associated exclusively with members of the Muslim Student Association. He hung out most often with students from Saudi Arabia and Somalia, many of whom shared his increasingly militant beliefs about jihad. He found it all very exciting. Because of his beard and Arab-style robes, some students took to referring to him as "Jesus."

Zac's mother was becoming more and more concerned about her son. One day, during the spring of 2010, Zac told her over coffee that he knew one of the five kids from northern Virginia who had recently traveled to Pakistan and attempted to join the Taliban (before being arrested by the Pakistani authorities). Barbara, a no-nonsense prosecutor, asked her son, "You're not hanging out with bad people, are you?" In her heart she felt she knew the answer. Zac assured her, "I'm not hanging out with bad people."

It was true that Chesser was not literally "hanging out" with most of the bad people he knew. Instead, he was spending time with a virtual community of like-minded militants on the Internet, who reinforced his own increasingly radical ideas. Chesser was part of the generation of militants that emerged in the decade after 9/11 who proved not to need face-to-face contact with fellow radicals to radicalize, rather self-radicalizing solely through the materials they read and watched on the Internet, just as Sageman had predicted in *Leaderless Jihad*. These militants in turn began creating their own websites in English, expanding a corpus long available only in Arabic, to help radicalize others. If you wanted to imbibe al-Qaeda's philosophy, it was no longer necessary to do so at a militant mosque or at a dusty training camp halfway around the world; thanks to this new generation of English-speaking, Internet-savvy jihadists, all of it was now a mouse click away.

Chesser would soon be among their leaders.

Jihadists have long embraced state-of-the-art propaganda tools to get their message out to supporters and potential recruits. During the 1980s the preferred tool was *Jihad*, a slick magazine published in Arabic and distributed in some two dozen countries. *Jihad* celebrated the successes of the mujahideen then fighting the Soviets in Afghanistan. After 9/11 it was password-protected Web forums in Arabic that discussed jihadist matters. Al-Qaeda in Iraq was the first terrorist group to use broadband video systematically to broadcast its grisly beheadings on the Web. Social media became in many ways the ultimate recruitment tool, allowing aspiring militants not only to access the rhetoric of Binladenism but also to disseminate it themselves. Above all, much of the jihadist material on social media was in English.

More than 40 percent of the 360 U.S.-based militants examined for this book either maintained an online social media presence where they posted jihadist content or used the Internet in an operational manner, beyond simple tasks such as sending e-mails—e.g., sending encrypted e-mails or publishing webzines. In Chesser's telling, "The Internet led to a rapid rise in Jihadism as it offered up a podium for the idea which was not available elsewhere."

Mitch Silber, who headed Intelligence Analysis at the NYPD, says that in the decade after 9/11, the Internet grew to be as integral to Islamist terrorism as it was to everything else, becoming "a medium of communication as important if not more important than face-to-face meetings—maybe more important because you have anonymity. And it's a place where people can learn about the ideology, can bounce off other people in sort of a virtual echo chamber, and even create conspiracies." For law enforcement officials, the migration of Islamist militants to the Internet had both upsides and downsides. Silber says, "The upside is that you can try to position yourself in places where you might come across individuals who are on a trajectory toward violence. The downside is that you can't monitor all of the Web. It's like trying to monitor the ocean."

An important force multiplier for all this was the rise of Awlaki on the Internet as the most prominent spiritual guide speaking and writing about holy war to an American audience. Chesser says that Awlaki "was hands down the most influential English-speaking scholar in America and he held that position for years." For Chesser, Awlaki's Web-published tract "44 Ways to Support Jihad" was a work of seminal importance and helped impel Chesser's transformation from a rank-and-file convert to an Islamist zealot spreading the message of holy war in every way that he could.

Yet another of Awlaki's American acolytes was Samir Khan. Although Awlaki became the most visible face of jihad online, Khan eventually rivaled, and aided, him in influence. Americans had launched the Internet, so perhaps it was only fitting that they would also launch the online Islamist movement in the English-speaking world. From his home in suburban Charlotte, North Carolina, Khan began a career as one of the central visionaries of Internet jihad.

S amir Khan was born in Saudi Arabia in 1985, but his family moved to Queens when he was seven and later settled in suburban Long Island. Khan attended W. T. Clarke High School in Westbury, New York, where he wrote for the school newspaper. In the summer of 2001, Khan spent a week at a fundamentalist Muslim summer camp organized by a mosque in Queens. He was "captivated" by the teachings he heard there. Khan, now fifteen, found that becoming more religiously observant was a good way to stay away from the peer pressure of his fellow teens. He stopped listening to hip-hop (except for a group of Muslim rappers named Soldiers of Allah) and stopped wearing the baggy pants in fashion among his classmates.

In the tenth grade, Khan went from being a typical teenager keen on video games and girls to a religion-obsessed Muslim who refused to recite the Pledge of Allegiance that began the school day. Classmate Bobby Khan (no relation) recalls, "Before 9/11 people saw this change, but didn't make much of it, but afterward, more people decided to question his ideology." Khan told his classmates that U.S. foreign policy was to blame for the attacks and started provoking arguments about the Israeli-Palestinian conflict. His classmates, angered, would ask him, "What's your deal, man? You hate America?" Khan's graduating yearbook photo shows an unsmiling young man in a tie, self-identified as "Mujahid," the Arabic word for holy warrior.

Around his graduation in 2003, Khan befriended members of the Islamic Thinkers Society. This was a grandiose name for a tiny group of young Muslim men living in the New York City area, most of whom could hardly be described as "thinkers." One of the men on the fringes of the group attended an anti-Israeli rally in Manhattan with a large sign declaring "Death to All Juice," clearly intended to read "Death to All Jews." The group later evolved into an even more militant arm, Revolution Muslim, which was interested in spreading jihadist ideas in the States. Revolution Muslim set up forums for discussion of jihad on the Internet and conducted street protests in busy parts of Manhattan.

One of Revolution Muslim's leading members was ex-convict Jesse Morton. Khan and Morton discussed a possible collaboration on a media project about jihad. It never happened, but several years later, Morton contributed articles to the first two issues of Khan's English-language webzine, *Jihad Recollections,* which appears to have been the first jihadist webzine ever published in English. Khan explained his inspiration in the inaugural issue: "Many of our hard working brothers in the English *Jihadi* community—may Allah reward them with mountains of good deeds—usually limit themselves to translating works rather than developing their own." He declared, "We have decided to take it upon ourselves" to offer more original content.

Khan's family moved to North Carolina in 2004, his father's lucrative career as a computer analyst allowing them to settle in a swanky subdivision of Charlotte. Khan attended Central Piedmont Community College, but his real passion was spreading jihadist ideas on the Internet. He created a blog called *Inshallahshaheed,* meaning "A martyr, God willing," which soon became one of the most popular militant jihadi blogs, receiving thousands of hits a day. He wrote about the possibility of banning alcohol consumption in the States, posted articles about leading Islamist thinkers, and debated readers on arcane points of Islamic jurisprudence. More brazenly, he praised attacks by al-Qaeda and posted photos of dead American soldiers in Iraq. Khan consulted with a local lawyer about how far he could push the First Amendment before he got in trouble with the law; the lawyer told him he could write anything on his blog as long as it didn't explicitly incite violence. By November 2006 the FBI had begun paying attention to Khan's posts, which an FBI agent characterized as indicating "an increasing hatred of the United States and potentially escalating steps toward a violent act of physical jihad."

Khan gave a Friday sermon at the Islamic Society of Greater Charlotte in which he told the congregants that they were "wussies" because they weren't fighting in a jihad overseas. The sermon angered many of the mosque attendees, who ensured that Khan was never allowed to speak at the mosque again.

The same year that Khan launched his first website, Gabriel Weimann, a professor of communications at the University of Haifa in Israel, published *Terror on the Internet,* the first book to examine this relatively new phenomenon. After careful study, Weimann had found that terrorist websites had exploded in number from some dozen in the 1990s to more than four thousand by 2006. Weimann pointed out that the Internet was "an ideal arena for the activities of terrorist organizations," given its ease of access, the difficulty of censorship, its global reach, its independence from traditional media and simultaneous ability to shape media coverage, and its potential for interactivity. This would prove an all-too-accurate forecast of how jihadist groups would use the Web, which would come to its fullest fruition almost a decade later with ISIS's large-scale use of social media.

In October 2007 the *New York Times* ran a story about the recent proliferation of jihadist websites and featured an interview with Khan. The *Times* story quoted some of Khan's militant writings, including his advice that Americans needed to listen to bin Laden "very carefully and take his message with great seriousness." Khan told the *Times* reporter that he dreamt of meeting bin Laden and that he wouldn't rule out joining the jihad himself.

When asked about a video he had posted showing a suicide attack on a U.S. military outpost in Iraq, Khan told the *Times,* "When I saw that video, it was something that brought great happiness to me, because I know that this is something that America would never want to admit. They would never want to admit that they've been crushed, and that the mujahedeen have such power to destroy the disbelievers, and to break their ranks, and to split them in half. This is something that the media would never ever report."

Jibril Hough was a well-known leader in the Muslim community in Charlotte. After the *Times* article about Khan appeared, Hough told Khan's father, "We need to talk to Samir." Khan's father readily agreed, and Hough assembled a small group of elders from the Charlotte mosque, who gathered at Hough's suburban home to intervene with Khan. It wasn't an especially comfortable meeting. Hough began, "Well, everybody knows why we're here. We're not really trying to, you know, beat Samir up, but he is on the spot." Turning to Khan, he said, "We're here to share some words with you."

Hough told Khan that praising a figure such as bin Laden, and therefore appearing to sanction the killing of innocent people, was unacceptable: "Islam is against that. You kill one innocent person; it's like killing all of mankind. You save one; it's like saving all of mankind." Another of the mosque elders told Khan, "Look, you're talented, but use your talent in a more constructive and a positive way." Khan listened quietly, making little effort to defend his views.

Following the *Times* story, a local TV station started doing stories on Khan. TV reporter Molly Grantham tracked him down to his place of employment, a customer service support company. The blond reporter shouted questions at Khan, a short, pudgy guy with glasses and a straggly beard, and followed him from his car as he headed in to work. Khan soon lost his job. Few American employers wanted to retain an employee attracting media attention for his celebratory views of Osama bin Laden.

By 2008, Khan was writing in his blog that he yearned for martyrdom, explaining that "with the first drop of blood from the martyr, all of his sins are forgiven." He also posted a poem about his desire for death in a holy war and the "Eternal Gardens of Paradise."

Khan was now the subject of considerable interest at the FBI. In secret memos, agents noted that his "pro-jihad blog" was attracting substantial traffic—according to the FBI, enough to put it among the top 1 percent of the hundred million websites then extant. Khan had also recently published the webzine *Jihad Recollections,* which compiled seventy pages of articles in English by bin Laden and other militants. Agents puzzled over whether Khan was trying to get someone to commit an act of terrorism and, if so, whether he was following orders from a higher authority. In July 2009, FBI officials flew in from around the country to Washington for a top-secret "case coordination meeting" at the NCTC to discuss what actions, if any, could be taken against Khan. The meeting was actually a double-header: in a mark of how seriously the Bureau was taking Khan's case, the other jihadist on the agenda was Anwar al-Awlaki. Officials had discovered in late 2008 that Khan and Awlaki were communicating with each other, which the FBI found alarming given that they were two of the most prominent proponents of jihad in the English-speaking world.

Also in the summer of 2009, Khan began telling people at his local mosque that he planned to go to Yemen. He was worried that the FBI might pick him up on some "flimsy excuse," so in October, Khan, age twenty-four, got on a plane before that could happen.

In the Yemeni capital, Khan initially worked as an English teacher, but he yearned to join the holy warriors. One day he took a car and driver into the Yemeni hinterland to join al-Qaeda. It was an existential moment: "I realized that my entire life would be changed by this one decision. . . . I was about to become a traitor of the country where I grew up most of my life." The driver repeatedly played "Sir Ya Bin Laden" on the car CD player, a religious chant paying homage to al-Qaeda's founder. As the distinctive tall mud houses of Yemen rolled by, Khan closed his eyes and let out a deep breath. Nearing the end of his journey to meet the mujahideen in a remote area of desert sand dunes, he contemplated "the enigma of jihad. It's just absolutely enthralling that the guerrillas can fight off global superpowers with the bare minimum."

The hardened holy warriors of al-Qaeda's Yemeni affiliate didn't know quite what to make of the pudgy kid from Charlotte, North Carolina, who had suddenly landed in their midst, but Awlaki assured them that young Samir would prove valuable to their cause, according to a U.S. official who was tracking Awlaki in Yemen at the time. And indeed he would. Khan took all his anger at his home country and his years of experience as an active blogger and channeled them into bringing the al-Qaeda propaganda machine into the twenty-first century.

Six months after arriving in Yemen, Khan launched *Inspire,* an English-language webzine that dressed up its grim al-Qaeda content with colorful graphics and photos, jazzy headlines, and a jaunty editorial tone. First published to the Internet on July 11, 2010, it immediately caused a sensation; written in colloquial American English, it allowed Western jihadists to read the kind of content that had previously been available only on obscure Arabic-language jihadist forums. "Make a Bomb in the Kitchen of Your Mom," read a headline in the debut issue, an article bylined "the AQ [Al-Qaeda] Chef." On first glance, this might have seemed like a spoof in *The Onion,* but the article's instructions were both specific and accurate. *Inspire* explained how to assemble an explosive device from readily available ingredients such as fireworks, metal pipes, and batteries, and showed step-by-step photos of the process. Three years after the article was first published, the Tsarnaev brothers, regular readers of *Inspire,* used similar ingredients to make the bombs they detonated at the Boston Marathon.

Inspire's debut also included a section with tips about what to pack for would-be jihadists setting out for holy wars in countries such as Yemen. The webzine cautioned against taking suitcases, advising the future holy warrior to "pack light" using a "solid well built backpack that can last in any weather conditions" and to wear "flexible boots." It featured a suggested "hit list" that included Molly Norris, a Seattle cartoonist who had initiated an "Everybody Draw Mohammed Day," and featured an essay by Awlaki adding his clerical imprimatur. Those who denigrated the Prophet, he wrote, "we will bomb and we will assassinate." It was all a marked contrast to the extraordinarily boring, long-winded televised speeches of al-Qaeda's number two, Ayman al-Zawahiri, hitherto a staple of al-Qaeda's propaganda output.

Mitch Silber and his colleagues at the NYPD found *Inspire* alarming. Silber himself was listed in a section of the first issue entitled "Friends and Foes," which quoted some comments he had made about al-Qaeda on CNN. He concluded that the webzine's creators were native English speakers, maybe even Americans, and that they were carefully monitoring the U.S. media.

Andy Liepman of the NCTC recalls how quickly *Inspire*'s reach seemed to spread among Western jihadists. "What we did figure out and the British as well was that it was not just a few of the people we were arresting, but all of the people we were arresting had seen *Inspire*."

The webzine set off a lively debate in the Obama administration between those who wanted to block it in some way and others who felt that such efforts were a waste of time. Ben Rhodes, the top strategic communications adviser on national security to Obama, came down on the side of doing nothing. "If someone really wants to find something on the Internet," Rhodes said, "they can figure out ways around: you pull something down on YouTube, it shows up someplace else." Another question the administration wrestled with, Rhodes added, was "whether to counter-message *Inspire* directly." He explained that "there's one school of thought that basically said 'The more we mention *Inspire,* the more we are raising its profile.' But my belief is its profile is pretty high anyway." The administration's compromise solution, he explained, was to "counter the themes and messages of *Inspire* without naming it."

Nicholas Rasmussen, one of Obama's top counterterrorism advisers, says there has also been some effort to downplay media coverage of *Inspire,* so as "not to contribute to whatever resonance *Inspire* had by freaking out, or by giving a bunch of background quotes to a reporter about how disturbed we were by it." He admits that "we were not particularly disciplined at that in the early days. Somewhere in the broader intelligence and CT [counterterrorism] communities, you could always find someone who would say, 'Oh my God.' And analytically, they would not have been wrong, but certainly from a policy perspective, it was not contributing to our objective of tamping this down."

British intelligence officials, similarly concerned about an attractively packaged English-language mouthpiece for jihad, took a different tack. They hacked into *Inspire* shortly after the first issue was published and replaced its bomb-making recipes with recipes for cupcakes. "Make a Bomb in the Kitchen of Your Mom" was swapped out for recipes from "The Best Cupcakes in America," as published by the Ellen DeGeneres television show. The recipes included one for the Mojito Cupcake, "made of white rum cake and draped in vanilla buttercream"—no doubt particularly irritating to the teetotalers of al-Qaeda in Yemen. For all this, and underlining Rhodes's point about the impossibility of removing something from the Internet, al-Qaeda was able to restore the hacked issue of *Inspire* within a couple of weeks.

The FBI warned in a 2010 report that *Inspire* "could appeal to certain Western individuals and could inspire them to conduct attacks in the United States in the future." Representative Peter Hoekstra of Michigan, the ranking Republican member of the House Permanent Select Committee on Intelligence, said in July 2010, "This is an unfortunately well-done magazine that is proof positive that al-Qaeda and its affiliates have launched a direct appeal for Americans to launch small-scale attacks here at home. It provides al-Qaeda's warped rationale to carry out the attacks and a how-to guide to get the job done."

The editor of *Inspire,* which was Khan, though he didn't publicly identify himself as such, urged other militants to contribute articles and offered a Hotmail e-mail address to which readers could send submissions. He also provided elaborate instructions for getting in touch with him via encrypted e-mail.

For the second issue of *Inspire,* Khan wrote an essay titled "I Am Proud to Be a Traitor to America," in which he described bin Laden as "my beloved Shaykh." In a potpourri style, suited for a generation of Web surfers, the issue also featured a harebrained scheme to equip a pickup truck with blades welded to its wheels, thereby turning it "into a mowing machine, not to mow grass, but to mow down the enemies of Allah." (When word of this notion reached his hideout two thousand miles from Yemen, in the Pakistani city of Abbottabad, bin Laden wrote in a memo that the scheme didn't comport well with al-Qaeda's image.) With a dash of chutzpah, the webzine quoted Bruce Hoffman's observation that *Inspire* was "the *Vanity Fair* of jihadist publications. It's glossy and snarky and designed to appeal to Generation Z."

In its most notable departure from the first issue, *Inspire*'s second issue urged readers in the West not to take the risk of traveling overseas to fight in holy wars, urging that it was better for them to stay in the West instead and perform terrorist operations at home. In the view of senior FBI officials such as Art Cummings, publications such as *Inspire* had effectively established a new al-Qaeda stronghold, largely beyond the reach of U.S. law enforcement and intelligence. In the virtual safe haven of the Web, al-Qaeda could teach its followers both its ideology and its tactics, which in a previous generation would have necessitated a trip to one of al-Qaeda's training camps. Cummings says, "We used to say that we would never let a terrorist group establish sanctuary ever again in a country like al-Qaeda did in Afghanistan. Well, they don't need to attach to geography anymore. It already exists. It's on the Web. It's pure sanctuary."

George Piro, another senior FBI official (who conducted the interrogation of Saddam Hussein in December 2003), agrees. "In the old days," he says, the recruitment process for a terrorist group was generally in person and therefore easier to detect. "There had to be a person, a radical imam or the old guy that had fought in the Afghan War that had come back and was telling heroic stories, who did the recruiting." But with the advent of the Internet, coaxing others to join a terrorist group "doesn't require trained operatives that have to go through training camps and take a pledge of allegiance to a particular organization. All of that now is done online, anonymously." People such as Samir Khan, the schlubby twentysomething from Charlotte, could help make the leaderless jihad a reality without leaving the safety of their computer chairs.

Ironically, one person this sanctuary would not protect was Khan himself. Before long, his role as editor of *Inspire* and his association with Awlaki were to cost him dearly. But the propaganda machine he built would continue to thrive.

Chesser soon followed in Khan's footsteps. During the summer of 2008, Chesser's writings began to appear on Awlaki's website, often addressing the militant community that gathered there. One post asked, "If someone is an apostate, and they are so openly, can I just kill them right then and there, or are there conditions?" Chesser was also active on other Islamist websites, contributing to several online forums and setting up three YouTube channels. It was the beginning of Chesser's campaign to wage a virtual holy war: He blogged about "Destroying the West" and floated ideas that included filling trucks with poison ricin. He promoted what he termed "Open Source Jihad," pointing militants to hundreds of books about weapons and military tactics and even the entire security-screening manual for the U.S. Transportation Security Administration (TSA).

From the beginning, Chesser's posts focused primarily on the al-Qaeda-aligned Somali terrorist group al-Shabaab. Somalia looked to Chesser like an easy country to enter—his nascent plan was to infiltrate it from neighboring Kenya. He daydreamed about traveling to this "field of jihad." Never mind that Somalia was then one of the most anarchic countries in the world and that a suburban white kid from Virginia would be hard-pressed to cross its borders unnoticed.

In December 2008, Chesser became worried that his online activities might attract the attention of law enforcement and interfere with his goal of joining al-Shabaab. He posted a query to readers on Awlaki's website: "My sole desire in my heart is to join al-Shabaab. . . . It is so engraved upon my heart that I began lamenting the time it is going to take to raise the money or means and then travel to Somalia. I don't know how to get there, so that is an issue. Another one is based on things I look up and post on the Internet. I am worried that I will be arrested when I try to leave the country. Does anyone know how to help me?"

Chesser began corresponding through Awlaki's blog with Proscovia Nzabanita, the twenty-four-year-old daughter of a Ugandan diplomat based in Washington who shared his admiration for Awlaki and his ultrafundamentalist beliefs. Chesser had posted that he was worried about his inability to find a wife who would support his hardening Islamist views. Proscovia, who had grown up a devout Catholic and was herself going through her own recent and intense conversion to Islam, responded that she knew of a "sister" who would support such views. So began an e-mail flirtation between the two.

Chesser sent his father an e-mail saying he was soon to be married. His dad reminded him that he had never even held a full-time job, but Chesser was undeterred, and his father soon received a voice mail with the news that his son was getting married later the same day. Chesser also gave his mother a few hours' notice of the wedding, although he warned her that she and her partner, Stacy, would have to be segregated in a separate room from the ceremony. Barbara Chesser says that in any event "I would not have gone. And that broke my heart because I swore that I would always go to my kids' weddings, even if I didn't like the girl they were marrying." Chesser's father reluctantly attended, in the hope of keeping open the lines of communication with his son.

After the wedding, Chesser and his bride lived in his George Mason dorm for the rest of the school year. As with Awlaki, Bledsoe, and Abdulmutallab, all of whom chose highly observant wives (and Major Hasan, who tried to do so), Chesser's marriage accords with the isolationism of most radicalizing militants, who gradually cut themselves off from those who don't share their beliefs to the letter. Changing one's appearance, trying to convert others, or isolating oneself from divergent views does not make one a terrorist—merely a fundamentalist. But in concert with other extremist hallmarks, these behaviors can be dangerous to ignore.

Chesser's online activities were now attracting the attention of the FBI. Special Agent Paula Menges spoke to Chesser twice, in May and June 2009. Chesser told the agent that he was watching online videos about jihad "almost obsessively," in particular anything by Awlaki. "Awlaki inspires people to pursue jihad," Chesser told the agent. He also said that he had sent the cleric several e-mail messages and had received replies to two of them.

Chesser volunteered to the FBI agent that he had started a YouTube page using the user ID "LearnTeachFightDie," where he posted videos. The name, he explained, was about his philosophy: "Learn Islam, Teach Islam, Fight for Islam, and Die in the name of Islam." Chesser told the agent that although he didn't support acts of violence, he wanted the U.S. military to fail overseas. He also claimed, somewhat inconsistently, that his Islamist beliefs had moderated recently. He told her that a short while ago he "had wanted to travel overseas to fight in a jihad," but had since changed his mind. For many aspiring militants, an interview with the FBI would have been enough to discourage them from potentially illegal activity. Not Chesser. On July 13, 2009, he contacted Awlaki through his website, telling the Yemeni American cleric that he had prayed recently to Allah to let him join al-Shabaab in Somalia.

Around the time he was being interviewed by the FBI, Chesser abruptly dropped out of George Mason. He started working as a caretaker at the Shirley Gate Mosque in Fairfax, Virginia, living there with his new wife in a tiny studio that was once a storage room. There was no mattress; his now-pregnant wife slept on the concrete floor. Chesser spent much of his time studying religious texts from the mosque's library, but after a few months he quit this job and he and his wife moved in with her mother.

Unbeknownst to his family, Chesser planned to travel to Somalia with his wife imminently. Unaware that no airline would allow his wife to fly just days before she was due to give birth, he had purchased two tickets to Uganda, from where he hoped to travel to Kenya and from there on to Somalia. In Chesser's fevered imagination the last leg of the journey between Kenya and Somalia would be made by speedboat. But he and his wife never even got to the airport; alarmed by the plan to take her nine-months-pregnant daughter to Africa, Chesser's mother-in-law had hidden her daughter's passport. Chesser wrote in his journal that he tried "just about everything to get it from her." Days later, Proscovia gave birth to Chesser's son, whom the couple named Talhah.

Zachary Chesser of suburban Virginia now styled himself Abu Talhah Al-Amrikee, "the father of Talhah from America." In December 2009, Chesser created themujahid.com ("theholywarrior.com"), a militant "website dedicated to those who give their lives for this religion." In a posted mission statement, Chesser said that while it was not his intention to instigate "specific acts of violence," the site was intended "to encourage general and ambiguous acts of violence." Several weeks later he followed through with an article titled "How to Help the Mujahideen," which laid out his vision of the steps necessary for supporting holy warriors: "This entails working out, studying military strategy and tactics, eating correctly. . . . We have to go for jogs, do push-ups, learn firearms, and all kinds of things. . . . And, perhaps most importantly, we have to actually go and fight against the disbelievers." Having been prevented from going to Somalia, Chesser substituted virtual jihad for "real" holy war.

Chesser was becoming ever more embroiled in the U.S. online jihadist scene. In January 2010 he decided to start posting on the popular militant website Revolution Muslim, which for the past three years had been operated by Samir Khan's sometime acquaintance Jesse Morton. Morton saw the site as a vehicle for the Islamist "awakening" for America, posting to it videos of Awlaki and longer papers about militant Islam. It became the leading virtual gathering space for militant Islamists in the States to meet and exchange their views.

Morton gave Chesser access to administer and update Revolution Muslim's website. Soon Chesser became a star in the small, self-referential world of English-speaking jihadist propaganda; this was, by his own modest account, because "I have above average artistic, computer graphics, video editing, writing, and programming skills. These, combined with a flair for propaganda, motivational work, recruiting, networking, and marketing led to my quick rise on the Internet." As further proof that the Internet was superseding the "real world" as a gathering place for militants, Chesser only ever met one member of Revolution Muslim in person, when he and Morton once attended a protest at the White House together.

American counterterrorism experts began to notice Chesser's blogging. One of them was Jarret Brachman, a professor at North Dakota State University and the author of *Global Jihadism: Theory and Practice*. In a posting on Brachman's website, Chesser explained his theory that al-Qaeda's long-term strategy was more to inspire attacks in the United States than to use its own operatives. Citing the relative ease of buying weapons in America, he concluded, "The role of AQC [Al-Qaeda Central, meaning al-Qaeda's leadership] is likely to shift into an organization that says, 'We congratulate so-and-so on their recent operation . . .'" Chesser fancied himself the go-to guy for counterterrorism experts hoping to get a better understanding of homegrown radicalization, and reveled in the attention. He blogged that he did "not know anybody else who attracted as much interest from the online CT [counterterrorism] crowd except people who were actually fighting. All of these things are inter-related more or less, and they fed each other until I would end up in a position of enormous influence."

Perhaps this best explains what drove Chesser further and further down the path of militancy: a quest for recognition. He boasted on Brachman's website, "In 2010 both my youtube page and several others have seen more traffic than in all of 2009. . . . The growth of my page and some others I pay attention to is looking to hit a rate that would produce more than 1,000,000 views per year. There are currently no jihadi youtube pages with even that many total views."

U.S. counterterrorism officials were growing increasingly worried about the militants posting on the Revolution Muslim site. As cases such as Major Hasan's had shown, someone posting actively on a jihadist website could graduate to acts of violence. The fulminations of Revolution Muslim's contributors were, thus far, protected speech, but they were drawing perilously close to the First Amendment exception Samir Khan had been warned against: words that are intended to and are likely to lead to violence.

A cofounder of Revolution Muslim was Joseph Cohen, a Jewish Brooklyn native who, after attending an Orthodox rabbinical school, had unpredictably converted to Islam. Cohen was a New York City cab-driver with four kids and a great desire to draw attention to himself. Of Osama bin Laden, he told CNN, "I love him more than I love myself." He termed 9/11 an "inside job" and encouraged Muslims to "throw liquid drain cleaner" in the faces of Jews. In January 2009, Cohen posted to the Revolution Muslim website a video encouraging viewers upset about the conflict in Gaza to seek out Jewish leaders in the United States and "speak in front of their homes." Cohen gave the addresses of synagogues in New York and, most provocatively, posted a video of the Brooklyn headquarters of the Jewish Chabad organization, with directions to the main temple and the observation that it was always full at prayer time. He included a link to *The Anarchist Cookbook,* which can be used for building bombs. A subsequent video accused Chabad of funding terrorism and urged viewers to find the leaders of the organization and "hold them responsible." The clip ended with gunshots.

Though no one followed through on Cohen's incitements, the first arrest of a Revolution Muslim subscriber took place ten months later. Forty-six-year-old Colleen LaRose, a divorced high school dropout from Pennsylvania who had recently converted to Islam, was known online as "JihadJane." LaRose had traveled to Europe in the summer of 2009 to scope out an attack on Lars Vilks, a Swedish artist who had drawn a cartoon of the Prophet Muhammad's head superimposed on the body of a dog.

Jesse Morton was also attracting increasing media attention. In November 2009 he gave a provocative interview to CNN reporter Drew Griffin, who asked him, "You're commanded to terrorize the disbelievers?" Morton replied, "The Koran says very clearly in the Arabic language 'terrorize them.' It's a command from Allah." Griffin followed up, "So you're commanded to terrorize anybody who doesn't believe. How do you define terrorism?" Morton answered, "I define terrorism as making them fearful." A year later Morton posted what was intended to be a clarification to CNN's report about Revolution Muslim, but was, if anything, more incendiary than the initial interview: "[CNN] suggested that we justify the killing of American soldiers, that we hold the attacks on September 11, 2001 as justified, that we want to restore a global caliphate, wipe Israel off the map, and that attacks on almost any American are justified. . . . I would be a liar if I said I did not hold these ambitions and aspirations."

Since the founders of Revolution Muslim were based in the New York City area, the NYPD began to take a strong interest in the group and the threats its site's contributors were making. Mitch Silber was worried about the similarities he saw between Revolution Muslim and a British militant Islamist group, Al-Muhajiroun, which had been mounting vocal demonstrations in the streets of London for many years. Though these were perfectly legal, some of Al-Muhajiroun's members had graduated to plotting acts of terrorism. Silber was hearing from his British colleagues that "even though they seem like a bunch of blowhards, people who spend time with those groups are moving on to bigger and more dangerous things." After Colleen LaRose, eighteen other contributors and subscribers to Revolution Muslim's site would be arrested, for crimes ranging from lying to federal investigators to fighting alongside al-Qaeda-affiliated groups to plotting attacks in the States.

Revolution Muslim's ultimate downfall was, improbably, the animated series *South Park*—Zachary Chesser's onetime favorite show. The saga would reveal that in addition to being a recruitment mechanism for today's jihadists, the Internet can be used as a literal call to arms. Al-Qaeda communicated its orders via encrypted e-mail; what militants such as Chesser and Revolution Muslim attempted was new. By making their orders (or "wishes") totally public, they were effectively crowd-sourcing jihad.

South Park had always skewered anyone and everyone, from Tom Cruise and Barbra Streisand to Moses and Jesus. On the occasion of its two hundredth episode, Trey Parker and Matt Stone, the show's creators, decided to have some fun with the notion that Islamist militants had deemed that depictions of the Prophet Muhammad should be met with violence. The episode, which aired on April 14, 2010, included Muhammad as a character but winkingly avoided showing his face by keeping him dressed in a bear costume. A character in the show points out, "If Mohammed is seen we could get bombed." A character playing Santa Claus chimes in, "That's right, friends. All you need to do is instill fear and be willing to hurt people, and you can get whatever you want. The only true power is violence."

Chesser saw the episode as an opportunity, telling Morton that the 1989 fatwa by Ayatollah Khomeini (which demanded the death of Salman Rushdie following the publication of his novel *The Satanic Verses*) "was a tremendous help in radicalizing Muslims." Might there be a similar opportunity in the States with the *South Park* episode? Chesser decided to test this theory by posting the most "media enticing post" he could write without getting arrested. The day after the *South Park* episode aired, Chesser wrote that the episode "outright insulted" the Prophet "by showing him in a bear suit." Chesser continued menacingly, "We have to warn Matt and Trey that what they are doing is stupid, and they will probably wind up like Theo van Gogh for airing this show. This is not a threat, but a warning of the reality of what will likely happen to them." Van Gogh was the filmmaker murdered by an Islamist militant in Amsterdam in 2004, whose case Silber had investigated. Chesser posted a photograph showing van Gogh lying dead in the street in Amsterdam with two knives stuck in his body. Chesser also posted the New York City address of *South Park*'s network, Comedy Central, and provided a link to an article about a residence in Colorado belonging to Trey Parker and Matt Stone. He suggested to his readers that they "pay them a visit."

Given that Chesser's readers were mostly Islamist militants, this was a serious threat. To underline his intentions, Chesser posted photos of Parker and Stone along with photographs of others who had been publicly targeted for death for purportedly insulting the Prophet, including Rushdie and the Danish cartoonist Kurt Westergaard. Following the fatwa against him, Rushdie had lived for many years in hiding; as a result of his cartoons of Muhammad, Westergaard was attacked at his home in early 2010 by an ax-wielding Somali man with ties to al-Shabaab. Westergaard survived the assault only because he had taken the precaution of building a fortified safe room in his house.

Chesser blogged that *South Park* creators Parker and Stone would "likely" be attacked, explaining, "They're going to be basically on a list in the back of the minds of a large number of Muslims. It's just the reality." For good measure Chesser uploaded audio clips of a sermon by Awlaki titled "The Dust Will Never Settle Down," which urged the assassination of anyone who "defamed" the Prophet Muhammad. In the lecture, Awlaki said, "Harming Allah and his Messenger is a reason to encourage Muslims to kill whoever does that." Chesser took to his Twitter feed to crow, "The kuffar [nonbelievers] are starting to really pick up the South Park story insha'a Allah [God willing] this can be the USA's version of the Rushdie affair." By now Chesser was the subject of considerable attention in the national media. He felt he deserved the spotlight. Brashness aside, however, both he and Morton were conscious that they couldn't too obviously incite their militant readers to violence. From one of his posts discussing the likelihood that the *South Park* creators would be attacked, Chesser deleted the clause "we pray Allah make this a reality." A week after the *South Park* episode aired, Chesser and Morton issued a lengthy "clarification" of Revolution Muslim's view of the matter on its website, which they hoped would "scare the kuffar."

"By placing the Prophet Muhammad (peace be upon him) in a bear suit, the creators of South Park sought to insult the sacred, and show their blatant and general disregard for religion. . . . As for the Islamic ruling on the situation, then this is clear. There is no difference of opinion from those with any degree of a reputation that the punishment is death. . . . Thus our position remains that it is likely the creators of South Park will indeed end up like Theo Van Gogh."

This "clarification" didn't settle the media frenzy that had begun building around Chesser's posts. Angry *South Park* fans started making death threats to various members of the Chesser family. For Chesser's mother, this marked an irrevocable break with her son, who had now placed other members of his family in jeopardy. Over the phone, she told him, "I thought you had grown up to be a fine man, and you're not. Don't contact me anymore."

The Muhammad story line continued in the next episode of *South Park*, but his character was hidden under a "CENSORED" graphic and an audio bleep was heard when his name was said. Bending over backward not to give any offense, Comedy Central made further changes to Parker and Stone's cut, placing additional bleeps throughout the episode. It was an unusual position for a channel whose stock in trade was the giving of offense.

As far as Chesser was concerned, the censorship meant that his campaign against *South Park* had "worked phenomenally." He was further heartened when he went to mosque on the Friday after he made the first postings attacking *South Park* and he heard the imam defending Revolution Muslim in front of a thousand worshippers. The Revolution Muslim site was suddenly one of the top one hundred websites in the world, getting so much traffic that it finally went down. Chesser giddily recalls that "CNN forgot about the rest of the world for a week." At age twenty-one, Chesser was now wielding the "enormous influence" he believed was his proper due in life.

Molly Norris, a cartoonist based in Seattle, was appalled by Comedy Central's caving in to a tiny blog. She felt this would set a precedent for a slippery slope to more censorship. She asked her readers, "If artists have to be afraid of what they draw, then what's the point of even living here?" In response, Norris urged that the public treat May 20, 2010, as "Everybody Draw Mohammed Day." To launch the effort, she drew a poster featuring the Prophet as, variously, a teacup, a box of pasta, and a domino.

Norris's thinking was that if a lot of people drew the Prophet on that day it would water down the pool of potential targets for enraged Islamist militants, to the point where any one attack would seem pointless. Her initiative succeeded beyond any expectation. The poster drawn by Norris went viral, and Facebook groups sprang up with tens of thousands of members supporting Everybody Draw Mohammed Day. In Pakistan, where Facebook is wildly popular, the site was temporarily shut down.

Chesser identified some of the American supporters of Everybody Draw Mohammed Day on a militant website, including a teenager in Mississippi and a man from Texas, along with the address of the man's "possible church/school," noting that this was "just a place to start."

Dave Ross of Seattle's KIRO radio interviewed Norris about the building sensation. He asked her, "Really, Molly? You sure you want to do this?" Norris explained that she wanted to protest the fact that Comedy Central was now running scared. Ross asked, "Would you ridicule the Holocaust?"

"There's nothing funny about it," Norris said.

"Here in this country, the line we draw seems to be the Holocaust . . . and in the Muslim world, they draw the line at Mohammed," Ross countered.

Norris shot back: "That's a great pun, Dave: drawing the line."

Norris soon became alarmed by the deluge of publicity surrounding Everybody Draw Mohammed Day, however, and started distancing herself from the effort even before the designated date for the event, which was May 20, 2010. On her website, she wrote, "I am a coward. I have backed off of being associated with any group. . . . I am so freaked out that I am not drinking my regular 4 cups of coffee per day." Norris's disavowal didn't make any difference to Awlaki, who wrote on a militant site that she "should be taken as a prime target for assassination."

Not content with turning the *South Park* episode into a major source of controversy, Chesser posted a message on a militant website titled "Desensitizing Federal Agents," in which he explained that conducting "fake" bombing operations, by leaving suspicious packages resembling bombs in public places, would "desensitize" law enforcement officials. After officials had become sufficiently desensitized to the fake bombs, a real explosive could be substituted that would kill police officers investigating the incident. Chesser concluded: "Boom! No more kuffar."

Two days later, Chesser posted an article, "Actually Leaving for Jihad," in which he discussed the process necessary to leave the country for an overseas holy war, including obtaining travel documents, purchasing airline tickets, and "keeping a low profile." (A good tip for this last item, he said, was to shave one's telltale beard.) At the peak of his notoriety, Chesser had decided to realize his longtime dream of joining al-Shabaab in Somalia. He instructed his wife, if she was questioned by anyone about his travel plans, to use the cover story that he was traveling to Uganda to pick up her birth certificate. He was in contact with someone he believed to be a top al-Shabaab leader living in the West, who told him that the organization was expecting him and would arrange for his travel.

On July 9, 2010, Chesser and his wife left their Virginia apartment and drove with their seven-month-old son to a hotel in Maryland, where they spent the night. The next day, at JFK Airport in New York, Chesser attempted to board a flight with service to Uganda while carrying, with his wife's blessing, his baby son. On arrival in Uganda he planned to walk into Kenya and then on into Somalia, a journey, in his mind, as simple as crossing from Missouri into Kansas.

None of this happened because when Chesser checked in, an airline representative told him that he was on the no-fly list. A day later, bombs went off in Kampala, Uganda, killing seventy-six ordinary Ugandans gathered in two restaurants to watch the World Cup. The group that claimed responsibility for the attacks was al-Shabaab.

Chesser told the FBI agent who interviewed him that he was planning to attend a camp in Somalia for basic training and that he would likely be recruited into al-Shabaab as a "foreign fighter" and placed into the media branch located in the Somali capital, Mogadishu. He explained that foreign fighters were highly respected members of al-Shabaab, and that they were often put on the front line, which he said he accepted, as he wasn't afraid of death. He said his contacts had asked him to bring laptops and video cameras into Somalia, for use in al-Shabaab's propaganda campaign. These statements were all useful to build the FBI's case against him. On July 21, 2010, he was arrested for attempting to join a terrorist group.

In Chesser's view, his arrest was not as important as the message it sent: that he had abandoned the Internet jihad to go fight in the "real world." In his own mind, Chesser was the world's foremost Internet holy warrior, and he believed that his willingness to leave his comfortable life in Virginia to try to fight in Somalia would have a powerful demonstrative effect on others. In a letter written from his maximum-security jail cell, Chesser explained, "The movement needs role models and inspirational figures more than speeches or videos. Somebody like me can fail miserably on a tactical level, but still have a huge impact. I think my arrest has turned out to be my biggest success so far." He believed that he helped to inspire the actions of the Boston Marathon bombers, writing, "One will find that I have a surprising footprint in that event." There is no evidence for this assertion.

Chesser was sentenced to twenty-five years in prison for attempting to join al-Shabaab and for his efforts to incite violence against the creators of *South Park*. In many ways it was a draconian sentence for someone who hadn't *done* anything actually violent, but it could have been worse; facing as many as ninety years in prison, he pleaded guilty before his trial started. Chesser's wife was charged with making false statements to law enforcement officials regarding her husband's travel plans. She pleaded guilty and was deported.

Joseph Cohen was sentenced to two and a half years in prison for his threatening postings about the locations of Jewish organizations on the Revolution Muslim website that, as the government put it, placed "others in fear of serious bodily injury." Jesse Morton was sentenced to more than ten years in prison for his role in the *South Park* affair.

After assaulting a fellow prisoner at the federal penitentiary in Marion, Illinois, Chesser was transferred in 2014 to the supermax prison in Florence, Colorado, which is home to a who's who of terrorists, including Ramzi Yousef, the mastermind of the 1993 World Trade Center bombing, and the Underwear Bomber, Umar Abdulmutallab. Life in Florence is a kind of living death: most prisoners are kept in solitary confinement and locked in their cells for twenty-three hours a day. Chesser is scheduled for release in 2032. He will be forty-two.

M uch of the *South Park* episode had played out as farce, but for Molly
Norris there was also real tragedy.

Because of her role in instigating Everybody Draw Mohammed Day,
Norris was placed on the "hit list" of al-Qaeda enemies that appeared
in the first issue of *Inspire,* which Jesse Morton then uploaded onto the
Revolution Muslim website. Soon after these threats became public, the
Seattle Weekly, where Norris worked, announced that she had had to go
underground permanently. The announcement by the newspaper explained, "You may have noticed that Molly Norris' comic is not in the
paper this week. That's because there is no more Molly. The gifted artist
is alive and well, thankfully. But on the insistence of top security specialists at the FBI, she is, as they put it, 'going ghost': moving, changing
her name, and essentially wiping away her identity."

For American militants, ultimately, Internet activism has been a
double-edged sword. Like Chesser, Cohen, and Morton, many self-
radicalized jihadists have publicly overshared their sympathies, seemingly oblivious that it is perfectly legal for the FBI to monitor public
accounts on Twitter, Facebook, and other social networking sites—or
they become too enamored of the spotlight to care. A senior FBI official
says, "I think all the social media is more useful than not. If only they
knew."

On the other hand, effective propaganda by a few militants can help
radicalize many others—and this, as the FBI's George Piro notes, has
been the difficulty for law enforcement. Whereas traditional terrorist
plots involved multiple operatives and a planning cycle of many months,
giving the FBI opportunities to intercept communications about the
plot or its funding, for homegrown militants the timeline for a potential
attack has become enormously compressed. Says Piro, "When it's a lone
individual who's operating," if they aren't inclined to share their plans,
"everything's in their head. The ability for us to become aware of that
behavior and those activities, or their propensity for violence, becomes
less and less. From when that person makes a decision that they want to
carry out some type of attack until the moment that they actually do it,
that window is very, very small."

In any case, for those targeted by virtual jihad, the attention is deeply troubling. Following the January 2015 attack on the *Charlie Hebdo* satirical magazine in Paris, in which twelve were killed, Chesser wrote from prison that he had newly "reviewed" Molly Norris's statement about Everybody Draw Mohammed Day. His letter concludes, "I doubt she has any real way out of the situation except perhaps embracing Islam."

In the memorandum he submitted for the sentencing of Jesse Morton, prosecuting attorney Neil MacBride explained, "As philosopher Karl Popper wrote in *The Open Society and Its Enemies,* 'if we are not prepared to defend a tolerant society against the onslaught of the intolerant, then the tolerant will be destroyed, and tolerance with them. . . . We should therefore claim, in the name of tolerance, the right not to tolerate the intolerant.'"

Norris has not been heard from since she went into hiding in 2010.

CHAPTER 8

EXPORTING JIHAD:
AMERICANS ABROAD

THE ONLY REASON WE ARE STAYING HERE, AWAY FROM OUR FAMILIES,
AWAY FROM CITIES, AWAY FROM, YOU KNOW, ICE, CANDY BARS, ALL
THESE OTHER THINGS, IS BECAUSE WE ARE WAITING FOR THE ENEMY.

—Alabama native Omar Hammami in a
video recorded in Somalia in 2009

Omar Hammami knew his enemies were closing in. The harsh deserts
and tangled forests of Somalia were a long way from the tidy lawns
and comfortable two-story homes of Daphne, Alabama, but by his seventh year in Somalia, Hammami knew the terrain and had developed a
fine-tuned understanding of the brutality of al-Shabaab.

By the spring of 2013, this much was clear: the leaders of al-Qaeda's
Somali affiliate, whose name means "The Youth," were out to kill Hammami, the group's most public face.

On April 25, from deep in the bush of southern Somalia, where he
was lying low to avoid the wrath of al-Shabaab's leaders, Hammami
posted to his Twitter account:

> **abu m @abumamerican 25 Apr** just been shot in neck by
> shabab assassin. not critical yet

> **abu m @abumamerican 25 Apr** sitting in tea place then
> 3 shots behind to left. pistol i think. they ran

> **abu m @abumamerican 25 Apr**   No windpipe or artery.
> peroxide, gauze, and pressure. a perimeter has been made

This was perhaps the first assassination attempt in history in which the wounded victim tweeted the whole event in real time. Hammami even tweeted a photo of himself with blood oozing from his neck. Referring to the feared leader of al-Shabaab by his nom de jihad, Abu Zubayr, Hammami continued updating his some three thousand Twitter followers:

> **abu m @abumamerican 25 Apr**   they are sending forces
> from multiple directions. we are few but we might get back up.
> abu zubayr has gone mad. he's starting a civil war.

> **abu m @abumamerican 29 Apr**   After the failed
> assassination attempt i woke in the morning to hear that i was
> surrounded. We ran to a hole behind the house and waited.

This is the story of how a boy from small-town Alabama became a leader, and then a target, of one of the world's most brutal terrorist organizations. No al-Qaeda affiliate has recruited more Americans than al-Shabaab, and Hammami was, for a time, the group's most visible face in the West, leveraging his all-American upbringing to serve as a cultural go-between who could translate Binladenism to the West in culturally relevant style. Like Awlaki and *Inspire* editor Samir Khan, Hammami was part of a wave of Americans who preached jihad from abroad to the English-speaking world, but he advanced the form with his prolific and creative use of social media.

Hammami's story is how Zachary Chesser's life might have continued if he had made it to Somalia. It is a case study in how rare it is for an American to succeed in jihad abroad, as much as many fantasize about it, but it is also a study in how effective those Americans who do thrive can be.

Omar Hammami's story began a long way from either Alabama or Somalia. Omar's father, Shafik Hammami, was born into a comfortably middle-class family in the medieval heart of the Syrian capital,

Damascus, in 1952. But as Shafik grew older a long darkness enveloped Syria. By the time he was in his late teens the country was in the grip of the dictator Hafez al-Assad, whose son Bashar would also terrorize Syrians. Fear was a daily part of Shafik's life—fear that a neighbor, a friend, or even a family member might be a spy for the regime.

America beckoned as the brightest escape. For Shafik, who excelled at science, the promise of the States was bound up in his fascination with space flight and the Apollo program—the United States had just put a man on the moon—so he started exploring the possibility of attending an American college. Having heard that a Syrian student had fared well at Faulkner State Junior College in Bay Minette, Alabama, Shafik applied, and some months later he received his unexpected acceptance letter.

Shafik arrived in Bay Minette just before Christmas. The town had one grocery store, a courthouse, and a bowling alley. Shafik didn't experience overt racism in Bay Minette, but he did feel out of place. The rural Alabaman dialect was hard to understand, and drunken frat parties were out of the question for Shafik, an observant Muslim. He missed his family and Damascus, but calls home were prohibitively expensive and a return to Syria would mean compulsory military service.

One day Shafik met Debra Elizabeth Hadley, a pretty, trim, brunette senior at the local high school. Warm and bubbly, Debra was a good foil for the homesick, serious student from Syria. The unlikely couple soon started dating, going to movies and out to lunch or dinner, but nothing more. Debra was a chaste woman; she didn't drink. She was as serious about being a Baptist as Shafik was about his Sunni faith, which appealed to him. In December 1976, just before he graduated from Faulkner, Shafik and Debra were married at a local church. Following the Christian service, an imam blessed the marriage, reading a few verses from the Koran.

Shafik went on to study civil engineering at the University of South Alabama in Mobile, where he excelled. Before he graduated an official at the Alabama Department of Transportation promised to hire him as an engineer to work on roads and bridges around the state. Soon babies came, first Dena, a daughter, in 1981 and then a son, Omar, in 1984.

Debra and Shafik had discussed the possibility of one of them converting to the other's faith, but this was a nonstarter. Shafik told his
wife, "I will not interfere with your faith if you do not interfere with
mine." The caveat: the kids would be brought up as Muslims. When
Debra brought the toddlers to visit her family on Sundays, however, she
began to take them to Sunday school. Shafik's mother-in-law also began
sneaking them into a local Baptist church, and at age six, Omar was
baptized. He became a star student in Bible school, once winning ten
dollars for memorizing the names of the books in the Old Testament.
Shafik felt deeply betrayed when he found out about all this; his wife
obeyed his order to stop taking the kids to Bible school, but his mother-
in-law kept taking the young children to church. Shafik's relations with
his in-laws became tense.

He might have been losing the wars of religion with his kids, but the
influence of his heritage was clear at home, where the Hammami family
took their shoes off at the entrance and avoided pork. Shafik taught his
children Arabic phrases.

Omar's childhood pursuits were typical of his corner of the rural
South: deer and squirrel hunting, tree climbing, and building forts in
the woods. He played baseball and read *The Adventures of Tom Sawyer*. He also began to grapple with big philosophical questions; for a
class assignment, he wrote that the 1995 Oklahoma City bombing was
"pointless and stupid," and added, "I wish violence would vanish clear
from the Earth." When a teacher intuited that his goofing-off in class
meant that he wasn't being challenged, Omar was shifted to the gifted
program, where he thrived. During his vacations he began to read in his
bedroom all day—*1984* and *The Catcher in the Rye* were two favorites.

Omar became the class clown and a self-described "social butterfly";
by fifteen he was the president of his class and was dating one of the
prettiest girls in the school. Like Zachary Chesser, he was one of the
cool kids. It was a position he would enjoy only briefly.

In his early teens Omar began questioning the tenets of Christianity. The change was a subtle one at first. He puzzled over the Christian
doctrine of the Trinity, asking his mom, "How can God be three and
one at the same time?" Debra told him, "You will know when you get

to heaven." The discussions affected his dreams; at one point he dreamt his mother was barbecuing him on a large grill. He began praying not to Jesus but to God.

A trip Omar made to his father's hometown of Damascus in 1999, when he was fifteen, was as transformational as St. Paul's trip to the same city. Omar reveled in the religious atmosphere, and for the first time in his life began praying the five daily prayers prescribed by Islam. When he came back to the States, he found he was struggling between two worlds. The Western one consisted of drugs, girls, friends, and TV. The world of Islam seemed a lot more meaningful. He made the choice to become a practicing Muslim.

As he entered the ninth grade, he began wearing an Islamic *kufi* hat; his friends laughed at him, but he affected not to care. He started performing his noon prayers just outside his high school. Students were used to seeing circles of their peers holding hands to say a Christian prayer, but a student prostrating himself on the ground and invoking Allah was a spectacle, and Omar was determined to make his conversion to Islam a public matter. A year after bin Laden had been fingered as the mastermind of the 1998 attacks on the U.S. embassies in Kenya and Tanzania that killed more than two hundred people, Omar would try to provoke Bible-carrying Baptist classmates by saying, "Bin Laden is awesome."

He soon started trying to convert some of his classmates to Islam. His first success was with his girlfriend, Lauren Stevenson, but this soon ended their relationship. Where they were once kissing and hugging before class, before long they were only holding hands occasionally. Eventually Omar told Lauren, "We can't do this. We're not going to get married. This isn't going to happen. I'm not going to have a girlfriend."

His next conversion was Bernie Culveyhouse, and this had far more lasting consequences. Bernie was in the gifted student program with Omar, but he was a loner, fostering a Goth persona with his black trench coat and interest in paganism and the practice of witchcraft. The only child of an acrimonious divorce, Bernie was being raised by his single mother, Sharon, but between her long hours working as a nurse and her heavy drinking, he sometimes wouldn't see her for a week at a time.

Looking back, Bernie says, "I had a fucked-up childhood. There was a lot of drugs and violence, and I'd seen people try to murder my mom several times. It wasn't a pretty sight. So when I was a teenager, I was looking for something." His difficult childhood was, in other words, the "cognitive opening" described in Mitch Silber's NYPD report.

No one in high school talked to Bernie, and now that Omar was publicly practicing Islam, few would speak to him, either. The two outsiders drew together. One day Bernie saw Omar at a computer watching videos of the Chechen War. He asked, "What's Islam about?" to which Omar replied, "It's just simple monotheism." Bernie found this a perfect sales pitch.

Bernie began escaping the chaos of his mother's house for the relative quiet of the Hammami household. He soon found himself praying five times a day and noticed that he felt more at peace. In their Model United Nations class, Omar and Bernie would sign on to Azzam.com, at the time a major online repository of jihadist content, and watch videos of the Chechen War. When a classmate called bin Laden a terrorist, Omar shouted, "How the hell do you dare say this about somebody who's like the major person in my religion, like this major holy figure?"

Relations between Omar and his mother deteriorated. A typical conversation started with Debra saying, "I don't know why you're mean to me all the time. I guess that's just something that the Muslims teach you to do. I just know that Jesus lives inside of my heart."

Omar retorted, "Oh really, Jesus lives inside. . . . So if I cut you open, we'd actually physically find . . ."

Debra interrupted, "Don't be a smartass, Omar, you're talking about the Son of God."

Omar snapped back, "God doesn't have a son."

One day in class, Omar was reciting verses from the Koran when another student began laughing at him; Omar charged and started to strangle him. He let the kid go and stormed out of the classroom after a few moments but was later taken to the police station. On the way there he fumed to his father, "We kill people for making fun of our religion." In the end no charges were pressed.

Desperate to leave high school, Omar took the ACTs when he was in the eleventh grade. He scored high, in the ninety-third percentile, and applied to his father's alma mater, the University of South Alabama in Mobile, where he was accepted for early admission on a scholarship to study computer science. College was a "big breath of fresh air." He was minutes away from a mosque and could wear his Islamic garb without being hassled.

The 9/11 attacks came just weeks into his freshman year. Omar's reaction was complex: he was torn between a genuine revulsion for terrorism and his "real hatred for America, the disbelievers, and their oppression of the Muslims." Al-Qaeda had justly taken revenge on America, but Omar was unhappy about the deaths of thousands of civilians. He asked some of the other students watching the TV coverage of the attacks, "Why did this happen?" They stared at him, dressed in a *thobe* (an ankle-length robe) and turban, as if they wanted to kill him. He remained quiet. When he later found a quiet moment by himself in a mosque, however, he couldn't contain his glee. He jumped up and said, "Allahu Akbar!" "God is Great!"

Bernie was in eleventh-grade English when the news came in. Outside the class he found some girls crying. One said, "Why are these people doing it to us?"

He told them, "Maybe it's because we've been fucking up their half of the world for God knows how long and they're pissed off about it. Have you ever heard of this place called Palestine?"

Omar adopted increasingly strident views. When he refused to be in a family photograph, believing, as some fundamentalists do, that such images are displeasing to Allah, Shafik was so angry at his disrespect that he ordered him to leave the house. Omar slept in a storage locker with no electricity or water for a couple of weeks before moving into a cheap apartment in Mobile with Bernie. The two made quite a pair as they went shopping at Walmart in their head-to-toe Muslim garb. Some onlookers thought they were Amish or were reenacting the Nativity scene; others were hostile. People screamed at them in the street, "You go back to your country, you damn Arab!" Bernie had never felt so much public rejection in his life. It was like walking around during the McCarthy era with a hammer and sickle slapped to your chest. Omar, however, seemed to revel in his new notoriety. When someone flipped him the bird on the street, he shouted back, "Fuck you, too!"

Finding it hard to get a job that didn't clash with his increasingly rigid beliefs—any jobs involving payment with credit cards or associated with alcohol, TV, or music were out of the question—Omar ended up cleaning the Mobile mosque at night. He and Bernie also took telemarketing jobs and worked at Walmart doing inventory.

In this Bernie Culveyhouse and Omar Hammami were typical of modern American jihadists. Despite being as educated as the average citizen, only a third were known to have jobs when they were charged. (The unemployment rate for their peers is around 5 percent.) That's because being a militant Islamist tends to take over your life. As in the case of Hammami and Culveyhouse, militants often refuse jobs for religious reasons—anything to do with charging interest, or necessitating close contact with women who aren't family members, or involving alcohol or pork. The kind of person obsessively maintaining one or more jihadist websites was also likely not going to be a good fit for most U.S. employers. Zachary Chesser, Omar Hammami, and Samir Khan all lost or quit jobs because of their increasing militancy. Chesser and Carlos Bledsoe both dropped out of college as they became radicalized; Major Hasan did everything he could to leave the military. Faisal Shahzad abruptly quit his job and moved to Pakistan for eight months. Jihad became their lives.

After two years of intensively studying Islam, Hammami and Culveyhouse found that Mobile was getting too small for them. They were effectively jobless and were both looking for observant Muslim wives, hardly locally available. In 2003 the two attended a religious conference in Toronto. They were energized by the city, with its sizable Muslim population and all that came with it: a host of mosques, Muslim bookstores, and halal butchers. And Hammami relished even the small differences with the United States, ribbing Canadians he met with "How 'bout that hockey, eh?" "Wanna' have a coffee at Tim Horton's? Or should I get ya' a Fresca?"

Hammami found a job delivering milk to some of the eighty thousand

Somalis residing in Toronto, many of whom lived in grim public housing in the city's most impoverished neighborhoods. Given that the job
required getting up at 3:00 a.m. during the frigid Toronto winter, he
didn't last long. Then it was on to working as a delivery boy at a Somali
pizza joint and, on the side, translating books from Arabic into English.

Hammami was drifting. But hanging out with some of the Somalis who had fled their country's civil war paid off for him and Bernie
in other ways: a lot of people thought they were cool, these born-and-
bred Americans who knew a lot about Islam. Culveyhouse married
Ayan Mohamed Abdille, a Somali living in Toronto, and Hammami
was soon introduced to her sister Sadiyo, a tall nineteen-year-old college
student. Their small wedding celebration took place in Toronto. Hammami's family flew up from Alabama for the occasion; the newlyweds
slaughtered a lamb for the wedding feast.

Unlike in Alabama, criticism of U.S. foreign policy was widespread
in Toronto, especially when it came to the American occupation of
Iraq. Hammami and Culveyhouse hadn't paid much attention to world
events when they were intensively studying Islam in Alabama, but they
now became preoccupied by the war in Iraq. Both of them had lots of
strong opinions about President George W. Bush, whom they saw as
an evil crusader trying to "fuck up the world" on the basis of his religious beliefs. Hammami began writing for the Infowars website, which
propagates the conspiracy theory that 9/11 was plotted by the American
government to turn the United States into a police state.

Hammami and Culveyhouse began asking themselves: Should they
become holy warriors on behalf of embattled Muslims? They were now
on the cusp that separates fundamentalism from jihadization, and they
began fantasizing about traveling to a field of jihad. In Alabama, Hammami had rejected the notion of going to fight in a holy war, on the
grounds that individuals joining a true jihad must be sanctioned to do
so by their head of state, a view common in orthodox Saudi circles. Now
both he and Culveyhouse were thinking differently.

Just under half the 360 militants examined for this book either traveled to an overseas field of jihad or attempted to do so. For those so willing, South Asia was the most popular destination, with about a third

traveling or attempting to travel to Afghanistan or Pakistan to sign up with the Taliban or al-Qaeda; a fifth volunteered to fight in Somalia; and another quarter were drawn to the Syrian war. While for many jihadists the decision to travel proved a Rubicon, an irrevocable crossing into militancy, it could be another kind of turning point for those who declined to make a final break from American life. For the two best friends from Alabama, it went both ways.

During one of his trawls through the world of jihadi content online, Culveyhouse found a documentary about the legendary jihadist fighter Khattab, a Saudi who had fought alongside Chechen Islamist militants against Russia in the late 1990s and had helped launch the second Chechen War in 1999. He and Hammami watched the video together; halfway through, Culveyhouse looked over to see his friend crying. Culveyhouse was crying, too. Khattab became an obsession for them. In the many online videos of him, Khattab, a thickset man with a bushy beard and flowing black hair, is typically shown wearing a heavy fur hat and camouflage, and is surrounded by worshipful foot soldiers. Here was a man of both religion and action, a man to emulate.

Compared to Khattab's battlefield heroics, living in Toronto seemed a tad too, well, Canadian. Hammami and Culveyhouse decided it was time to make *hijra,* a spiritual pilgrimage to the Arab heartland, where everybody prayed five times a day and religious Muslims were looked upon favorably. They felt that there they could at last be true Muslims. Their first goal was to become bona fide scholars of Islam, the type who might teach a circle of students in Mecca; they weren't yet sure they wanted to wage violent jihad.

Hammami told his dad he was set on getting a scholarship to study at the medieval Al-Azhar University in Cairo, in many ways the Vatican of Sunni learning and a sure ticket to finding future work as a cleric. When Culveyhouse told his mother about the plan, Sharon, now a recovering alcoholic and so impressed by her son's newly disciplined behavior that she had converted to Islam herself, decided to go with him. Culveyhouse, his mother, wife, and daughter set off with Hammami and his wife for Egypt.

In early 2006 this unusual group settled in the port city of Alexandria, where a friend of Hammami's owned a long-disused apartment. Hammami rejoiced—he had finally made it to the land of the Muslims—but for his travel companions, Alexandria was less romantic. The city was a lot dirtier and more chaotic than they had anticipated. Hammami's wife, Sadiyo, was pregnant and became ill from all the sanitation problems. The apartment, which had previously been abandoned, had no electricity and was in one of the poorest, most crowded districts of Alexandria. Culveyhouse's six-month-old daughter started having serious respiratory problems. It hit Culveyhouse that there was no equivalent to the 911 emergency service in Egypt.

Hammami did attempt to enroll in Al-Azhar University, but as he wryly recalled, "The bureaucracy of Egypt is amazing and to enroll in Azhar you have to chop down the largest tree in Cairo with a falafel." Culveyhouse noticed that his friend was increasingly less concerned about studying Islam, preferring to spend hour after hour in Internet cafés engaging in arcane theological debates on Islamic forums.

Omar and Sadiyo had their first child, a daughter, in Alexandria. They named her Taymiyya, a nod to the thirteenth-century theologian of jihad, Ibn Taymiyya, who wrote many of his key works while imprisoned in Damascus. Debra and Shafik flew to Egypt to see their new granddaughter. Omar, in high spirits, took them to see the pyramids.

Culveyhouse, on the other hand, was becoming more and more disenchanted with Egypt. When he and Hammami consulted a leading religious scholar about his disaffection, the scholar advised him to return to the States, saying, "You should actually go to college and study medicine, or computer science or engineering. When you come here you see people eating off of the street and dying of poverty. If you want to do something for Muslim people, go better yourself so you can help other people. We don't need another person living on the street."

Culveyhouse had lived with Hammami for the past four years. They had spent so much time together that their relationship was almost like a marriage; they were bound together by their common experience of converting to Salafist Islam as Bible belt teenagers; learning to speak

Arabic fluently and quote much of the Koran from memory; moving to Canada; marrying sisters; living abroad. And both were seriously contemplating taking the next step: to become holy warriors fighting against the enemies of Islam. They had evolved a private language to discuss this step, calling it "going to medical school." To actually become a militant holy warrior was to "become a doctor." But now that they were at the critical point where a fundamentalist decides whether to prepare to do violence in the name of Allah, their paths finally diverged.

It was Culveyhouse's family obligations that dissuaded him from jihad. His own father had abandoned him; he wasn't going to do that to his wife or revisit his difficult childhood on his young daughter. But he also turned off the path of militancy in part because his time in Egypt, a majority Muslim country, had allowed him to place his interpretation of Islam in the context of a more widely shared, moderate understanding of the religion. The hardships of living in Egypt had deglamorized the idea of serving in a "field of jihad" sufficiently to disillusion him from the whole militant movement. By contrast, for Hammami, the excitement of joining the jihad simply outweighed his obligations to his wife and daughter. Being a holy warrior meant becoming someone like his hero Khattab; for him, that appears to have been a lot more enticing a prospect than being just another dad and husband.

Hammami felt that Culveyhouse was abandoning him. As his friend prepared to leave, Hammami played the religion card, telling Culveyhouse, "You're not a true Muslim, you're not a true believer. You're just not into this. You're caving in." He also played the best friend card: "Dude, you're my best friend, you can't leave me here alone."

Secretly, however, Hammami was developing a departure plan of his own. In Alexandria he joined Islamic Networking, an Internet forum, and began chatting with Daniel Maldonado, another American Islamist who happened to be living in Alexandria. They shared an excitement that after decades of civil war, an Islamist group, the Islamic Courts Union, was on the verge of taking over Somalia. When the two met up, they secretly agreed to go to Somalia. After the majority-Christian Ethiopian army invaded Somalia in 2006, al-Shabaab had cast the conflict as a takeover by a "crusader" army, which had spurred recruitment. Somalia was the jihad du jour, just as years later the Syrian civil war would excite the imaginations of Western militants.

Hammami tried to persuade his wife to come to Somalia with him; she refused. As the child of Somali refugees, Sadiyo had no nostalgia for her homeland. Hammami regretted leaving his family behind but rationalized that jihad was "an obligation" for him. He couldn't resist hinting at his plans to Culveyhouse, now back in the States, though the two were quickly drifting apart. He sent him an instant message, saying, "Brother, I'm done with studying. There's Muslims all over the world dying. There's a time for seeking knowledge and there's a time for taking action. It's the time for taking action."

Still jobless, Hammami told his family that he was going to Dubai for a couple of days to look for work. From Dubai, he caught a flight to Mogadishu. In his own words he was "the only white man among a sea of Somalis," bound for the world's most dangerous country. At check-in, airport workers looked at him with astonishment. On the plane, he got to chatting with a Somali woman to whom he used to deliver milk in Toronto, telling her he was on his way to visit his wife's family. It was the same story he told officials when he landed in Mogadishu. When he did indeed arrive at the house of his wife's family, they were surprised to find him without their daughter, Sadiyo, but welcomed him anyway.

Back in the States, Culveyhouse called Shafik to let him know that Omar was not in Dubai. Shafik was upset, asking, "How did you let my son go to Somalia?" Shafik knew enough about Somalia to be seriously concerned. Now that the Islamic Courts Union had taken over much of the country, neighboring Ethiopia, a largely Christian country, had invaded to forestall the emergence of an Islamist state on its borders. The country was effectively a war zone; the U.S. embassy there had long closed. Shafik did what he could, contacting his local congressman and the State Department, but to no avail. He received a call or two from Omar, who insisted that he had gone to Somalia only to see his in-laws, and then . . . nothing. Sadiyo also heard nothing further from her husband and decided to leave Egypt for Canada.

In Mogadishu, Hammami had met up with his Alexandria acquaintance Daniel Maldonado, who put him in touch with the local mujahideen. He was about to get a crash course in the on-the-ground reality of jihad. Shortly after he arrived, the Ethiopians had taken over Mogadishu, and deposed the Islamic Courts Union. In Islamic jurisprudence the invasion of non-Muslim Ethiopian forces into Somalia was grounds for an intensified holy war.

The mujahideen of the Islamic Courts Union fled south en masse, in the direction of the port city of Kismayo, which lies just north of the Somali-Kenyan border. Among them was Omar Hammami. He was issued an AK-47, a step up from the shotguns and rifles of his youth. Under cover of night, he bumped along the terrible roads out of Mogadishu in a convoy of trucks. His fellow holy warriors positioned themselves on the roofs of the trucks and, staring at the stars, chanted *nasheeds,* Islamic songs, about Paradise. For Hammami, this indeed felt like Paradise—"the dream of any Muslim who has the love of the religion burning in his heart." He was just like his hero Khattab, fighting a holy war far from the mundane comforts of home.

On the road, al-Shabaab's holy warriors survived on camel's milk, which gave Hammami diarrhea, and the occasional small deer or wild turkey. Hammami's training began in earnest once they arrived in the Kismayo area days later. He took courses on the standard weapons of guerrilla warfare (the AK-47, PK submachine gun, and rocket-propelled grenade) and received more advanced explosives training. Occasionally, there were Ethiopian helicopter attacks to dodge.

To avoid such attacks and the blistering heat of the day, the mujahideen made long marches through the bush at night. Hammami would sometimes glimpse baboons, oryx, and even lions, but edible food was hard to find. When they neared the edge of starvation, he and the other men would resort to eating maggots or snails. Some developed malaria or were afflicted with a strange slime in their stools. To ward off hunger, Hammami would daydream about Krispy Kreme doughnuts; one day he was given a cup of milk tea with just a hint of sugar and felt it was worth more than gold. He developed a toxic skin infection that left rotten white flesh exposed along his ankle. Jihad, it turned out, wasn't always glamorous.

The class clown in Alabama was also having a hard time being understood by the Somalis. For around a year, until he learned the local language, no one understood any of his jokes, suggestions, or ideas. It was thoroughly distressing. Still, when after many months of training, he received permission to call Sadiyo, and she told him she was going to divorce him unless he returned to Canada, Hammami refused. So ended his first marriage. He soon married a local woman and began a second family, integrating himself more fully into his adopted culture. He chose a nom de jihad, "Abu Mansoor al-Amriki," "the American father of Mansoor," naming himself after one of his new sons.

One day in October 2007, Shafik was at home in Alabama watching his favorite TV channel, Al Jazeera, when a news item aired about an American citizen fighting in Somalia. Onto the screen came a man dressed in combat fatigues; his face was completely covered with a greenish headscarf, but his voice was unmistakable as he said, "All Muslims of America, take into consideration the example of Somalia. After fifteen years of chaos and oppressive rule by the American-backed warlords, your bothers stood up in order to establish peace and justice in the land." With horror, Shafik recognized his son.

Extreme as Omar's commitment was, he was not alone. Al-Shabaab has had, arguably, the deepest links to the United States of any al-Qaeda affiliate, finding supporters in places as diverse as Seattle, St. Louis, San Diego, Minnesota, Maryland, and Ohio, and some forty Americans have made the long, dangerous trek to Somalia.

Al-Shabaab found its American recruits useful in a number of ways. Some would aid the cause by soliciting donations from sympathetic members of the Somali diaspora in the States; others would help with recruitment efforts, appearing in English-language videos to target recruits in the States but also in the United Kingdom and Australia. A few, including Hammami, would even take on leadership roles. Less-promising volunteers were dispatched as suicide bombers.

The largest source of American aid to al-Shabaab was Minnesota. Nineteen Minnesota residents have been indicted for traveling to fight in Somalia or have died in the war there. The most concentrated source of volunteers was the Cedar-Riverside neighborhood of Minneapolis, known as "Little Mogadishu," one of the poorest places in the United States. Somali American family incomes there averaged less than fifteen thousand dollars a year, and the unemployment rate was 17 percent. For the young locals who became volunteers, fighting in a holy war may simply have sounded more appealing than working a dead-end job in Minneapolis, or having no job at all.

For Philip Mudd at the FBI, the relatively large number of Somali Americans from Minnesota joining the jihad reminded him of the disadvantaged Muslims of Europe—the North Africans living in grim French suburbs or the Pakistanis living in what were effectively ghettos in Northern England. Mudd says, "We don't typically have Muslim ghettos in the States. American Muslims are spread across the country, by and large, and they integrate well. So I finally realized the characteristic of a potential problem Muslim community was not the nation of origin. It was the purpose of emigration and whether new immigrants would be concentrated in communities that had similarities to what Europe has witnessed. In the Somali American case, these were poor people working in meat-packing plants along with a lot of single-mom households living in ghettos, with direct connectivity, especially with the Internet, back to the strife-torn zone of Somalia."

The story of Minnesotan support for al-Shabaab began in late 2007, when Cabdulaahi Ahmed Faarax, an American citizen of Somali descent who had previously fought for al-Shabaab, convinced seven other men to travel to Somalia and join the "true brotherhood" of jihad. One of the seven was Shirwa Ahmed, an ethnic Somali and naturalized American citizen who graduated from high school in Minneapolis in 2003 and then worked at the Minneapolis airport. During this period, he became increasingly religious, and in his spare time he would counsel drunken Somali kids in Cedar-Riverside to embrace their culture.

Ahmed left Minneapolis for good on December 4, 2007, eventually reaching Somalia and al-Shabaab. On October 29, 2008, he drove a truck loaded with explosives toward a government compound in Puntland, northern Somalia, and became the first American ever to conduct a terrorist suicide attack, blowing himself up and killing twenty other people. A finger inside the truck was recovered, and the FBI later matched it with fingerprints on file for Ahmed.

The bombing caused consternation at the FBI. If an American citizen was willing to die in a suicide operation overseas, what did that imply about the possibility of home front suicide attacks? Recent British experience presented a worrisome scenario. In 2003 a British citizen had conducted a suicide bombing at a jazz club in the Israeli capital, Tel Aviv; two years later were the deadly bombings in which four British citizens took their own lives and those of fifty-two commuters.

The State Department designated al-Shabaab a Foreign Terrorist Organization in March 2008, making it illegal for a person in the United States knowingly to provide the group with money, communications equipment, weapons, or explosives, or to join it. The FBI started a serious effort to crack down on suspicious immigration to Somalia. Codenamed Operation Rhino, the disruption-minded approach accorded with the FBI's post-9/11 directive to prevent terrorist attacks before they happened, and prefigured the even larger effort that the FBI would undertake half a decade later to prevent Americans from joining ISIS.

The Special Agent in Charge of the Minneapolis FBI field office leading Operation Rhino on the ground was Ralph Boelter. He began meeting regularly with members of the Somali community in Minneapolis, ranging from tribal "elders" to the young men most likely to fall prey to al-Shabaab's recruitment pitches. Boelter went on local Somali radio stations to explain that Somali Americans could live the American Dream, citing the Minneapolis-based University of Minnesota as a pathway to the middle class. He contrasted this with the foolish choice of going to Somalia, by which one would likely end up as cannon fodder on al-Shabaab's front lines. This was all too true; at least fifteen Americans died while fighting for the group.

Well intentioned though such efforts were, they could reach only so far into al-Shabaab's American support network. A resident of Ohio, Ahmed Hussein Mahamud, was indicted in 2011 for funding Somali Americans traveling to join al-Shabaab; St. Louis resident Mohamud Abdi Yusuf pled guilty of providing funds in 2012; and in 2013, Basaaly Saeed Moalin, a cabdriver in San Diego, was convicted along with three coconspirators of sending $8,500 to the group. Beyond the Somali American community, Ruben Shumpert, an African American convert to Islam from Seattle, was killed in Somalia in 2008. And a former U.S. soldier, Craig Baxam, of Laurel, Maryland, was arrested by Kenyan authorities in 2011 as he tried to make his way to Somalia; he told FBI agents that he considered joining al-Shabaab to be a religious duty.

Al-Shabaab also started carrying out operations outside Somalia, bombing two groups of fans watching the World Cup on television in Kampala, Uganda, on July 11, 2010, killing more than seventy. The group carried out that operation because Uganda had provided troops to a UN-authorized African Union mission then fighting al-Shabaab in Somalia. The group also started showing an interest in targets in the West. Eight months before the attack in Uganda, a twenty-eight-year-old Somali man armed with a knife and an ax forced himself into the home of Kurt Westergaard, the Danish cartoonist who had depicted the Prophet Muhammad with a bomb in his turban, and tried unsuccessfully to break into the fortified safe room where Westergaard was hiding. Danish intelligence officials said the suspect had links with al-Shabaab.

By 2010, al-Shabaab's tactics were becoming so violent that even Osama bin Laden scolded members of the group, saying in a letter dated August 7, 2010, that they were killing too many civilians in Mogadishu. By then, al-Shabaab controlled much of southern Somalia, but a year later, the UN-sanctioned African Union mission partnered with Somali troops to fight al-Shabaab militants, and in August of that year, African Union and Somali government forces defeated al-Shabaab units in Mogadishu, forcing the militants from a stronghold they had controlled since 2009.

As al-Shabaab was assuming control of southern Somalia, Omar Hammami was emerging as a propaganda star. In March 2009, a year and a half after his first video appearance, he revealed his face in an al-Shabaab video for the first time. The video portrays him as a hipster Pied Piper of jihad. Sporting a full beard and wearing camouflage, his black hair tumbling past his shoulders, he leads recruits in military training and religious study. He looks like a leaner, cooler version of his jihadi hero Khattab.

Adding to this persona, Hammami also started releasing jihadi raps on the Internet. The songs had catchy titles: "Send Me a Cruise [Missile]," "Make Jihad with Me," and "Blow by Blow." The lyrics were about as good as the titles promised:

> Month by month, year by year
> Keeping them kaffirs living in fear . . .
> Bomb by bomb, blast by blast
> Only gonna bring back the glorious past
> Mortar by mortar, shell by shell.
> Only gonna stop when I send them to hell.

On June 4, 2009, U.S. president Barack Obama gave a much-anticipated speech in Cairo, which was supposed to inaugurate a "new beginning" between the United States and the Muslim world. Hammami soon released a video addressing himself to Obama, saying, "How dare you send greetings to the Muslim world while you are bombing our brothers and sisters in Afghanistan. And how dare you send greetings to Muslims while you are supporting Israel, the most vicious and evil nation of the modern era." He invoked bin Laden's words: "America will not dream of peace nor will those who live in America, until we are living the dream of peace in Palestine." He went on to defend the 9/11 attacks on the grounds that the World Trade Center wasn't housing "daycare centers and maternity wards" and was therefore a legitimate target.

The kid from the gifted program in Daphne, Alabama, was, a decade later, publicly denouncing the president of the United States. Andy Liepman, the number-two official at the NCTC, said, "What scared us about Hammami was the same thing that scared us about *Inspire.* Our people who looked at resonance and messaging said, 'This is the kind of thing that's going to appeal to people. Hammami's cool, and he's handsome, and he's charismatic.' We put a huge effort, particularly when Obama came in, to messaging. Not just: How does their message resonate with potential recruits in the West? But how does our message counterresonate?"

The FBI had also taken notice. On November 27, 2007, Omar Hammami was indicted in Alabama for the role he was playing in al-Shabaab, and was charged again two years later. Beyond his slacker-cool propaganda role, by 2009 the U.S. government also publicly described him as a military tactician, recruitment strategist, and financial manager for al-Shabaab who had commanded guerrilla forces in combat and had been involved in the planning of Shirwa Ahmed's suicide attack. The FBI had determined further that Hammami was the battalion commander of al-Shabaab's foreign fighters—from not only the States but also the United Kingdom, Scandinavian countries, Pakistan, and a number of Arab states. Few of these recruits spoke Somali, but most spoke either English or Arabic; Hammami's dual fluency and natural charisma made him a ready choice to oversee al-Shabaab's foreign fighters.

Bernie Culveyhouse, meanwhile, had been evolving in a different direction. After returning to the States in 2006, he landed a job in computer programming. He remained, for the moment, an Islamic fundamentalist, but he became increasingly bothered by news of al-Qaeda's brutal campaign of attacks in Iraq against Muslims who weren't following its dictates to the letter. A transformational moment for him came when he watched a documentary about the 2002 murder of American journalist Daniel Pearl in Pakistan. Pearl was beheaded and his execution filmed by al-Qaeda terrorists. Culveyhouse began thinking, "This is not a righteous war. This is people murdering people because they think what they think is right and the other people are wrong."

It was the beginning of a long process of deradicalization that led Culveyhouse to reject all violence in the name of Islam. Today he works at a tech firm in Silicon Valley, living nearby with his wife, three kids, and mother. He did his best to keep up, via the Internet, with the doings of his old friend, but Hammami seemed less and less familiar to him. When he listened to Hammami's response to Obama's 2009 speech in Cairo, delivered in a stilted, slightly foreign accent, Culveyhouse almost didn't recognize his voice.

Hammami started thinking more broadly about jihadist strategy. In this he was heavily influenced by the example and writings of Abu Musab al-Suri, someone Hammami resembled in ways he felt were significant: Suri was Syrian like Hammami's father, and like Hammami, he had lived for many years in the West.

Hammami set out to emulate Suri with a fifty-page strategy paper about how to establish a caliphate in the Muslim world where true Islamic law would reign supreme. Written under the pseudonym "Abu Jihad al-Shami" ("The father of Jihad from the Syrian region"), the study attracted little attention, as its advice (that the mujahideen should avoid conventional warfare and stick with guerrilla tactics) was Jihad 101. But it showed that Hammami, now twenty-six, was trying to position himself as a major thinker in the world of militant Islam.

In 2012 he released a 127-page autobiography to the Internet, recounting his life growing up in Alabama and the six years he spent rising up through the ranks of al-Shabaab. In the autobiography, he reveals a busy home life: He had had three children with his new Somali wife, the first of whom he named Jihad. Two other wives soon followed, and three more children. He had learned the local language and moved into a mud hut with his growing family. But he also wrote of the nostalgia he felt for Alabama, how he yearned for a short visit home to see his mother, father, and sister. He imagined, "After all the hugs and kisses, me and Dena would probably go running around town laughing our heads off and talking about a billion things without ever finishing a conversation about any of them." The Alabama visit would involve some Chinese food, hot wings, ice cream, and gourmet coffee.

Around the same time, Hammami made his debut on Twitter. Shortly after the Boston Marathon bombing of April 15, 2013, Omar tweeted a burst of commentary:

> **abu m @abumamerican 19 Apr**   These brothers are making history. Let them shine.

> **abu m @abumamerican 20 Apr**   boston proves global jihad is still alive and well . . . in the belly of the beast as it were.

abu m @abumamerican 20 Apr   Fact they managed 2
prepare what they did under radar is in itself a feat, the
courage even to take the 1 step, remarkable.

When he wasn't praising acts of terrorism, Hammami sounded more like a high school kid from Alabama, peppering his tweets with phrases such as "thanks for the props," "homie," and "pass the barf bag," and making references to Tupac, Kid Rock, and baby back ribs.

Hammami also began to use his Twitter account for a less predictable kind of rant: against the leaders of al-Shabaab. He had gradually become disillusioned with his superiors, and on Twitter he began a deadly serious campaign to vilify them. In one tweet he claimed that they were enriching themselves at the expense of al-Shabaab's foot soldiers: "War booty is eaten by the top dogs, but the guys who won it are jailed for touching it. A gun, bullets, some beans is their lot." He also charged al-Shabaab's leaders with imprisoning foot soldiers on a whim. In a Shakespearean turn of phrase, he called the group's leader, Abu Zubayr, a "usurping king."

Hammami's prolific use of Twitter, more than seventeen hundred tweets in all, marked the first time that a leader of a jihadist group had used social media in a systematic way. It was an evolutionary step forward from the static jihadi websites that American militants such as Samir Khan and Zachary Chesser had created over the past half decade: Hammami used Twitter to interact with his hundreds of followers both privately and publicly, often in real time.

As a result of his Twitter critiques, Hammami was growing concerned that he might be targeted for death. On March 16, 2012, he released a short video in which he said, "I feel that my life is endangered by Harakat Shabaab Mujahideen due to some differences that occurred between us regarding matters of the Sharia and matters of strategy." A day later al-Shabaab's official Twitter account stated that Omar Hammami was not at risk from the group. The U.S. intelligence community, meanwhile, was picking up signals intelligence, from tapped cell phone calls between al-Shabaab operatives, that the group's leadership was increasingly riven by disputes and that a number of al-Shabaab's leaders simply didn't like Hammami. At the end of the day, despite his relatively high profile in the West—*Wired* magazine ran a feature about him, and CNN frequently showcased his rants—he was still a kid from the Deep South, not a native Somali, and therefore, in the minds of many, not worthy of so prominent a voice in al-Shabaab.

Soon al-Shabaab's leaders responded to Hammami's critiques outright. In December 2012 they released a lengthy pamphlet in English declaring that he did not "in any way, shape or form, represent the views" of the group and that his "video releases are merely the results of personal grievances that stem purely from a narcissistic pursuit of fame." Three months later the group released, also in English, a more vicious takedown: "It is preposterous, to say the least, that a novice soldier who could barely identify the direction of an incoming bullet a few years ago or couldn't competently lead a simple ambush would now instruct his veteran trainers on matters of strategy." This document described Hammami as "paralyzed by an egotistical obsession with self image" and even insulted him as a rapper, observing that the raps "Send Me a Cruise" and "Make Jihad with Me" had been composed by another American recruit. It concluded menacingly, "So long, the American!"

On September 2, 2013, Hammami gave what would be his last interview, to Voice of America's Somali service. He said that he had renounced any allegiance to al-Shabaab and al-Qaeda. To the question "Are you a terrorist?" he replied, "Yeah, I'm definitely a terrorist."

Omar followed up the VOA interview with a tweet:

> **abu m @abumamerican 5 Sep**   Regardless of the fact that voa decided to turn a 30 min interview into 2 words, i'm still a terrorist

With a handful of companions, his three Somali wives, and his six children, Hammami was now hiding deep out in the bush of southern Somalia. Assassins from al-Shabaab tracked him to a village that he occasionally visited to attend mosque. On the morning of September 12,

2013, when he emerged from the mosque after making his predawn prayers, al-Shabaab assassins shot and killed him. He was twenty-nine. Someone using Hammami's Twitter account soon tweeted:

> **abu m @abumamerican 15 Sep**   We confirm the martyrdom of Omar Hammami in the morning of Thur 12 2013. Shafik's family please accept our condolences.

Two weeks later another tweet came from Hammami's account:

> **abu m @abumamerican 28 Sep**   Shafik, rest assured ur grandkids are all doing well, n r cared by their moms families. We will never let them down

The same day, Shafik replied with his own tweet:

> **shafik hammami @ShafikHammami 28 Sep**
> @abumamerican Please keep me abreast of what you know about my grand children's affairs, I never met them nor seen them, but I will love'em

Shafik believes his son was a *shaeed,* a martyr, who fought a true holy war and who died defending himself and his family. He explains, "Although the West looks at him as a terrorist, I know that wasn't his goal. Yes, he joined a terrorist organization, but he went with a pure intention to defend Muslims against invasion from other countries." Referring to Omar's tweets criticizing the excesses of the al-Shabaab leadership, Shafik continued: "When he found out that this group is not following the Islamic ruling in sharia, he tried to correct their actions from within. He tried to correct the movement with what little influence that he had."

"To me it's just one of those almost Shakespearean tragedies where everybody is hurt," says Culveyhouse. "Nobody won. He didn't actually accomplish anything. There was no good that came out of this at all.

And as a result of it, this poor little girl has to grow up without a dad, these good people that I care about have to grow up without a son."

To those who ask her how she's doing, Omar's mother, Debra, says, "Darlin', we have been through hills and valleys. All I know is that I ask everyone I meet, 'Do you go to church?' And if they say yes, I ask them, 'Please put us on your prayer list.'"

Turn on your TV," the text read. Glancing at his phone, Chicagoan David Coleman Headley recognized the sender as one of his handlers in the Pakistani jihadist group Lashkar-e-Taiba, "The Army of the Pure." Headley switched on the television and watched the first confused reports of a terrorist attack in Mumbai, India's largest city, the capital of the country's financial world and vibrant film industry. Ever since a stray bomb had landed on his school in Pakistan during the 1971 India-Pakistan War, killing two, Headley had nursed a grudge against the Indians. If revenge is a dish best served cold, thirty-seven years certainly qualifies.

Omar Hammami showed the kind of public platform an American citizen could gain within a terrorist group overseas, at least before resentments and ego soured his fortunes. He also showcased how "normal" a jihadist can seem, even one who takes the step of fighting abroad—someone who, if the dice had rolled even a little differently, might have, say, settled comfortably in Silicon Valley. David Headley was in all things a counterpoint. His authority was clandestine but lasting, his plans specific and deadly, and he was anything but an "average American." Headley is a reminder that despite the demographic data showing that American jihadists are as emotionally stable as average Americans, sometimes there are outliers. A compulsive liar, stone-cold sociopath, and career criminal, Headley, the child of a socialite from Philadelphia's Main Line and a prominent Pakistani TV anchor, would prove a unique asset for his terrorist organization of choice and something of a worst-case scenario for an American jihadi abroad.

On November 22, 2008, four days before Headley watched the carnage unfold in Mumbai, a Lashkar team of ten gunmen had left the Pakistani port city of Karachi in a small boat. Once at sea, they hunted for one of the many Indian trawlers that fish in the Arabian Sea. They hijacked a trawler named the *Kuber* and killed all the crew members except the captain, whom they forced to navigate the vessel during the four-day haul to Mumbai.

Five nautical miles offshore of Mumbai, the gunmen transferred to a dinghy, with which they motored toward the beachfront fishermen's slum that Headley had identified six months earlier as the perfect landing spot. After they landed, they made their way to the taxi stand Headley had scoped out and, boarding taxis in groups of two, fanned out across Mumbai. One of the gunmen left a bomb in his taxi, designed to explode at the same time they started assaulting their main targets, to give the impression that Mumbai was under assault by a large force and so add to the mayhem and confusion.

Two of the gunmen arrived at Café Leopold, a British Raj–era restaurant popular with foreigners. They emptied their AK-47s into the dining room, killing eleven. Another pair of gunmen hunted down passengers at the central railway station, killing fifty-two, and yet others attacked the restaurant inside the Oberoi Hotel. Alan Scherr, a retired art professor, and his thirteen-year-old daughter, Naomi, were visiting India as part of a Virginia-based spiritual group when two gunmen came running into the packed restaurant. Bullets flying, diners screamed and dove under the tables. Alan was trying desperately to calm his daughter when survivor Andreina Varagona felt the warm spray of blood on her face and hair; she turned to see Naomi lying lifeless. Thirty-six guests and hotel staff were killed at the Oberoi.

At the landmark Taj Hotel, gunmen opened fire in multiple restaurants and meeting rooms, and ignited bombs that eventually turned the nineteenth-century structure into a giant firetrap in which thirty-four hotel guests and employees died. A mile away, Lashkar's operatives assaulted the Mumbai branch of Chabad House, a community center for the ultra-Orthodox, Jewish Lubavitcher sect, taking hostage Rabbi Gavriel Holtzberg and his pregnant wife, Rivka, who had moved to Mumbai from Brooklyn five years earlier. The Holtzbergs' two-year-old son survived the attack, but the couple from Brooklyn was executed, along with three others.

The assaults, which stretched over three days of mayhem, were carried live by almost every major news station around the world. Their protracted nature and the stunning imagery of the Taj going up in flames made a perfect subject for round-the-clock TV coverage, as Lashkar's planners had intended. When the attacks were finally over, 166 people were dead, including 6 Americans. In addition, all but one of the gunmen were killed. It was the most spectacular terrorist operation since 9/11.

Headley, born in Washington, DC, played an instrumental role in planning the Mumbai operation, the most involved an American citizen had ever been in planning a large-scale overseas jihadist terrorist attack. Indeed, the attacks' success, their very feasibility, was greatly owed to Headley. He had the American passport, the Western-sounding name, and the Caucasian looks that allowed him to travel around Mumbai surveying and videotaping potential targets without arousing suspicion. Without Headley, there would have been no intelligence about how best to enter and exit the targeted locations, or the precise locations of obstacles such as police posts and security guards. There would have been no careful survey of where and when to land a boat filled with Lashkar gunmen to go undetected by Mumbai authorities.

Watching the TV coverage with Headley in Pakistan on the night of November 26, 2008, was his glamorous Moroccan wife, Faiza. She knew enough about her husband's work with Lashkar and his frequent trips to Mumbai, on one of which she had accompanied him, to realize that he had played some kind of role. Shaken, she told her husband, "My God, police will come to me and FBI will come to me. Oh my God. They will catch me." Headley laughed it off, telling his wife to "keep quiet." To him, all his hard work had paid off; the hated Indians were taking it on the chin. As the operation dragged on, however, he became concerned that his own role could be exposed.

Back at Headley's other home, in Chicago, Shazia, the mother of his four children, who was unaware of Faiza's existence, wrote her husband a coded e-mail congratulating him on the unfolding attacks: "I have been watching these cartoons all day long. I'm so proud of you that you have graduated into being something important."

To call David Coleman Headley a natural-born spy doesn't really do him justice. He was multilingual, flitting easily between English, Urdu, Punjabi, Arabic, and Hindi, while his distinctive features, one brown eye and one blue eye, underscored his fluid identity as the son of an American woman and a Pakistani father. This made him a perfect double agent, as comfortable hanging out in an American bar as he was attending a Lashkar military training camp high in the mountains of Kashmir. Certainly, Headley hated Indians, but his core motivation was perhaps simpler: he reveled in games of deception. He was a major drug dealer who spied for the Drug Enforcement Administration, a fanatical Pakistani militant who partied in Mumbai with Bollywood stars, and a serious Muslim who maintained extramarital affairs. Headley found this life of international intrigue a lot more entertaining than the only two legitimate jobs he had ever had, bartending and running a video store.

Headley was above all an opportunist, ready to turn coat whenever it benefited him. He gave up fellow drug dealers to the DEA in exchange for lighter prison sentences for himself, he routinely betrayed the wives he swore he would be faithful to, and he betrayed the friends he made in India, whose friendship he had sought solely to provide him cover as he surveyed Mumbai for the best targets for Lashkar's gunmen. He betrayed the country of his birth when he scoped out the Mumbai Chabad House and marked the Americans living there for death at the hands of Lashkar's gunmen.

David Coleman Headley's journey to become the James Bond of jihad began in Washington around half a century before the Mumbai terrorist attacks. Serrill Headley, a beautiful, WASPy seventeen-year-old from Philadelphia, met Syed Saleem Gilani, a dashing Pakistani TV broadcaster and sometime poet living in Washington on assignment. It was a love match of the type rare in Pakistan in the late 1950s. Soon came a son, Daood, who was born in Washington on June 30, 1960. (Many years later Daood would Anglicize his name to David Coleman Headley, adopting family names from his mother's side.)

In the early 1960s, Serrill Headley and her husband and baby son moved to Lahore, Pakistan, where she donned a sari and learned the language and how to cook the local food. (When family members visited Serrill, she told them that she knew of the Beatles, although she had never heard their music.) Yet after a few years the shine was off Serrill's marriage. When David was ten, his mother moved back to the States, and the young boy was left in the care of his father. David went to school in Karachi, where the errant bomb fell during the 1971 war, killing two and etching a permanent hatred of the Indians on the young boy—a hatred only amplified by the military boarding school he later attended in Lahore, where anti-Indian sentiments were instilled as a matter of course.

At age seventeen, Headley had had enough of Pakistan. His father had remarried and his stepmother was not to Headley's liking. So he headed to Philadelphia, where Serrill had launched an improbable new life as a barkeep. Headley moved into an apartment above his mother's bar (the Khyber Pass Pub, featuring Pakistani decorations and South Asian dishes) and soon got drawn into the party scene. It was the late 1970s in Philly; disco was new. Headley became known around town as "the Prince." It was all a very long way from Pakistan, which was then under the grim dictatorship of General Zia-ul-Haq.

In 1985, Headley married a Penn State graduate who had been bartending at the Khyber. Like many women, she was intrigued by the air of mystery Headley cultivated, but the marriage soon ran into trouble. Whenever Headley went to Pakistan he would come back full of resentment. Seeing an Indian person in the street, he would spit and call him an infidel. His wife decided that Headley couldn't reconcile his American and Pakistani identities; they divorced in 1987.

Pakistan was then the center of the global heroin trade, and Headley began traveling back and forth more often, to work as a mule for Philly drug dealers. He was first arrested in Germany in 1988, picked up at Frankfurt airport while moving two kilos of heroin. Facing significant prison time, he agreed to cooperate with DEA agents. He delivered a suitcase of heroin to two big dealers in Philly, occasioning their arrest and getting his own sentence cut in half, to four years.

Three years after his release from prison, Headley flunked a probation drug test and was sent back to jail for another six months. In 1997 he was convicted again for moving heroin from Pakistan to the States; his best friend, Tahawwur Hussain Rana, whom he had known since they were both teenagers attending the same Pakistani military boarding school, put his house up as bond for Headley's bail. In order to serve a shorter sentence (fifteen months), Headley pleaded guilty and again agreed to work as an informant for the DEA, putting other drug dealers in prison.

By the time he was forty, Headley had spent more than five years in prison but seemed resolved to get his life back together. He finally set himself up in a legitimate business, buying a video store on the Upper West Side of Manhattan. He also began cultivating an interest in his father's religion, reasoning that it might help him stay away from drugs. As he was going through this spiritual awakening, he traveled to Pakistan in 2000 and, for the first time, encountered members of the jihadist group Lashkar-e-Taiba. In Lahore, he attended a sermon by Lashkar's leader, Hafiz Saeed, who proclaimed, "One second spent conducting jihad is superior to one hundred years of worship." The sermon made a deep impression on Headley, or so he told Islamist acquaintances over the years. Whether piety was another of the convenient postures he adopted is an open question.

Headley was living in New York at the time of the 9/11 attacks, and he watched the news coverage obsessively. He told a girlfriend, "America got what it deserved." The girlfriend recounted his reaction to a local bartender, who conveyed it to members of the New York City Joint Terrorism Task Force, but when FBI and DEA agents subsequently confronted him, three weeks after the attacks, he simply denied her account. The DEA, which had arguably the best intelligence on Pakistan of any U.S. agency at the time, because of its focus on the Pakistani drug trade, was more than happy to overlook the incident because Headley had recently signed an informant agreement. As the "war on terror" geared up, it was clear that Pakistan was going to be a central focus, and Headley seemed a potentially golden informant about what was really going on there.

Four months after 9/11, Headley went back to Pakistan, but rather than providing intel to the DEA about the jihadist scene, he decided that his new goal was to join Lashkar. In February 2002 he attended an initial course of study at a Lashkar campus in western Pakistan, and a few months later was trained in small arms in Kashmir. In 2003, for three months, he attended another, more serious military training camp, where he was taught how to handle an AK-47, grenades, and explosives. Later that year he trained as a Lashkar spy, learning how to set up a safe house, perform a "dead drop," and mount surveillance operations. Around this time, Headley's mother expressed concern to some of her friends that her son had become a religious fanatic and had even attended militant training camps. One of those friends reported Headley to the FBI office in Philadelphia, but as before, nothing came of the tip.

After a couple of years of training with Lashkar, Headley was ready for an operation, but his messy personal life almost put an end to his hopes. In August 2005 he had an altercation with his then wife, Portia Peter, outside his Manhattan video store, during which she asserts that he hit her. One thing led to another, and soon she was telling officials at the Joint Terrorism Task Force that Headley had made multiple trips to receive training from Lashkar. Peter was interviewed three times by members of the task force, but Headley was never questioned and the lead was dropped—despite the fact that the same task force had been told four years earlier of Headley's militant views.

In June 2006, now separated from Headley, Portia Peter, a Canadian, applied for a green card under a law that allowed the abused foreign-born spouses of American citizens to apply on an expedited basis. In her application, she explained that Headley had received militant training and that he was virulently anti-Semitic and anti-Indian. Meanwhile, Headley officially changed his name from the foreign-sounding Daood Gilani to the WASPy-sounding David Coleman Headley, a name he rightly believed would draw less attention as he traveled the world on Lashkar's business. Headley also moved his Pakistan-based wife, Shazia, and their four kids to Chicago.

At a friend's house in Lahore in early 2007, Headley met Faiza, who was studying medicine. He married once again. He suggested they spend their honeymoon in Mumbai. The couple stayed at the iconic

Taj Hotel, a massive Victorian Indo-Gothic concoction and longtime gathering place for Mumbai's elite. Headley made sure to take plenty of videos and photos in and around the hotel to commemorate his honeymoon. These would be shared with his Lashkar handlers, who had chosen him as the member of the organization best suited to gather the intelligence on the ground for their prospective attack. To Faiza, her husband seemed strangely tense; the couple argued, and the honeymoon ended acrimoniously.

In December 2007, Faiza had an altercation with one of Headley's servants in Lahore. The servant hit her, and already embittered by the disastrous honeymoon, Faiza filed a criminal charge against Headley that landed him in a Pakistani jail for about a week—until one of his Lashkar handlers, a major in the Pakistani military, intervened to get him released.

As was becoming a pattern for Headley's angered wives and girlfriends, Faiza sought revenge by going to the authorities—this time, to the U.S. embassy in Islamabad, where she told American officials that her husband was planning some kind of terrorist attack. She even showed the officials the pictures he had taken at the Taj, telling them that Headley "is a criminal. I heard he is in drugs. I heard he is in arms. I heard he's a criminal. He's got a bomb. He's going to bomb Karachi." Faiza visited the embassy three times, but U.S. officials there distrusted her histrionic tone. A senior FBI official also explains that Headley's status as a productive, reliable source for the DEA "made some of the things that were being alleged by his estranged love interests a little bit difficult to believe."

Somehow Headley and Faiza managed to reconcile, and he reunited with her in 2008. Back in Chicago, Shazia was having her suspicions about Faiza. Headley assured her that he was not involved with the other woman, writing in an e-mail, "I swear on the Koran, if I'm lying you can do whatever you want."

By now Headley was deep into planning the Mumbai operation. His handlers in Pakistan, Sajid Mir and "Major Iqbal," gave him twenty-five thousand dollars to cover his expenses in Mumbai, and he secured a job as "South Asia Regional Director" for the Chicago-based company First

World Immigration, which was owned by his old boarding school friend Tahawwur Rana. He set up an office in Mumbai for the company, which he rarely went to but which gave him the appearance of working for a legitimate business and was good cover for his regular visits to the city. Between 2006 and 2008 he made several trips to Mumbai, performing carefully videotaped surveillance not only of the Taj but also of other prominent landmarks, including the Oberoi Hotel, Mumbai's central railway station, and the Chabad House.

During one of these trips, Headley struck up a friendship with Rahul Bhatt, a Bollywood actor and the son of a prominent director. With his Armani suits, Rolex Submariner watch, and gym-buffed body, the six-foot-two Headley adeptly played the part of a rich, fun-loving American businessman; he and Bhatt began regularly hitting the Mumbai party scene, where Headley effortlessly made contacts throughout Mumbai's elite. He even befriended a prominent official of Shiv Sena, an ultranationalist Hindu party with extremist anti-Muslim views. His handlers encouraged this connection, mulling the possibility of Headley setting up a hit on the Shiv Sena leadership.

In all this, Headley contrasted sharply with the dour Salafists for whom a repudiation of Western culture was integral to the radicalization process. His embrace of jihad may have been sparked by his hatred of India, but it was kept alive by the fact that he loved being the perfect terrorist. He appears to have had a classic case of antisocial personality disorder, once termed psychopathy. Marked by lying, egocentrism, difficulties with the law, lack of remorse about harming others, and abusive relationships, it is an almost perfect description of David Headley's life.

In his 2005 book, *The Psychology of Terrorism*, academic John Horgan concluded that, based on an examination of previous research and an in-depth study of the IRA, contrary to earlier researchers' claims, terrorist groups preferred recruits who were, measurably speaking, psychologically "normal." The same holds true on average among the 360 militants examined for this book; Headley is almost the exception that proves the rule.

I n January 2008, Headley met with his Lashkar bosses to plot the attack on the Taj but was told that the Mumbai operation had been postponed or even canceled. But Lashkar felt it needed a high-profile operation to stem the drifting-away of recruits who were now joining the new jihadi outfits then springing up in Pakistan. In March 2008, Headley met with a frogman from the Pakistani navy, who used sea charts to illustrate how best to travel from Pakistan to Mumbai and pointed out which landing points in and around the city might work best for the mission. A month later, Headley made his seventh trip to Mumbai; posing as a tourist interested in the city's waterfront, he surveyed it from a variety of boats. He eventually decided on a ramshackle fishing village as an ideal landing place for the gunmen, close to a main road and a twenty-four-hour taxi stand and also far from any police station. Once he had chosen this he took more boat trips in the area to ensure there were no navigational hazards to impede the landing.

In the years after al-Qaeda's attacks on New York City and the Pentagon, the U.S. government had worried about foreigners coming to the States to wreak havoc, but this time it was an American citizen exporting holy war—to a U.S. ally and the world's largest democracy.

In a stroke of diabolical brilliance, Headley went to a Hindu temple and purchased a number of red string bracelets that are worn by practicing Hindus, which he would have the gunmen wear to help them blend in with Mumbai locals. Lashkar had by now found ten recruits for the assault, all of whom had trained in close-quarters fighting and urban warfare. The men understood that they had been recruited for a *fedayeen* ("those who sacrifice themselves") attack, which would end with a "stronghold" option in which they would hunker down in a final fighting position and fight to the death.

The ten-member team was kept in isolation in a Karachi safe house during the weeks before the operation. They reviewed Headley's surveillance videotapes and studied maps made from his careful GPS readings and Google Earth images of the targets. The gunmen were all given Indian ID cards and had their hair cut in a short, Western style. They were outfitted with cargo pants and sweatshirts. In their new clothing, they looked like millions of other ordinary, upwardly mobile young Indian men.

Headley's planning worked smoothly, but the gunmen made a mistake that would definitively link the attack to Pakistan. One of them dropped a GPS in the boat they used to travel to Mumbai, which was later recovered by the Indian authorities. The Indians gave it to the FBI after determining that it had been wiped clean; using specialized software, FBI lab techs at Quantico found a "ghost image," however, that mapped the boat's journey. Art Cummings presented the image to his Indian counterparts, saying, "Here's the map of where that boat started. It started in Karachi. If that's not good enough, we traced the outboard motor to a store in Karachi." An Indian official asked, "How the hell did you do that?" Cummings explained, "We got with the manufacturer, and we know exactly where it was distributed to." The Indians were impressed.

The FBI still had no idea, however, that an American was so deeply involved in plotting the Mumbai attacks. In the fall of 2008, during the final phase of planning, Headley started brainstorming another terror spectacle with his Lashkar bosses, this one an attack on the leading Danish newspaper, *Jyllands-Posten*, which three years earlier had published cartoons of the Prophet Muhammad. In a message to a Pakistan-based Yahoo group on October 29, 2008, Headley wrote, "Call me old fashioned but I feel disposed towards violence for the offending parties."

In January 2009, following the Mumbai attacks, Headley traveled to Copenhagen, where he reconnoitered the *Jyllands-Posten* on the pretext of looking to place advertising for his immigration business. In coded correspondence with Lashkar, he referred to the new plot as the "Mickey Mouse project." On one of his e-mail accounts, he listed a set of procedures that included "Route Design," "Counter Surveillance," and "Security." Headley planned to take over the *Jyllands-Posten* building using tactics similar to those in Mumbai, in which multiple attackers would fight to the death. The plan involved beheading newspaper employees and throwing their heads out the windows. This would guarantee significant media coverage. While in Denmark, Headley picked up some hats emblazoned with the word *Copenhagen,* grim souvenirs for his handlers back in Pakistan.

On March 3, 2009, anticipating the operation's risks, Headley wrote to his old friend Tahawwur Rana a note that was effectively his last will and testament. He gave him instructions for the disposition of his property in Dubai and Pakistan, and noted, "I would like my sons to get into Aitchison," a posh boarding school in Pakistan.

But Lashkar officials suddenly put the Copenhagen attack on hold. The group knew it was being targeted by a variety of governments as a result of the Mumbai attacks, which had succeeded beyond Lashkar's wildest expectations. But Headley had a dream in which his grave had the extraordinary honor of being situated next to the grave of Muhammad; resolved to defend the honor of the Prophet in light of the blasphemous Danish cartoons, he became determined to go ahead with the Copenhagen operation with or without Lashkar's participation. He made contact with Ilyas Kashmiri, who ran his own jihadist group in Pakistan and had close ties to al-Qaeda.

The cartoons had become a particular obsession of al-Qaeda. In March 2008, Osama bin Laden publicly denounced their publication as a "catastrophe" and promised swift punishment. Three months later an al-Qaeda suicide attacker bombed the Danish embassy in Islamabad, killing six. For al-Qaeda, the cartoons assumed some of the symbolic significance that Salman Rushdie's fictional writings about the Prophet had had for Khomeini's Iran two decades earlier.

Headley met with Kashmiri in the Pakistani tribal regions to brief him on his surveillance of the *Jyllands-Posten* building. Kashmiri congratulated him on the Mumbai attacks and told him that "the Elders," al-Qaeda's leaders, wanted the Copenhagen attack to "be carried out soon as possible." Kashmiri suggested deploying a truck bomb, but Headley said the building's design would render this ineffective; far more likely to succeed, he proposed, was a Mumbai-style assault. Kashmiri told Headley that he knew men in the United Kingdom who might be interested in taking part in such an operation. This group, however, was being monitored by British intelligence because of its links to al-Qaeda, and in July 2009 the British tipped off the FBI that someone named "David" had called the men from a Chicago pay phone.

Now under surveillance by both British and American intelligence, Headley traveled to the city of Derby, in Northern England, to meet the men he hoped to recruit. Their response to the proposed operation was lukewarm. Instructed to raise ten thousand pounds in financing, they had come up with only two thousand. When Headley returned to the States in early August 2009 he was questioned by airport inspectors about his many trips to Pakistan, but, in a textbook case of intelligence-led policing, he was released so the FBI could investigate whom else he might be conspiring with.

Philip Mudd remembers asking his FBI colleagues about Headley. "The two questions are 'Who else is he in touch with?' and 'What's the extent that Lashkar is in the United States?'" FBI officials decided to follow Headley for as long as it took, to see if he might have co-conspirators, naming the investigation Operation Black Medallion. Agents examined his phone records and e-mail and began tracing his relationships with everyone he knew, from his old friends to employees at his local pizza parlor.

Mudd and his colleagues at the FBI were keenly aware of an episode three years earlier in which British police officers had been tailing a group of UK-based Islamist militants who included Mohamed Siddiqi Khan, a man of Pakistani descent who seemed to be only a peripheral player. Following suspects is labor intensive, and because Khan, a married schoolteacher with no criminal record, wasn't deemed of much importance, the police stopped tailing him. Khan would go on to lead the 2005 London suicide bombers.

With this worst case fresh in their minds, FBI officials wanted to make absolutely sure they fully mapped any Lashkar support network Headley might have in the States. When David Headley came into the FBI's sights, Mudd felt that instead of "Can we indict him?" the right question was "How do we blow this out?" Mudd wanted a true "enterprise investigation"—that is, a takedown of the entire spiderweb behind an operation, not just the strand that started it. For Mudd, a good takedown happened at the point when you were almost bored with the plot, when you were doing surveillance and nobody new was emerging and there was no money flow or travel that couldn't be accounted for.

Andy Liepman of the NCTC was particularly concerned by the Headley case. A Chicago resident had been active with Lashkar and plotting attacks with al-Qaeda for years. Did these groups have other operatives like Headley? For Liepman, it opened up a vulnerability that the intelligence community hadn't thought of. At least in terms of al-Qaeda plots, it had always looked at the reverse: people who were living overseas and entering the United States. Liepman recalls his colleagues joking around and saying, "Do we have to identify the United States as a terrorist safe haven?"

After an exhaustive investigation of Headley, FBI officials concluded that his only support network in the States was his friend Rana. When they found out that Headley was preparing to leave for Pakistan again, they moved in. He was arrested at O'Hare Airport on October 3, 2009. He soon told investigators that he was planning to kill the *Jyllands-Posten*'s cultural editor, Flemming Rose, who had first commissioned the Danish cartoons, and cartoonist Kurt Westergaard. When he was arrested, Headley had in his luggage a book titled *To Pray As a Jew: A Guide to the Prayer Book and the Synagogue Service*—he mistakenly believed Rose to be Jewish—and a memory stick containing a video of close-up shots of the entrance to the *Jyllands-Posten* offices. He also confessed his involvement in the Mumbai attacks, which came as news to the FBI.

Tahawwur Hussain Rana was arrested fifteen days later, on October 18, 2009. The FBI surveillance of Headley's e-mails and the wiretaps placed on him provided evidence that Rana had known of the Copenhagen operation, and it was his immigration business that Headley had used as cover while casing the *Jyllands-Posten* offices. But the feds still needed Headley's testimony to put Rana away. Because six Americans had been murdered during the Mumbai attacks, Headley faced a possible death penalty. He had only one thing left that he could bargain for with the feds: he agreed to testify against his best friend from high school, the same man he had trusted to bail him out of jail and safeguard his will.

It was David Headley's final betrayal. He escaped the death penalty and instead was sentenced to thirty-five years. Rana was sentenced to fourteen.

Many American militants don't make it out of the country, whether because they want to conduct jihad in America, because they lack the adaptability for long-term "fieldwork," or because they get caught on their way abroad. Even those Americans who manage to get to an overseas jihad are more often pawns than leaders. But those who do succeed outside the United States can be some of the most dangerous militants of all. Omar Hammami significantly raised the media profile of al-Shabaab in the West, while David Headley's American passport and Caucasian looks enabled him to plan the Mumbai attacks.

The FBI has taken an aggressive approach to preventing Americans from reaching fields of jihad in the first place, and it seeks to arrest (if and when he comes back) anyone who has succeeded. American jihadists who stay overseas, however, cause special problems for U.S. law enforcement. Headley's planned attack in Denmark was averted because, finally and belatedly, the FBI recognized the threat he posed—and because he was in the United States, available for arrest and prosecution. Though the Department of Justice indicted Omar Hammami in 2007, FBI agents were powerless to curb his actions in Somalia.

To extend the arm of American power to remote battlefields, the Obama administration deployed what would become the emblematic weapon of the war on terror: the armed drone.

CHAPTER 9

TRACKING THE TERRORISTS

JUST BECAUSE WE HAVE THE BEST HAMMER DOES NOT MEAN THAT
EVERY PROBLEM IS A NAIL.

—President Obama at the graduation
ceremony at West Point, May 28, 2014

The most infamous American jihadist abroad was, of course, Anwar al-Awlaki. In the spring of 2010, Awlaki's star was rising so fast that Abu Bashir, the leader of the Yemeni branch of al-Qaeda, Al-Qaeda in the Arabian Peninsula (AQAP), even floated the idea that Awlaki should lead AQAP. Osama bin Laden nixed this idea; Abu Bashir had once served as his secretary, and bin Laden felt there was little point in appointing someone he didn't know as leader of AQAP. Bin Laden did, however, request a "detailed" résumé for Awlaki so that he could get a better sense of the American cleric. He also instructed both men to provide written accounts of their "vision" of how the holy war in Yemen was playing out so that he could decide whether it was worth trying to escalate the struggle there.

As his profile rose Awlaki became one of the central preoccupations of senior Obama administration officials. None was more fixated than President Obama himself. This was not what most of the world had anticipated when Obama first assumed office. Five months into his presidency, on June 4, 2009, Obama delivered the speech in Cairo that was billed as the start of a "reset" with the Islamic world. President George W. Bush had been widely unpopular among Muslims for his invasion of Iraq and the prisons at Guantanamo and Abu Ghraib, but many had higher hopes for a president who had opposed the Iraq War as a candidate—and who had the middle name Hussein. Before a carefully selected audience at Cairo University, Obama declared, "I have come here to seek a new beginning between the United States and Muslims around the world; one based upon mutual interest and mutual respect; and one based upon the truth that America and Islam are not exclusive, and need not be in competition."

Obama said he had come to this conclusion partly based on his own life experiences. "I am a Christian, but my father came from a Kenyan family that includes generations of Muslims. As a boy, I spent several years in Indonesia and heard the call of the azaan at the break of dawn and the fall of dusk." Interrupted by applause and at one point a standing ovation, Obama said, "America is not—and never will be—at war with Islam. We will, however, relentlessly confront violent extremists who pose a grave threat to our security. Because we reject the same thing that people of all faiths reject: the killing of innocent men, women, and children. And it is my first duty as President to protect the American people."

Listeners heard that Obama was extending an olive branch to the Muslim world, largely ignoring the fact that he had also made a robust defense of the American war on al-Qaeda. Something similar happened a few months later, when the president went to Norway to accept the Nobel Peace Prize. The jurors who awarded the prize, like many 2008 voters, seemed to have conflated Obama's opposition to the Iraq War with an opposition to war in general. The president was surely the first prizewinner to use his acceptance speech in Oslo to explain his philosophy of just and necessary wars. Obama said, "I face the world as it is, and cannot stand idle in the face of threats to the American people. For make no mistake: Evil does exist in the world. A nonviolent movement could not have halted Hitler's armies. Negotiations cannot convince al-Qaeda's leaders to lay down their arms. To say that force may sometimes be necessary is not a call to cynicism—it is a recognition of history, the imperfections of man, and the limits of reason."

Obama would prove to be one of the most militarily aggressive

American presidents in decades. He authorized military operations in seven Muslim countries—Afghanistan, Iraq, Libya, Pakistan, Somalia, Syria, and Yemen; mandated a troop surge in Afghanistan; and vastly ramped up the CIA drone program. And he became the first president since the Civil War to authorize the assassination of a U.S. citizen: Anwar al-Awlaki.

The road from the Cairo speech to the drone wars begins at the start of Obama's first term, with the botched underwear bomb attack. As the drama in Detroit unfolded on Christmas Day 2009, Obama was on vacation in Hawaii, where he had spent much of his youth. The Obamas were singing carols when a military aide interrupted to say that John Brennan, Obama's top counterterrorism adviser, was on the phone.

At first Obama chose not to comment publicly on the attempted attack. He continued taking walks on the beach with his family and playing golf. He wanted to project an image of calm—to get away from the panic-inducing color-coded alerts and breathless press conferences of the Bush administration. Ben Rhodes, an adviser on national security, says there didn't seem to be much point in making a major public statement about an al-Qaeda attack that had ultimately failed: "We did have a theory that—let's not pump oxygen into these guys."

The 24/7 American news cycle abhors a vacuum, however, so on December 27, Janet Napolitano, the secretary of homeland security, was dispatched to make the rounds of the Sunday talk shows. To ABC News she asserted, "Once the incident occurred, the system worked," which hardly seemed reassuring. Hadn't "the system" failed completely in the run-up to the botched attack? A terrorist carrying a bomb had managed to get through security at a Western airport and then onto an American plane. Representative Peter King, the Republican congressman from Long Island who sat on the House Committee on Homeland Security, contradicted her flatly on CBS's *Face the Nation:* "The fact is, the system did not work."

Flouting the convention that politics take a backseat during a national security crisis, former vice president Dick Cheney accused Obama of "trying to pretend we are not at war" with terrorists. He sharpened the point: "When President Obama pretends we aren't [at war], it makes us less safe."

After seventy-two hours of silence, on the same day that al-Qaeda took credit for the failed attack, Obama interrupted his vacation to state that he was ordering a thorough review of how an armed terrorist had managed to board an American plane. He observed, "A systemic failure has occurred, and I consider that totally unacceptable." As soon as he heard the speech, Michael Leiter of the NCTC thought, "This is going to be nasty."

According to the White House's subsequent investigation, the government had possessed enough information to determine that the would-be bomber Umar Farouk Abdulmutallab was working for al-Qaeda in Yemen and that the group was looking to expand its attacks beyond the Arabian Peninsula. Yet the intelligence community "did not increase analytic resources working" on that threat. Even the possible use of a hard-to-detect PETN bomb was well-known; White House counterterrorism adviser John Brennan had been personally briefed by Saudi prince Mohammed bin Nayef about the failed assassination attempt in which the same type of bomb was used.

The Christmas Day plot came in the first year of Obama's presidency. Obama knew that if it had succeeded, it would have dealt a crippling blow to his ability to govern. Conservatives had already let it be known that Democrats didn't have the guts to make hard-nosed choices about the war on terror. When Obama returned to the White House from Hawaii in early January, he dressed down his top national security advisers in the Situation Room, saying, "This was a screwup that could have been disastrous. We dodged a bullet, but just barely. It was averted by brave individuals, not because the system worked. And that is unacceptable."

The officials around the table, who included Michael Leiter, CIA director Leon Panetta, John Brennan, and Janet Napolitano, were largely silent. They knew they were being taken to the woodshed.

Leiter was both candid and apologetic, saying, "Mr. President, we didn't connect the pieces. We had this SIGINT. We had the report from the father to the embassy in Nigeria. We didn't connect it. That's our

role. We screwed that up." He said that the national security community was committed to improving, but he added, "I can't tell you that
something like this can't happen again. This is a hard problem, and
finding individuals like this is a huge challenge."

Obama replied, "I want these things fixed and I will hold you
accountable—you, this group around the table, accountable for fixing that process, and that's where my focus is going to be, not on who
messed up."

Just as for George W. Bush, combating terrorist groups would become the dominant foreign policy issue of much of Obama's two terms.
Following the Christmas Day incident, Obama became resigned to this.
Where once terrorism had been one issue among many, about half the
discussions in the National Security Council were taken up by terrorist
groups and how to defeat them.

One of Obama's major campaign platforms had been a promise to
end America's ground wars in both Iraq and Afghanistan, so he was not
about to embark on another such war in the Arabian Peninsula. As he
explained to his national security team, "We can't do in Yemen what we
did in Afghanistan. We shouldn't have to spend tens of billions of dollars in Yemen because one scared kid from Nigeria was recruited to do
something bad." Liberals had wanted Obama to recast his antiterrorism
efforts as a global law enforcement effort, but in articulating his plan,
the president chose a middle path between this and a conventional war,
declaring "war against al-Qaeda and its allies." The rhetorical shift signaled an abandonment of Bush's open-ended fight against terrorism in
favor of a war with particular violent jihadists.

Under the Bush administration, there was an American drone attack in Pakistan every forty-three days. During the first two years of
the Obama presidency, there was one every four days. And in 2011 and
2012, just as strikes in Pakistan began to slow, Obama vastly accelerated the campaign in Yemen. Just one U.S. drone strike occurred in
Yemen under Bush; under Obama the numbers climbed to more than
160 drone and cruise missile strikes.

A controversial hallmark of Obama's drone program was so-called
signature strikes, which he authorized for use in Pakistan's tribal regions

in 2011 and in Yemen a year later. Such strikes did not target known militants but rather people displaying the behaviors of suspected militants. The strikes were reportedly governed by stricter rules in Yemen than in Pakistan, and were given a different name: Terrorist Attack Disruption Strikes (TADS). These were the brutal overseas analogue to the FBI's disruption policies in the United States—the mission was to seek out and "disrupt" suspected terrorists before they could attack, but outside U.S. borders this was a lethal directive.

Obama increasingly turned to the military's secretive Joint Special Operations Command (JSOC, pronounced "Jay-Sock"), made up of the Navy's SEAL Team 6, the Army's Delta Force, and other elements of special operations. After 9/11, JSOC had become a small army within the military, with its own drones, its own air force, and its own intelligence operations. It was in some ways even less accountable than the CIA, as it did not have to brief Congress on its covert operations.

According to conservative estimates, by the end of 2016 the Obama administration had presided over the killing of more than 3,000 people in drone strikes in Pakistan and Yemen. More liberal estimates put the number at over 4,000. Obama remarked drily to his aides, "Turns out I'm really good at killing people. Didn't know that was going to be a strong suit of mine."

In the days following the failed Christmas Day attack, Abdulmutallab's FBI interrogations revealed that it was Anwar al-Awlaki who had ordered the young Nigerian to carry out the operation. For senior counterterrorism officials this came as a surprise. They had pegged Awlaki as an al-Qaeda ideologue, but it was now clear that he was also an operational planner. Such a marriage of roles (both mouthpiece and muscle, bookish intellectual and hard-nosed operator) was rare.

Awlaki himself was eager to take credit for the fruits of his influence. In a fiery interview posted to YouTube on May 23, 2010, he claimed Major Hasan as "a student of mine" and praised the Christmas Day plot. The operation had "achieved great successes, even without killing a single person," he said, and Abdulmutallab was "likewise a student of mine, and this also is an honor."

Awlaki brushed aside criticism in the media that the botched attack had targeted only civilians, on the basis that all American voters were complicit in U.S. foreign policy. He also invoked a common Binladenist theme: that the United States deserved to experience mass casualties. "For fifty years, an entire people—the Muslims in Palestine—has been strangled, with American aid, support, and weapons," Awlaki said. "Twenty years of siege and then occupation of Iraq, and now the occupation of Afghanistan. After all this, no one should even ask us about targeting a bunch of Americans who would have been killed in an airplane."

With his combination of inciting rhetoric and military authority, Awlaki began to be seen by some U.S. national security officials as more of a threat than even bin Laden. It was Awlaki and not bin Laden who was now orchestrating the group's plots against American aviation, and it was concurrent with Awlaki's ascension within AQAP that the organization had begun trying to launch attacks in the States. But how to find someone hiding in the remote parts of Yemen? And even if he could be found, the administration couldn't very well send FBI agents in to arrest him. The tribes in Yemen are well armed; tribal disputes are often settled with artillery. With only a few dozen U.S. Special Forces in the entire country a ground operation would be difficult to mount, and in any event it would be opposed by the Yemeni government.

That left the drone option.

Senior White House officials began debating whether they should target Awlaki for death. Not since the Civil War had a president and his advisers seriously contemplated authorizing the assassination of an American citizen. The president, Attorney General Eric Holder, and a small team of senior national security officials were in the unusual position of acting as Awlaki's jury, judges, and de facto executioners. Just days after the Christmas Day plot, Obama, the former constitutional law professor, gave his verbal approval to target Awlaki for death.

While the president had agonized over some of his earlier decisions to target militants for death, he did not struggle with the decision to kill Awlaki. He had only to consider the cases of Carlos Bledsoe, fresh from a Yemeni prison; Nidal Hasan, who had sought guidance from Awlaki;

and now an operation hatched in Yemen that could have killed hundreds of Americans. Three weeks after the president's authorization, the *Washington Post* reported that Awlaki was on a JSOC kill/capture list.

In July 2010 two lawyers at the Justice Department, David Barron and Marty Lederman, wrote a classified memo laying out the rationale for its being lawful, under specific circumstances, for the president to authorize the killing of an American citizen. Merely being an American citizen, the memo explained, did not make one immune from being targeted. As an operational leader of al-Qaeda actively working to kill Americans, Awlaki posed an "imminent" threat of violent attack against the United States. Moreover, he was hiding in a remote area of Yemen where capture was simply not feasible. Barron and Lederman stipulated that any plan to kill Awlaki would have to comport with the "law of war," that is, try to avoid civilian casualties.

A confidential Justice Department memo written around the same time introduced a broader concept of "imminence" than had previously been in use. An imminent threat no longer required the "United States to have clear evidence that a specific attack on U.S. persons and interests will take place in the immediate future." Instead, the memo argued that an "informed, high-level" U.S. official could lawfully target an American who had been "recently" involved in "activities" posing a threat of an attack on the United States and where there was "no evidence suggesting that he has renounced or abandoned such activities." In other words, an American could be targeted for death not only for planning an attack but also for having been previously involved in such a plan, and if there was no good reason to believe he wouldn't try again.

There was a certain irony to this reasoning. The FBI had been monitoring Awlaki's e-mail account for years. To do this, its agents had had to obtain a court order. Yet the decision to target Awlaki for death was made without any kind of judicial proceeding. As Vicki Divoll, a former assistant general counsel for the CIA, put it after the news first leaked that the Obama administration had authorized Awlaki's killing, "Awlaki's right to privacy exceeds his right to life."

At least one senior Obama administration official was troubled by the decision to kill Awlaki. Harold Koh, a rumpled, combative academic and leading international lawyer, became a darling of the left after 9/11 for his aggressive critiques of the Bush administration's detention and interrogation policies. But when Koh gave up his position as the dean of Yale School of Law in the summer of 2009 to join the State Department, he became the public face of the Obama administration, defending the legality of CIA drone strikes. Indeed, during the first two years of the administration he was the only Obama official to acknowledge publicly the program's existence. On March 25, 2010, Koh gave a speech at a conference of the American Society of International Law in which he defended how suspected militants were added to the kill list, saying that selection procedures were "extremely robust."

Still, something bothered Koh about the decision to kill Awlaki. As an American citizen, wasn't he protected by the Fifth Amendment stipulation that no citizen shall "be deprived of life, liberty, or property, without due process of law"? What was the real case against Awlaki? Koh went to a secure facility at the State Department and paged through a stack of classified files about Awlaki's plots, many of which involved plans to kill large numbers of Americans and Europeans. After five hours of reading, he concluded that Awlaki was "satanic." Koh, the onetime toast of *bien pensant* liberals, was now comfortable with Awlaki's death penalty.

In the fall of 2010 another failed plot confirmed the administration's instincts about Awlaki. The cover of the third issue of *Inspire* showed a photo of a UPS cargo plane parked at an airport with the figure $4,200 stamped over it. Inside the magazine was AQAP's account of its grandiloquently named "Operation Hemorrhage," a plot to bring down cargo planes bound for the States. Awlaki had played a lead role in planning the operation, even taking part in the development and testing of the explosive devices to be used. In late October AQAP mailed two packages with PETN bombs cleverly hidden inside HP LaserJet printer cartridges; mobile phone circuit boards served as detonators, and the bombs were almost impossible to detect, as the explosives were odorless and the circuitry for the detonator looked like ordinary wiring. The packages were sent from a FedEx office and a UPS facility in Sana'a, the Yemeni capital, to the street addresses of two synagogues in Chicago. With grim humor, they were addressed to Reynald de Chatillon, a Christian knight during the Crusades, and to Don Diego Deza, who persecuted Muslims in Spain in the sixteenth century.

AQAP claimed that one of the devices had brought down a UPS flight near Dubai on September 3, 2010. In fact, both were discovered before they could detonate, one in Dubai and the other at a British airport, because of information provided by the Saudis, who had managed to plant a spy in the ranks of AQAP. The leading Saudi counterterrorism official, Prince Mohammed bin Nayef (previously an AQAP target), called John Brennan to warn him of the plot. In any case, *Inspire* celebrated the plot's financial success: the $4,200 that AQAP had spent, it claimed, would impose "billions of dollars" in extra security costs on the air transportation business.

O bama told his national security team, "I want Awlaki. Don't let up on him." He asked for updates at his weekly counterterrorism meetings, known as "Terror Tuesdays," and asserted his belief that Awlaki posed a greater threat than even Ayman al-Zawahiri, bin Laden's successor as the head of al-Qaeda. Despite the injunction of the Justice Department memo, Obama also signaled that he was willing to compromise when it came to avoiding civilian deaths. "Bring it to me and let me decide in the reality of the moment rather than in the abstract," he told Brennan.

On May 5, 2011, just three days after Osama bin Laden's death in a U.S. Navy SEAL raid, Obama received word of a good lead on Awlaki's whereabouts in Yemen. There was a sense of excitement at the White House: Could this be a one-two punch that would put both al-Qaeda Central and its most virulent offshoot on the ropes? JSOC initially took the lead on the operation, tracking the signals of cell phones associated with Awlaki and his circle. Unlike in Pakistan, where drone strikes were under the exclusive control of the CIA, in Yemen both the CIA and JSOC were launching strikes; at any given moment there were some seventy JSOC "operators" working with the Yemeni military and intelligence services. Drones tracking Awlaki and his associates flew out of bases in East Africa and Saudi Arabia as well as from U.S. Navy ships cruising in the Arabian Sea.

Important leads on Awlaki's whereabouts had originated from Ahmed Warsame, a Somali in his mid-twenties who was Al-Qaeda in Yemen's key go-between with al-Shabaab. JSOC tracked Warsame as he moved around Yemen, and in the spring of 2011 the unit picked up information that he was planning to take a boat from eastern Yemen across the Gulf of Aden back to his native Somalia. The navy deployed a ship off the coast of Yemen, and on April 19, 2011, operators from SEAL Team 6 descended on Warsame's puttering fishing boat. He put up no resistance.

On board the USS *Boxer,* now effectively a floating prison, the High-Value Detainee Interrogation Group (HIG), made up of FBI agents and CIA officers, interrogated Warsame for more than two months using standard noncoercive interrogation techniques. Warsame, who had been educated in the United Kingdom, gave his interrogators a detailed account in fluent English of the inner workings of al-Qaeda's Yemeni affiliate. He said that he had met with Awlaki on multiple occasions, and e-mail correspondence with the cleric was found on his computer and thumb drives. As the interrogation wore on, Warsame revealed that he had met with Awlaki only days before he was captured, and he gave up useful details of Awlaki's "pattern of life"—what kind of security measures he used and the types of vehicles typically in his convoys.

In early May, Warsame's disclosures combined with signals intercepts established that Awlaki was in the Shabwah region of southern Yemen. On the evening of May 5, special operations planners sent Predator drones, Harrier jets, and a JSOC aircraft to follow Awlaki, who was riding in a pickup truck across the deserts of Shabwah. It was a great deal of firepower to kill one man, but Obama himself was pushing hard to "remove him from the field." Awlaki's truck was driving fast, and the flight crews tracking the vehicle could not keep their laser-guided weapons locked on the fast-moving target. The JSOC plane fired a missile but missed.

Meanwhile, Awlaki summoned a similar truck from his convoy to distract the American planes and drones overhead. Flames from the drone missile's explosion licked Awlaki's vehicle, but operators knew that even a very close hit could be survivable. An official involved in planning the operation said, "We only blew his bumper off." The Harrier jets, running low on fuel, turned back for the base; at the same time, clouds rolled in that obscured the view of the drone operators. Awlaki, who had in fact survived the attack, was able to take advantage of the cover to switch trucks with two of his confederates. The men gave their lives for Awlaki when another drone incinerated their vehicle.

Awlaki witnessed the fatal explosions from the safety of a nearby cave. The planning official says, "It was one of the worst nights of my life." After the success of the bin Laden raid three days earlier, Awlaki had slipped from JSOC's grasp. There was considerable rivalry between JSOC and the CIA at the time. Each had slightly different "kill" lists, and they fought for turf on a number of issues. The official says that after JSOC's botched attack on Awlaki, "They were smiling at Langley [CIA headquarters]."

The next good intelligence about Awlaki's location came in September 2011, from an al-Qaeda operative in Yemeni custody. Now the hunt centered on the governorate of Al Jawf, on Yemen's northern border with Saudi Arabia, which abuts the Empty Quarter, the world's largest desert and a good place to get lost. Awlaki had made an uncharacteristic mistake; instead of changing his hideout often, he remained in a house in the same town, Khashef, for two weeks. A number of children were in the house, which no doubt made Awlaki think there was a lower risk that the United States would take a shot at him with a drone.

This time the CIA was in charge of what it termed Operation Troy. On the morning of Friday, September 30, 2011, Awlaki had just finished breakfast with his younger American acolyte, Samir Khan, the editor of *Inspire*, when the two men and their companions got into several vehicles. CIA drones locked on, and missiles killed both Awlaki and Khan at 9:55 a.m. In a single morning the American government had assassinated not one but two U.S. citizens.

Obama announced that Awlaki had been killed that same morning, during the retirement ceremony for the chairman of the Joint Chiefs, Admiral Mike Mullen. Interrupted by applause, Obama said that Awlaki's death was a "major blow" to al-Qaeda in Yemen, which

Cleric Anwar al-Awlaki poses for a *Washington Post* profile at his mosque in Northern Virginia on October 4, 2001. Awlaki would rise to become a leader of al-Qaeda in Yemen. The mug shot dates from his 1997 arrest in San Diego for soliciting prostitutes. (Top: Tracy Woodward/*The Washington Post*)

Nineteen-year-old Mohammed Hamzah Khan of Chicago was arrested by the FBI in October 2014 for attempting to join ISIS. (Courtesy of the Khan family)

New York City Police Department deputy commissioner of intelligence David Cohen (in foreground) briefs NYPD commissioner Raymond Kelly. Cohen implemented surveillance of places where Muslims gathered. (Lucas Jackson/Reuters)

Mitchell Silber directed the NYPD's Analytic Unit. He coauthored the controversial 2007 report *Radicalization in the West: The Homegrown Threat.* (Michael Appleton/ *The New York Times*/Redux)

Former CIA case officer Dr. Marc Sageman wrote the influential books *Understanding Terrorist Networks* (2004) and *Leaderless Jihad* (2008). He asserted that jihadists unconnected to foreign organizations posed the most significant terrorist threat to the United States.

Georgetown University professor Bruce Hoffman challenged Sageman's view, arguing that al-Qaeda and like-minded organizations still posed a greater threat than "homegrown" terrorists. (Courtesy of Bruce Hoffman)

Carlos Bledsoe (*right*) and his father, Melvin, at Carlos's high school graduation in Memphis, Tennessee. After radicalizing in Yemen, Bledsoe killed an American soldier in Little Rock, Arkansas, on June 1, 2009. (Courtesy of the Bledsoe family)

Mug shot of Matthew Llaneza following his arrest by San Jose police on weapons charges. In a sting operation, the FBI arrested Llaneza in February 2013 for plotting to bomb a bank in Oakland, California.

Major Nidal Hasan killed thirteen people at Fort Hood, Texas, on November 5, 2009.

Faisal Shahzad of Connecticut trained with the Pakistani Taliban before attempting to detonate a car bomb in Times Square on May 1, 2010.

New York City–raised Najibullah Zazi plotted to bomb the New York City subway system in September 2009 after having trained with al-Qaeda in Pakistan. (Karl Gehring/*The Denver Post*)

Charlotte, North Carolina–raised Samir Khan became an innovative propagandist for al-Qaeda in Yemen, developing the group's first English-language magazine, *Inspire*.

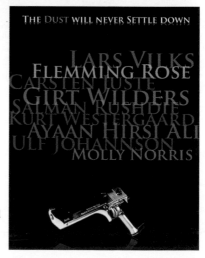

THE DUST WILL NEVER SETTLE DOWN

LARS VILKS
FLEMMING ROSE
CARSTEN JUSTE
GIRT WILDERS
SALMAN RUSHDIE
KURT WESTERGAARD
AYAAN HIRSI ALI
ULF JOHANNSON
MOLLY NORRIS

A "hit list" of proposed Western targets from Issue 1 of *Inspire*, released in July 2010. Seattle-based cartoonist Molly Norris was targeted for drawing cartoons of the Prophet Muhammad.

Virginian Zachary Chesser preaches outside the White House. Chesser increased his online platform as part of the Islamist group Revolution Muslim and was arrested for encouraging attacks against the creators of *South Park* and for attempting to join the Somali terrorist group al-Shabaab.

Alabaman Omar Hammami poses with a high school date in 1999. Hammami would become a leader of al-Shabaab. (Courtesy of the Hammami family)

Omar Hammami (*right*) with the deputy leader of al-Shabaab during a press conference on May 11, 2011, in Mogadishu. (AP Photo/Farah Abdi Warsameh)

Chicagoan David Headley was one of the key planners of the 2008 attacks by Lashkar-e-Taiba in Mumbai—the most spectacular terrorist operation since 9/11.

Anwar al-Awlaki (*left*) with Umar Farouk Abdulmutallab (*center*), the "Underwear Bomber" who attempted to bring down Northwest Airlines Flight 253 on Christmas Day 2009.

A young Dzhokhar "Jahar" Tsarnaev (*left*) with his brother, Tamerlan (*right*), in a photo released during Jahar's 2015 trial for the Boston Marathon bombing.

On December 2, 2015, Tashfeen Malik and Syed Rizwan Farook carried out what was then the most lethal terrorist attack on American soil since 9/11, killing fourteen who were attending an office training session in San Bernardino, California. Malik pledged allegiance to ISIS on Facebook before the attack.

Propaganda image of a wedding in ISIS-held Syria, posted on the Tumblr page of a woman who calls herself "Bird of Jannah [Paradise]."

A tweet characteristic of the social media effort that has drawn an unprecedented number of women to ISIS's ranks.

Imam Mohamed Magid presides over one of the largest mosques in the United States, the All Dulles Area Muslim Society in Northern Virginia. He has successfully intervened with young Americans who've hoped to join ISIS.

Kerry Cahill, the daughter of Michael Cahill, a victim of Major Nidal Hasan's attack on Fort Hood, with Nader Hasan, Nidal's cousin. The two have traveled around the United States to speak out against extremism. (Courtesy of Nader Hasan)

had now lost its "leader for external operations"—a description of the militant cleric the administration had never before used in public.

Jibril Hough, the Islamic community leader in Charlotte who had overseen the "interventions" with Samir Khan when he first showed signs of radicalism, was at work when he heard a news report about a significant drone strike in Yemen. After a national security reporter at NPR confirmed Khan's death, Hough called Samir's father.

Hough recalls, "I always felt that I was going to get some kind of call, especially after he went to Yemen. But by the same token, I didn't see him as someone that would actually do an act of violence. He seemed more a propaganda type that would believe it in theory, write about it. I mean there are thousands of people in America that do their own form of that. Some people said, 'Oh he was a terrorist. He deserved to die.' I'm like, 'Hold on. When was he ever found guilty of doing an act of terrorism? Have we given up the hope of letting people have their day in court?' "

A few days later, at Hough's urging, Khan's grieving family issued a statement, saying their son "never broke any law and was never implicated in any crime." The statement also pointed out that he was a U.S. citizen, killed by his own government, and yet no U.S. official had "contacted us with any news about the recovery of our son's remains or offered us any condolences." The statement asked, "Was this style of execution the only solution? Why couldn't there have been a capture or a trial?" A week earlier, senior Obama administration officials had confirmed that Khan was never the intended target of the strike, only Awlaki, and that Khan had never been on a kill list.

Shortly before the drone strike that killed his father, Colorado-born Abdulrahman al-Awlaki left his grandparents' house in the Yemeni capital to try to find him. Two weeks later, on October 14, in a bleak coda to his father's death, Abdulrahman was killed in a drone strike that was, according to the U.S. government, targeting an al-Qaeda operative. Only sixteen, he was "collateral damage" in a new era of warfare.

Obama was unhappy about Abdulrahman's death, telling his national security team that the strike had been "sloppy" and ordering an internal review of the drone program. The resulting Presidential Policy Guidance on drone strikes stated that future strikes would be authorized only with "near-certainty that no civilians will be killed or injured."

Meanwhile, killing Awlaki Sr. had done little to kill his ideas. Al-Qaeda in the Arabian Peninsula continued to publish *Inspire,* and more than three dozen militants indicted or convicted in the States since Awlaki's death have cited his influence or possessed his propaganda.

After Awlaki's death, the Obama administration continued the massive ramp-up of the CIA drone campaign against al-Qaeda and allied groups in the tribal regions of Pakistan that had begun in earnest in 2010. Over time the strikes decimated al-Qaeda's core, so much so that by 2015, the drone campaign in Pakistan had decreased in tempo significantly. By then, al-Qaeda Central in Pakistan really was on life support—albeit six years after Marc Sageman had first asserted this.

The best testament to the drone program's success came from bin Laden himself, in a trove of documents the Navy SEALs recovered at bin Laden's compound after he was killed. A major theme of the documents was how much punishment CIA drones were inflicting on al-Qaeda. In a forty-eight-page memo to an aide written in October 2010, bin Laden said that al-Qaeda's longtime sanctuary in Pakistan's tribal areas was now too dangerous because of the campaign of American drone strikes there. "I am leaning toward getting most of our brothers out of the area," he wrote.

A number of other al-Qaeda documents fill in the portrait of an organization under significant pressure from U.S. counterterrorism operations. One of the memos referred to "the killing of many jihadi cadres, leaders and others" via drone, and noted that "this is something that is concerning us and exhausting us." Other documents suggested that operatives travel in the Afghan-Pakistani border regions only on "cloudy days," when American drones were less effective. Bin Laden warned that "the Americans have great accumulated expertise of photography of the region due to the fact they have been doing it for so many years. They can even distinguish between houses that are frequented by male visitors at a higher rate than is normal." Compounding their problems, al-

Qaeda members were short on cash, one of them writing to bin Laden of "the financial problem."

Bin Laden was also deeply aware that as the tenth anniversary of 9/11 approached, his central goal of attacking the United States again remained unfulfilled. He urged al-Qaeda affiliates in the Middle East to stop wasting their time in attacks against local government targets, and instead to focus on "killing and fighting the American people." One letter advised jihadist militants in North Africa to stop "insisting on the formation of an Islamic state" and instead attack the U.S. embassies in Sierra Leone and Togo, and American oil companies. Bin Laden offered similar advice to AQAP, telling it to avoid targeting Yemeni police and military targets and instead prioritize attacks on American targets. Much of bin Laden's advice either didn't make it to these groups or was ignored; al-Qaeda's affiliates in Yemen and North Africa continued to attack local targets.

Certainly if judged as a tool to eliminate the leadership of al-Qaeda and its affiliates, the CIA drone campaign was effective. Strikes killed more than four dozen prominent members of al-Qaeda in Pakistan, and another four dozen in Yemen. But the price of this success was high. While drones have become more accurate over time, an estimated 129 to 161 civilians have been killed in Pakistan during the Obama administration, and at least 87 in Yemen. In Pakistan, anger about the program drove approval ratings for the United States to record lows—at one point less than 10 percent of the country's 180 million residents had a favorable view of the States. The repercussions of this deep-seated anger may still be unfolding. The Pakistani American Faisal Shahzad, who launched the unsuccessful attempt to blow up an SUV in Times Square on May 1, 2010, said during his trial that protesting the drone strikes was one of his chief motivations.

A Pew poll conducted in forty-four countries in Africa, Asia, Europe, the Middle East, and Latin America in 2014 showed overwhelming disapproval for the CIA drone campaign, even among American allies such as the United Kingdom and Germany. Many Western nations consider the program illegal under international law because it has taken place without a formal declaration of war.

Just as drone warfare has raised a host of legal and ethical concerns about America's national security apparatus, so have other aspects of the Obama administration's covert campaign against terrorists—including those that hit much closer to home.

After the failed Christmas Day bombing, Obama told his national security advisers that "we need to tighten up here on watch-listing, in particular, and information sharing." For Obama, optimizing domestic intelligence was crucial to avoiding all-out war abroad. This meant the continuance of a highly classified program of the National Security Agency, which brought its powerful resources to bear on every U.S. citizen. On June 5, 2013, the *Guardian* broke the first story in what would become a flood of revelations regarding the extent and nature of the NSA's surveillance programs. The most controversial of these was its bulk collection of American telephone metadata, which includes the time, date, and phone numbers of telephone calls, though not their content. Of course, whom you call, when, and for how long can reveal a great deal, from your choice of doctor to your most intimate relationships.

Facing bipartisan criticism over the threat such programs posed to privacy, the Obama administration scrambled to defend them as legal and essential to U.S. national security. Two weeks after the first leaks by former NSA contractor Edward Snowden, President Obama said during a visit to Berlin, "We know of at least fifty threats that have been averted because of this information, not just in the United States but, in some cases, threats here in Germany. So lives have been saved."

General Keith Alexander, the director of the NSA, testified before a congressional committee that "the information gathered from these programs provided the U.S. government with critical leads to help prevent over fifty potential terrorist events in more than twenty countries around the world."

The Obama administration also tried to present the issue as one of preventing future 9/11s. A typical NSA talking point was "NSA and its partners must make sure we connect the dots so that the nation is never attacked again like it was on 9/11." Spokespeople were encouraged to use "sound bites that resonate"— specifically, "I much prefer to be here today explaining these programs than explaining another 9/11 event that we were not able to prevent." As with every counterterrorism measure developed over the previous decade, the need to prevent a future 9/11 functioned as the central frame for the administration's case. In an October 29, 2013, House Intelligence Committee hearing on the NSA programs, featuring General Alexander and the director of national intelligence, James Clapper, the 9/11 attacks were mentioned fourteen times.

Some reporters parroted the statistic that NSA surveillance had averted more than fifty terrorist plots. CBS News anchor Bob Schieffer said on *Face the Nation:* "Fifty-six terror plots here and abroad have been thwarted. . . . So what's wrong with it, then, if it's managed to stop fifty-six terrorist attacks? That sounds like a pretty good record." In fact, the government's claims were vastly overblown. With regard to the 360 individuals involved in jihadist crime in the United States since 9/11, surveillance of American phone data had no discernible role in preventing acts of terrorism and only a marginal role in preventing terrorist-related activity, such as fund-raising for a jihadist group.

The single plot the government publicly cited was that of Basaaly Moalin, the San Diego cabdriver who provided funds to al-Shabaab. Yet, far from justifying the phone data program, that plot called its necessity into question. In late 2007, Moalin began a series of conversations with Aden Hashi Ayro, one of the leaders of al-Shabaab, unaware that the NSA was listening in. At one point Ayro told Moalin that it was "time to finance the jihad," and at another, "You are running late with the stuff. Send some and something will happen." Over several months in 2008, Moalin transferred thousands of dollars. This was damning evidence for the cabdriver, but the case hardly justified the surveillance of all phone calls made in the States for the past five years. Moalin's $8,500 contribution was a drop in the bucket, and the case involved no attack plot; nor was there a threat to the United States or American targets. The NSA had conducted a wide-ranging fishing expedition that netted a minnow.

U.S. district judge Richard Leon, who presided over a federal court case challenging the constitutionality of the bulk collection program, ruled on December 16, 2013, that it constituted an unreasonable search under the Fourth Amendment. He also cited in his opinion the "utter lack of evidence that a terrorist attack has ever been prevented because searching the NSA database was faster than other investigative tactics."

A White House review panel similarly concluded, in a report released on December 18, 2013, that information from Americans' phone data "was not essential to preventing attacks." Geoffrey Stone, a member of the panel and a University of Chicago law professor, said that in searching for evidence that phone metadata collection had actually stopped any terror attacks, "We found none." He did note, however, that the NSA's intercepts of overseas e-mail traffic were far more useful in preventing attacks.

As more information about the NSA programs came to light, the American public grew increasingly skeptical. A HuffPost/YouGov poll released in July 2014 found that more than half of Americans believed that metadata collection was an unnecessary intrusion into their lives. Recognizing this, and the program's poor track record, the administration announced that it would reform surveillance so the government no longer collected phone data in bulk; phone companies would store this data, but "absent an emergency situation," a court order would be required to access it.

In June 2015, after a lengthy debate in Congress, this proposal became law. It was the first time a key element of the post-9/11 national security edifice and legal apparatus had been rolled back. Almost a decade and a half after 9/11, in the debate about the balance between security and privacy, the pendulum was swinging back in the direction of privacy.

The Demographics Unit at the New York City Police Department was also a casualty of Americans' growing concern about privacy. As we have seen, the NYPD's large-scale monitoring of Muslim restaurants, businesses, and mosques in the New York City area netted little for its efforts. Thomas Galati, a senior official in the Intelligence Division that oversaw the Demographics Unit, testified in a 2012 deposition that since his arrival six years earlier, "I have never made a lead from rhetoric that came from a Demographics report," and further that "I don't recall other ones prior to my arrival." As with the NSA program, it took a combination of poor results and public outcry—this time from Muslim communities throughout the New York City area—for change to come. In 2014, three years after it became public knowledge, the Demographics Unit was disbanded by the administration of incoming New York City mayor Bill de Blasio.

The problem for counterterrorism officials during the Obama administration was not that they lacked information, but that they didn't adequately understand or share the information they already possessed, derived from conventional law enforcement and intelligence techniques. Despite the fact that U.S. authorities had, on at least five occasions, received plausible tips from his family members, friends, and acquaintances, David Coleman Headley successfully aided the 2008 terrorist attacks in Mumbai. Nidal Hasan's multiple e-mails to Anwar al-Awlaki, which discussed the permissibility, under Koranic law, of killing U.S. soldiers, were intercepted by U.S. intelligence agencies but ultimately dismissed. Carlos Bledsoe was able to buy a rifle over the counter at Walmart despite having been under investigation by the FBI. Umar Farouq Abdulmutallab's father contacted the U.S. embassy in Nigeria with concerns that his son had become radicalized and might be planning something.

These cases argue not for the gathering of ever-vaster troves of information or an aggressive program of sting operations, but for making smarter judgments about information collected through established, legal means. Homegrown jihadist extremists have mounted seventy-two plots to conduct attacks within the United States since 2001. Of those plots, sixteen involved a terrorist act that was not prevented by any type of government action, such as the failed attempt by Faisal Shahzad to blow up a car bomb in Times Square on May 1, 2010. Of the remaining fifty-six plots, the public record shows that forty were uncovered by traditional law enforcement methods, such as the use of informants, community tips about suspicious activity, and standard policing practices.

Informants played an important role in preventing just under half of the plots by homegrown jihadist extremists since 9/11, including the

Fort Dix plotters, one of whom told a government informant in 2007 that they were plotting to kill soldiers stationed at the nearby army base. As we have seen, informants also ensnared hopeless deadbeats whose chances of launching a successful terrorist operation were nil, such as the Newburg Four and the Liberty City Seven. A further one in ten jihadist terrorism investigations relied on tips to law enforcement. Saudi student Khalid Aldawsari's plot to attack a variety of targets in Texas in 2011, including former President George W. Bush's home in Dallas, was foiled when a company reported his attempt to buy chemicals suitable for making explosives.

The key role that families and communities played in preventing violent extremism was also overlooked in the effort to justify more exotic counterterrorism measures. As we have seen, in more than a quarter of the terrorism cases since 2001, a tip from the local Muslim American community or a family member was pivotal.

In contrast to the most overreaching counterterrorism efforts, many routine policing and intelligence initiatives have dramatically reduced the threat posed by terrorists. On September 11, 2001, there were sixteen people on the U.S. no-fly list. By 2016 there were forty-eight thousand. In 2001 there were thirty-two Joint Terrorism Task Force "fusion centers," around the country, where law enforcement agencies work together to chase down leads and build cases. A decade and a half later there were more than one hundred. Before 9/11, the Department of Homeland Security, the NCTC, and the TSA did not exist. Annoying as it is for many Americans to go through a TSA checkpoint, it has been a strong deterrent to smuggling any kind of weapon on board a plane. While it's impossible to measure the impact of programs designed to *prevent* attacks, the relatively small number of successful jihadist attacks in the States in the years since 9/11 indicate that American defensive measures are working.

Another important change: At the dawn of the twenty-first century, the American public didn't comprehend the threat posed by jihadist terrorists. This has changed dramatically. In December 2001 the passengers on an American Airlines jet disabled the "shoe bomber," Richard

Reid, as the plane flew between Paris and Miami. Eight years later it was his fellow passengers who tackled the Underwear Bomber, Umar Abdulmutallab, on Northwest Flight 253. The following year, a street vendor spotted Faisal Shahzad's suspicious SUV parked in Times Square. The public's awareness of terrorism as a domestic threat has been a huge force multiplier to the other measures put in place to defend the "homeland."

Another aid to homeland defense has been, of course, overseas offense. In 2013 the United States allocated $72 billion to intelligence collection and other covert activities. Before 9/11, the budget was around a third of that figure: $26 billion. Aside from the significant, if controversial, pressure applied on al-Qaeda by the CIA drone program, this has also financed communications monitoring, the hiring of additional analysts and spies, and other effective measures against terrorist groups.

From a purely American perspective, by the time Obama had begun his second term, the threat from al-Qaeda and allied groups had receded significantly. The threat inside the States had become largely lone-wolf attacks, while the threat overseas took the shape of attacks on U.S. facilities, such as the one mounted by an al-Qaeda–aligned group on the American consulate in Benghazi, Libya, that killed four Americans on September 11, 2012. Shocking and tragic as these attacks have been, they still pale in comparison to the murder of almost three thousand people in one morning.

President Obama, for his part, was feeling sufficiently comfortable about the parlous state of al-Qaeda and its allies that on May 23, 2013, in a speech at the National Defense University in Washington, DC, he made the case that it was time to wind down the "boundless global war on terror" and "perpetual wartime footing" that has been a feature of American life since 9/11. The president said that al-Qaeda was "on the path to defeat," and that remaining terrorism threats would be "less capable al-Qaeda affiliates" and "homegrown extremists." In the president's view, these threats did not necessitate a wartime mindset. For a president who had never wanted either war or terrorism to be defining issues of his tenure, it was a satisfying statement to make—yet also bittersweet, given that the "wartime footing" was, to a not insignificant degree, of his own making.

In January 2014, Obama maintained this line when he assured David Remnick, the editor of the *New Yorker,* that the local groups waving al-Qaeda's flag that had recently gained ground in Iraq and Syria posed far less of a threat than al-Qaeda's core. He quipped, "The analogy we use around here sometimes, and I think it's accurate, is if a jayvee team puts on Lakers uniforms that doesn't make them Kobe Bryant."

That offhand remark would come back to haunt Obama. ISIS, a top-down organization with tens of thousands of men under its command, would come to pose a grave threat to the Middle East, but also, to an increasingly troubling degree, the West. Its shrewd recruitment strategies and policy of directing attacks in Europe and inspiring them in the States blended the leader-led jihad of Bruce Hoffman with elements of the leaderless jihad of Marc Sageman—a virulent mutation of Binladenism that made al-Qaeda seem almost quaint. No overseas movement would inspire as many Americans to pursue jihad in as short a time.

Yet even as an intensifying sectarian civil war was bringing jihadist groups to prominence across Syria and Iraq, America received a powerful reminder that the homegrown threat was alive and well.

CHAPTER 10

THE BOSTON BOMBERS

Jahar @J_tsar 15 Jan 2013   I don't argue with fools who say islam is terrorism it's not worth a thing, let an idiot remain an idiot

—Tweet from Dzhokhar "Jahar" Tsarnaev three
months before the Boston Marathon bombings

Jahar had nowhere left to hide. His feared, beloved older brother, Tamerlan, who had once nurtured dreams of becoming a world-class boxer, was dead, following an intense firefight with the police eighteen hours earlier. Now Jahar was alone, hiding inside a dry-docked boat in the Boston suburb of Watertown as the police closed in. Huddling under a tarpaulin, Jahar was bleeding profusely from multiple gunshot wounds, the most severe of which was caused by a bullet that had entered through the left side of his mouth and exited through his lower face. Other shots had damaged his left hand and nicked his neck.

As he lay in the boat with the sounds of police sirens and helicopters all around him, Jahar believed the end was very near. Losing blood rapidly, he wrote what he believed to be his final testament on the inside of the boat with a pencil: "The U.S. government is killing our innocent civilians, but most of you already know that. As a M[uslim] I can't stand to see such evil go unpunished, we Muslims are one body, you hurt one you hurt us all. . . . Know you are fighting men who look into the barrel of your gun and see heaven, now how can you compete with that. We are promised victory and we will surely get it." It was an efficient rendering of the Binladenist creed.

Four days earlier, on April 15, 2013, Jahar and Tamerlan made the fifteen-minute trip from their home in Cambridge, Massachusetts, across the Charles River to Boylston Street, in downtown Boston, on a mission they believed to be sanctioned by Allah. They arrived near the final stretch of the Boston Marathon, in which some twenty-three thousand runners were participating. The brothers were both carrying large backpacks. Tamerlan was wearing sunglasses and a baseball cap, while Jahar wore a backward white baseball cap, showing his youthful, nineteen-year-old face. They looked like any other American college-age kids crowding the marathon route, but unlike the hundreds of thousands of other spectators, they weren't cheering.

The two men dropped their backpacks on the ground at two locations on Boylston Street, not far from the marathon finish line. At 2:49 p.m. the first bomb went off; the second, thirteen seconds later. The bombs were filled with nails and ball bearings that produced shrapnel devastating to those in the immediate vicinity of the blasts. Three died in the blasts: Martin Richard, an eight-year-old boy; Boston University graduate student Lingzi Lu, twenty-three, who was close to completing her degree in statistics; and Krystle Campbell, twenty-nine, from Medford, Massachusetts, who managed a steakhouse in the town of Arlington, just outside Boston. More than 170 other people were wounded. Martin Richard's seven-year-old sister lost a leg.

Twenty minutes after he deposited the backpack bomb on Boylston Street, Jahar stopped by Whole Foods in Cambridge to pick up some milk. Later that afternoon he sent a text to his friend Baudy Mazaev in Boston, saying, "Yo buddy are yu ok man? Two bombs went off." Baudy replied, "People losing limbs." Jahar wrote back, "I automatically thought of yu man Boston and what not," adding: "Alrighty man stay safe my man, keep in touch."

Lisa Monaco had been in her new job as President Obama's top counterterrorism adviser for only three weeks. She was on the secure phone with her British counterpart when she saw the CNN headline:

Breaking news about bombs in Boston! Monaco immediately hung up and called the FBI and NCTC. Monaco was a native of the Boston suburbs and had attended Harvard. Her oldest brother had raced in a previous Boston Marathon, and her twin brother was among the spectators that day. Monaco, a deliberate and considered former federal prosecutor, had previously worked in key positions in the national security bureaucracy. She was the longest-serving chief of staff to FBI director Robert Mueller and head of the National Security Division at the Department of Justice, which guides all terrorism cases through the legal process, before she had moved into the basement office in the West Wing that gave her close proximity to the president.

Within twenty minutes of seeing the breaking news, Monaco briefed the president in the Oval Office, though the only hard-and-fast information at the time was that there had been two explosions near the finish line of the marathon. Monaco's immediate questions: Is this a diversion for something else? Are we looking at other attacks in other cities? Whoever did this—were they acting alone?

I n the days after the attack, Jahar continued doing what he usually did: attending classes at UMass Dartmouth, where he was a sophomore; going to the gym; playing video games; and tweeting. During those first days, he tweeted:

> **Jahar @J_tsar 16 Apr 2013**   So then I says to him, I says, relax bro my beard is not loaded

> **Jahar @J_tsar 16 Apr 2013**   Nowadays everybody wanna talk like they got somethin to say but nothin comes out when they move their lips; just a bunch of gibberish

> **Jahar @J_tsar 17 Apr 2013**   I'm a stress free kind of guy

The day after the bombings, Jahar went to pick up his car from the shop, where he had left it two weeks earlier. The mechanic who handed over the car thought Jahar appeared nervous, but the rest of Jahar's day was unremarkable: *FIFA Soccer* on PlayStation with a friend, working out. The following day, he had a meal with some friends in his dorm. Having just carried out the most spectacular act of terrorism on American soil since 9/11, Jahar seemed determined to demonstrate that he was a stress-free kind of guy.

The façade was not to last. After carefully reviewing a deluge of video feeds from cameras in the Boylston Street area, at 5:00 p.m. on April 18, FBI officials released video and photos of the suspected bombers. Jahar texted one of his buddies at UMass Dartmouth, advising him, "If yu want yu can go to my room and take what's there . . ."

At around 10:00 p.m. the Tsarnaev brothers armed themselves with five homemade bombs, a 9-millimeter pistol, ammunition, a machete, and a knife. They drove a Honda Civic to the campus of MIT, and at 10:25 they shot and killed Sean Collier, a twenty-seven-year-old MIT police officer. An hour later they carjacked a Mercedes and demanded that the owner, Dun "Danny" Meng, a Chinese immigrant, hand over his ATM card. Tamerlan asked Danny, "Did you hear about the Boston explosion?" With pride, he added, "I did that." While the Tsarnaevs stopped to get gas, Danny escaped on foot and alerted the police, who gave chase.

As they careened through the streets of Watertown, the two brothers threw small homemade bombs out of the vehicle. When the police finally cut them off, an intense firefight ensued. Tamerlan fired at the cops from a position on the street; they fired back, wounding him. Jahar gunned the car to escape and unintentionally ran down his brother, who soon died of his injuries. He was twenty-six.

Early on the morning of April 19, Jahar abandoned the car and fled on foot. He smashed his two cell phones so that he couldn't be tracked, and sought refuge inside the boat behind a house on a quiet residential street.

Hours later the Tsarnaev brothers were publicly identified as the bombing suspects. That afternoon, Jahar's friend Baudy sent him a text: "Jahar man if u can read this just turn urself in for the sake of ur parents, ull be so much safer there's no reason for all of this just do it for everyone's sake it'll be better for u it's time to seek repentance PLEASE JUST TURN YOURSELF IN AND DON'T MAKE IT ANY WORSE."

A nzor Tsarnaev, an ethnic Chechen, was born in Kyrgyzstan following the 1944 mass deportation of Chechens by Joseph Stalin. Anzor
married his wife, Zubeidat, in the mid-1980s. Tamerlan, their oldest
child, was born in 1986, and Jahar, their youngest, in 1993, with two
sisters between them.

On 9/11 they were living more than four thousand miles to the east
of Manhattan, in the grim Caspian port city of Makhachkala, Dagestan, home to a combustible mélange of competing ethnic groups, gangsters, and Salafists. For murky reasons that may have involved crossing
some local gangsters, the Tsarnaevs applied for refugee status in the
States. They wanted out.

Over the course of 2002 and 2003 the family immigrated to Massachusetts. At first everything seemed to be going somewhat well. They
settled in a third-floor apartment on Norfolk Street in Cambridge. Anzor
was an adept car mechanic, and Zubeidat, a cosmetologist, performed
facials in their home. Tamerlan dreamed of becoming an Olympic
boxer, a goal that seemed less and less far-fetched as he swiftly ascended
in the New England boxing scene. Meanwhile, Jahar captained his high
school wrestling team at the Cambridge Rindge and Latin School, and
upon graduation he won scholarships from both the University of Massachusetts Dartmouth and the city of Cambridge.

At UMass Dartmouth, Jahar was seen as an easygoing, party-loving
skateboarder. Facebook documents his active nightlife, and his prolific tweets were the typical musings of an indifferent (indeed, failing)
American college student: homework that was late, sleeping in, sex, girls,
marijuana, and alcohol. A not untypical tweet from Jahar five months
before the Boston bombing read:

> **Jahar @J_tsar 17 Nov 2012** This night deserves Hennessy a
> bad bitch and an o [ounce] of weed the holy trinity

These are hardly the preoccupations of an Islamist zealot, and indeed, until just before the bombing, it's hard to find evidence that Jahar
believed in much of anything. He stands in stark contrast to many of

the militants in this book, who more closely followed the incremental road from fundamentalism to terrorism outlined in Mitch Silber's 2007 study for the NYPD. To all outward appearances, Jahar went straight from slacker to violent jihadist. In retrospect, however, his involvement in the world of anti-American jihadism is less mysterious. It seems to have been influenced largely by his older brother, who, by contrast, fit well into the NYPD's profile.

Tamerlan was the star of the tight-knit Tsarnaev family. He was the big and strong son. His mother adored him, and his father, a onetime boxer, encouraged his interest in the sport. The whole family laughed at his jokes. But for someone who dreamed of one day becoming a big-name boxer, who drove around town in a white Mercedes—a perk from his father's car repair business—dressed in the style of a small-time Russian pimp, favoring skin-tight jeans, pointy shoes, and billowing white shirts open to the navel, Tamerlan led a fairly unglamorous life. He had dropped out of community college after two years, in 2008, and then worked as a pizza delivery man.

Tamerlan spent his leisure time drinking and smoking. Worried about this, his mother, experiencing her own deepening of faith, began urging him in early 2010 to embrace his Islamic heritage. Tamerlan, like Nidal Hasan and many of the militants Silber studied, was a "revert," coming to militancy from a Muslim but nonobservant background. He was at the time becoming increasingly disenchanted with life in his adopted country. In a 2010 photo essay about his burgeoning boxing career, titled "Will Box for Passport," Tamerlan said he felt alienated from American society, volunteering, "I don't have a single American friend. I don't understand them."

He added, however, that he wanted to become an American citizen. This was a prerequisite for getting on the U.S. Olympic team, the dream he saw becoming ever more attainable. In 2010 he won the Rocky Marciano Boxing Trophy, which made him the Golden Gloves heavyweight champion of New England and one of the top amateur boxers in the States. He was blocked from advancing to the national championship that year, however, because of a rule change that prohibited non-U.S.

citizens from competing, which may have stoked his anger at the American government.

B y 2011 the life that had once seemed a case of the American Dream working its magic began losing its luster for the Tsarnaev family. Fixing up cars and doing facials can't pay for much in the *haute bourgeois* neighborhood of Cambridge, Mass. Anzor got into an altercation at a Boston restaurant and was struck in the head with a steel pole, an injury from which he never quite recovered. Then his business took a dive and he became ill, diagnosed with cancer. The family now subsisted on food stamps and welfare payments, and in August 2011, Anzor and Zubeidat filed for divorce. Anzor went back to Dagestan, while his wife found a new identity in fundamentalist Islam, forgoing her high heels and tight skirts to adopt a veil. In 2012 she was accused of shoplifting sixteen hundred dollars' worth of clothes from Lord & Taylor. Bella and Ailina, the couple's daughters, moved out of the family home and settled in New Jersey, where Bella was subsequently arrested on a charge of distributing marijuana. Tamerlan told a confidante that he heard a "voice" in his head that told him to do certain things. The Tsarnaev family was coming apart at its many seams.

In June 2010, Tamerlan had married Katherine Russell, his on-again, off-again girlfriend. They had met in a downtown nightclub. The match did not thrill Katherine's family; the Eurotrashy hustler turned Islamist zealot didn't quite jibe with the WASPy Russell family. Both Katherine's grandfather and her father, Warren K. Russell III, an emergency room physician, were graduates of Phillips Exeter Academy and Yale. The couple soon had a baby girl, and Tamerlan and Katherine lived on welfare payments until they ran out. Katherine started working as many as eighty hours a week as a home health aide; Tamerlan was unemployed.

As he drew deeper into the world of Islam, Tamerlan, the onetime Olympic contender, quit boxing entirely and traded his flashy clothes for a uniform of sweatpants and T-shirts. He was now a very long way from his conception of himself as a larger-than-life hero, an illusion his adoring family had so long kept intact. This was, in Silber's phrase, Tamerlan's cognitive opening to the world of militant Islam, in which he seems to have found a refuge—an arena where he could, perhaps, still be in control, still be influential and larger than life. The first recipient of that influence was Katherine, who converted to Islam, took a new name, Karima, and started wearing a head scarf. Tamerlan's most promising acolyte by far was Jahar.

"His brother pressured [Jahar] a lot," says Jahar's friend Baudy. "His brother would have had the most influence, especially when his dad left. That's the cultural thing. . . . Before, [Jahar] wouldn't pray. But then he did. The only reason Jahar started to was because he lived in the same house." Jahar's own cognitive opening appears to have been his parents' acrimonious divorce, after which he suddenly had no father around. His sisters, too, had left Boston. Jahar's wrestling team traditionally asked the families of departing seniors to attend the last match of the year; on the night of Jahar's final match, there were no Tsarnaev family members to give flowers and snap pictures. Into the void left by his absent parents and sisters stepped Tamerlan.

While tapping the phone of a militant in Chechnya, Russian intelligence officials overheard a conversation with Tamerlan's mother, who told the militant that her son was ready to die for Islam. The Russians told the FBI that Tamerlan had embraced radical Islam and that he might travel to Russia to join a militant group. In March 2011, FBI agents consequently opened an "assessment" of Tamerlan, which, though not a formal "investigation," allowed them to run Tamerlan's phone number through a series of U.S. government databases to see if he was in contact with anyone suspicious. He was interviewed by agents, but the FBI found no grounds for further action. The file on Tamerlan was closed on June 24, 2011. When Russian officials went to the CIA in September 2011 to emphasize their concerns about Tamerlan, his name was added to the TIDE list (the largest, least urgent watchlist), which was enough, probably, to slow the wheels of his application for citizenship, but not enough to reopen his FBI case.

Tamerlan was lucky to have evaded far more serious legal action around this time. On September 11, 2011, Brendan Mess, Erik Weissman, and Rafi Teken were murdered in Waltham, Massachusetts. Investigators reported that the victims' throats were slashed so viciously that they were almost decapitated, and their bodies and the apartment were strewn with copious high-quality marijuana. There was no sign of forced entry; the murderer appeared to know the three victims. Mess was one of Tamerlan's best friends, and Tamerlan had been investigated for violence before—cops had intervened in 2009, after he hit his live-in girlfriend, though the charges were dismissed. But law enforcement officials never questioned him about the 2011 case, which remained unsolved until after the Tsarnaevs were suspected in the Boston bombings.

It was another case of missed signals, of a lack of communication between the arms of U.S. law enforcement. If FBI allegations are correct, Tamerlan was involved in the triple slayings and was a dangerous killer well before 2013—yet he evaded even the no-fly list.

Instead, in January 2012, Tamerlan told his family that he had decided to return to Dagestan, supposedly to renew his Russian passport. Once in Dagestan, he became close to Magomed Kartashov, a distant cousin who in 2011 had founded an organization called the Union of the Just, a group of anti-American Islamists who wanted to bring sharia law to the Caucasus but were not engaged in violence. At the same time, Tamerlan began attending a Salafist mosque. Russian security officials have claimed that he met with violent Islamist extremists in Dagestan, but U.S. intelligence services have not been able to confirm those allegations. With the same combination of heroic aspirations and practical mediocrity that had characterized his life in the United States, it seems that Tamerlan went to Dagestan with the notional plan to join an Islamist group fighting the Russians, but failed in his quest. The trip was, nonetheless, his passage into jihadization.

In mid-July 2012, Tamerlan returned to the States, his full beard an outward sign of his heightened radicalization. In November he confronted a Muslim grocery store manager who had advertised halal Thanksgiving turkeys. Tamerlan asked the manager, "Why are you pushing Muslims to celebrate this holiday when it is just for Americans?" When a preacher at the Islamic Society of Boston said that same month that it was permissible for Muslims to celebrate American holidays such as the Fourth of July and Thanksgiving, Tamerlan stood up in the middle of the mosque and loudly declared that the celebration of any such holiday was not allowed in Islam. (Salafists do not celebrate birthdays or holidays, believing that such celebrations are un-Islamic.)

Two months later, a speaker at the mosque said that Dr. Martin Luther King Jr. was a great man. Tamerlan again stood up, this time shouting that the preacher was a "nonbeliever" and was "contaminating people's minds." Other worshippers in the congregation shouted, "Leave now!" at Tamerlan until he left the mosque. Later, several elders from the mosque met with him and told him to stop interrupting prayer services, after which he ceased such public displays.

At the Cambridge mosque, Tamerlan struck up an unlikely friendship with Donald Larking, an elderly invalid who had recently converted from Catholicism. Like so many other militants, Tamerlan was increasingly hanging out only with those who confirmed his radicalizing views, a role Larking, a rabid conspiracy theorist, ably filled. Tamerlan started recommending to acquaintances *The Protocols of the Elders of Zion,* which purports to reveal a secret plan by the Jews to take over the world. Both Tamerlan and Jahar came to share their mother's belief that 9/11 was engineered by the U.S. government to create mass hatred for Muslims. Seven months before the Boston bombing, Jahar tweeted:

> **Jahar @J_tsar 2 Sep 2012**   Idk why it's hard for many of you to accept that 9/11 was an inside job, I mean I guess fuck the facts y'all are some real #patriots #gethip

Tamerlan maintained a YouTube account that took on an increasingly militant tone. He posted a well-produced video about the prophecy that an Islamic army carrying black banners would bring true Islam to the Muslim world. The video showed al-Qaeda fighters training in Afghanistan. Such explicit promotion of jihadist ideology, public though it was, either went unnoticed by law enforcement or was not deemed menacing enough to reopen Tamerlan's FBI case.

The Tsarnaevs downloaded an issue of *Inspire,* of which they were dedicated fans, that featured an article about making bombs out of pressure cookers and gunpowder from fireworks. In February 2013, Tamerlan bought forty-eight firework mortars, loaded with eight pounds of explosive powder. Six weeks later, on March 20, the Tsarnaevs went to a firing range in Manchester, New Hampshire, where they rented two 9-millimeter pistols and spent an hour practicing shooting them. During this period the two brothers constructed a number of homemade bombs from pressure cookers, explosive powder, shrapnel, and electronic components.

Jahar was finally going to be someone other than a slacker student and small-time drug dealer, and he couldn't resist telegraphing his upcoming action hero role. In the weeks before the bombings, he held forth to his Twitter followers:

> **Jahar @J_tsar 21 Mar 2013**   Evil triumphs when good men do nothing

And:

> **Jahar @J_tsar 8 Apr 2013**   If you have the knowledge and the inspiration all that's left is to take action

Even more overtly, he created a second Twitter account a month before the bombing in which he shed his slacker persona entirely, exchanging it for rote yet ominous zealotry:

> **Ghuraba @Al_firdausiA 13 Mar 2013** It's our responsibility my brothers & sisters to ask Allah to ease the hardships of the oppressed and give us victory over kufr [the infidels]

Around the same time, he bragged to a friend that he knew how to build a bomb. He even discussed "martyrdom" operations, telling a friend that martyrs "die with a smile . . . and go straight to heaven." Two days before the bombing, Jahar tweeted:

Jahar @J_tsar 13 Apr 2013   Got me a haircut, I don't usually do those

He had good reason to cut his distinctive shaggy locks; he wanted to be less recognizable when he planted his backpack bomb.

A resident of Watertown discovered Jahar hiding in his dry-docked boat and called the police. The police apprehended Jahar and took him to Beth Israel Hospital in downtown Boston, where he lay unconscious for one day. Members of the FBI's High-Value Detainee Interrogation Group (HIG) waited outside his bedroom door for him to wake up. When he did, the agents used the "public safety exception" to forgo reading him his Miranda rights. Jahar, still seriously wounded, answered questions in writing or by making facial expressions.

He described freely how he and his brother had contemplated suicide attacks and had decided to set off bombs during Boston's July 4 celebration. Because they managed to build a number of bombs in their Cambridge apartment faster than they had anticipated, they opted to target the Boston Marathon instead. He told investigators that they had had no assistance from any terrorist organization and had acted entirely on their own, motivated by their anger about the wars in Afghanistan and Iraq.

This was yet another lone-wolf attack, yet another case where the terrorists' very isolation from any organization made their plans—while necessarily far smaller in scale than a 9/11—invisible to the law enforcement apparatus. The persistence and deadliness of the lone-wolf threat were by now abundantly obvious. After the Boston bombings, central questions once again came to the fore: What could law enforcement agencies learn from these cases? And how could they be better at preventing them? Neither new nor established counterterrorism measures had caught the Tsarnaevs.

One possible way forward could be found within the FBI itself, where a little-known unit had been developing an alternative method of identifying terrorists before they struck.

---

eep inside the vast, wooded marine base in Quantico, Virginia, within earshot of the outdoor firing ranges that dot the base, is the nondescript office building housing the FBI's Behavioral Analysis Unit (BAU). The BAU is split into four sections: white-collar crime, crimes against children, crimes against adults, and counterterrorism. The latter section, BAU 1, was founded in 2003 to deal with the flood of requests that had started to come in from FBI case agents around the country who were now working on terrorism cases and needed guidance. The analysts at BAU 1 work with agents to advise when and how to intervene in cases in which there is often great uncertainty about what might be going on inside a suspected terrorist's head.

The approach of BAU 1 stands in marked contrast with the NYPD's influential examination of the radicalization process. The NYPD focused largely on the outward manifestations of radicalization: extremists' turn to Salafist beliefs; their wearing of traditional Islamic clothing and involvement in social activism; the politicization of their views about U.S. foreign policy; their separation from society; and finally, jihadization, which could take the form of travel abroad for training or bonding activities at home with other militants.

The FBI behavioral analysts use a different framework. They focus on behaviors that show that someone is on what they term the "pathway to violence." The ideology enabling this pathway is a secondary concern; whether they are dealing with neo-Nazis or jihadists, it is the *actions* along the pathway that can determine whether someone might carry out a terrorist attack. Indeed, analysts believe the pathway framework is useful for analyzing any individual who might be planning a violent crime. While the NYPD focused on religiosity, tracing a process that could merely describe someone's conversion to ultrafundamentalism, the BAU looks for universal indicators of someone who might engage in violence, as well as the inhibitors that might keep that individual from doing so.

The pathway-to-violence concept is rooted in the work of psychologists and law enforcement officials who have made a deep study of criminal behavior. In 1988, Reid Meloy, a forensic psychologist and the chief of the Forensic Mental Health Division for San Diego County, published a classic text in the field, *The Psychopathic Mind,* which makes an important distinction between "affective" aggression and "predatory" aggression. An FBI analyst described the difference:

"If you're in a bar and somebody spills a drink on you, nine times out of ten people are going to say, 'Don't worry about it. Buy me a new drink and we'll call it even.' One time out of ten it's going to lead to a fight. Most of those fights are going to be 'affective,' and they're going to fight it out in the bar or out in the street. A very, very small percent are going to say, 'Don't worry about it, no harm no foul.' And they're going to watch where you sit in the bar, and they're going to follow you home and then they're going to drive around your house a few times to see if neighbors are watching or dogs are barking or lights are on. And then they're going to see if the back door is open and they're going to come and slit your throat. That's 'predatory' violence."

The distinction between affective and predatory violence helped to inform the work of Frederick Calhoun, one of the pioneers in the emerging field of "threat management," an offshoot of criminology that focuses on preventing violent crime. Calhoun entered the field in a circuitous manner. In the mid-1980s he was a professional historian with a PhD dissertation on Woodrow Wilson's military interventions to his name when the U.S. Marshals Service, which was preparing to celebrate its bicentenary, asked him to write its history. In the course of his research, Calhoun heard that the marshals had kept some three thousand records of threats to federal judges, whom they are sworn to protect, going back to 1980.

Calhoun was intrigued. After wrapping up the history book, he painstakingly constructed a database of all the threats the marshals had documented, then brainstormed questions the data might answer. The big one: Did threats actually result in violence? Calhoun came to something of a counterintuitive conclusion: people who made threats to federal judges almost invariably did not act on them; those who killed judges made no threats. This finding would come to save a lot of U.S. marshals valuable time; instead of running down every idle threat, they could focus on other behaviors that might better indicate whether someone might do violence: Was the person scoping out the courthouse? Had he told anyone that he was familiar with a judge's schedule?

Like many American innovations, the science of threat management began in California, more specifically in Hollywood. Its prehistory starts with Gavin de Becker, whom Hollywood stars made their leading choice for protection from the late 1970s onward. De Becker's roster of clients has included Elizabeth Taylor, Richard Burton, John Travolta, Oprah, and Madonna, all of whom contended with stalkers and even threats from rabid fans. In 1981, a Jodie Foster–obsessed John Hinckley underlined how dangerous some of these fans could be when, outside the Washington Hilton, he attempted to assassinate President Ronald Reagan to win the actress's affection. Reagan was lucky to survive.

By 1989 de Becker and his firm had profiled more than five thousand individuals who had made a threat to someone on his roster of stars. From this vast array de Becker invented a screening system that examined "pre-incident indicators" that helped to filter out "signals" from "noise" to focus on the individuals whose threats needed to be taken most seriously. He called the system MOSAIC. De Becker came to believe that the most effective process for predicting violence was to establish whether a history of violence or violent intent was present in a given case. To protect his clients it was more important to understand this *process* than to get too hung up on *motive*. The MOSAIC program was so effective that the Supreme Court police and the U.S. Capitol police adapted it for their purposes.

Calhoun kept hearing about de Becker's work during his research into threats against judicial officials. He invited himself to de Becker's office in Los Angeles, where they spent the day talking. De Becker helped Calhoun sell the idea of using his database of threats to create a customized version of MOSAIC for use by the Marshals Service. The two went on to develop another MOSAIC for assessing risks to abortion clinics, which the marshals also protected.

Calhoun, together with a colleague, Stephen Weston, who had commanded a unit of the California Highway Patrol that investigated threats against state officials, synthesized their work on predicting violence in the 2009 primer *Threat Assessment and Management Strategies,* which became a must-read in the field. Based on a series of case studies of violent criminals, the book identifies a six-stage process through which a predatory aggressor, which the authors term a "hunter," generally moves before committing an act of violence. The first is grievance, the motive or rationale underlying the act. The second is ideation, during which the grievance matures into the idea that violence is both justified and necessary. Then comes research and planning, the phase during which the plot is constructed. Next is preparation, finding the right weapon or mode of assault. Then breach, enacting the plan to get inside whatever security perimeter surrounds the target. And finally, attack.

A key element of Calhoun and Weston's analysis is that it is neither psychological nor sociological. They write that they had "no pretense of understanding what goes on inside the head of a hunter. Why each hunter acts the way he or she does is unique to each and, in fact, may never be fully known or understood." Echoing de Becker, they concluded that understanding the process that led to violence was a useful way of predicting a hunter's actions, as his motive could be murky and multilayered and often not fully knowable, even to the perpetrator himself. This kind of theorizing helped shape the thinking of the FBI's behavioral analysts. In the words of one counterterrorism analyst, "We don't get as wrapped round the axle with philosophies, with radicalization and the fundamentalist. Our focus is more on behavior. What have they done? What can we observe? What have we documented?"

The FBI analyst outlined the application of behavioral analysis to one suspect's case. The suspect had written a letter to his local city council to protest a neighbor dumping leaves on his property; separately, angry at the local school board, he had written another letter; later he filed a lawsuit against a different neighbor. "That was interpreted by the case agent as 'Look, he's mad at everybody. He's just a cork waiting to pop,'" the analyst explained. "But behaviorally we looked at it and said, 'No, that's rule-following behavior. That's a guy who resolves conflict exactly the way our system is built to resolve conflict. If we saw him taking matters into his own hands that would be far more concerning.'"

The BAU's pathway-to-violence framework follows Calhoun and Weston's six-stage process, beginning with a grievance. According to the analyst, "We don't mean grievance like, 'I'm mad because the guy cut me off in traffic.' Grievance that is the kind that sort of eats at your core. You complain about it. You let it fester." This can then lead to ideation and then to planning: "Let's say you're angry at your wife. Let's say that you can't stand the way she cooks meatloaf or the way she incessantly talks to her mother. Whatever it is about your wife that drives you crazy. So just having that grievance might exist for a lot of people. Fewer of those people are going to move on to ideation. And sometimes that's just a fantasy, that's thinking, 'You know if she weren't in my life, if I could make something bad happen to her, I wouldn't have to deal with this.' And for a lot of people, that fantasy is sufficient. But fewer still move on from ideation to research and planning. 'Okay, so I'm online and I'm checking what are the local laws on this: Would it be justifiable if she did this? Would it be accidental? What's the difference between first-degree and second-degree murder in this state? What are the penalties associated with that?'"

Then there is preparation and breach, in which "they'll do dry runs. They'll say, 'Okay, on the date when this has to happen it has to go smoothly, so I'm going to go a week in advance or two weeks in advance just to see what security looks like.'" The analyst offered that "the 9/11 hijackers, for example, tested security."

In 2013, Calhoun and Weston published another book, *Concepts and Case Studies in Threat Management,* which developed their theories further. In it, they lay out a series of "inhibitors" that tend to prevent someone from going down the pathway to violence, such as "family ties, financial resources, holding down a good job, religious beliefs." Sometimes these inhibitors "topple like dominoes, with one inhibitor knocking over the next in a sequence of decline—frequently, rapid decline." The loss of a job, for instance, might trigger a divorce, and that might trigger, in turn, the loss of a house, and so on.

Agents working at the BAU also found this a fruitful way to consider the pathway to violence, as it accounted for cases in which progress along the pathway accelerated or decelerated depending on what was going on in an individual's life. One analyst explained, "If we can look at your life and see you're at the preparation phase—you're shooting paintballs, you're exercising daily, you're preparing—that's concerning to us. We look at the things in your life that will keep you from acting out, versus the things that are encouraging that. And if it's entirely lopsided, then you're either much higher risk or much lower risk."

Analysts working in counterterrorism wouldn't reference specific cases, but they offered examples of the kind of work they do: "A case agent will come to us and say, 'We have somebody that we're concerned about for X, Y, and Z reasons. He's saying bad things online. He's started dressing in a fundamentalist way, and he's got a picture of himself on Facebook with a plastic AK-47. Is he going to blow something up?' We look at the pathway-to-violence concepts: Where is he on this pathway, if at all? And we tell them often, 'Just because you're on this pathway— probably most of society is somewhere on this pathway—it does not mean you're going to end up there.'"

The BAU agents cited a case in the Midwest in which a terrorism suspect was doing and saying things that a case agent found worrying. The agent called the BAU in for a threat assessment, which it made by seeking input from the agent, a linguist, and the surveillance team following the suspect. When the analysts then met with the agent, they asked for his assessment of the suspect "on a scale from one to ten," with ten being "he's going to blow something up tomorrow" and one being no threat at all. The agent said he believed the suspect was a "nine." The analysts countered, "We think a one." Unlike the case agent, embroiled in his particular investigation, the BAU analysts based their assessment on a holistic view of similar cases nationwide.

Beyond the pathway to violence and a lack of "inhibitors," another key indicator of future violence, the behavioral analysts have found, is what they term "leakage." Leakage was identified by the FBI in 1999 in the context of school shootings, emerging from the observation that a student who was going to do something violent had often intentionally or unintentionally revealed something significant about the impending act, anything from confiding in a friend to making ominous "they'll be sorry" remarks.

What was true of school shootings turned out to be true for terrorist crimes as well. In an ongoing study of some eighty terrorism cases since

2009, the FBI found that leakage happened more than 80 percent of the time. Those to whom information was leaked, termed "bystanders," were broken down into peers, family members, authority figures, and strangers. FBI analysts found an average of three bystanders per case, and in one case as many as fourteen. Some bystanders saw radicalization behavior. Others saw actual plotting and planning, such as the accumulation of weapons, self-educating about how to make explosives, or preparations to travel to a field of jihad.

FBI analysts were dismayed by how common it was for bystanders to know that a radicalized individual was up to something. Analysts graphed out the bystanders who were most likely to come forward with information versus those least likely to do so. Peers were aware of the most concerning information, but they were the least likely to volunteer it. Family members were often aware of both radicalization and planning, but they came forward less often than authority figures such as college professors, supervisors, military commanders, or clerics. These figures were reasonably likely to offer information but were more aware of a suspect's radical sympathies than of any actual plotting.

Strangers were the most likely to come forward, which could be helpful; a tip from a clerk at a New Jersey Circuit City who in 2006 was asked to make copies of a videotape on which he saw men shooting off weapons and shouting "Allahu Akbar!" developed into the Fort Dix case. Strangers made up only 5 percent of the bystanders with useful information about a suspect, however, which raised an interesting problem for the "If You See Something, Say Something" counterterrorism campaign that was targeting that 5 percent, rather than the 95 percent of the peers, family members, and authority figures who generally had the most useful information about a militant. The "If You See Something, Say Something" campaign also generated a number of false positives from suspicions of, say, a Middle Eastern man taking a photo of a bridge.

The prevalence of leakage in terrorism cases opened up some potential investigative avenues for the FBI. As one agent put it, "If you're going to commit a significant act of terrorism, I don't think it's possible to do that without having some leakage someplace. In the future perhaps we can pick that up either through behavioral study, through technical coverage, or through some type of investigative technique."

The pathway-to-violence framework, the presence or absence of inhibitors, the leakage phenomenon—these lenses have all proved to be fruitful ways of looking at jihadist terrorism cases. Yet even with the founding of BAU 1 in the wake of the 9/11 attacks, too often its behavioral analysis has been applied only after the fact.

The Boston Marathon bombers began with a grievance, which was the belief that Muslims were under attack by the United States. They then moved to ideation, where they came to believe that it was necessary to avenge this grievance. This prompted them to the research and planning stage: reading *Inspire* for instruction on how to build bombs. For preparation, they bought the fireworks and pressure cookers to build the bombs. Breach was easy, as it required simply showing up at the marathon, where they then launched their attack.

The inhibitors that might have kept the Tsarnaevs from becoming the Boston bombers had indeed "fallen like dominoes." Tamerlan was both unemployed and unemployable. Jahar, often wreathed in smoke from his joints, was struggling in school and lacked a stabilizing family life after his parents' acrimonious divorce. And while he didn't fit the radicalization process laid out in the NYPD report, he did follow the pathway to violence from grievance through attack. He was also, for all his atypical profile, incorrigibly prone to leakage in the weeks before the bombings—from his ominous tweets, to his boasts that he could build a bomb, to his discussions of martyrdom operations with friends.

A year after the Boston bombings, forensic psychologist Reid Meloy, with British colleague Jessica Yakeley, published a study of terrorists with no connections to formal terrorist organizations. Meloy, who worked as a consultant with the FBI's behavioral analysts, also framed the initial stage leading to violence as "grievance," but his explanation of what that meant is worth quoting at length, as it nicely summarizes Tamerlan Tsarnaev's particular rancor. According to Meloy, the pathway begins with "an event or series of events that involve loss and often humiliation of the subject, his or her continual rumination about the loss, and the blaming of others. Most people with grievances *eventually grieve their loss,* but for those unwilling or unable to do so, often the most narcissistically sensitive individuals, it is much easier to convert their shame into rage toward the object which they believe is the cause of all their suffering. Such intense grievances require that individuals take no personal responsibility for their failures in life . . . they are 'injustice collectors.'"

What follows this stage, Mcloy explains, is "moral outrage": "He embeds his personal grievance in an historical, religious, or political cause or event. The suffering of others, which may be misperceived or actual, provides emotional fuel for his personal grievance. He closely identifies with the 'victimized' group, whether they be aborted fetuses, an endangered animal species, rain forests, gun owners, Muslims. . . . What is ironic is that the lone terrorist often has never actually suffered oppression or victimization as a member of the group with whom he identifies. This is a *vicarious* identification." Tamerlan was hardly oppressed; the country he decided to attack had welcomed him and his family as refugees, he and his siblings had attended free American schools, and his family had survived on welfare payments when the going got tough. Jahar was given scholarships to help him with college.

Personal grievance and moral outrage are then "framed by an ideology." As with the pathway-to-violence framework, the nature of the ideology is secondary; its function is to allow the perpetrator some justification for the violent act he is planning. Meloy explained, "Upon closer examination, these conscious belief systems are quite superficial; subjects will cherry pick phrases from the relevant authoritative text to justify their desire to kill others. . . . This framing is absolutist and simplistic, providing a clarity that both rationalizes behavior and masks other, more personal grievances." This was true of the Tsarnaevs, who, like many lone wolves, had a limited, opportunistic understanding of their faith. For both brothers, the combination of Binladenist propaganda such as *Inspire,* anti-American resentments, and the absence of moderating influences was enough to flatten their conception of Islam into a justification for lethal vengeance.

Hindsight is twenty-twenty, yet one cannot help but wonder if, had law enforcement been more attuned to the Tsarnaevs' behaviors in the years and months before the bombings, things might have ended differently. Would BAU 1 have recommended keeping Tamerlan's FBI investigation open? Could Jahar's darkening tweets have been flagged for the warnings they were? It certainly seems to justify further study of the *process* of lone wolves, more than a fruitless comparison of superficially similar individuals—every reader of Awlaki's blog, every ultra-fundamentalist, every loner who prefers to wear a *thobe*—most of whom have no motive for violence.

Yet the question of "why?" can't help but confound. Two books and hundreds of news articles have been written about the Tsarnaevs, and the trial of Jahar produced many thousands of pages of testimony, yet we are still no closer to a complete explanation of why two brothers from Cambridge murdered their fellow citizens. After all, plenty of people object to American foreign policy in the Muslim world, many people have disappointments in life, and families often fall apart, but few people turn to violence for these reasons.

Perhaps this says something about the fundamental nature of evil acts; you can point to someone's disappointments in life or how they might have been swayed by bin Laden's ideology, but acts such as those of the Tsarnaevs remain as fundamentally inexplicable as they are pointless. To repeat Calhoun and Weston's important observation, "Why each hunter acts the way he or she does is unique to each and, in fact, may never be fully known or understood." We can, perhaps, add an addendum to this dictum, which is that even the perpetrator himself often cannot really explain the "why" in any meaningful way. Jahar sat through his months-long trial as if it were happening to someone else, never defending his actions or expressing any hint of remorse. On May 15, 2015, not long after the second anniversary of the bombings, a jury sentenced him to death. For the first time he addressed the families of the victims who were in court that day, saying, finally, "I am sorry for the lives that I've taken, for the suffering that I've caused you, for the damage that I've done. Irreparable damage."

As he handed down the death sentence, Judge George O'Toole told

Jahar, "Whenever your name is mentioned, what will be remembered is the evil you have done. No one will remember that your teachers were fond of you. No one will mention that your friends found you funny and fun to be with. No one will say you were a talented athlete, or that you displayed compassion in being a Best Buddy, or that you showed more respect to your women friends than your male peers did. What will be remembered is that you murdered and maimed innocent people and that you did it willfully and intentionally. You did it on purpose."

The judge closed his remarks by invoking Verdi's opera *Otello,* in which the evil Iago tries to justify his malice by saying that "I believe in a cruel God." O'Toole said, "Surely someone who believes that God smiles on and rewards the deliberate killing and maiming of innocents believes in a cruel God. That is not, it cannot be, the God of Islam. Anyone who has been led to believe otherwise has been maliciously and willfully deceived."

CHAPTER 11

FUTURE JIHAD

PERHAPS WE WILL HAVE TO LIVE WITH AN ACCEPTABLE LEVEL OF
VIOLENCE.

—British home secretary Reginald Maudling,
following a visit to Northern Ireland in 1971

S econds before he detonated the bomb concealed in his truck, Moner
 Mohammad Abusalha, a Florida native and rabid Miami Heat fan,
radioed nearby fighters, saying, "I see Paradise and I can smell Paradise."

On the day of the suicide bombing, May 25, 2014, al-Qaeda's Syrian affiliate tweeted out a picture of Abusalha holding a cat, with the
caption, "Abu Hurayra Al-Amriki ['the American father of the cat'] performed a martyrdom operation in Idlib." Back in Florida, Abusalha's
family learned their son's fate from news reports. He was the first American suicide attacker to die in Syria.

In the martyrdom video that al-Qaeda soon released, Abusalha is
shown tearing up his U.S. passport and setting it on fire, after which he
appears holding an AK-47 and delivers a diatribe to the camera. He appeals to fellow militants in the States, saying in English that coming to
fight with al-Qaeda is so simple that he arrived in Syria "with only twenty
dollars in my pocket." He promises that "Allah made it easy for me" to
travel from the States to Turkey and from there into neighboring Syria.

Abusalha paints a grim picture of his former life compared with the
newly embraced joys of being a holy warrior: "Just sitting down five
minutes drinking a cup of tea with mujahideen is better than anything

I've ever experienced in my whole life. I lived in America! I know how it is. You have all the fancy amusement parks, and the restaurants, and the food, and all this crap and the cars and you think you're happy. You're not happy, you're never happy. I was never happy. I was always sad and depressed. Life sucked. . . . All you do is work forty, fifty, sixty hours a week."

Over footage of a woman in a black burka shooting an automatic rifle, Abusalha tells the story of a Russian woman fighting for al-Qaeda who supposedly conducted a suicide operation in Pakistan. He says, "She's a thousand men. Not like you men who sit at home." In the Paradise of martyrdom, he promises, "A tree will pick the fruit off of itself and hand it to you," while you enjoy the company of a woman so lovely "you would die from her beauty."

Abusalha also threatens an al-Qaeda attack on his home country: "You think you are safe where you are in America or Britain. . . . You are not safe. We are coming for you: Mark my words."

Toward the end of the video, Abusalha contemplates his impending death. Fighting back tears, he addresses his family back in Florida, saying, "I love you, Mom," and to his oldest brother, "I love you, bro. . . . Look after our sister and our little brother." The camera then shows a truck decorated with the distinctive black-and-white al-Qaeda flag driving off before, in the distance, it is lost in a massive explosion. Age twenty-two, Moner Mohammad Abusalha, of Vero Beach, Florida, was dead, and along with him, a contingent of Syrian soldiers.

Despite its DIY aesthetic, Abusalha's videotape represented a carefully honed recruiting pitch for the Westerners whom al-Qaeda and its splinter group, ISIS, wanted to draw into the Syrian war. Its message: that it was easy to come and fight in Syria; that life in the West was nothing compared with the life you led as a holy warrior; that only real men fought jihad; and that "Paradise" would welcome "martyrs" with beautiful women. Propaganda for previous fields of jihad, from Afghanistan in the 1980s to Bosnia in the 1990s and Iraq after the U.S. invasion of 2003, had made similar claims. Recruitment efforts to the Syrian war, however, were to prove successful on a scale al-Qaeda had never before achieved—and that Western governments did not anticipate.

As the events of the "Arab Spring" began unfolding in early 2011, Anwar al-Awlaki and his colleagues at *Inspire* pushed back on a wave of analysis from Western national security experts that they were becoming increasingly irrelevant. In February 2011 this author posted a piece on CNN.com titled "Al Qaeda the Loser in Arab Revolutions," making the point that al-Qaeda's leaders were watching the events of the Arab Spring unfold with a mixture of glee and frustration: glee because overthrowing the dictatorships and monarchies of the Middle East had long been their central goal; frustration because none of the Arab revolutions had anything to do with al-Qaeda.

Sure enough, the trove of documents recovered in the compound in Abbottabad, Pakistan, where Navy SEALs killed bin Laden on May 2, 2011, showed how al-Qaeda's leader had wrestled with what to do or say about the momentous events then roiling the Middle East—in line with his politics, yet unfolding independent of his influence. He made no public statements, but privately he wrote lengthy memos analyzing what was happening; pointing to the "new factor" of "the information technology revolution," which had helped spur the revolutions; and characterizing them as "the most important events" in the Muslim world "in centuries."

Awlaki, ever more al-Qaeda's global mouthpiece, was more public in his analysis. In an essay titled "The Tsunami of Change," Awlaki made the uncontroversial point that the protests then spreading from Cairo to Bahrain were threatening the Arab world's authoritarian regimes. But disputing commentators such as CNN's Fareed Zakaria, who had recently written that the protests represented "a total repudiation of al Qaeda's founding ideology," Awlaki asserted that "the opposite is the case." Awlaki then turned to this author, writing, "It is interesting to see how [Peter Bergen] doesn't get it right this time. For him to think that because a Taliban-style regime is not going to take over following the revolutions is a too short-term way of viewing the unfolding events." In other words, according to Awlaki, just you wait: Taliban-type theocracies would be coming to the Middle East as the revolutions there unfolded further. As brash and calculating as his statements were, Awlaki better anticipated how the Arab Spring would devolve than did many Western commentators, including this one.

Awlaki also outforecast the Obama administration. With the success of the drone program, U.S. officials were growing justifiably confident that terrorist activity in Pakistan and Yemen was being significantly reduced, but they hadn't foreseen—few did—how the Arab Spring was to give a new lease on life to jihadism across the Middle East. As the Arab Spring rapidly turned into the Arab Winter, plunging states such as Egypt, Libya, and above all Syria into chaos, new jihadist groups emerged, able to operate with relative impunity. The strongest front to emerge was ISIS, which took advantage not only of the political chaos but also of the tools of the revolutions themselves: namely the widespread dissemination of social media, which had helped the Arab Spring's early idealists organize against their authoritarian regimes, and which represented a new frontier in what bin Laden had identified as a revolution in "information technology."

The Nazis went to great lengths to hide their crimes against civilians; ISIS shared them on social media, to be shown around the world and to intimidate anyone who would stand in their way. Videos propagated on YouTube, Facebook, and Twitter were critical to the group's international appeal, enabling ISIS to recruit some thirty thousand "foreign fighters," including thousands from Western countries. Professionally shot, often from multiple angles and in high definition, and fluidly edited to the strains of haunting Islamic chants, the videos projected ISIS's divinely inevitable victory and depicted the executions of Shia civilians. Like snuff movies directed by MTV, they could not have been more different from al-Qaeda's dated productions, which tended to feature the ponderous new leader of the group, Ayman al-Zawahiri, delivering droning monologues to a static camera. ISIS leaders seemed to have instinctively understood that if Vietnam was the first TV war, and the 1991 Gulf War was the first 24/7 cable news war, the war in Syria was the first war in which the main action was captured on social media, a mode of communication that states could do little to control.

Al-Qaeda had only two hundred members around the time of the 9/11 attacks, and had functioned like Harvard, choosing only the elite from among a pool of thousands of militants who had passed through its training camps in Afghanistan. By contrast, ISIS functioned more like the American public school system, taking all comers at all levels of ability to create its insurgent army. Marshall McLuhan's famous, gnomic observation that the "medium is the message" aptly describes the way ISIS created on social media a diverse, distributed network through which anyone, anywhere could sign up for the jihad.

In just the months from September to December 2014, ISIS supporters around the world used at least forty-six thousand Twitter accounts. For Obama's chief counterterrorism adviser, Lisa Monaco, and her colleagues, this posed new and unexpected challenges: "I don't think we've seen the end of this evolution, but I think this is of a different order of magnitude, for instance, from Awlaki and Samir Khan. I remember just a few years ago, as policy makers, we were grappling with *Inspire* and how to handle that, and yet that is something that now feels like the eight-track tape version of inspiring followers and adherents to take action. It's a totally different problem now with beheading videos, and Twitter followers in the tens of thousands."

A key reason for the explosion of ISIS was the particular nature of its jihad against the regime of Syrian dictator Bashar al-Assad. Assad was a secular dictator and also an Alawite, which many Muslims believe to be a heretical branch of Shiism. For the Sunni militants drawn to fight in Syria, including Moner Abusalha, Assad's secularism made him an apostate, the gravest crime in Islam, while his Alawi roots also made him a heretic. The brutal tactics he used against his own people, meanwhile, made him an international pariah. This trifecta made funding the Sunni insurgency in Syria highly attractive for donors in the Gulf. Location was also a major factor. Syria had been the entry point for the thousands of "foreign fighters" who joined Al-Qaeda in Iraq earlier in the decade, and as a result, the group had established a substantial infrastructure in Syria as well as Iraq.

Al-Qaeda had no presence in Iraq before the American invasion in 2003, but it grew there substantially in the years following the arrival of

U.S. troops in the country (which fact the Bush administration tended to gloss over). On October 17, 2004, Iraqi insurgent leader Abu Musab al-Zarqawi issued an online statement pledging allegiance to bin Laden, thus establishing what became known as Al-Qaeda in Iraq, but even after this, al-Qaeda's control seemed tentative. Ayman al-Zawahiri, then al-Qaeda's number two, sent a letter to Zarqawi (which was intercepted by U.S. forces in Iraq in July 2005) urging him to exercise more restraint in his campaign against the Shia, with whom Zarqawi was waging a virulent sectarian war. Zawahiri also gently advocated an end to Zarqawi's televised executions: "Among the things which the Muslim population who love and support you will never find palatable are the scenes of slaughtering the hostages." Although he continued to operate under the al-Qaeda banner, Zarqawi largely ignored these admonishments, continuing to attack the Shia without restraint and to brutalize Sunnis who did not conform to his Taliban-like social policies. It was exactly the playbook that ISIS would use a decade later, albeit on a far more industrial scale.

This long-simmering dispute between al-Qaeda Central and Al-Qaeda in Iraq would eventually contribute to the split that begat ISIS. It was not until early 2014, however, that the schism became official, when al-Qaeda's central leadership posted a notice on jihadist websites saying that ISIS "is not a branch of the al-Qaeda group." Prior to this, ISIS and another local al-Qaeda affiliate, the al-Nusra Front, had been fighting each other in Syria for several weeks. ISIS had in fact recently announced a merger with al-Nusra, but this precipitated conflict as to which organization was to have primary authority in Syria. A leader of al-Nusra rejected the merger with ISIS. ISIS, in turn, rejected Zawahiri's annulment of the merger. (This is a fine example of what Freud usefully termed "the narcissism of minor differences.")

Zawahiri was fed up with ISIS's lack of respect for his leadership of the al-Qaeda network and, by extension, his leadership of the global jihad. He was likely also concerned by its recent brutal campaign of beheadings, fearing it would alienate ordinary Syrians. Rather than displaying any heartfelt interest in the issue, his concerns about Muslim civilian casualties were tactical: al-Qaeda's leader had seen this movie before. When Al-Qaeda in Iraq imposed its brutal rule on the country's population, it had caused the Sunni tribes in western Iraq to rebel in 2006. Known as the "Sunni Awakening," that uprising led, with a heavy assist from the U.S. military, to al-Qaeda losing control of western Iraq by 2008.

Meanwhile, the al-Nusra Front engaged in the kind of alliance building that al-Qaeda affiliates had rarely been able to pull off, given that most militant leaders saw compromise as a deviation from their God-given beliefs. Al-Nusra allied with more moderate elements of the Syrian opposition to fight against ISIS, and it didn't systematically target Muslim civilians. Al-Nusra represented what al-Qaeda's core leadership wanted in one of its affiliates: a group that didn't tarnish their brand. The choice was clear for Zawahiri; he repudiated ISIS. It was the first time in its quarter-century history that al-Qaeda had officially rejected one of its affiliates.

Yet ISIS was proving the far more successful offshoot. The seizure of many of Iraq's most important cities, including Mosul in 2014 and Ramadi a year later, demonstrated that ISIS had branched out from being a terrorist group and had turned into a highly effective insurgent army. ISIS also seemed to have learned from the mistakes al-Qaeda made during the first years of the Iraq War, and was providing some level of effective, if brutal, governance to the local Sunni population, something that Al-Qaeda in Iraq had never bothered to do.

ISIS was also perhaps the most well-funded terrorist group in history, benefiting not only from Gulf donors but also from the millions of dollars it had seized from banks in the Iraqi cities and from other revenue streams, including taxation, extortion, oil sales, antiquities sales, and ransoms from kidnappings. The group quickly used its growing reputation as the most fearsome jihadist group in the world to seed itself in roughly a dozen countries. Think of ISIS as a pathogen that preys on vulnerable hosts in the Muslim world. Thus far it has held true that the weaker a Muslim state, the stronger the presence of ISIS. Between the summer of 2014 and the fall of 2015, more than thirty terrorist groups issued statements of support for ISIS or went further and pledged their allegiance to ISIS. Most worrying were the groups that pledged allegiance to ISIS, since this allowed its leadership some measure of control, making these groups more likely to align with ISIS's most radical goal, creating a present-day caliphate across the Muslim world—and, as the ISIS core had, using the most reprehensible tactics to do so.

Terrorist groups in Afghanistan, Algeria, Egypt, Lebanon, Libya, India, Indonesia, Nigeria, Pakistan, the Philippines, and Yemen all pledged allegiance. The Libyan branch of ISIS, which affiliated in November 2014, revealed its new loyalty in particularly brutal fashion. There had been debate in the U.S. intelligence community about whether the Libyan group was a "wannabe" ISIS, a local front rebranding itself rather than an outpost taking orders from the ISIS central command. Clarity came on January 27, 2015, when ISIS gunmen attacked the upscale Corinthia Hotel in the Libyan capital, Tripoli, killing ten. Five victims were foreigners; one was an American. A month later, ISIS released a video showing a dozen members of Egypt's Coptic Christian minority being beheaded on a Libyan beach. Both attacks were celebrated in granular detail in ISIS's premier propaganda venue, *Dabiq* webzine. This, combined with the steady flow of fighters shuttling back and forth between Libya and Syria and Iraq, underlined the links to ISIS central.

The fact was that despite its dispute with al-Qaeda's core leadership, by 2014 ISIS had become the group most responsible for keeping Binladenism alive. Bin Laden was very much a revered figure in ISIS propaganda, and indeed the group saw itself as his rightful heir. Ambitious, resource-rich, and increasingly adept at capturing the imaginations of recruits worldwide, ISIS became, essentially, next-generation al-Qaeda.

Even more than ISIS's fearsome profile abroad, it was cases such as Abusalha's that explained why by 2014 senior U.S. counterterrorism officials were "all Syria, all the time." By the time he died, Abusalha was one of about one hundred Americans who had traveled to Syria or had tried to do so as the civil war there ground on. A year after he died, that number had jumped to some 250 Americans, the majority trying to join ISIS. The group's prioritization of Western recruitment began to preoccupy U.S. counterterrorism officials. ISIS's multiprong, Internet-age propaganda machine seemed proof that it was going about this in a more systematic, informed way than al-Qaeda Central ever had.

The mastery of ISIS's recruitment messaging was twofold: it made the act of joining the group in Syria seem feasible, giving detailed instructions on what to bring and what to expect, and it also made it appealing to Western recruits by promising social services, a brotherhood of like-minded recruits, and potential marriage partners in relatable, easy-to-visualize terms. All this was geared to help the potential recruit jump over the hurdle from idle fantasy to actionable plan—the kind of practical and psychological reservations that had deterred someone like Bernie Culveyhouse from joining al-Shabaab.

ISIS posted online in early 2015 a handy fifty-page booklet, "Hijrah to the Islamic State." *Hijrah* is an Arabic word that means "emigrating for religious reasons." The booklet's jaunty subtitle was, "What to Packup. Who to Contact. Where to Go. Stories & More!" Inside, ISIS aspirants in the United States and other English-speaking countries could read how to make the journey to Syria. Some of the advice was obvious: ISIS told its would-be recruits not to tell "anyone, even family" of their plans. Other tips were subtler. ISIS suggested that anyone trying to reach its de facto capital in Syria, Raqqa, near the Turkish border, should not buy a ticket to Turkey, as enough "foreign fighters" had already passed through Turkey that this might attract attention from law enforcement. It instead advised volunteers to buy a ticket for a less "suspicious" vacation spot, such as Spain or Greece, buying a ticket to Turkey once they arrived there. Round-trip, of course, for appearance's sake.

ISIS recommended bringing a sleeping bag and a good backpack with plenty of pockets "as you will definitely have to move around in *Sham* [Syria] once you get here." A solar charger for electronics was also advised "since electricity is a big problem here," as well as a headlamp suitable for use in dark conditions. Because of the cold of the Syrian winter, recruits were urged to pack a good, warm jacket and a "beanie hat."

Once in Turkey, recruits were told, they would wait in a hotel and make contact with an ISIS facilitator, often a "Twitter contact." ISIS even helpfully provided the Twitter handles of seventeen ISIS recruiters to whom potential recruits could send private direct messages in order to set up their travel from Turkey into Syria. The booklet urged operational security for such messaging, telling recruits to use the Tor browser to disguise their IP addresses and recommending Androids as "securer" than iPhones.

If asked in Turkey about the purpose of their trip, ISIS recruits were advised to say "tourism." To give credibility to this cover story, they were urged to bone up on well-known tourist spots. They were also advised not to pack knives that could be used as weapons, or combat boots that might give away their ultimate purpose in Syria. There was also special advice to ISIS "sisters" (female recruits) not to travel as a "pack" on a plane and to "be chill to the airport officers" because "you're just tourists."

The group painted an idealized yet accessible picture of life under ISIS's rule: recruits would receive free housing, electricity, and water (but not free gas); they would receive free groceries such as pasta, canned foods, rice, and eggs; they would be given monthly allowances and free medical care; and they would pay no taxes. Presenting itself as a real state with plentiful social services and constructed infrastructure was a smart innovation on ISIS's part—it made al-Qaeda's high-flown rhetoric about the restoration of the caliphate seem like concrete reality. *Dabiq* asserted that administrators governed towns after the main ISIS fighting force had moved on. One issue of the webzine included photos with captions showing "services for Muslims," including street cleaning, electricity repairs, care homes for the elderly, and cancer treatment centers for children, while another had a sort of classified ad calling "all Muslim doctors, engineers, scholars, and specialists" to join ISIS. A video showed smiling kids taking amusement park rides at a city fairground in Mosul. According to ISIS propaganda, life in the Islamist utopia was, almost above all, *normal.*

ISIS also promised a place where pious young Muslim men and women could come to find their perfect marriage partner. Given how exacting the standards of many radicalizing Muslims become—Bledsoe, Chesser, Hammami, Awlaki, and others searched outside their milieus for suitably pious "sisters"—and the young target audience of ISIS's campaigns, this was a popular selling point. One of the most active of ISIS's recruits on social media was a Malaysian doctor in her mid-twenties who had married a foreign fighter she met only once briefly before the marriage ceremony. The doctor explained in one of her frequent posts in English that no one would force women recruits to marry, and that marriages consummated under ISIS's black banners were truly "blessed." She helpfully noted that the banks of the Euphrates River were "almost every newly married couples' [sic] favorite spot."

Another 2015 ISIS publication, a one-hundred-page booklet titled simply "The Islamic State," outlined the training regime new male recruits would go through. This included learning how to use "basic firearms" such as AK-47s and also "medium heavy" weapons such as machine guns, mortars, and rocket-propelled grenades, as well as "chemical" and "electronic" warfare. ISIS advised that those who wanted to perform a suicidal "martyrdom" operation "are put on a waiting list," implying that there were more volunteers for suicide operations than ISIS could handle. Page after page showed dead militants "smiling," having seen their home in Paradise just before their souls left their bodies. The bodies of these martyrs, the booklet assured, did not decay. This was an update of a classic jihadist sales pitch; the bin Laden–funded *Jihad* magazine had claimed in the late 1980s that the bodies of those martyred in the Afghan War smelled of perfume.

Collectively, ISIS's English-language propaganda machine offered an answer to the big question: Why would anyone in the United States or the West want to give up his comfortable life to join ISIS? Making it look easy might help one overcome practical objections, but inspiration was another matter. The answer for ISIS's recruits was, as for so many other militants, the desire to belong to something greater than themselves. In the minds of ISIS's recruits the group was doing something of cosmic importance by defending Sunni Muslim civilians from the onslaughts of the Assad regime. The final, inevitable battle between the West and Muslims would presage the arrival of the Mahdi, the Islamic savior, and the victory of Islam; the battle against Assad was its opening salvo.

All this bloviation was made easier to swallow because ISIS was *victorious*. In the summer of 2014 the group released a video showing a bulldozer breaking down the great sand berm that demarcated the Iraq-Syrian border, first established by Britain and France in a secret agreement to carve up the Ottoman Empire following the end of World War I. This was ISIS's symbolic first step toward expunging all vestiges of Western influence in the Arab world. Al-Qaeda had never controlled large swaths of the Middle East. ISIS's territory, by some estimates, was around the size of the United Kingdom and it ruled over millions of people. To quote bin Laden—who was referring to the 9/11 attacks, but might as well have been talking about ISIS's appeal over that of al-Qaeda—"When people see a strong horse and a weak horse, by nature, they will like the strong horse."

As with all totalitarian regimes, mythmaking became essential to ISIS's authority. It celebrated its creation of the perfect state as a way of enchanting new believers. In a propaganda video released in August 2014, shortly after the group had seized control of key Iraqi cities and declared its official name to be simply the Islamic State, a global brigade of fighters (British, Finnish, Moroccan, South African, Trinidadian) all extolled the wonders of living in the caliphate. Filmed during "golden hour," near sunset, the video showed groups of boys with guns and happy ISIS fighters. An ISIS fighter from South Africa said, "I don't have the words. I don't have the words to express myself about the happiness to be here." The video closes with two boys armed with guns in a park waving to the camera. Text on the screen read, "I wish you were here." In other words, "Yes, we have created an Islamist utopia here on earth! And you should be part of it." Another ISIS fighter helpfully noted, "You can still survive even if you don't speak Arabic. You can find almost every race and nationality here."

I t was not much of an exaggeration. In the first four years of the war, fighters from more than ninety countries were believed to have joined the rebels who aimed to topple Assad's regime. Most were from Muslim-majority countries, but by 2015 the total number of Westerners who had fought in Syria came to around 4,500: 1,500 fighters had traveled to

Syria from France; 750 from the United Kingdom; 700 from Germany; 500 from Belgium; more than 150 from the Netherlands; and 150 each from Austria, Denmark, and Canada. Not every fighter had joined ISIS, but most had.

By the summer of 2015 more than four dozen American citizens or residents had been charged with joining or attempting to join ISIS, and some half dozen with attempting to join the al-Nusra Front, which remained al-Qaeda's sanctioned Syrian affiliate. The recruits hailed from around the country and were, by any measure, a diverse group. Among those who joined, attempted, or helped others join were Joshua Van Haften, a thirty-four-year-old white man and registered sex offender from Wisconsin; Tairod Pugh, a forty-seven-year-old African American convert to Islam who had once served in the U.S. Air Force; and Ariel Bradley, a twenty-nine-year-old white woman from Chattanooga who had been raised as an evangelical Christian.

The diversity of ISIS's American recruits was in sharp contrast to an earlier wave of overseas jihadist recruitment from the States. Beginning in 2007, a cohort of U.S. militants was drawn to the Somali civil war to fight alongside al-Shabaab. These volunteers were overwhelmingly Somali Americans, most of whom were from Minnesota.

By contrast, according to FBI director James Comey, in 2014 the FBI was investigating cases in all fifty states. The one hundred and seventeen Americans who had been publicly identified by September 2016 as having joined or tried to join ISIS or al-Nusra hail from twenty-three states: Alabama, Arizona, California, Colorado, Florida, Georgia, Illinois, Maine, Massachusetts, Michigan, Minnesota, Mississippi, Missouri, New Jersey, New York, North Carolina, Ohio, Pennsylvania, South Carolina, Texas, Virginia, Washington, and Wisconsin.

For counterterrorism officials this diversity posed a new set of problems, says Lisa Monaco: "The challenge that we faced five to ten years ago was very different and arguably less complex than what we're facing now. I experienced, when I was at the FBI, a new phenomenon with the young Somali American males traveling to Somalia, but it was a unique enough travel pattern. It was a diaspora community that you could conduct outreach to. It was a difficult problem, but it felt like one where you could have a game plan and try to address it. Similarly, in terms of identifying American fighters going to Pakistan, somebody was gone for weeks and it takes so much effort to get into the FATA [the Federally Administered Tribal Areas, the tribal regions of Pakistan along the Afghan border]. That is of a different ilk than thousands of flights a day going to Istanbul."

This was doubtless true. Flying to Turkey from the States was easy to do, and from there, travel into Syria was also relatively straightforward. By contrast, travel into Somalia or the remote tribal regions of Pakistan's FATA was alone enough to dissuade many militants, and the few available routes could be far more easily monitored. And as the Americans volunteering to fight with ISIS were not from a concentrated diaspora community, there was no obvious vector to reach into the Muslim community to try to find interlocutors to help persuade would-be ISIS recruits to turn back.

Those drawn to ISIS or al-Nusra have also skewed younger and more female than previous generations of American militants. One in five were teenagers—including six teenage girls, the youngest of whom was fifteen. On average, the American individuals involved in Syrian militancy were age twenty-five. And while the majority of ISIS supporters in the States were men, more than one in six of them were women—an unprecedented development. Women were present rarely, if at all, among jihadists in previous holy wars in Afghanistan against the Soviets, in Bosnia against the Serbs, and in the initial insurgency in Iraq against the U.S.-led occupation.

It was likely the wide accessibility of ISIS's messaging that changed its recruitment base, a feature that became compounded as more female role models reached the caliphate. Hoda Muthana, a twenty-year-old from Birmingham, Alabama, who had been studying business at the University of Alabama, made it to Syria. She joined ISIS and became a prolific social media poster and recruiter with the handle "Umm Jihad," or "the mother of jihad." She had told her parents she was going on a college field trip to Atlanta. From Syria she tweeted, "Soooo many Aussies and Brits here. But where are the Americans. Wake up u cowards." In December 2014, Muthana married an Australian fighter; when he was killed on the front lines three months later, she tweeted that he had achieved his long-desired martyrdom. She posed for pictures completely covered in her black *niqab* and holding an AK-47, with four other female friends similarly garbed and posing on top of a fancy white BMW with the caption "chillin in the Khilafa [caliphate]." The takeaway: Jihad was not only your ticket to Paradise; it was also a cool time on the way there. It was the same message Omar Hammami had broadcast for al-Shabaab, but while Hammami's wit and slang had been unique in his group, quickly making him a star, in ISIS, Hoda Muthana was one of many virtual ambassadors of both genders reaching out to impressionable young Americans.

Insurgencies such as the one against the Assad regime can last for many years. Indeed, since World War II, the average insurgency has lasted at least a decade. In 2016 the Syrian civil war was in its fifth year, looking likely to prove to be an important training ground for foreign fighters for many years in the future. That the Syrian conflict provided a large safe haven for groups such as ISIS therefore deeply worried Obama administration officials. It was, unlike Iraq or Afghanistan, an issue that had developed entirely under that administration's watch. Government agencies began paying closer and closer attention to those who traveled to Syria and also those who returned.

U.S. officials were determined to prevent "blowback," or Western recruits returning to their countries of origin trained and radicalized. The historical touchstone for this was the Afghan War against the Soviets and the ensuing civil war, which helped launch bin Laden's al-Qaeda, and during which the 9/11 hijackers trained in Afghanistan. Several of the plotters of the first World Trade Center attack also trained there, but until 9/11 American law enforcement demonstrated little interest in investigating individuals who traveled abroad to fight in an overseas jihad. That changed with the realization that all of the 9/11 hijackers had trained in Afghanistan. Afterward, the government considered all those who had traveled to fields of jihad to be potential terrorists and tracked their activities. As FBI director James Comey explained in 2014, "We see Syria as [we see Afghanistan], but an order of magnitude worse in a couple of respects. Far more people going there. Far easier to travel to and back from. So, there's going to be a diaspora out of Syria at some point, and we are determined not to let lines be drawn from Syria today to a future 9/11."

Fears of blowback accelerated when French authorities arrested a suspect in the May 24, 2014, shooting at the Jewish Museum in Brussels, in which four people were killed. The suspect, Mehdi Nemmouche, had traveled to Syria the previous year, one of many hundreds of French citizens to do so. The attacks in Paris the following year demonstrated that the organization had both the intention and the capability to launch mass casualty attacks in the West and was training Westerners in Syria to carry them out.

For many Americans, the big question after the Paris attacks is: Could it happen here? Several factors make such a massive assault considerably less likely in the States. First, geography: You can drive from France to Syria and back. You can't drive from Syria to New York City. That presents a hurdle for terrorists trained in Syria, who would have to board a plane to the States and who might well be on a watch list. No such barrier exists in Europe; following their training in Syria, a number of the Paris plotters—citizens of France and Belgium—took advantage of Europe's open borders to move around the Continent freely.

Second, there is the sheer volume of Europeans fighting in Syria. By the end of 2016, as we have seen, they numbered around 7,000, including some 3,000 French, German, and British citizens. More than half of the British fighters were estimated to have returned to the United Kingdom. The flow of militants was overwhelming to the national security services tasked with monitoring them. French law enforcement was aware of the terrorists who carried out the *Charlie Hebdo* attacks in February 2015, as well as some among the perpetrators of the massacres in Paris almost a year later, yet these men were still able to execute their plots. By contrast, ISIS and other jihadist groups have trained, at most, a few dozen Americans in Syria, only a couple of whom are known to have returned to the States.

Another safeguard against a mass casualty ISIS attack in America: the defensive measures put in place after 9/11. The formation of new government entities such as the Department of Homeland Security and the National Counterterrorism Center has made the States a far more elusive target for overseas terrorists than it was a decade and a half ago. So too has the vast expansion of resources devoted to counterterrorism in both the intelligence and law enforcement communities, misapplied though such resources have sometimes been.

The United States is not, it must be said, completely insulated from the danger of an attack overseen by ISIS. Aside from the Americans who have fought in Syria, many of ISIS's European recruits are from "Visa Waiver" countries, which means they can travel to the States for up to three months without first obtaining a visa, providing their names do not turn up on a watch list.

Thus far, however, significant blowback from Syria seems unlikely to happen in the United States. For the Americans who have actually traveled there it has often been a one-way ticket; of the twenty-three individuals who have been publicly identified as having reached Syria, nine have died while fighting for ISIS or other militant groups. They simply lacked combat savvy and were killed in the war, as Nicole Mansfield, thirty-three, from Flint, Michigan, was in 2013, or they died in a suicide attack as the Floridian Moner Mohammad Abusalha did. The deaths suggested that ISIS and al-Qaeda's affiliate in Syria did not place any particular value on the lives of their American recruits. There was certainly scant evidence that they planned to turn these recruits around and send them back to carry out attacks in the States.

Even those ISIS-trained fighters who did return have not posed a proven threat to the United States. The only case in which a returned fighter has been charged with plotting an attack in the States is that of twenty-two-year-old Abdirahman Sheik Mohamud of Columbus, Ohio. The government alleges that Mohamud, who left to fight in Syria in mid-April 2014 and returned about two months later, was told by a cleric in al-Qaeda's Syrian affiliate that he should go back to the States to conduct an act of terrorism, and that he discussed a plan with an informant in the States to kill American soldiers at a military base in Texas. According to Mohamud's lawyer, however, he possessed no weapons and no concrete plan of attack and he has pleaded not guilty to a charge of providing material support to a terrorist group.

The relative lack of threat to the American homeland by returning fighters from Syria mirrors the case of the Somali Americans who fought against the U.S.-backed Ethiopian invasion of Somalia, in which blow-back was also feared. In 2011, Representative Peter King, the Republican chairman of the House Committee on Homeland Security, warned about the Americans then fighting in Somalia: "With a large group of Muslim-Americans willing to die as 'martyrs' and a strong operational partnership with al Qaeda leaders in Pakistan and in Yemen, al-Shabaab now has more capability than ever to strike the U.S. homeland." As it turned out, just as was the case in Syria, for many Americans who went to fight in Somalia it was a one-way ticket, and those Americans who returned from the Somali jihad did not attempt or carry out any kind of terrorist attack in the States.

There have certainly been worrisome cases of militants returning to the United States to attempt serious attacks. As we have seen, Najibullah Zazi grew up in New York City and traveled to Pakistan, where he was trained by al-Qaeda to conduct bombings on the New York City subway in 2009. The following year, Faisal Shahzad, trained in bomb-making techniques by the Pakistani Taliban, left a car bomb (albeit a faulty one) undetected in Times Square. It is also worth noting, however, that in none of the successful terrorist attacks in the States since 9/11—the Boston Marathon bombings, the massacre at Fort Hood, the attack in San Bernardino—did any of the perpetrators receive training overseas.

The real threat from ISIS, it has become more and more clear, isn't likely to be Americans trained abroad by the group but rather those inspired by it—once again, the lone-wolf threat. As James Comey noted in 2014 while referring to the December 2013 arrest of Terry Loewen, who was accused of plotting an attack on the Wichita airport in Kansas, "We have made it so hard for people to get into this country, bad guys, but they can enter as a photon and radicalize somebody in Wichita, Kansas."

The "photon" Comey was talking about was, of course, the Internet. The only profile that tied together American militants drawn to the Syrian conflict is that they were active in online jihadist circles. Nine out of ten were posters of jihadist material on Twitter or Facebook, or were in direct contact with ISIS recruiters over social media. Americans drawn to join ISIS or al-Nusra either self-recruited or, in some cases, were wooed via direct contact over the Internet with members of ISIS or al-Nusra.

This raises the question of how we should conceptualize lone wolves in the age of social media. A militant radicalizing in front of his computer by himself at home is now not really alone. He is swimming in a virtual sea of jihadist recruiters, cheerleaders, and fellow travelers who are available for interaction with him 24/7. Contrast this with a classic lone-wolf American terrorist of the past such as the "Unabomber," Ted Kaczynski, who mailed his targets more than a dozen bombs between the late 1970s and the mid-1990s that killed three people and injured some two dozen others, all in the service of his obscure, Luddite beliefs. Kaczynski did this entirely by himself while living like a hermit in a remote cabin in Montana with—forget the Internet—no electricity. Today's lone wolf is instead plugged into a vast self-referential and interactive ecosystem where he or she can virtually, instantly find thousands of other people around the world who share his or her beliefs.

In 1895, Gustave Le Bon, a French sociologist, published *The Crowd: A Study of the Popular Mind,* which remains the seminal text in the field of social psychology. *The Crowd* is rich with insights about how individuals lose both their own personalities and their sense of responsibility when they are part of a crowd. The crowd forms a "collective mind," which is simple-minded, excessively suggestible, primitive, and emotional. The Internet has fostered the formation of virtual crowds—an "imagined community"—and with social media, that crowd is now available around the clock to inspire and cajole in real time.

ISIS creates a virtual, global crowd by appealing to primitive emotions that spur individuals to lose their sense of self and responsibility, all in the service of the ancient dream of the restoration of the caliphate.

Take the case of Alex, a twenty-three-year-old sometime Sunday school teacher living in a remote part of Washington State who converted to Islam. In 2015 multiple members and fans of ISIS spent thousands of hours online with Alex, promising that they would find her a suitable husband and even sending her gifts of chocolate and books about Islam. The teenage Khan siblings of Chicago, for their part, were in touch with virtual recruiters in Turkey and Syria and militants in the United Kingdom before attempting their emigration to the caliphate. In the useful formulation of the Israeli counterterrorism expert Gabriel Weimann, the lone wolf is now part of a virtual pack.

ISIS initially downplayed the merits of homegrown extremism, concentrating on wooing its recruits abroad. Whereas *Inspire* focused largely on inspiring attacks in the West, *Dabiq,* which modeled itself on *Inspire* in many ways, was geared more toward perpetuating ISIS's successful insurgencies in Iraq and Syria. Where *Inspire* included instructions on making bombs and building weapons at home, *Dabiq* encouraged followers to join the jihad at its source. A writer in the third issue of *Dabiq* declared, "This life of jihad is not possible until you pack and move to the #Khilafah."

By early 2015, however, ISIS's message had somewhat shifted. Issue seven of *Dabiq* carried a four-page article extolling the virtues of Amedy Coulibaly, who had conspired with the attackers at the satirical magazine *Charlie Hebdo* and had recently killed four Jews at a kosher supermarket in Paris. Though he self-radicalized in France, Coulibaly had released a video in which he declared his ISIS allegiance. In the spring of 2015, ISIS released a seventy-one-page booklet on the Web titled "How to Survive in the West," essentially a guide for ISIS supporters looking to disguise their views and activities. Tips included making sure to have a Western-sounding nickname so as to attract less suspicion and wearing colored contact lenses after an attack to confuse the police. There were also instructions on how to build a bomb using a microwave oven. ISIS's attacks in Paris in late 2015 confirmed that the organization was now as preoccupied with attacking the "far enemy" in the West as with imposing its brutal rule over the "near enemy" in the Middle East.

I n Garland, Texas, on May 3, 2015, the United States saw its first attack inspired by ISIS, along the lines of previous ISIS-inspired attacks in Copenhagen, Ottawa, and Paris. The attackers opened fire at a contest to draw cartoons of the Prophet Muhammad. The controversial event offered a ten-thousand-dollar top prize for the best caricature of the Prophet, and featured the far-right-wing Dutch politician Geert Wilders, who had released a 2008 film showing terrorist acts superimposed over verses from the Koran and had subsequently been named on an al-Qaeda hit list.

The intentionally provocative contest had attracted considerable discussion on social media, including from ISIS supporters. One of the shooters, Elton Simpson, had tweeted his allegiance to ISIS and had been in touch over Twitter with members of the group. Simpson, a thirty-year-old Illinois native and resident of Phoenix, Arizona, who converted to Islam during his youth, was joined in the attack by his roommate, thirty-four-year-old Nadir Soofi, born in Texas. Minutes before the attack, Simpson, using the hashtag "texasattack," tweeted out a line from Osama bin Laden: "If there is no check on your freedom of your speech, then let your hearts be open to the freedom of our actions." He also tweeted, "May Allah accept us as mujahideen."

The attack was a spectacular flop. Contest organizers had taken the sensible precaution of hiring additional security, and a police officer killed the two ISIS-inspired militants immediately after they opened fire. Nevertheless, ISIS made a statement claiming Simpson and Soofi as "soldiers of the caliphate."

While the shooting was the first attack by ISIS supporters, it had been preceded by several ISIS-inspired plots, each stymied by law enforcement. In January 2015, Christopher Lee Cornell of Ohio was charged with an alleged plot to attack the U.S. Capitol. Cornell had posted material supportive of ISIS online and was being monitored by an informant. After he was arrested, Cornell told a local news station, "I would have took my gun. I would have put it to Obama's head." He has pleaded not guilty. A month later, the United States charged three Brooklyn men with conspiring to provide material support to ISIS, and alleged that the men had discussed potential attacks in the United States. In April 2015 the United States charged John Booker and Alexander Blair with an ISIS-inspired plot to bomb Fort Riley, Kansas. They deny the charges.

The same month, the United States charged two New York City women, Noelle Velentzas and Asia Siddiqui, with another bomb plot. Velentzas described herself as a "citizen of ISIS," while Siddiqui had contact with members of Al-Qaeda in the Arabian Peninsula, including Samir Khan, with whom she had been in touch when he was still based in North Carolina. (She contributed a poem to *Jihad Recollections*, Khan's first webzine.) When the FBI arrested Velentzas and Siddiqui in Queens, agents seized multiple propane tanks, soldering tools, a pressure cooker, fertilizer, and bomb-making instructions. They have pleaded not guilty.

In each of these cases, a Bureau informant monitored the alleged plotters. Depending on your perspective, this was either another overzealous law enforcement effort victimizing largely harmless blowhards or the FBI ferreting out real threats to the community before the would-be perpetrators could act. Either way, the FBI seemed to be staying on top of these cases. Though their number did, indeed, suggest that ISIS-inspired attacks were a far greater concern than blowback from Syria-trained insurgents, two years into the group's dominance in the world of militant Islam, things seemed to be, in the United States at least, more or less under control.

That is, until 11 a.m. on December 2, 2015. Sixty miles east of Los Angeles, Syed Rizwan Farook and his wife, Tashfeen Malik, stormed into a Christmas party for employees of the San Bernardino County health department, where Farook worked as an inspector of restaurants and other public places. Wearing military-style clothing and black masks and wielding assault rifles, the couple unleashed a barrage of bullets. After killing fourteen people, they sped off in a Ford Explorer.

The men and women killed ranged in age from twenty-six to sixty, and their names reflect the ethnic diversity that is one of the great strengths of the States: Robert Adams, Isaac Amanios Gebreslassie, Bennetta Betbadal, Harry Bowman, Sierra Clayborn, Juan Espinoza,

Aurora Godoy, Shannon Johnson, Larry Kaufman, Damian Meins, Tin Nguyen, Nicholas Thalasinos, Yvette Velasco, Michael Wetzel. Twenty-one others were injured.

Just before the shootings, Malik had pledged her allegiance to ISIS's leader, Abu Bakr al-Baghdadi, in a post on Facebook (using a pseudonymous account). She and her husband then carried out what was, at the time, the most lethal terrorist assault in the States since 9/11.

The couple had prepared over a long period. In the garage behind their house they had constructed nineteen pipe bombs, which they planned to detonate using the bulbs from Christmas tree lights. They had acquired two assault rifles and two handguns as well as 4,500 rounds of ammunition, modifying one of the rifles so that it would take a larger magazine. They had honed their shooting skills at gun ranges. And they had gone to great lengths to hide their tracks—destroying the hard drive in their computer, smashing their cell phones, and minimizing their presence on social media. As a married couple, they had no need to send each other emails or make phone calls to discuss their plot, so they were able to maintain perfect operational security. Also helpful for their plans was that they were "clean skins," unknown to law enforcement.

Judging by their arsenal, Farook and Malik had planned further attacks, but police forces ended their mission four hours after the assault on the holiday party, killing the couple in a shootout. Two days after the attacks, an ISIS radio station embraced Farook and Malik as "supporters." There was no evidence that ISIS had trained Farook and Malik in Syria, as had been the case for several of the terrorists who had killed 130 in Paris only three weeks earlier. Nor were there any indications that ISIS members had been in direct contact with the couple, as with the perpetrators of the botched Garland, Texas, operation. It was a tragic reminder of how lethal the lone wolf threat could be.

B efore they opened fire on Farook's coworkers, he and Malik seemed to be building a life in the United States. Farook, aged twenty-eight, was earning more than $70,000 a year as a public health official, and he and Malik, aged twenty-nine, lived in a two-story townhouse in a neighborhood of neatly trimmed lawns. The couple had celebrated the birth of their first child in May 2015.

Farook was born in Chicago to Pakistani immigrants who later moved to California. He studied environmental health at Cal State in San Bernardino. Malik was born in Pakistan and moved to Saudi Arabia as a child. She attended college in the Pakistani city of Multan, graduating in 2013, before returning to Saudi Arabia. The couple met through a site called BestMuslim.com, which provides "matrimonial service" to Muslims, and married in Saudi Arabia in 2014. Malik arrived in the United States on a visa for spouses and later became a permanent resident.

It was during college that Malik became increasingly religious. On the grounds that images of living beings are prohibited in Islam, she declined to pose for a photograph for her graduation picture. For Farook, it was after two trips he made to Saudi Arabia in 2013 and 2014—first to meet and then to marry Malik—that he seemed to become more devout, according to coworkers, who noticed he had also grown a full beard. After the newly married couple returned to the States, their fundamentalism became more apparent. Malik remained fully veiled even in the presence of male members of her husband's immediate family, and she refused to drive in accordance with Saudi law. She also began posting extremist statements on Facebook. At the same time her husband was trying to reach out to terrorist groups such as al-Shabaab in Somalia and the al-Nusra Front in Syria.

Farook and Malik were married parents, college graduates, solidly in the American middle class, without criminal records or documented mental health issues—in other words, like so many of the 360 American militants examined for this book. Farook and Malik were both typical Americans and typical American jihadists. The only thing about them that was atypical, according to the canon of post-9/11 terrorist profiling, was that Malik played a key role in the attack. What studies like Mitch Silber's 2007 NYPD report didn't capture, because they were completed many years before the emergence of ISIS, was the unexpected and unprecedented role that women in the West would come to play in the world of militant Islam. In a survey conducted for this book of 600

Western recruits to ISIS from twenty-six Western countries, we found that one in seven were women—and as we have seen, this proportion has been even higher in America, at one in six. In the wake of Malik and Farook's joint attack in San Bernardino, female jihadists in the West must be considered as potentially dangerous as their male counterparts.

What can be done about lone wolves inspired by ISIS, such as Farook and Malik? The FBI says that in 2015 it had mounted some nine hundred investigations into militants in the States, and the Bureau has a solid record of monitoring and arresting those ISIS recruits who come to its attention. That said, recruits who practice careful operational security present a serious challenge to the FBI, and Malik and Farook were simply not on the Bureau's radar. The hard fact is that there may be other such militants out there, and there is only so much the feds can do to prevent them from striking if they are without a record.

The San Bernardino attack and the massacres in Paris three weeks earlier combined to cause a wave of anti-Muslim sentiment. Leading Republican presidential contender Donald Trump called for an immediate end to all Muslim immigration to the States, while many of the nation's governors and Republican presidential candidates voiced their opposition to the resettlement of Syrian refugees, despite the fact that refugees had played no role in any jihadist attack in the States since 9/11.

A pioneer of this particular strain of anti-Muslim paranoia was Pamela Geller, long the most visible and vocal of a number of activists claiming that the United States was threatened by creeping "Islamization." Geller, who grew up in Long Island, was working in the genteel offices of the *New York Observer* as an associate publisher on 9/11. The attacks sent her on a personal jihad against what she believed to be a fifth column of "Islamofascists" intent on imposing sharia law on the American population, among whom she counted President Obama a fellow traveler. She began an organization called Stop! Islamization of America and wrote a book titled the same. In 2010, from her blogging perch in her modernist Upper East Side apartment, Geller organized the protests against the establishment of the so-called Ground Zero mosque in Manhattan. (The planned building was in fact two blocks from the

World Trade Center site and wasn't a mosque but an Islamic community center.) The protests turned Geller into a national figure with the imprimatur of a *60 Minutes* profile. Three years later she was denied entry to the United Kingdom after her books and speeches were classified by British authorities as criminal "incitements to racial hatred."

It was Geller who organized the ill-fated Garland, Texas, cartoon contest in May 2015. In the wake of the shooting, Geller justified her decision to hold the contest by explaining that Muslims had become a "special class" that Americans were not allowed to offend. This fit well in the long tradition of what Richard Hofstadter termed in 1964 "the paranoid style in American politics," his well-known analysis of the vocal conspiracy theorist element of the American far right. More than half a century later, Hofstadter's observations about how the paranoid right interpreted the world still rang true: "The central image is that of a vast and sinister conspiracy, a gigantic and yet subtle machinery of influence set in motion to undermine and destroy a way of life. . . . The paranoid spokesman sees the fate of this conspiracy in apocalyptic terms. He traffics in the birth and death of whole worlds, whole political orders, whole systems of human values. He is always manning the barricades of civilization. He constantly lives at a turning point: it is now or never in organizing resistance to the conspiracy. Time is forever running out."

Geller updated the paranoid right for the post-9/11 era. Instead of a Communist plot to take over America, the 1950s conspiracy du jour, the threat was now Muslims. Geller was only the most visible of a number of such commentators. Former Reagan administration official Frank Gaffney published a pamphlet titled *The Muslim Brotherhood in the Obama Administration;* former federal prosecutor Andrew McCarthy offered *How Obama Embraces Islam's Sharia Agenda;* frequent Geller collaborator Robert Spencer wrote the book *Stealth Jihad: How Radical Islam Is Subverting America Without Guns or Bombs;* and journalist Paul Sperry added *Infiltration: How Muslim Spies and Subversives Have Penetrated Washington.*

These assertions defied common sense. To claim that nationwide sharia law is imminent is to ignore simple facts: Muslims make up around 2 percent of the U.S. population; there isn't a jurisdiction in the

States where sharia is the law; nor is anyone demanding its imposition. Short of a mass conversion of hundreds of millions of citizens to Islam, the chances of One Nation Under Sharia seem slight. Yet the arguments of the scaremongers have seeped into mainstream political life. The former Speaker of the House Newt Gingrich asserted in July 2010 that "Sharia is a mortal threat to the survival of freedom and the United States as we know it." The same year, former CIA director James Woolsey coauthored a report for the Center for Security Policy that made similar claims. By 2014, thirty-two state legislatures had introduced bills to outlaw sharia; seven of those bills were passed. In other words, seven states outlawed a practice that didn't exist.

Americans have also long tended to overestimate the threats posed by jihadists while underestimating the sources of other forms of terrorism, generally defined as any act of violence against civilians motivated by ideology. Since 9/11, extremists affiliated with a variety of far-right-wing credos, including white supremacists, antiabortion extremists, and antigovernment militants, have killed around half the number of people in the United States as have extremists motivated by al-Qaeda's ideology. As we have seen, by the end of 2016, ninety-four people had been killed in jihadist terrorist attacks in the United States, while right-wing racists and antigovernment militants had killed forty-eight.

On June 17, 2015, Dylann Roof, a slight white man in his early twenties with a mop of blondish hair, walked into the Emanuel African Methodist Episcopal Church in Charleston, South Carolina, one of the oldest and most storied black churches in the South. After sitting in on a Bible study session for an hour, Roof started shooting the parishioners, saying, "You've raped our women, and you are taking over the country." Roof killed nine African Americans, including Pastor Clementa Pinckney, forty-one, who was also serving as a South Carolina state senator. Roof later told investigators that he wanted "to start a race war." Unaffiliated with any organization, he was a classic example of what white racist Louis Beam termed "leaderless resistance."

By any reasonable standard, the attack on the church in Charleston was terrorism. Trying to start a race war is a fundamentally political objective, realistic or not. Do the thought experiment: If this attack had been conducted by a Muslim man shouting "Allahu Akbar!" what was a big news story would have become even bigger, as it would have appeared to fit so well into the political and media narrative that almost a decade and a half after 9/11 Muslim militants are the major terrorist problem in the United States.

Despite a national history of violence motivated by ideologies other than Binladenism, it is jihadist violence that has continued to dominate the news and the attention of policy makers. Some of this is quite understandable. After all, 9/11 remains far and away the most destructive terrorist attack on American soil. And as we have seen, al-Qaeda and its affiliates have continued to plot attacks in the States that, had they succeeded, could have killed scores or even hundreds. Yet a disparity in media coverage persists between even failed jihadist attacks and successful killings by other militants.

Americans often suffer from historical amnesia. A 2015 *Washington Post*/ABC News poll found that more than three quarters of Americans were worried about possible jihadist attacks, but the golden age of terrorism in the States was in the 1970s, not in post-9/11 America. During the '70s the leftist Weather Underground targeted the Pentagon, the U.S. Capitol, and banks and was responsible for some 45 bombings. Other antiwar activists carried out major bombings at Fresno State College, the University of Wisconsin, and City Hall in Portland. The Black Panthers, who were active for only three years during the 1970s, mounted 24 bombings, assaults, and hijackings. Fuerzas Armadas de Liberación Nacional Puertorriqueña, a Puerto Rican separatist group, mounted 82 bombings, mostly in New York and Chicago. There were an astonishing 112 hijackings in the States during the 1970s, and terrorists killed 184 people and injured more than 600 others. In the decade and a half since 9/11, jihadists and far-right terrorists have, by contrast, killed 142.

Americans' persistent fear of terrorism can be explained partly by the disparity between expert and lay evaluations of risk. In the words of Clinton Jenkin, a psychologist writing in the peer-reviewed journal *Homeland Security Affairs,* "Experts view risk as the likelihood of actual harm based on mortality estimates, whereas lay perceptions of risk are based on a number of qualitative (and subjective) characteristics." The average person's perception of risk, he explains, is influenced by "the voluntariness of exposure," how much control we feel we have, how great we judge the potential damage, how unpredictable the situation seems, and so on. Since terrorists can strike anyone, anywhere, in a random and dreadful manner, we tend to fear them more than we fear far more common and predictable causes of death. In any year since 9/11, Americans were twelve thousand times more likely to die in a car accident, for instance, than in a domestic terrorist incident.

The extent to which our government and the media participate in this endemic paranoia is damaging in that, apart from doing the terrorists' job for them, which is to terrorize, it helps to crowd out the far more serious issues the planet faces. Climate change is far less telegenic than ISIS. More to the point, homicide is the fifteenth leading cause of death for Americans. The scale of this death toll resembles both a national security problem and a public health issue. Around 70 percent of American homicides are accomplished with firearms, according to an authoritative study by the United Nations; some eighty-eight thousand Americans died in gun violence between 2003 and 2010. That means that in the years after 9/11, an American residing in the United States was around *five thousand* times more likely to be killed by a fellow citizen armed with a gun than by a terrorist inspired by the ideology of Osama bin Laden. It's probably more or less inevitable that most Americans will die of cancer or a heart attack, but why is it even plausible that Americans in high schools, colleges, movie theaters, and churches should die at the hands of young armed men?

Americans generally regard themselves as belonging to an exceptional nation. And in terms of living in a religiously tolerant and enormously diverse country, Americans can certainly take some justified pride. But this exceptionalism can also lead to myopia. Americans kill each other with guns at rates unheard of in other advanced industrialized countries; Britain, with around a fifth of the population of the United States, had forty-one gun murders in 2010, while the States had around *eleven thousand*. In other words, Americans are fifty times more likely to be murdered with a gun than are British citizens.

This is not to say the public should overlook the dangers of Islamist extremism. There have been benefits to public awareness of jihadist terrorism as a threat in the States, with everyone from strangers raising the alarm on plots in progress to, more often, family and community members of radicalizing militants alerting the authorities. To take this a step further: What if our collective vigilance could help prevent threats before government counterterrorism machinery needed to get involved? Early intervention seems, now more than ever, an avenue worth exploring. The increasing sophistication of social media has made it ever more difficult for law enforcement to determine when a subject is idly dabbling in Binladenism versus going operational, but people who actually *know* aspiring militants are still likely to recognize when they're changing in a way that merits real concern.

Efforts at intervention were made in a number of the cases profiled in this book. Mosque elders in Charlotte tried to deradicalize Samir Khan; an FBI agent spoke to Carlos Bledsoe both in Yemen and in Nashville; mosque leaders in Boston spoke to Tamerlan Tsarnaev, hoping to moderate his militant views. FBI agents tried to dissuade Shannon Conley from joining ISIS—though not Hamzah Khan and his siblings. In these cases, of course, nothing worked, but then again, measuring a successful intervention is, as with gauging the success of preventative law enforcement, almost impossible. How can you measure something that didn't happen?

Moreover, one of the fruits of the FBI's study of terrorist cases since 2009 was the finding that doubt about whether to go through with an act is common. An FBI analyst explains: "Subjects have expressed doubt along the way, during radicalization, prior to committing an act. To somebody, they have said, 'I don't know if I should do this. Maybe this isn't for me.' But then they still went ahead."

That's where a cleric such as Imam Mohamed Magid could step in. A tall man given to wearing suits with no tie and a vibrantly patterned African hat, Imam Magid presides over one of the largest mosques in America, the All Dulles Area Muslim Society in Northern Virginia, which is attended by thousands of congregants. The son of a leading Sudanese Islamic scholar, Imam Magid arrived in the States in 1987 seeking treatment for his father's failing kidneys. The imam was amazed that his father was treated by three doctors of different faiths; a Muslim, a Catholic, and a Jew. It was the first Jew whom Magid had ever met, and the meeting was to spark Magid's long-lasting interest in interfaith dialogue. His father's treatment failed, but Magid opted to stay as the clerical leader of the All Dulles Area Muslim Society.

On the night of 9/11 one of the mosque's rented spaces was vandalized: graffiti with racial and ethnic slurs was sprayed, and a door was broken. Christians and Jews from the neighborhood quickly rallied to the mosque's defense, offering to escort women wearing *hijab* between their day-to-day activities so they wouldn't be harassed. Law enforcement was also quick to respond to the vandalism. This fostered a cordial relationship with the Washington field office of the FBI and deepened the long-standing relationship Imam Magid and his flock had with the local Christian and Jewish communities. Indeed, Magid's mosque rented space from synagogues and churches in the greater Washington, DC, area for some of its prayer meetings, and the cleric was a regular at interfaith meetings. Magid and his parishioners practiced the kind of tolerant Islam that has been a feature of the faith for more than a millennium and that was a sharp contrast to everything ISIS stood for.

Magid is outraged by ISIS's actions and its claims to represent true Islam. He was one of more than one hundred leading Islamic scholars from around the globe who signed an open letter of repudiation to ISIS leader Abu Bakr al-Baghdadi in September 2014. In a densely argued eighteen-page critique in classical Arabic (also translated into English), the letter said that ISIS was guilty of dozens of violations of sharia law. The signers' central protest concerned the meaning of *jihad,* which they stressed "cannot be applied to armed conflict against any other Muslim," in contrast to ISIS's brutal intolerance. They went on to say that the struggle "against one's ego" was a far greater form of jihad than the word's lesser meaning of a struggle "against the enemy," and that in any case, "*jihad* without legitimate cause, legitimate goals, legitimate purpose, legitimate methodology and legitimate intention is not *jihad* at all, but rather, warmongering and criminality." Magid said that the letter, which was reported on by media outlets around the world, created "doubt" about Baghdadi's pretensions to speak for all Muslims as the caliph.

Imam Magid had been here before. Four years earlier he had made a video responding to Awlaki's calls for jihad because of American foreign policy. In the video, he said, "There's no justification for us to commit injustice in response to injustice." He also explained that by telling people in Europe and America that their loyalty was not to where they lived, but to the *ummah,* the global community of believers, on whose behalf they should wage jihad, Awlaki was misunderstanding the concept of loyalty. Imam Magid explained that, in fact, in Islam, your identity and your loyalty begin in your own neighborhood, according to Muhammad's dictum that one should first take care of parents and family, and after that, next-door neighbors. This was far more important than some abstract devotion to jihad in some faraway land.

To those who preached jihad, Magid also pointed to the social and political victories gained by African Americans through the use of nonviolent tactics during the civil rights era. "If nonviolence does not work," he said, "African Americans would not be where they are now."

In the fall of 2014, Magid, the father of five children, started hearing about youngsters in his community who were being ensnared by ISIS's siren call. Suddenly they started speaking what he termed "ISIS language," about Khalifa, the caliphate. They started telling their parents that watching movies was *haraam,* "not permissible." Magid decided to intervene in a number of these cases, spending long hours at his mosque trying to counter ISIS's arguments with several young men ranging from their teens to their early twenties.

To one ISIS-enamored teenager, Magid said, "Do you have any doubts about Baghdadi or ISIS being true Muslims?" The teen said that he did have some doubts. The cleric asked him, "Is there any doubt in Islam that you need to take care of your mother?" The teen replied that there was none. The cleric explained, "The Prophet said, 'Leave the matter of doubt for the matter of no doubt.' The path of ISIS, the least we can say about it is, it's doubtful. It might take you to hellfire. But the relationship with your mother—there is no doubt about that path."

Magid found the ISIS recruiters frustratingly persistent. Members were constantly in touch with one of the youngsters he was counseling. They knew what he was doing almost all the time: "They will text him, call him, tweet him—all kind of things, almost twenty-four hours," Magid reported. Magid would talk to this youngster for two hours, and ISIS members would then "undo him after two hours, three hours, four hours."

Still, religious arguments made in person by a real scholar of Islam could be persuasive to potential ISIS recruits. Amir, a twenty-two-year-old computer programmer who had converted to Islam, initially found ISIS's message and actions to be very attractive, but he started having doubts after the group murdered the American aid worker Peter Kassig. Those doubts solidified after Imam Magid discussed with him the many Islamic texts instructing that innocent lives should not be taken. Amir now began to conceive of ISIS as a "deviant" sect. With their highly informed understanding of the Koran and the *hadith,* clerics such as Magid are crucial to the intervention process because they can talk to militants in the theological terms to which they are most likely to respond.

Indeed, if Magid had had the opportunity to intervene in the case of the Khan teenagers, observant young Muslims with no history of violence and no evidence of planning violent acts, they might not have been arrested at O'Hare Airport on their way to join ISIS. Hamzah Khan, as we have seen, faced up to fifteen years in prison for the crime of attempting to provide support to ISIS, and his two younger siblings also faced the possibility that they might be prosecuted. As of 2016, Hamzah had pled guilty in exchange for a lesser (though still significant) prison sentence, while his siblings were likely to be sentenced to lengthy supervised probation.

In the hours after the Fort Hood attack, Kerry Cahill, a twenty-nine-year-old actress based in New Orleans, received a frantic call from her mother, Joleen. Joleen's husband, Michael, worked at Fort Hood as a civilian assistant to doctors working at the base. Joleen had tried calling him repeatedly to see if he was all right, but, ominously, he wasn't picking up his phone. Kerry, who was then visiting Chicago, called every

Texas hospital around Fort Hood, but found out nothing about her father. At 11:15 that night, an army chaplain and sergeant arrived at Joleen's house to inform her that her husband had been shot and killed at Fort Hood. Kerry says, "The sun of our solar system was gone. He was the center, the heart and soul of our family."

A week after the shooting, Kerry was deeply angered when she was confronted by a photograph of Major Nidal Hasan, the man who had killed her dad, staring out at her from the cover of *Time* on a drugstore magazine rack. For a while Kerry went on a crusade to try to stop the use of photos of the major in stories about the Fort Hood shooting, telling news editors that the continued use of these images was a mark of disrespect to the victims of the attack and their families. But when her father was awarded a posthumous medal for bravery for trying to stop the rampage, Hasan's photo still appeared in stories about the award.

Back in her adopted home of New Orleans, Kerry Cahill landed a role in the HBO show *Treme*. This helped her focus on something other than her dad's death, but early in 2011 she traveled to Washington for a congressional hearing held to determine whether the Pentagon or the FBI could have done anything to prevent the Fort Hood attack. What she found out made her angry all over again: that Major Hasan's superiors had worried for years about his militant views and even his emotional stability, that the FBI had known about Hasan's correspondence with Awlaki. Beyond all that, as Kerry read through the government report on the shootings, she was shocked to learn that Hasan was a mediocre psychiatrist who showed up late for work. She wondered why he had been allowed to remain in the army.

Nader Hasan had little idea how troubled his cousin was until he read the same report, which laid out in detail how concerned some of his peers and superiors were about Nidal during the many years he worked at Walter Reed. Nader was also irritated by how few Muslim leaders were stepping forward to denounce violence in the name of Islam. This was driven home by a conversation he had while defending a client on a drug charge at the courthouse in Arlington, Virginia. The agent on the case had attended the same church as one of the victims killed at Fort Hood. He asked Nader, "Your community is against this, right?" Nader

replied, "Absolutely." The agent countered, "Well, why aren't they saying anything? The silence is deafening."

The statement "The silence is deafening" kept resonating with Nader.
He started asking people, "As a Muslim American, what group or organization serves your needs?" He found that there wasn't any organization that represented Muslim Americans with an avowedly nonreligious
approach. Nader kept wine at his house and beer in the fridge, but he
still identified as Muslim, and he had many friends who felt the same.
Nader decided that these more secular Muslims were not being heard.

Despite his family's misgivings about attracting any more attention,
Nader created the Nawal Foundation in 2011 to encourage American
Muslims to speak out against extremism and to voice their patriotism. It
was named after Nader's mother, Nawal.

Nader explains: "The Nawal Foundation was born from frustration
that American Muslims lacked a true voice to represent their feelings
and position about terrorists and terrorism." Media depictions of Islam,
he says, too often focus solely on terrorist rhetoric. He decided to create
a forum where American Muslims could "denounce violence without
question, and say our religion doesn't promote this. We also had to accept that our community has a lot to do, and recognize that we have to
own this identity and change it for ourselves, not just hope it will go
away." At the same time, Nader wanted to push back on the notion held
by some Muslims that they were routinely unfairly treated in the States:
"I ask every Muslim, 'Do you think that America's not here for you?
Before you answer that: if you call nine-one-one, and say somebody's
breaking into your house, are the police going to come in and help you?
They're not going to ask you if you're Muslim.'" Nader felt vindicated
when a Pew poll taken around the time he started the foundation found
that nearly half of Muslim Americans thought national Muslim leaders
had not done enough to denounce Islamist militants.

In the week before the tenth anniversary of 9/11, Nader was interviewed on ABC News about his plans for the foundation. When asked
if he had any desire to talk to the families of his cousin's victims and, if
so, what he would say to them, Nader replied that his message would be
"God bless you. God bless the ones you lost, who've been harmed. And

God bless our country to get through this." What Nader initially felt was an unfair question turned out to be the best thing that came out of the interview, because Kerry Cahill was watching the broadcast.

After watching the ABC News story about Nader's new foundation, Kerry talked with her family, and together they wrote an e-mail to Nader. Reading their e-mail, Nader was both surprised that they would reach out to him and also impressed by the compassion of the Cahills. The Cahills asked, "How are you doing?" and expressed real concern for the Hasans. Kerry felt that she wanted to offer some support to the Hasans because they were going through hell as well.

That first step led to a meeting of the two families a few days before the second anniversary of the Fort Hood shooting. Nader picked up Kerry and her siblings and mother at a Metro station near his house in Northern Virginia. On the drive, he pointed out George W. Bush's favorite Chinese restaurant and, more somberly, the mosque where Major Hasan had once worshipped. When they arrived at the Hasans' home, Nader saw that the Cahills didn't quite know what to make of it. There was an American flag flying outside his house and no pictures of, say, Saddam Hussein adorning the walls. The news channels had kept saying that he was of Palestinian origin, so she expected a foreign accent, but there wasn't one. Kerry realized that Nader was as American as she.

Nader's wife brought out homemade baklava. The Cahills presented them with the children's book *Mouse Soup,* which had been Michael Cahill's favorite book to read to them as kids. They had found it at the train station that day and, deciding it was a good omen, gave it to Nader to read to his son. The Cahills started asking questions about Major Hasan. Nader told them, "I'll answer anything." He talked about what he wanted to do with his foundation; Kerry asked how she could get involved.

After the visit, Kerry told her sister that she had realized that Major Hasan had not only murdered their father and the other victims at Fort Hood, but also tarred the rest of the Hasan family with a crime they had nothing to do with. She said, "I'm now angrier, and I didn't think I could be, because he did this to them, too. And they didn't deserve it."

Kerry joined the board of Nader's foundation, and together she and

Nader started speaking out against both fanatical Islamism and Islamo-phobia. Both of them felt that people could find comfort and strength by seeing that they could work together and be friends despite the tragedy that had brought them together. Kerry believes that extremism exists in the United States because the political atmosphere doesn't do enough to foster mutual respect. "We have to move into understanding and respect," she says. "And that does not mean we agree, and that does not mean I have to do what you do, but what it means is you move into a place where you understand the other side better, and I think that's what's missing in the discourse in our country."

The United States has survived three existential crises: the Civil War, which threatened to irretrievably break the nation; the Second World War, which, had the Nazis succeeded in their aims, would have meant the end of Western liberal democracies; and the Cold War, which could have ended not with a whimper but with mutually assured destruction. Jihadist terrorism is not such a threat. On 9/11 the United States survived a terrible breach of national security, but it has put in place a variety of measures that ensure that another such large-scale attack is quite unlikely. What we are left with, however, is a persistent low-level threat that will likely take many, many years before it withers and dies. In the meantime, Kerry Cahill and Nader Hasan's message of understanding, mutual respect, and open dialogue seems a good way to move forward.

AN ORDINARY AMERICAN TERRORIST

Four hours before dawn on Sunday, June 12, 2016, a 911 operator in Orlando received a strange call. In Arabic, the caller said, "In the name of God the merciful, the beneficent. Praise be to God and prayers as well as peace be upon the prophet of God." Then he switched to English: "I wanna let you know I'm in Orlando, and I did the shootings."

"What's your name?" the operator asked. The caller replied, "My name is 'I pledge allegiance to Abu Bakr al-Baghdadi [the leader of ISIS].'" The operator repeated, "Ok. What's your name?" Again the man said, "I pledge allegiance to Abu Bakr al-Baghdadi, may God protect him." The dispatcher asked where, exactly, the man was calling from; he hung up. The exchange had taken less than a minute.

The mysterious caller was Omar Mateen, and this was his way of announcing to the world that, in the city most famous as the home of Walt Disney World, he was waging violent jihad. On the dance floor of Pulse, a nightclub that caters to Orlando's gay community, Mateen had begun systematically murdering patrons around 2 a.m., armed with a legally purchased military assault rifle. Moments earlier his victims had been dancing to the pulsating rhythms of the club's "Latin Night."

Mateen was laughing as he began shooting inside the club. After firing a number of rounds, he used his cell phone to place the 911 call and then took three calls from police negotiators. In these calls he described himself as an "Islamic soldier" and demanded that the United States "stop bombing Syria and Iraq." He claimed that he was wearing an explosive-laden vest, similar to those worn by the ISIS terrorists who had killed 130 people in Paris eight months earlier. He had no such vest and never detonated any explosives, but during his three-hour rampage, Mateen killed forty-nine and wounded fifty-three people. Police shot Mateen dead around 5 a.m. It was not only the worst terrorist attack on American soil since 9/11; it was also the deadliest mass shooting in American history.

As the world woke up to news of the massacre on Sunday morning, people began asking what they ask after every terrorist attack: Why? Why would someone take the lives of innocent civilians, often total strangers? It is a question that might not be completely answerable.

Omar Mateen was in many respects typical of the terrorists we have encountered in this book. He was an American citizen born in Queens, New York, to parents who had emigrated from Afghanistan and eventually settled in the small city of Port St. Lucie on the east coast of Florida. Mateen, aged twenty-nine, was married and had a three-year-old son. He was steadily employed as a security guard at a local golf resort. He had no criminal convictions, and there is no evidence that he suffered from mental illness. In his case, as in so many others of the more than three hundred fifty Americans charged with jihadist terrorism since September 11, the easy explanations—that jihadists in the United States are mad or bad, somehow clinically or criminally other—do not suffice.

If we focus on the ten lethal jihadist attacks in the United States since 9/11, we see that only three of the twelve perpetrators had a documented history of mental illness. Naveed Afzal Haq, who killed a woman at the Jewish Federation building in Seattle in 2006, had been treated for bipolar disorder. Muhammad Youssef Abdulazeez, who killed four Marines and a sailor at two military installations in Chattanooga, Tennessee, in 2015, suffered from clinical depression. In August 2016, a judge ruled that Alton Nolen, who beheaded a coworker in Oklahoma in September 2014, was not competent to plead guilty after hearing testimony from a psychiatrist who testified that Nolen was schizophrenic. Killing people in the service of jihadist ideology is, of course, deviant behavior, but in the majority of cases the root cause was not a documented mental illness.

Instead, as we have seen, American jihadist terrorists are motivated by a mix of factors, including a dislike of U.S. foreign policy in the Muslim world; a cognitive opening to militant Islam, often precipitated by a personal disappointment or loss; and the desire to attach themselves to an ideology or organization that could give them a sense of purpose. For many, embracing the ideology of Osama bin Laden or ISIS allowed them to become the heroes of their own story as well as actors in a cosmic crusade.

Mateen's motivations, too, seem to have been multilayered, and will probably never be fully explicable. Mateen himself offered one inspiration: ISIS. There was the 911 call, pledging himself to Abu Bakr al-Baghdadi; later, Mateen called a local TV station and told a producer that he was carrying out his attacks for ISIS. At another point during the massacre Mateen pledged his allegiance to ISIS on Facebook, as the terrorists in San Bernardino had.

Yet a more complex stew of personal traits, resentments, and obsessions also propelled him toward violence. As a child Mateen was angry and disruptive in class, and at age fourteen he was expelled from high school for fighting. On the morning of the 9/11 attacks, Mateen told classmates that Osama bin Laden was his uncle. As an adult, relatives say Mateen expressed homophobic views, while coworkers remember that he claimed to have connections to both al-Qaeda and Hezbollah, groups that are at war with each other. Both his first wife and his second wife say he was abusive and couldn't control his temper, and there are suggestions that he might have been confused about his sexual identity. Mateen's reported use of gay dating apps and visits to the Pulse nightclub in the months before the attack make this a tempting central narrative—self-loathing for his own homosexuality turned violent—but these behaviors are also consistent with the careful planning of predatory murderers. In the weeks after the massacre FBI investigators concluded that there was no evidence Mateen had had a gay relationship.

Like Tamerlan Tsarnaev, Mateen had a dream that had faded. He desperately wanted to be a police officer and took selfies while wearing New York Police Department shirts, but he was dismissed from a Florida police-training academy in 2007 because he threatened to bring a gun to campus and was falling asleep in class. Eight years later, in 2015, Mateen tried once again to become a police officer, applying to the police academy at Indian River State College in Fort Pierce. He was turned down because he admitted to having used marijuana and also because of what the college termed "discrepancies" in his application form. It was only days before the Orlando massacre that Mateen learned he had finally been accepted into a police training program, but by then his grievances had long festered. Three weeks before his attack, one of the leaders of ISIS publicly urged that sympathizers of the group carry out attacks in the West during the coming holy month of Ramadan. By following this directive, carrying out an attack as a self-styled "Islamic fighter" pledging allegiance to ISIS, Mateen was finally the heroic holy warrior that he believed himself to be. A day after the massacre ISIS's official radio station, Al-Bayan, claimed him as one of the "soldiers of the caliphate in America." But Mateen's connection to ISIS was only aspirational; he wasn't trained, directed, or financed by the group. Instead he was, like every other lethal jihadist in the States since 9/11, operating as a self-radicalized "lone wolf."

Mateen had something else in common with the most infamous jihadists before him: He was on the radar of the FBI as a possible militant, just as Tamerlan Tsarnaev, Nidal Hasan, and Carlos Bledsoe had been. Mateen was investigated in 2013 for the comments he made to coworkers about his purported connections to al-Qaeda and Hezbollah. A year later the FBI took another look at Mateen because he was a passing acquaintance of Moner Abusalha, who had died in a suicide attack in Syria in 2014. But in the end, just as with Tsarnaev, Hasan, and Bledsoe, the FBI did not pursue a case against Mateen.

Ahmad Khan Rahami of Elizabeth, New Jersey, fit a similar profile. A full two years before he set off a bomb in the Chelsea neighborhood of Manhattan on September 17, 2016, injuring thirty-one people, he came to the attention of the FBI when he became embroiled in a family dispute and stabbed his brother. Rahami's father, Muhammad, says the incident prompted him to share with FBI agents his concerns— simmering for some time—that his son was interested in terrorism. The FBI looked into Rahami but seems to have concluded that the stabbing episode reflected family dysfunction rather than any extremist beliefs. After Rahami's attack in Manhattan, the FBI denied his father's claims that he had warned federal agents two years earlier about his son's growing preoccupation with al-Qaeda and the Taliban.

Like Mateen, Rahami was both an American citizen of Afghan descent and a married father in his late twenties. As with so many American militants, he became more religiously observant after a trip to a field of jihad—in his case, Afghanistan and Pakistan. According to his father he began obsessively watching extremist videos, following yet another common pattern.

The device Rahami detonated bore a close resemblance to those used in the Boston Marathon attacks three years earlier. Both Rahami and the Tsarnaevs used pressure cookers to house their devices and added shrapnel to increase the lethality of the charges. Lone wolves often make a study of previous attacks, and Rahami seems to have been no exception. Adding to the similarities, Rahami is believed to have planted a pipe bomb in Seaside, New Jersey, the day before the Chelsea bombing, targeting a Marine Corps charity run. That bomb detonated without injuring anyone.

The crucial difference between Rahami's attack and the Boston Marathon bombing is that Rahami did not succeed in killing his victims. Instead of placing his bomb directly on the street he had targeted, where it could have inflicted significant damage, he planted it in a dumpster, which largely contained the blast. It was the error of an amateur—albeit an amateur who pulled off the first jihadist attack in Manhattan since 9/11.

It's telling that in the notebook Rahami kept, in which he referenced a prominent ISIS leader, he also made notes about Anwar al-Awlaki. This underlined the continuing importance of Awlaki, whose sermons and writings have turned up in some one hundred jihadist terrorism cases in the United States since 9/11, more than sixty of them since his death in 2011.

The homegrown terror threat poses a knotty problem for U.S. law enforcement. Lone wolves generally don't communicate with foreign terrorist organizations via email or phone—the type of communications

286 | UNITED STATES OF JIHAD

that could be intercepted by the U.S. intelligence community. Nor do they have meetings with coconspirators who could be monitored by the FBI. The FBI said in 2016 that it was conducting some one thousand investigations of suspected Islamist militants; in many cases the Bureau will conclude, rightly, that there is no cause for alarm. The attack in Orlando reminds us that despite all these FBI investigations, sometimes America's homegrown terrorists will still slip through the net.

The attack in Orlando also reminds us that even while suspected jihadist terrorists are under FBI investigation, they can easily buy military-style assault weapons. Omar Mateen, Nidal Hasan, and Carlos Bledsoe were all FBI subjects of interest, yet all legally purchased semi-automatic weapons shortly before their attacks. Several bills that would have prevented the subjects of FBI terrorism inquiries from purchasing assault weapons were introduced in Congress in the days following the Orlando massacre. It is a symptom of the dysfunction of the American political system that all of them failed to pass.

To paraphrase an observation made by the American writer H. L. Mencken: For every complex problem, there is a solution that is simple, neat, and wrong. A day after the Orlando attack, the then presumptive Republican presidential nominee, Donald Trump, made a speech that was billed as his big statement on counterterrorism. Trump said, "I will suspend immigration from areas of the world where there is a proven history of terrorism against the United States, Europe, or our allies." Trump failed to elaborate, but presumably this ban would apply to countries such as Afghanistan, Iraq, Libya, Pakistan, Syria, and Yemen, all of which have significant ISIS or al-Qaeda presences within their borders. The ban could also have included countries such as Indonesia and Saudi Arabia—longtime American allies that also have been sites of terrorist attacks against Western and American targets.

A plan to suspend immigration to solve the problem of terrorism in America is, first and foremost, a fundamentally un-American idea. The United States didn't ban Italian immigration in the 1920s because a small minority of Italians became members of the Mafia. Not to mention that by imposing what looked like a religious test on immigrants the plan would open itself to serious legal challenges. But even putting such objections aside, we have no reason to believe that such a ban would stop terrorism. Since 9/11, every lethal jihadist terrorist attack in the States has been carried out by an American citizen or legal resident.

Trump's proposal, which he later revised to a ban on immigration from countries with "a proven history of terrorism" (would that have included France, where there have been multiple terror attacks since 2014?), was the half-baked notion of a man with no policy experience. Yet there was a sense in which it demanded to be taken seriously. It gave voice to a real, dangerously xenophobic sentiment that terrorism is an "us" vs. "them" problem. As this book has demonstrated again and again, it is not. Jihadist terrorism in the United States is overwhelmingly a phenomenon of ordinary Americans making extraordinarily bad choices.

When ISIS emerged on the world stage in 2014, it rapidly revealed itself to be the standard bearer of global jihad, including for radicalizing Americans. But by the fall of 2016, there was a real sense that ISIS was on the run in its self-styled state in Iraq and Syria, where it had lost, respectively, around half and a fifth of its territory. On one level that looked like a very good thing; if ISIS no longer controlled vast swaths of territory, its claim to being the caliphate seemed increasingly questionable. Even as it was losing ground, however, the number of ISIS-inspired attacks in the West increased. The loss of territory appeared to have little effect on ISIS's ability to influence Americans like Omar Mateen. This will be ISIS's legacy in the United States: the crowdsourcing of jihad, so that men like Mateen can convert personal grievances into what they believe is a righteous holy war. Meanwhile we can hope in the future to better judge the potential for violence posed by militants such as Mateen, and, at the very least, to make the weapons of their war harder to come by.

NOTES

CHAPTER 1: AMERICANS FOR ISIS

1 **an e-mail to the U.S. State Department . . . working at a local big-box home supply store:** *United States of America v. Mohammed Hamzah Khan,* CR No. 14-564, Transcript of Proceedings (Northern District of Illinois, 2014), [hereafter *U.S. v. Khan,*] Government Exhibit 1, Nov. 17.

1 **met someone online:** *U.S. v. Khan,* criminal complaint, Oct. 6.

1 **Mina, and his sixteen-year-old brother, Khalid:** These names are pseudonyms as the younger siblings of Hamzah Khan were minors at the time of their arrest.

1 **excited to make their pilgrimage:** *U.S. v. Khan:* "The defendant and his siblings not only have a desire but a self-described obligation to join and support a designated foreign terrorist organization."

1 **planned to marry an ISIS fighter:** Kevin Sullivan, "Three American Teens, Recruited Online, Are Caught Trying to Join the Islamic State," *Washington Post,* Dec. 8, 2014.

1 **to serve in a combat role . . . doodled in his notebook a picture of a fighter:** *U.S. v. Khan,* criminal complaint, Oct. 6.

2 **watched *Saleel Sawarim* . . . tweeted that she had watched it:** *U.S. v. Khan,* government exhibits 20 and 21, Oct. 6.

2 **following a brutal imprisonment:** Rukmini Callimachi, "The Horror Before the Beheadings," *New York Times,* Oct. 25, 2014.

2 **while a black-clad terrorist:** Mark Landler and Eric Schmitt, "ISIS Says It Killed Steven Sotloff After U.S. Strikes in Northern Iraq," *New York Times,* Sept. 2, 2014.

2 **"just as your missiles continue":** Chelsea J. Carter and Ashley Fantz, "ISIS Video Shows Beheading of American Journalist Steven Sotloff," CNN.com, Sept. 9, 2014.

2 **the most widely followed news story:** Janet Hook and Carol E. Lee, "WSJ/ NBC Poll: Almost Two-Thirds Back Attacking Militants," *Wall Street Journal,* Sept. 10, 2014.

2 **saw the soldiers of ISIS not as fanatical:** In *U.S. v. Khan,* Nov. 17; Khan's attorney points to their letters as evidence of the "inference that we're asking you to draw, that there's every bit as much of an interest that they wanted to go live in a caliphate, which isn't a crime yet."

2 **wrote a three-page letter . . . "evil of this country makes me sick" . . . wrote of her longing for death . . . begged their parents:** *U.S. v. Khan,* government exhibits 4 and 5, Nov. 17.

3 **Their father, Shafi, and mother, Zarine . . . shopped at Walmart:** Author interview with the Khan parents, Chicago, IL, May 13, 2015.

3 **Yet even as Zarine and Shafi:** Sullivan, "Three American Teens, Recruited On-line."

3 **He was a fan of TV shows . . . After high school:** *U.S. v. Khan,* memo of law in support of motion to suppress statements defendant's exhibit C, April 17.

4 **The Khans were then homeschooling . . . tickets to Vienna and Istanbul:** Sullivan, "Three American Teens, Recruited Online."

4 **Abu Qa'qa . . . to Raqqa, Syria:** *U.S. v. Khan,* memo of law in support of motion to suppress statements defendant's exhibit C, April 17.

4 **U.S. Customs and Border Protection officials . . . At first Hamzah told FBI:** *U.S. v. Khan,* transcript of proceedings, Nov. 17.

4 **A search of the Khan household:** Sullivan, "Three American Teens, Recruited Online."

4 **for trying to provide "material support":** *U.S. v. Khan,* criminal complaint, Oct. 6.

5 **At seventeen years old:** Author interview with Thomas Durkin, attorney for Hamzah Khan, Chicago, May 13, 2015.

5 **The Khan kids had never been in trouble:** Sullivan, "Three American Teens, Recruited Online."

5 **Hamzah seemed motivated more . . . But to federal prosecutors:** *U.S. v. Khan,* transcript of proceedings, Nov. 17.

5 **death cult recently designated:** "Terrorist Designations of Groups Operating in Syria," Media Note, May 14, 2014, Office of the Spokesperson, Department of State, Washington, DC, http://www.state.gov/r/pa/prs/ps/2014/05/226067.htm.

5 **some three hundred supporters:** Fisal Hammouda and Thomas Anthony Durkin, "Justice for Hafiz Mohammed Hamzah Khan," fund-raiser to create awareness and support for Hafiz Mohammed Hamzah Khan, Berkeley, IL, Jan. 16, 2015, attended by the author.

5 **retained Thomas Durkin:** Durkin interview.

5 **greeted the congregation with a rousing:** Hammouda and Durkin, "Justice for Hafiz Mohammed Hamzah Khan."

5 **the case of Shannon Conley of Denver:** *United States of America v. Shannon Maureen Conley,* Criminal Complaint, p. 4, New America, https://s3.amazonaws.com/static.newamerica.org/securitydata/attachments/terrorplots/1765/Shannon%20Conley%20-%20Criminal%20Complaint.pdf.

6 **no attempts were made:** Khan parents interview.

6 **idealistic Americans who flocked to Spain:** Dan Kaufman, "The Last Volunteer," *New York Times Magazine,* March 13, 2015. About three thousand Americans fought on the side of the Republicans, in a group known as the Abraham Lincoln Brigade.

6 **In the absence of social media . . . "Hamzah Khan is our son!":** Hammouda and Durkin, "Justice for Hafiz Mohammed Hamzah Khan."

6 **On January 12, 2015, Hamzah pled . . . "We have a message for ISIS":** Michael Martinez and George Howell, "Illinois Mom Tells ISIS: 'Leave Our Children Alone,'" CNN.com, Jan. 13, 2015.

7 **issuing its own license plates:** Rick Gladstone, "Islamic State Says It Plans to Issue Its Own Currency," *New York Times,* Nov. 14, 2014.

7 **throwing homosexuals:** Perry Chiaramonte, "Death Plunge: ISIS Throws Gay Men off Buildings under Guise of Sharia Law," FoxNews.com, June 6, 2015.

7 **lopping off the hands:** Graeme Wood, "What ISIS Really Wants," *The Atlantic,* March 2015.

7 **beheading women:** "Islamic State 'Beheads Women for Sorcery' in Syria," BBC .com, June 30, 2015.

7 **enslaving and raping minority women:** Wood, "What ISIS Really Wants."

7 **ISIS had drawn to its banners:** Peter Bergen, "ISIS Goes Global," CNN.com, March 8, 2015, http://www.cnn.com/2015/03/08/opinions/bergen-isis-boko -haram/.

7 **ISIS had splintered:** Liz Sly, "Al-Qaeda Disavows Any Ties with Radical Is-lamist ISIS Group in Syria, Iraq," *Washington Post,* Feb. 3, 2014.

7 **Osama bin Laden saw the establishment:** Office of the Director of National In-telligence, "Letter Addressed to Atiyah," http://www.dni.gov/files/documents/ ubl/english/Letter%20Addressed%20to%20Atiyah.pdf.

7 **claiming its leader, Abu Bakr al-Baghdadi:** Cole Bunzel, "From Paper State to Caliphate: The Ideology of the Islamic State," Brookings Project on U.S. Relations with the Islamic World, 2015, http://www.brookings.edu/~/media/ research/files/papers/2015/03/ideology-of-islamic-state-bunzel/the-ideology -of-the-islamic-state.pdf, p. 31.

7 **al-Qaeda believed that killing Muslims:** Combating Terrorism Center at West Point, "Zawahiri's Letter to Zarqawi (English Translation)," https://www.ctc .usma.edu/posts/zawahiris-letter-to-zarqawi-english-translation-2.

7 **ISIS's bid for dominance was the mass murder:** Bunzel, "From Paper State to Caliphate," p. 10.

7 **executing hundreds of Iraqi Shia soldiers:** Rod Nordland and Alissa J. Rubin, "Massacre Claim Shakes Iraq," *New York Times,* June 15, 2014.

7 **murdering more than a hundred:** "Syria: Deliberate Killing of Civilians by ISIS," Human Rights Watch, July 3, 2015, https://www.hrw.org/news/2015/07/03/ syria-deliberate-killing-civilians-isis.

8 **burning its Muslim victims:** "ISIS Burned up to 40 People Alive, Official in Iraq Says," CNN.com, Feb. 19, 2015.

8 **analysts asked why:** Peter Bergen, "Why Does ISIS Keep Making Enemies?" CNN.com, Feb. 16, 2015.

8 **ISIS burned to death . . . The group's ideology:** Rod Nordland and Anne Bar-nard, "Militants' Killing of Jordanian Pilot Unites Arab World in Anger," *New York Times,* Feb. 4, 2015.

8 **ISIS's distinctive black flags:** Michael Crowley, "Khorasan: Behind the Mysteri-ous Name of the Newest Terrorist Threat," *Time,* Sept. 25, 2014.

9 **English-language webzine, *Dabiq*:** "The Islamic State's (ISIS, ISIL) Magazine," *The Clarion Project,* http://media.clarionproject.org/files/islamic-state/isis-isil -islamic-state-magazine-issue%2B9-they-plot-and-allah-plots-sex-slavery.pdf.

9 **an allusion to ancient prophecy:** Shimon Shamir, "Reflections on Islamism:

From the Muslim Brotherhood to the Islamic State," 2014 Zeev Schiff Memorial Lecture, Oct. 29, 2014, Washington Institute, Washington, DC, http://www.washingtoninstitute.org/policy-analysis/view/reflections-on-islamism-from-the-muslim-brotherhood-to-the-islamic-state.

8 **the Prophet Muhammad predicted:** "The Book Pertaining to the Turmoil and the Portents of the Last Hour (Kitab Al-Fitan wa Ashrat As-Sa'ah), Book 041, number 6924," University of Southern California Center for Muslim-Jewish Engagement, http://www.usc.edu/org/cmje/religious-texts/hadith/muslim/041-smt.php.

8 **When American aid worker Peter Kassig:** Bergen, "Why Does ISIS Keep Making Enemies?"

9 **The group practices** *takfir*: Bunzel, "From Paper State to Caliphate."

9 **repeatedly published images of Shia shrines:** Peter Bergen and Emily Schneider, "ISIS Reveals Its Strategy," CNN.com, Oct. 22, 2014, http://www.cnn.com/2014/10/20/opinion/bergen-schneider-isis-magazine.

9 **a few dozen Americans:** Barbara Starr, " 'A Few Dozen Americans' in ISIS Ranks," CNN.com, July 15, 2015, http://www.cnn.com/2015/07/15/politics/isis-american-recruits/index.html.

10 **investigated supporters of ISIS:** Associated Press, "Comey: Extremists Exist in All 50 States," *Washington Post,* Feb. 25, 2015.

10 **more than eighty extremists . . . plotting an attack in the States:** "Homegrown Extremism 2001–2015," International Security, New America, http://securitydata.newamerica.net/extremists/analysis.html.

10 **ISIS is one on a long list:** Ibid. The database of 360 cases was created to enable the making of some broad claims about jihadist militants in the States since 9/11. David Sterman of New America played the key role in creating the database.

10 **some kind of jihadist terrorist crime:** Ibid. The database does not include extremists tied to violent Islamist groups that do not target the United States (for example, Hamas and Hezbollah); nor does it include individuals who were acquitted or charged with lesser crimes (for example, immigration violations that cannot be shown to involve some kind of terrorism-related crime). While the vast majority of (335 out of 360) individuals in the database have been charged with a terrorism-related crime by the U.S. government, also included are 19 individuals who either died or were killed without being charged but are widely and credibly reported as having engaged in violent extremist activity. So too are 6 individuals charged with a terrorism-related crime by a foreign country, but not by the United States. The database encompasses the period from September 11, 2001, to September 1, 2015.

10 **An astonishing four out of five:** Ibid. Forty-six percent of the jihadist extremists in the database were born American citizens; another 25 percent are naturalized citizens; 12 percent are legal permanent residents. Only 18 percent are on temporary visas, illegal residents, refugees, or of unknown immigration status.

10 **more than one hundred:** Ibid. One hundred and eleven had been charged by July 2015.

10 **and a further thirty-nine:** Ibid.

11 **"Binladenism," the dogma laid out:** The passage on Binladenism and historical comparison with other ideologies is taken from Peter Bergen, "Does Islam Fuel Terrorism?" CNN.com, Jan. 13, 2015.

11 **Bin Laden spoke of a global conspiracy . . . support for Israel:** "Jihad Against Jews and Crusaders, World Islamic Front Statement," Federation of American Scientists, Feb. 23, 1998, http://fas.org/irp/world/para/docs/980223-fatwa.htm.

12 **Queens-born Samir Khan:** Matthew Chayes et al., "Samir Khan, al-Qaida Figure, Grew Up on Long Island," *Newsday,* Oct. 7, 2011.

12 **a trigger for Boston Marathon bomber Tamerlan Tsarnaev's:** Alan Cullison, Paul Sonne, and Lukas I. Alpert, "Tsarnaev's Six-Month Visit to Dagestan Is Scrutinized," *Wall Street Journal,* April 24, 2013.

12 **four "waves" of global revolutionary terrorism:** David C. Rapoport, "The Four Waves of Rebel Terror and September 11," *Anthropoetics* (Spring 2002): 419–25.

13 **There have been Muslims in the United States:** Denise A. Spellberg, *Thomas Jefferson's Qu'ran: Islam and the Founders* (New York: Knopf, 2013), p. 6.

13 **the Virginia Act for Establishing Religious Freedom:** In Philip B. Kurland and Ralph Lerner, *The Founders' Constitution,* Volume 5 (Chicago, IL: University of Chicago Press, 1986), Amendment I (Religion), Document 44, http://press-pubs.uchicago.edu/founders/documents/amendI_religions44.html.

13 **Thomas Jefferson, the law's principal author:** In Kurland and Lerner, *The Founders' Constitution,* Volume 5, Document 45, http://press-pubs.uchicago.edu/founders/documents/amendI_religions45.html.

13 **The act became the basis:** "Thomas Jefferson and the Virginia Statute for Religious Freedom," Virginia Historical Society, http://www.vahistorical.org/collections-and-resources/virginia-history-explorer/thomas-jefferson.

13 **Imam Mohamed Magid, a Sudanese American cleric:** Author interview with Imam Magid, Sterling, VA, July, 14, 2015.

13 **In a number of Muslim nations:** In Egypt, the Muslim Brotherhood was designated a terrorist organization in 2013.

13 **Ahmadis, a minority sect:** Asad Hashim, "Pakistan's Ahmadiyya: An 'Absence of Justice,'" AlJazeera.com, Aug. 7, 2014.

13 **Muslims currently number around five million:** "Muslims in America: A Statistical Portrait," Embassy of the United States–Baghdad Iraq, http://iraq.usembassy.gov/resources/information/current/american/statistical.html.

13 **one of the fastest-growing religions:** Daniel Burke, "The World's Fastest-Growing Religion Is . . . ," CNN.com, April 3, 2015.

13 **around 7 percent of the population:** Conrad Hackett, "5 Facts About the Muslim Population in Europe," Pew Research Center, Jan. 15, 2015, http://www.pewresearch.org/fact-tank/2015/01/15/5-facts-about-the-muslim-population-in-europe/.

14 **70 percent of its prison population:** Harriet Alexander, "What Is Going Wrong in France's Prisons?" *The Telegraph,* Jan. 17, 2015.

14 **Muslim citizens in France:** Claire L. Adida, David D. Laitin, and Marie-Anne

Valfort, "Identifying Barriers to Muslim Integration in France," *Proceedings of the National Academy of the Sciences of the United States of America* 107, no. 52 (Dec. 2010).

14 **many French Muslims live in grim *banlieues*:** Audie Cornish, "In France, Young Muslims Often Straddle Two Worlds," NPR, March 3, 2015, http://www.npr .org/sections/parallels/2015/03/03/390449785/in-france-young-muslims-often -straddle-two-worlds.

14 **half the neighborhoods with a high Muslim population:** Jonathan Laurence and Justin Vaisse, *Integrating Islam* (Washington, DC: Brookings Institution Press, 2006), p. 37.

14 **The French term for these neighborhoods:** Steven Erlanger, "A Presidential Race Leaves French Muslims Feeling Like Outsiders," *New York Times,* April 4, 2012.

14 **France has supplied more foreign fighters:** "The Foreign Fighters Phenomenon Is a Challenge for France and Its Partners," Statement of Permanent Representative of France to the United Nations Françoise Delattre Before the UN Security Council, May 29, 2015, http://www.franceonu.org/The-foreign-fighters -phenomenon-is-a-challenge-for-France-and-its-partners.

14 **as wealthy and educated as the average American:** "Muslim Americans: No Signs of Growth in Alienation or Support for Extremism," Pew Research Center, Aug. 30, 2011, http://www.people-press.org/2011/08/30/section-1-a -demographic-portrait-of-muslim-americans/.

14 **a tiny minority:** American Muslims number around 5 million; 360 have been charged with a jihadist crime since 9/11. Therefore, there is a 1-in-15,000 chance that an American Muslim has committed some kind of jihadist crime in the years since 9/11.

14 **Only a dozen men attended . . . One of these was Mohammed Loay Bayazid:** Peter Bergen, *The Osama bin Laden I Know: An Oral History of al Qaeda's Leader* (New York: Free Press, 2006), pp. 74–82.

14 **grew up in Kansas City:** Lawrence Wright, *The Looming Tower: Al-Qaeda and the Road to 9/11* (New York: Random House, 2006), p. 126.

14 **Al-Qaeda's most important military trainer:** Bergen, *The Osama bin Laden I Know,* p. 103.

14 **Wadi el-Hage:** Ibid., p. 78.

15 **Floridian Adnan Shukrijumah:** Sophia Saifi, Ben Brumfield, and Susan Candiotti, "Pakistan's Army Kills al Qaeda Commander Who Grew Up in U.S.," CNN.com, Dec. 8, 2014, http://www.cnn.com/2014/12/06/world/asia/ pakistan-al-qaeda-death/.

15 **Adam Gadahn:** Greg Botelho and Ralph Ellis, "Adam Gadahn, American Mouthpiece for al Qaeda, Killed," CNN.com, April 23, 2015, http://www.cnn .com/2015/04/23/world/adam-gadahn-al-qaeda/.

15 **Their average age is twenty-nine; more than a third are married:** "Homegrown Extremism 2001–2015." Thirty-seven percent are married, 5 percent are divorced, 1.5 percent are split but not officially divorced, and one individual was widowed. Fifty-six percent were unmarried or information on their marriage status was unavailable.

15 **12 percent have served time in prison:** Ibid.

16 **As Immanuel Kant observed:** Immanuel Kant, "Idea of a Universal History on a Cosmopolitical Plan," 1784, Sixth Proposition, http://philosophyproject.org/wp-content/uploads/2013/02/IDEA-OF-A-UNIVERSAL-HISTORY-ON-A-COSMPOLITAN-PLAN.pdf.

16 **Zachary Chesser:** Tara Bahrampour, "Fairfax Man Guilty in Terror Case Is Cited in Report on Future of Islamist Extremism," *Washington Post*, Feb. 26, 2012.

16 **driving toward his first meeting with members:** Samir Khan, "I Am Proud to Be a Traitor to America," *Inspire* (al-Qaeda magazine), 2010, https://azelin.files.wordpress.com/2010/10/inspire-magazine-2.pdf, p. 45.

16 **another suburban office worker:** Associated Press, "Retaliation Warning Issued After Former Charlotte Man Killed in Yemen," www.wbtv.com/story/15586296/former-charlotte-man-killed-in-yemin-drone-attack.

16 **Tamerlan Tsarnaev, unemployed:** Peter Bergen, "The Lasting Mystery of the Tsarnaev Brothers," CNN.com, May 18, 2015.

16 **In the 1970s:** "How Young People Went Underground During the '70s 'Days of Rage,'" NPR, April 13, 2015.

16 **Nader Hasan:** Lee Hancock, "After the Massacre," *Salon*, July 1, 2012, http://www.salon.com/2012/07/01/after_the_massacre/.

16 **Bernie Culveyhouse grew up:** Author interview with Bernie Culveyhouse, Palo Alto, CA, Dec. 27, 2013.

17 **forty-five Americans have been killed:** The death toll includes two people killed by Hesham Mohamed Hadayet at the the El Al ticket counter at Los Angeles International Airport on July 4, 2002; one person killed at a Jewish Federation center in Seattle by Naveed Haq on July 28, 2006; thirteen killed by Maj. Nidal Hasan at Fort Hood, Texas, on November 5, 2009; a soldier killed by Carlos Bledsoe in the June 1, 2009, shooting at the Little Rock, Arizona military recruiting center; three people killed in the Boston Marathon bombing on April 15, 2013, and one more killed as the Tsarnaev brothers went on a rampage through Boston in the days after; one person beheaded in Oklahoma on September 25, 2014, by an individual with jihadist propaganda on his computer; four people killed in 2014 during a multistate killing spree by Ali Muhammad Brown, who claimed the killings were revenge for American policy in the Middle East; and five people killed in the attacks by Mohammod Youssuf Abdulazeez at military facilities in Chattanooga, Tennessee, on July 16, 2015.

17 **forty-eight Americans have been killed . . . FBI has instigated more terrorist** "plots" . . . "Entrapment," **however, has never succeeded:** "Homegrown Extremism 2001–2015."

17 **the FBI deployed thousands of informants:** Trevor Aaronson, *The Terror Factory: Inside the FBI's Manufactured War on Terrorism* (Brooklyn, NY: Ig Publishing, 2013), p. 24.

17 **the New York City Police Department (NYPD):** Adam Goldman and Matt Apuzzo, "NYPD Docs: 'Focus' Scrutiny on Muslim Americans," Associated Press, March 9, 2012.

17 **The National Security Agency (NSA) has swept up:** Ellen Nakashima, "Independent Review Board Says NSA Phone Data Program Is Illegal and Should End," *Washington Post*, Jan. 23, 2013.

17 **there is, in fact, little to show for them:** Bailey Cahall, David Sterman, Emily Schneider, and Peter Bergen, "Do NSA's Bulk Surveillance Programs Stop Terrorists?" *New America*, Jan. 13, 2014.

18 **A large majority of Americans consider:** "One Year Later: New Yorkers More Troubled, Washingtonians More on Edge," Pew Research Center, Sept. 5, 2002, http://www.people-press.org/2002/09/05/one-year-later-new-yorkers-more-troubled-washingtonians-more-on-edge/.

18 **four out of ten Americans:** Lydia Saad, "Americans' Fear of Terrorism in U.S. Is Near Low Point," Gallup News Service, Sept. 2, 2011, http://www.gallup.com/poll/149315/americans-fear-terrorism-near-low-point.aspx.

18 *Foreign Policy* **magazine regularly surveyed:** *Foreign Policy* and Center for American Progress, "The Terrorism Index," Center for American Progress, Aug. 18, 2008, https://www.americanprogress.org/issues/security/news/2008/08/18/4854/the-terrorism-index/.

18 **about 60 percent of Republicans . . . Muslim Americans polled less favorably:** "The American Divide: How We View Arabs and Muslims," Arab American Institute, Aug. 21, 2012, http://www.aaiusa.org/tags/american_opinion_polls.

18 **Another poll, also from 2012:** "Little Voter Discomfort with Romney's Mormon Religion," Pew Research Center, July 26, 2012, http://www.pewforum.org/2012/07/26/2012-romney-mormonism-obamas-religion/.

18 **presided over or launched:** Kevin Liptak, "Countries Bombed by the U.S. under the Obama Administration," CNN.com, Sept. 23, 2014.

18 **The most conservative estimate:** "Drone Wars Pakistan: Analysis," International Security, New America, http://securitydata.newamerica.net/drones/pakistan-analysis.html.

19 **some two hundred people:** "Homegrown Extremism 2001–2015."

19 **"Jihad is becoming as American as apple pie":** Ken Millstone, "Anwar al-Awlaki Hails Rise of 'Western Jihad,'" CBS News, March 22, 2010.

CHAPTER 2: ALL-AMERICAN AL-QAEDA

20 **assignations with "escorts" . . . traveled to Florida:** FBI, "Report on Anwar Aulaqi," May 6, 2003.

20 **Dar al-Hijrah mosque:** FBI, "Report on Interview with Anwar Aulaqi," Sept. 15, 2001.

21 **street address of his mosque . . . Arribat al-Islami:** FBI, "Report on Anwar Aulaqi," May 6, 2003.

21 **El Cajon Boulevard:** Tony Perry, "Radical Cleric Killed by Drone Was Twice Arrested with Prostitutes in San Diego," *Los Angeles Times,* Sept. 20, 2011.

21 **claimed that he had been set up:** Anwar al-Awlaki, "Spilling Out the Beans," *Inspire,* Spring 2012 issue.

21 **Being a U.S. citizen:** FBI, "Report on Interview with Anwar Aulaqi," Sept. 15, 2001.

21 **al-Qaeda sympathizer:** Awlaki, "Spilling Out the Beans."

21 **few weeks before 9/11 . . . go-to figure:** Scott Shane and Souad Mekhennet, "Imam's Path from Condemning Terror to Preaching Jihad," *New York Times,* May 8, 2010.

21 **On 9/11, Awlaki:** FBI, "Report on Interview with Anwar Aulaqi," Sept. 15, 2001.

21 **first heard the news . . . close the mosque:** J. M. Berger, *Jihad Joe: Americans Who Go to War in the Name of Islam* (Washington, DC: Potomac Books, 2011), p. 128.

21 **Awlaki posed . . . hands clasped:** "Curriculum Guide: Muslim: Fact and Stereotype," *Washington Post,* Sept. 25, 2001.

21 **hadn't owned a TV . . . "was considered to be an extremist":** Brian Handwerk and Zain Habboo, "Attack on America: An Islamic Scholar's Perspective—Part 1," *National Geographic News* (blog), Sept. 28, 2001, http://news.nationalgeographic.com/news/2001/09/0927_imampart1.html.

22 **"going through a serious PR crisis":** Alexander Meleagrou-Hitchens, *As American as Apple Pie: How Anwar al-Awlaki Became the Face of Western Jihad* (London: International Centre for the Study of Radicalisation and Political Violence, 2011), p. 35.

22 **question-and-answer session . . . "the US should have":** Anwar al-Awlaki, "Understanding Ramadan: The Muslim Month of Fasting," *Washington Post,* Nov. 19, 2001.

22 **He first attracted:** *9/11 Commission Report,* p. 517n33.

23 **Awlaki was visited:** Susan Schmidt, "Imam from Va. Mosque Now Thought to Have Aided Al-Qaeda," *Washington Post,* Feb. 27, 2008.

23 **"Blind Sheikh":** *9/11 Commission Report,* p. 72.

23 **religious credentials:** The Blind Sheikh is a sharia jurist with a degree in Koranic studies from the prestigious al-Azhar University in Cairo.

23 **Awlaki had spent time:** *9/11 Commission Report,* p. 221.

23 **shopping at Safeway:** FBI, "Surveillance Log of Anwar al-Aulaqi," Nov. 7, 2001, http://www.scribd.com/doc/149699460/1488-05312013.

23 **eating pizza:** FBI, "Surveillance Log of Anwar al-Aulaqi," Nov. 13, 2001.

23 **NPR show *Talk of the Nation*:** FBI, "Surveillance Log of Anwar al-Aulaqi," Nov. 15, 2001.

23 **consorting with prostitutes:** FBI, Office of Intelligence Policy and Review, "Memorandum to James A. Baker: Re: Anwar Nasser Aulaqi," Feb. 4, 2002, Washington, DC.

23 **discussed only trivial matters:** FBI, "Report on Interview with Anwar al-Aulaqi," Sept. 17, 2001.

23 **"Al-Hazmi was so slight of build":** FBI, "Report on Interview with Anwar al-Aulaqi," Sept. 21, 2001.

23 **"spiritual leader":** FBI, "Report on Anwar Aulaqi," Oct. 17, 2001.

23 **circulated a notice:** FBI, "Request of Query for Future Travel of Anwar Aulaqi," Oct. 25, 2001.

23 **garnered him an invitation . . . turkey and bacon sandwiches:** Department of Defense, "Internal e-mail, 'Re: Luncheon Speaker—Islam and Middle Eastern Politics and Culture,'" Jan. 24, 2002, https://publicintelligence.net/dod-email -discussing-anwar-al-awlakis-2002-presentation-at-the-pentagon/.

24 **trailing Awlaki . . . stopped surveillance:** FBI, "Surveillance Log of Anwar al-Aulaqi," Feb. 5, 2002.

24 **many years before 9/11:** FBI and Savannah Information Technology Center, "Investigative Information Request Form for Anwar al-Aulaqi," June 15, 1999.

24 **for the first time:** Phil Hirschkorn, "New York Remembers 1993 WTC Victims," CNN.com, Feb. 26, 2003.

24 **masterminded by Ramzi Yousef:** Benjamin Weiser, "Mastermind Gets Life for Bombing of Trade Center," *New York Times,* Jan. 9, 1998. Yousef trained at al-Qaeda's Sadda training camp on the Afghan-Pakistani border.

24 **five American citizens:** Abdul Yasin ("Most Wanted Terrorists: Abdul Rahman Yasin," Federal Bureau of Investigation, https://www.fbi.gov/wanted/ wanted_terrorists/abdul-rahman-yasin/view); Earl Grant (Ralph Blumenthal, "Defendant in a Bombing Plot Released on Bail," *New York Times,* October 19, 1993; Victor Alvarez (Joseph P. Fried, "The Terror Conspiracy: The Overview; Sheik and 9 Followers Guilty of a Conspiracy of Terrorism," *New York Times,* October 2, 1995; Clement Rodney El-Hampton (Francis X. Clines, "Specter of Terror; U.S.-Born Suspect in Bombing Plots: Zealous Causes and Civic Roles," *New York Times,* June 28, 1993); and Nidal Ayyad (Alison Mitchell, "The Twin Towers; Sifting Through Mideast Politics in Ashes of World Trade Center," *New York Times,* March 14, 1993).

24 **shot and killed Meir Kahane:** Michael Specter, "Jewish Leader Kahane Slain in New York," *Washington Post,* Nov. 6, 1990.

24 **Nosair's circle included:** Richard A. Serrano, "Early Terrorist in U.S. Condemns Today's Jihad," *Los Angeles Times,* May 16, 2013.

24 **CNN ran an interview . . . "I was a student in Pakistan":** "Transcript of John Walker [*sic*] Interview," CNN.com, July 4, 2002, http://edition.cnn.com/2001/ WORLD/asiapcf/central/12/20/ret.walker.transcript/.

25 **In a poll:** Toni Locy, "Few Have Sympathy for Lindh," *USA Today,* Jan. 28, 2002. Lindh's actions did not reach the threshold for charges of treason; after all, the Taliban were not, at the time Lindh was associated with them, launching attacks on American targets as al-Qaeda was.

25 **born in Washington, DC, . . . fewer than eighty-five survivors:** "John Walker Lindh Profile," CNN.com, n.d., http://www.cnn.com/CNN/Programs/people/ shows/walker/profile.html.

25 **Lindh's plea agreement:** *United States of America v. John Phillip Walker Lindh,* CR No. 02-37-A [hereafter *U.S. v. John Lindh*], plea agreement (Eastern District of Virginia, July 15, 2002).

25 **slapped sanctions on the Taliban:** Katherine Q. Seelye, "Lindh Lawyers Claim 'Selective Prosecution,'" *New York Times,* May 17, 2002.

25 **refused offers by al-Qaeda:** "John Walker Lindh Profile," CNN.com.

25 **convict him:** *U.S. v. John Lindh,* indictment, Feb. 5, 2002.

25 **ranged from Hamzah Khan:** *United States of America v. Mohammed Hamzah Khan,* Case No. 14 CR 564 [hereafter *U.S. v. Hamzah Khan*], indictment (Northern District of Illinois, Jan. 9, 2015).

26 **ABC News broadcast:** Brian Ross, "Tape Released: American Al Qaeda Member Warns of Attacks," ABCNews.org, Sept. 12, 2005, http://abcnews.go.com/GMA/Investigation/story?id=1115448.

26 **California convert . . . death metal . . . 9/11 . . . big attack:** Raffi Khatchadourian, "Azzam the American," *New Yorker,* Jan. 22, 2007.

26 **wept with joy:** Terry McDermott, "The Mastermind," *New Yorker,* Sept. 13, 2010.

26 **"Azzam al-Amriki" . . . "Fighting and defeating America" . . . first American to be charged:** Khatchadourian, "Azzam the American."

27 **known as Abu Abdul Rahman:** Yosri Fouda and Nick Fielding, *Masterminds of Terror: The Truth Behind the Most Devastating Terrorist Attack the World Has Ever Seen* (Edinburgh: Mainstream Publishing, 2003), p. 10.

27 **"Manual for a Raid" . . . "will be with your heavenly brides":** Hans G. Kippenberg and Tilman Seidensticker, *The 9/11 Handbook* (London: Equinox Publishing, 2007).

28 **"the Jews and the Crusaders":** Bernard Lewis, "License to Kill: Usama bin Ladin's Declaration of Jihad," *Foreign Affairs,* Nov./Dec. 1998.

28 **one and a half billion:** "The Future of the Global Muslim Population," Pew Research Center, Jan. 27, 2011, http://www.pewforum.org/2011/01/27/the-future-of-the-global-muslim-population/.

28 **idiosyncratic reading of the Book of Genesis:** Stuart Wexler, *America's Secret Jihad: The Hidden History of Religious Terrorism in the United States* (Berkeley, CA: Counterpoint Press, 2015), p. 3.

29 **"lost tribe" . . . "mud people":** Kerry Noble, *Tabernacle of Hate: Why They Bombed Oklahoma City* (Quebec: Voyageur Publishing, 1998), pp. 88–91.

29 **informed the beliefs . . . Ku Klux Klan . . . The Order:** For an overall discussion of this point, see Wexler, *America's Secret Jihad* and Henry Schuster with Charles Stone, *Hunting Eric Rudolph: An Insider's Account of the Five-Year Search for the Olympic Bombing Suspect* (New York: Berkley Books, 2005).

29 **bombed a park . . . two abortion clinics:** Schuster with Stone, *Hunting Eric Rudolph,* p. 17.

29 **Larry McQuilliams:** Greg Botelho, "Man Who Shot at Consulate, Federal Courthouse, Austin Police HQ Killed," CNN.com.

29 **father was studying . . . moved to St. Paul:** Jeremy Scahill, *Dirty Wars: The World Is a Battlefield* (New York: Nation Books, 2013), pp. 31–32.

30 **"holy warriors":** Awlaki, "Spilling Out the Beans."

30 **exploits of the mujahideen . . . to attend Colorado State:** Shane and Mekhennet, "Imam's Path from Condemning Terror to Preaching Jihad."

30 **first Gulf War:** Awlaki, "Spilling Out the Beans."

30 **as it was for bin Laden:** Osama bin Laden, "Jihad Against Jews and Crusaders,"

Al-Quds Al-Arabi, Federation of American Statistics, Feb. 23, 1998, http://fas .org/irp/world/para/docs/980223-fatwa.htm.

30 **to become more religious . . . traveled to Afghanistan:** Awlaki, "Spilling Out the Beans."

30 **words of Abdullah Azzam:** "Awlaki Acknowledges His Radical Past," The Investigative Project on Terrorism, May 4, 2012, http://www.investigativeproject .org/3568/awlaki-acknowledges-his-radical-past.

30 **first wife . . . first son:** Scott Shane, *Objective Troy: A Terrorist, a President, and the Rise of the Drone* (New York: Tim Duggan Books, 2015), p. 87.

31 **tracking Khalid al-Mihdhar . . . did not alert the FBI:** *9/11 Commission Report,* pp. 159, 181–82.

31 **rented an apartment:** *United States of America v. Zacarias Moussaoui,* Case No. 01-455-A [hereafter *U.S. v. Moussaoui*], Defense Exhibit 950 at 29 (Eastern District of Virginia, March 6, 2006).

31 **wrote a check:** FBI, "Report on Anwar Aulaqi Money Transfers," Sept. 20, 2001, http://www.scribd.com/doc/132509692/Awlaki-Production#page=28.

31 **Hani Hanjour:** *9/11 Commission Report,* p. 229.

31 **Hazmi, Hanjour, and Awlaki:** Ibid., p. 517 n33.

31 **"something very big is going to happen":** "Memorandum for the Record, 9/11 Commission, Dieter Snell," Nov. 19, 2003, http://media.nara.gov/9-11/MFR/ t-0148-911MFR-00449.pdf.

31 **"Never Again":** John Ashcroft, *Never Again: Securing America and Restoring Justice* (New York: Hachette Book Group USA, 2006).

32 **reconfigured from crime-solving organizations:** "Intelligence Reform and Terrorism Prevention Act of 2004," Public Law 108-458, Dec. 17, 2004, pdf at http://www.nctc.gov/docs/pl108_458.pdf.

32 **"take off and land":** *9/11 Commission Report,* pp. 273–76.

32 **Moussaoui was arrested:** Ibid., p. 247.

32 **second wave:** Phil Hirschkorn, "Moussaoui: White House Was My 9/11 Target," CNN.com, March 27, 2006.

32 **traveled to Pakistan . . . "Islamic Extremist Learns to Fly":** *9/11 Commission Report,* pp. 273–75.

32 **"probable cause":** Senator Chuck Grassley, "Letter to FBI Director Robert Mueller," Jan. 8, 2003, http://www.grassley.senate.gov/news/news-releases/ grassley-questions-rationale-behind-fbi-award.

32 **Binalshibh's phone number:** *9/11 Commission Report,* p. 273.

32 **credit card fraud:** Department of Justice, Office of Public Affairs, "Ali Al-Marri Pleads Guilty to Conspiracy to Provide Material Support to Al-Qaeda," Justice News, April 30, 2009, http://www.justice.gov/opa/pr/ali-al-marri-pleads-guilty -conspiracy-provide-material-support-al-qaeda.

33 **"far exceeds the interests":** Jeffrey Rapp, "Declaration of Mr. Jeffrey N. Rapp, Director, Joint Intelligence Task Force for Combating Terrorism," Sept. 9, 2004, pdf at http://www.washingtonpost.com/wp-srv/nation/documents/jeffreyrapp _document.pdf.

33 **plea agreement in 2009:** *United States of America v. Ali Saleh Kahlah al-Marri,*

Case No. 09-CR-10030 [hereafter *U.S. v. al-Marri*], Plea Agreement (District Court for the Central District of Illinois, April 3, 2009).

33 **"Stop it!":** "FBI Director Robert Mueller Describes Agency's Post-9/11 Transformation," *On Campus,* The Harbus, Oct. 16, 2012, http://www.harbus.org/2012/fbi-director-robert-mueller-describes-agencys-post-911-transformation/.

33 **Bush told Mueller:** George W. Bush, *Decision Points* (New York: Crown, 2010), pp. 144–45.

33 **two thousand agents:** Robert S. Mueller, "Statement Before the Senate Committee on Homeland Security and Governmental Affairs," Sept. 13, 2011, https://www.fbi.gov/news/testimony/ten-years-after-9-11-are-we-safer.

34 **former Navy SEAL who spoke Mandarin:** FBI, "FBI Director Names Arthur Cummings Executive Assistant Director for National Security Branch," Jan. 11, 2008, https://www.fbi.gov/news/pressrel/press-releases/fbi-director-names-arthur-cummings-executive-assistant-director-for-national-security-branch.

34 **"Holy shit!"** . . . **"Blind Sheikh"** . . . **"ASAP"** . . . **"overstays":** Author interview with Arthur Cummings, Southport, CT, Feb. 26, 2015.

35 **"What is the Bureau doing":** "FBI Director Robert Mueller Describes Agency's Post-9/11 Transformation."

35 **twenty-three-foot boat . . . once a month:** Cummings interview.

36 **"When you catch a terrorist":** Christopher Dickey, "The Next Terror Threat," *The Daily Beast,* May 6, 2011, http://www.thedailybeast.com/articles/2011/05/06/al-qaeda-terror-threat-to-new-york-city-and-us-trains-remains-high.html.

36 **Kelly recruited David Cohen . . . raised Jewish . . . "David, there is a man"** . . . **"station"** . . . **"rack and stack":** David Cohen, interview by author, Manhattan, New York, Oct. 1, 2014.

37 **Alec Station . . . "I want you to":** Lawrence Wright, *The Looming Tower: Al-Qaeda and the Road to 9/11* (New York: Knopf, 2006), p. 3.

37 **NYPD's CIA:** Christopher Dickey, "The Inside Story of the CIA and the NYPD," *The Daily Beast,* June 27, 2013, http://www.thedailybeast.com/articles/2013/06/27/the-inside-story-of-the-cia-and-the-nypd.html.

37 **assassination of Meir Kahane:** John Kifner, "Meir Kahane, 58, Israeli Militant and Founder of the Jewish Defense League," *New York Times,* Nov. 6, 1990.

37 **bin Laden's Pakistan-based group on Atlantic Avenue in Brooklyn:** Peter Bergen, *Holy War Inc.: Inside the Secret World of Osama bin Laden* (New York: Free Press, 2001), pp. 145–46.

37 **Palestinian had plotted to blow up:** Serrano, "Early Terrorist in U.S. Condemns Today's Jihad."

38 **"New York has been targeted"** . . . **"eighteen months later!":** Cohen interview.

39 **center be created . . . "connect the dots":** *9/11 Commission Report,* pp. 403–8.

39 **founded in 2004:** "Intelligence Reform and Terrorism Prevention Act of 2004," Public Law 108-458, Dec. 17, 2004.

39 **edited the *Harvard Law Review*:** Board of Editors, *Harvard Law Review,* Vol. 113, 1999–2000, http://harvardlawreview.org/about/staff/vol-113/.

39 Leiter was clerking . . . "All the time" . . . importance of Yemen: Author interview with Michael Leiter, Washington, DC, Sept. 15, 2014.

40 gathering intelligence . . . kept cropping up: Gregory D. Johnsen, *The Last Refuge: Yemen, Al-Qaeda, and America's War in Arabia* (New York: W. W. Norton, 2013), p. 233.

40 "The climate here": Johari Abdul-Malik, interview for "Connections Between Radical Cleric, Hasan Closely Examined," *PBS News Hour*, aired Nov. 12, 2009, PBS, http://www.pbs.org/newshour/bb/religion-july-dec09-imam_11-12/.

40 "You speak English": Tom Junod, "The Lethal Presidency of Barack Obama," *Esquire*, Aug. 12, 2012.

41 Mann Act: FBI, "Report on Anwar Aulaqi," May 6, 2003.

41 charged Awlaki with fraud: Shane and Mekhennet, "Imam's Path from Condemning Terror to Preaching Jihad."

41 father was a government minister: Awlaki, "Spilling Out the Beans."

41 750,000: Scahill, *Dirty Wars*, p. 186.

41 doctoral program: "Memo on Anwar Aulaqi Ph.D. Program Sponsorhip," July 12, 2000, Center for International Programs, New Mexico State University, Las Cruces, NM.

41 2002 sermon . . . Yemeni jail: Shane and Mekhennet, "Imam's Path from Condemning Terror to Preaching Jihad."

41 Awlaki characterized this: "Anwar Al-Awlaki interview with Moazzam Begg," *Cageprisoners*, Dec. 12, 2007, http://old.cageprisoners.com/articles.php ?id=22926.

41 Awlaki became involved: U.S. Department of the Treasury, "Treasury Designates Anwar Al-Aulaqi, Key Leader of Al-Qa'ida in the Arabian Peninsula," Press Center, July 16, 2010, http://www.treasury.gov/press-center/press-releases/Pages/tg779.aspx.

42 read the Koran: "Anwar Al-Awlaki interview with Moazzam Begg."

42 Sayyid Qutb . . . interrogate him: Scahill, *Dirty Wars*, pp. 187–88.

42 Awlaki was released: Meleagrou-Hitchens, "As American as Apple Pie."

CHAPTER 3: WHO ARE THE TERRORISTS?

44 strangest job interview . . . Theo van Gogh: Author interview with Mitchell Silber, Manhattan, Nov. 8, 2013.

45 Bouyeri had no links . . . Dutch officials: Mitchell D. Silber, *The Al Qaeda Factor: Plots Against the West* (Philadelphia: University of Pennsylvania Press, 2012), p. 222.

46 Silber's next stop was West Yorkshire: Ibid., pp. 107–27.

46 the radicalization process . . . He found that the plotters: Silber interview.

46 he traveled to Canada: Silber interview; see Silber, *The Al Qaeda Factor*, pp. 245–59.

46 experimented with homemade bombs: Linden McIntryre, "Canada: The Cell Next Door," *Frontline*, broadcast Jan. 2007, PBS, http://www.pbs.org/frontline world/about/episodes/602_transcript.html.

46 **planned to detonate truck bombs:** Silber, *The Al Qaeda Factor,* p. 245.

47 **department officials encouraged:** Silber interview.

47 **Published in August 2007:** Mitchell D. Silber and Arvin Bhatt, *Radicalization in the West: The Homegrown Threat* (New York: New York City Police Department, 2007), pdf at http://www.nypdshield.org/public/SiteFiles/documents/NYPD_Report-Radicalization_in_the_West.pdf.

47 **report lays out a taxonomy of jihadist terrorists:** Ibid., pp. 22–23.

47 **"cognitive opening":** Ibid., p. 6. The concept of the cognitive opening draws on the work Quintan Wiktorowicz, who did fieldwork among Islamist militants in the United Kingdom and, based on that work, published *Radical Islam Rising: Muslim Extremism in the West* (Washington, DC: Rowman & Littlefield, 2005). Wiktorowicz would later become an Obama administration official working on countering violent extremism.

48 **no perfect linear progression:** Silber and Bhatt, *Radicalization in the West,* pp. 6–7, 30, 36–37, 63.

48 **Secretary of Defense Donald Rumsfeld wondered:** "Rumsfeld's War-on-Terror Memo," *USA Today,* May 20, 2005.

48 **the majority of conspirators:** Silber and Bhatt, *Radicalization in the West,* pp. 26, 27, 59, 76.

48 **none was the product of a madrassa:** Ibid., and e-mail from Mitchell Silber to author June, 29, 2015.

48 **examined the educational backgrounds . . . engineering . . . "muscle hijackers":** Peter Bergen and Swati Pandey, "The Madrassa Scapegoat," *Washington Quarterly* 29, no. 2 (2006): pp. 117–25.

49 **"We fight against poverty":** "Remarks by Mr. George W. Bush, President, at the International Conference on Financing for Development," Monterrey, Mexico, March 22, 2002, http://www.un.org/ffd/statements/usaE.htm.

49 **"Today, billions of people":** "Howard Dean's Speech —Part Two," *Guardian,* Dec. 15, 2003.

49 **the United Nations General Assembly held a meeting:** Press release, "Terrorism Must Be Addressed in Parallel with Poverty, Underdevelopment, Inequality, General Assembly Told, As General Debate Concludes," UN General Assembly, GA/9971, Nov. 16, 2001, http://www.un.org/press/en/2001/ga9971.doc.htm.

50 **the Library of Congress issued a study:** Rex A. Hudson, *Who Becomes a Terrorist and Why: The 1999 Government Report on Profiling Terrorists* (Guilford, CT: Lyons Press, 1999), pp. 75, 77.

50 **son of Polish Holocaust survivors:** Author interview with Marc Sageman, Rockville, MD, Jan. 6, 2014.

50 **dynamic of group loyalty:** On this point, see Christopher Browning, *Ordinary Men: Reserve Police Battalion 101 and the Final Solution in Poland* (New York: Harper Perennial, 1998).

50 **an entirely new career path . . . "what drove me":** Sageman interview.

51 **The sample grew from 25 militants:** Ibid.; Marc Sageman, *Understanding Terror Networks* (Philadelphia: University of Pennsylvania Press, 2004).

51 **who joined terrorist organizations:** Ibid., pp. 73–74, 79, 83.

51 the importance of group dynamics: Ibid., pp. 107–21.

51 "social bonds": Ibid., p. 178.

51 Friends decided to join the jihad together: Ibid., pp. 110, 135, 156.

51 The planners and pilots: Ibid., pp. 103–7.

51 "bunch of guys": Sageman interview.

52 formed a group dedicated to holy war: *United States of America v. Kevin James et al.,* Case No. 8:05-cr-00214-CJC [hereafter *U.S. v. James et al.*], Plea Agreement for Defendant Kevin James (Central District of California, Dec. 14, 2007), pp. 13–17.

52 James recruited five others: Ibid.; Peter Bergen, *The Longest War: The Enduring Conflict between American and al-Qaeda* (New York: Free Press, 2011), p. 241.

52 group of largely Albanian immigrants: *United States of America v. Mohamad Ibrahim Shnewer,* Case No. 1:07-mj-02045-JS [hereafter *U.S. v. Shnewer*], Criminal Complaint (District of New Jersey, May 7, 2007); Bergen, *Longest War,* p. 241.

52 The Fort Dix plotters: *U.S. v. Shnewer,* Criminal Complaint, May 7, 2007, paras. g, h, i, 13.

52 the ringleader surveilled the Fort Dix base: Ibid., para. b, 15.

52 were convicted and given: U.S. Department of Justice, "One Plotter Sentenced to Life Plus 30 Years; Second Gets 33 Years in Prison for Conspiring to Kill U.S. Soldiers," press release, April 29, 2009, pdf at http://www.investigativeproject .org/documents/case_docs/843.pdf.

52 Abu Musab al-Suri, was publishing his magnum opus: Abu Musab al-Suri, *The Call to Global Islamic Resistance* (2004), which has been published on several jihadist websites. For an excellent translation of a condensed version, see Jim Lacey, ed., *A Terrorist's Call to Global Jihad: Deciphering Abu-Mus'ab al-Suri's Islamic Jihad Manifesto* (Annapolis, MD: Naval Institute Press, 2005).

52 An intense intellectual, Suri: Author's observations of Suri in London and Afghanistan in early 1997.

52 moved back to Afghanistan: Lacey, ed., *A Terrorist's Call to Global Jihad,* pp. 21, 23.

52 a sixteen-hundred-page book: See Suri, *The Call to Global Islamic Resistance,* chap. 8.5.

53 critique of bin Laden's al-Qaeda: Bergen, *Longest War,* p. 244.

53 a top-down bureaucracy: Ibid., p. 202.

53 A videotape recovered in Afghanistan . . . Suri instead recommended: Peter Bergen, *The Osama bin Laden I Know: An Oral History of al-Qaeda's Leader* (New York: Free Press, 2006), pp. 244–46.

53 reprinted at length and regularly: See Aaron Y. Zelin, "Inspire Magazine," *Jihadology* (http://jihadology.net/category/inspire-magazine/) for issues of *Inspire* magazine. *Inspire* 1, pp. 48–53: "The Jihadi Experiences: The Schools of Jihad"; *Inspire* 2, pp. 17–21: "The Jihadi Experiences: The Open Fronts and Individual Initiatives"; *Inspire* 4, pp. 35–39: "The Jihadi Experiences: The Military Theory of Open Fronts"; *Inspire* 5, pp. 29–32: "The Jihadi Experiences: Individual Terrorism Jihad and the Global Islamic Resistance Units"; *Inspire* 8, pp. 18–19:

"The Jihadi Experiences: The Main Areas of Operation for Individual Jihad"; *Inspire* 9, pp. 23–24: "The Jihadi Experiences: The Most Important Enemy Targets Aimed at by Individual Jihad"; *Inspire* 10, pp. 22–24: "The Jihadi Experiences: The Strategy of Deterring with Terrorism"; *Inspire* 12, pp. 42–43: "The Jihadi Experiences: The Concept of Preparation, Its Cause and Goal."

53 **As Suri himself pointed out:** Bergen, *The Osama bin Laden I Know*, p. 387; Suri, *The Call to Global Islamic Resistance*.

54 **Suri's vision was:** Marc Sageman, *Leaderless Jihad: Terror Networks in the Twenty-First Century* (Philadelphia: University of Pennsylvania Press, 2008), p. 144.

54 **told UPI in 2002 that there were likely as many as two thousand al-Qaeda cell members:** "U.S. Exposes Al-Quaeda Sleepr [*sic*] Cells from New York to Florida to L.A.," UPI, Nov. 1, 2002, http://www.freerepublic.com/focus/news/779780/posts.

54 **Two years later Walid Phares:** *Paula Zhan Now,* Jan. 23, 2006, CNN.com, http://www.cnn.com/TRANSCRIPTS/0601/23/pzn.01.html.

55 **David Cohen invited Sageman:** Marc Sageman e-mail to author, Aug. 23, 2015.

55 **taught terrorism workshops:** Associated Press, " 'Scholar in Residence' Is NYPD's Terrorism Guru," July 7, 2008.

55 **"Utilizing the Leaderless Resistance concept":** Louis Beam, "Leaderless Resistance," *The Seditionist,* Feb. 1992, http://www.louisbeam.com/leaderless.htm.

CHAPTER 4: LONE WOLVES

56 **Blues City Tours:** "Sightseeing and Tours," Blues City Tours, http://www.bluescitytours.com/index.php.

56 **In late April 2009:** James Kitfield, "Tennessee Is the Capital of American Jihad," *Politico,* July 23, 2015, http://www.politico.com/magazine/story/2015/07/chattanooga-shooter-carlos-bledsoe-120530.

57 **a little conductor's uniform:** *Losing Our Sons,* by Americans for Peace and Tolerance, June 2012 (a documentary about the Bledsoe and Long families).

57 **"From Friday to Monday"** . . . **"My heart dropped":** Author interview with Melvin Bledsoe, Memphis, TN, Feb. 22, 2014.

57 **June 1, 2009:** *State of Arkansas v. Abdulhakim Mujahid Muhammad (a.k.a. Carlos Bledsoe),* Case No. 60 CR-09-2626 [hereafter *Arkansas v. Muhammad*], Arrest Report (Arkansas Sixth Circuit, June 1, 2009).

57 **at close range with a semiautomatic rifle:** Ibid.

57 **heard the gunshots:** Associated Press, "APNewsBreak: Ark. Soldier Shooter Sent FBI Letter," July 29, 2011, http://www.foxnews.com/us/2011/07/29/apnewsbreak-ark-soldier-shooter-sent-fbi-letter/.

57 **did not strike:** *Arkansas v. Muhammad,* Arrest Report.

57 **Bledsoe drove off:** *Arkansas v. Muhammad,* Search Warrant Affidavit.

57 **Going to prison:** *Arkansas v. Muhammad,* Forensic Report.

58 **resulting in a fatality on American soil has been carried out by lone wolves:** "Homegrown Extremism 2001–2015."

58 **have served in America's wars:** Statement of Melvin Bledsoe before the House Committee on Homeland Security, "The Extent of Radicalization in the American Muslim Community and that Community's Response."

58 **put to work at an early age:** Melvin Bledsoe interview.

58 **Carlos worked at a Chuck E. Cheese's:** *Arkansas v. Muhammad*, Forensic Report, p. 4.

58 **Southern Baptist beliefs:** Melvin Bledsoe interview.

58 **also played basketball:** Daveed Gartenstein-Ross, "Abdulhakim Mujahid Muhammad (Carlos Bledsoe): A Case Study in Lone Wolf Terrorism," *Jihadology*, Dec. 23, 2013, http://jihadology.net/2013/12/23/guest-post-abdulhakim -mujahid-muhammad-carlos-bledsoe-a-case-study-in-lone-wolf-terrorism/.

59 **tight-knit Bledsoe family:** Author interview with Monica Holley (Bledsoe), Memphis, TN, Feb. 22, 2014.

59 **dabblings with marijuana:** *Arkansas v. Muhammad*, Forensic Report, p. 4.

59 **involved in a brawl:** Gartenstein-Ross, "Abdulhakim Mujahid Muhammad (Carlos Bledsoe)."

59 **"I'm gonna kill you":** Kristina Goetz, "Memphian Drifted to Dark Side of Islamic Extremism, Plotted One-Man Jihad vs. Homeland," *Memphis Commercial Appeal*, Nov. 14, 2010.

59 **"The climate in Memphis":** Melvin Bledsoe interview.

59 **graduated from high school:** Gartenstein-Ross, "Abdulhakim Mujahid Muhammad (Carlos Bledsoe)."

59 **For Melvin, Carlos's graduation:** *Losing Our Sons*.

59 **at Tennessee State University:** Marvin Bledsoe interview.

59 **In the car, the officer found . . . took a plea deal:** Gartenstein-Ross, "Abdulhakim Mujahid Muhammad (Carlos Bledsoe)."

59 **religious anchor:** *Losing Our Sons*.

59 **feeling that Judaism did not embrace blacks . . . formal declaration of faith:** Abdulhakim Muhammad, letter to Kristina Goetz, May 18, 2010, https:// aseerun.wordpress.com/2010/05/18/abdulhakim-mujahid-muhammad-may -18-2010-how-allah-guided-me/.

60 **all the Muslims she knew:** Monica Holley (Bledsoe) interview.

60 **in favor of reading the Koran:** *Losing Our Sons*.

60 **did not dress like that . . . She and her brother debated religion:** Monica Holley (Bledsoe) interview.

60 **a picture of Dr. Martin Luther King Jr. . . . . "What kind of religion" . . . covered it:** Melvin Bledsoe interview.

61 **"unclean":** Statement of Melvin Bledsoe before the House Committee on Homeland Security, "The Extent of Radicalization in the American Muslim Community and that Community's Response."

61 **white ankle-length robe:** Melvin Bledsoe interview.

61 **marry a Muslim "sister":** Monica Holley (Bledsoe) interview.

61 **dropping out of school:** Melvin Bledsoe interview.

61 **legally changed his name:** Carlos Bledsoe (Abdulhakim Mujahid Muhammad), Tennessee Official Name Change Record, April 23, 2006, in author's collection.

61 **planning to move to Yemen:** Melvin Bledsoe interview.
61 **"I love you guys, too":** Monica Holley (Bledsoe) interview.
61 **arrived in Yemen on September 11, 2007 . . . Yemenis were hospitable:** Abdulhakim Muhammad, letter to Kristina Goetz, May 18, 2010.
61 **cost of living:** Kristina Goetz, "Memphian Drifted to Dark Side of Islamic Extremism, Plotted One-Man Jihad vs. Homeland."
61 **teaching English for three hundred dollars:** James Dao, "A Muslim Son, a Murder Trial and Many Questions," *New York Times,* Feb. 16, 2010.
62 **arrested in Yemen . . . wage jihad:** *Arkansas v. Muhammad,* Forensic Report.
62 **99 percent Muslim:** "The Global Religious Landscape: A Report on the Size and Distribution of the World's Major Religious Groups as of 2010," Pew Forum on Religion and Public Life, Dec. 2012, pdf at http://www.pewforum.org/files/2014/01/global-religion-full.pdf.
62 **make bombs and gun silencers:** Abdulhakim Muhammad, letter to Kristina Goetz, undated; see also Goetz, "Memphian Drifted to Dark Side of Islamic Extremism, Plotted One-Man Jihad vs. Homeland."
62 **contact information for several militants:** *Arkansas v. Muhammad,* Forensic Report, p. 2.
62 **Political Security Organization:** Abdulhakim Muhammad, letter to Kristina Goetz, undated; see also Goetz, "Memphian Drifted to Dark Side of Islamic Extremism, Plotted One-Man Jihad vs. Homeland."
62 **mixed with hardened jihadists:** Abdulhakim Muhammad, letter to Kristina Goetz, undated.
62 **holy war . . . Greg Thomason . . . caught its attention:** *Arkansas v. Muhammad,* Forensic Report, p. 9.
63 **no choice in the matter:** *Arkansas v. Muhammad,* Forensic Report, p. 9.
63 **confidential informant for the Bureau:** Author interview with senior FBI official, Washington, DC, 2015.
63 **Bledsoe was deported:** *Arkansas v. Muhammad,* Forensic Report, p. 9.
63 **at Memphis International Airport . . . "raped by infidels":** Melvin Bledsoe interview.
63 **he fumed sullenly:** Dao, "A Muslim Son, a Murder Trial and Many Questions."
63 **Following instructions to report . . . stopped tracking him:** Author interview with senior FBI official.
63 **"broad dissemination on this":** Leiter interview.
63 **about ten thousand FBI investigations . . . and the Bureau had determined:** Author interview with senior FBI official.
64 **angry at CNN:** *Arkansas v. Muhammad,* Forensic Report, p. 9.
64 **setting Carlos up in Little Rock:** Melvin Bledsoe interview.
64 **searched the Internet:** *Arkansas v. Muhammad,* Forensic Report, p. 10.
64 **leaving his few possessions to mosques:** Kristina Goetz, "Muhammad Admits on Interrogation Video That Killing Was Retaliation," *Memphis Commercial Appeal,* July 22, 2011.
64 **buying weapons and stockpiling ammunition:** *Arkansas v. Muhammad,* Forensic Report, p. 10. Muhammad declined a request for an interview.

64 **"I'm not under surveillance. It's on"** . . . **practice shooting:** This is what Bledsoe told psychiatrist R. Clint Gray of Arkansas State Hospital about what he was thinking after he purchased the gun at Walmart. See *Arkansas v. Muhammad,* Forensic Report.

64 **assassinate three rabbis** . . . **the shots missed:** Abdulhakim Muhammad, letter to Kristina Goetz, undated; Goetz, "Memphian Drifted to Dark Side of Islamic Extremism, Plotted One-Man Jihad vs. Homeland."

65 **gasoline cost close to four dollars a gallon** . . . **he drove through Little Rock:** *Arkansas v. Muhammad,* Forensic Report.

65 **left his SUV's tailgate down:** Goetz, "Memphian Drifted to Dark Side of Islamic Extremism, Plotted One-Man Jihad vs. Homeland."

65 **hundreds of rounds of ammunition:** *Arkansas v. Muhammad,* Search Warrant Inventory.

65 **Molotov cocktails:** *Arkansas v. Muhammad,* Forensic Report, p. 9.

65 **"wanted to kill as many people in the army as possible":** *Arkansas v. Muhammad,* Hudson Interrogation (June 1, 2009).

65 **"without justified reason":** *Losing Our Sons.*

66 **stabbed a prison guard:** Abdulhakim Muhammad, letter to Kristina Goetz, May 18, 2010.

66 **had bragged about killing:** Abdulhakim Muhammad, letter to Kristina Goetz, undated.

66 **"I don't really feel nothing, you know":** Goetz, "Muhammad Admits on Interrogation Video That Killing Was Retaliation."

66 **a letter Bledsoe had sent the judge:** *Arkansas v. Muhammad,* Defendant Guilty Plea (Jan. 14, 2010).

66 **twelve life sentences, plus an additional 180 years:** *Arkansas v. Muhammad,* Judgment and Sentencing Order (Jan. 25, 2010).

67 **The Bledsoe family was bitter:** Melvin Bledsoe interview.

67 **Andy's father, Daris:** *Losing Our Sons.*

67 **Kevin Lamar James:** *U.S. v. James et al.,* Criminal Complaint (Aug. 2, 2005).

68 **grew up middle class** . . . **begins in Ramallah** . . . **settled in Arlington** . . . **grew up playing together** . . . **observant** . . . **parents divorced** . . . **the Capitol Restaurant:** Author interview with Nader Hasan, Arlington, VA, May 25, 2014.

69 **her generous handouts:** Nora Hasan, Obituary, *Roanoke Times,* May 31, 2001.

69 **passed through high school like a ghost:** McKinley and Dao, "Fort Hood Gunman Gave Signals Before His Rampage."

70 **enter the military:** Nader Hasan interview.

70 **an officer-training program in Texas** . . . **transferred to medical school:** McKinley and Dao, "Fort Hood Gunman Gave Signals Before His Rampage."

70 **Nidal's father died:** Malik Hasan, Obituary, *Roanoke Times,* April 18, 1998.

70 **his mother also died:** Nora Hasan obituary.

70 **"get to know God":** Lee Hancock, "The Survivors," *Texas Monthly,* June 2012.

70 **the Dar al-Hijrah mosque:** Nora Hasan obituary.

70 **Awlaki was already an imam:** McKinley and Dao, "Fort Hood Gunman Gave Signals Before His Rampage."

70 which catered to graduate students . . . attend a Yankees game . . . "burning in hell" . . . Iranian girlfriend: Nader Hasan interview.

71 "score all the points in Islam": Maria Newman and Michael Brick, "Neighbor Says Hasan Gave Belongings Away Before Attack," *New York Times,* Nov. 6, 2009.

71 One such argument: Asra Nomani, "Inside the Gunman's Mosque," *The Daily Beast,* Nov. 7, 2009, http://www.thedailybeast.com/articles/2009/11/07/major -hasans-hidden-militancy.html.

72 help him meet potential spouses: Nader Hasan interview.

72 graduated from medical school: McKinley and Dao, "Fort Hood Gunman Gave Signals Before His Rampage."

72 Nidal gave a presentation: U.S. Senate Committee on Homeland Security and Governmental Affairs, "A Ticking Time Bomb: Counterterrorism Lessons from the U.S. Government's Failure to Prevent the Fort Hood Attack" [hereafter Lieberman Report], Feb. 3, 2011, p. 29, pdf at http://www.hsgac.senate.gov//imo/ media/doc/Fort_Hood/FortHoodReport.pdf?attempt=2.

72 During a PowerPoint presentation: Nidal Hasan, "Nidal Hasan's June 2007 'Grand Rounds' presentation, part 1," Fox News, Sept. 10, 2013, http://video .foxnews.com/v/2663135028001/nidal-hasans-june-2007-grand-rounds -presentation-part-1/?#sp=show-clips.

73 his religious beliefs took precedence: Lieberman Report, p. 30.

73 upset by the battlefield injuries: McKinley and Dao, "Fort Hood Gunman Gave Signals Before His Rampage."

73 burned so intensely: Ibid.; Mary Pat Flaherty, William Wan, and Christian Davenport, "Suspect in Fort Hood Shooting, a Muslim, Asked Army to Discharge Him, Aunt Said," *Washington Post,* Nov. 6, 2009.

73 "Camel Jockey, Get Out!": McKinley and Dao, "Fort Hood Gunman Gave Signals Before His Rampage."

73 divulged that patients had told him: Joseph Rhee, Mary-Rose Abraham, Anna Schecter, and Brian Ross, "Officials: Major Hasan Sought 'War Crimes' Prosecution of U.S. Soldiers," ABC News, Nov. 16, 2009.

73 didn't seem like a good "fit": Lieberman Report, p. 34.

73 consisted almost entirely of references to the Koran: Ibid., p. 29.

74 his admiration for Awlaki and his ideas deepened . . . sent another query . . . another lengthy query . . . their paths had crossed . . . got a response out of Awlaki . . . Referring to the . . . Hasan asked if Awlaki could help him find a wife: Nidal Hasan, e-mail correspondence with Anwar al-Awlaki, Dec. 17, 2008–June 16, 2009, Intelwire.com, http://news.intelwire.com/2012/07/the -following-e-mails-between-maj.html.

75 earning about ninety thousand dollars a year: Philip Jankowski, "$4M and Counting: Hasan Trial Delays Add to Costs," *Killeen Daily Herald,* July 7, 2013.

75 Awlaki sent his thanks . . . send money to him via PayPal . . . phone him (collect) . . . collateral damage to innocent bystanders: Nidal Hasan, e-mail correspondence with Anwar al-Awlaki, Dec. 17, 2008–June 16, 2009.

75 the entire correspondence was known to the FBI . . . "Here's another e-mail

sent to Aulaqi" . . . "set a lead" . . . "involved in terrorist activities" . . . Agents in the FBI San Diego field office found the response puzzling . . . "The response looks a little slim" . . . Hasan was not "a friend of WFO" . . . "This is not San Diego" . . . all FBI investigation of Hasan was dropped: Webster Commission on the Federal Bureau of Investigation, Counterterrorism Intelligence, and the Events at Fort Hood, Texas, on Nov. 5, 2009, Final Report, July 19, 2012 [hereafter Webster Commission], pp. 41–61, https://www.fbi.gov/news/pressrel/press-releases/final-report-of-the-william-h.-webster-commission.

76 "a screwup": Author interview with senior FBI official, Washington, DC, 2015.

77 "Mike and I were pretty furious": Author interview with Andy Liepman, Santa Monica, CA, Aug. 4, 2014.

77 always glowing . . . useful to U.S. counterterrorism efforts: Lieberman Report, p. 33.

77 Hasan's evaluation report from 2008: Officer Efficiency Report, Nidal Hasan, covering period from July 1, 2007, to June 30, 2008, Hasan Department of Defense file, Stamp 20100108-331, Washington, DC.

77 regarding him as a fanatic: Lieberman Report, p. 34.

77 without any serious scrutiny: Ibid., p. 33.

78 arriving there on July 15: Webster Commission, p. 61.

78 "Nidal was afraid of war": Nader Hasan interview.

78 ramped up the number of soldiers deployed to Afghanistan: Peter Baker, "How Obama Came to Plan the 'Surge' in Afghanistan," *New York Times,* Dec. 5, 2009.

78 ordered to deploy to a combat zone . . . "You're getting our worst": Lieberman Report, p. 34.

78 had made a deep impression on Hasan: Colonel Terry Lee, interview by Shepard Smith, Fox News, Nov. 5, 2009, on YouTube at https://www.youtube.com/watch?v=cPrT0T3371Q.

78 purchased a Belgian FN Herstal 5.7-millimeter pistol: Webster Commission Report, p. 61.

78 began attending the Islamic Community of Greater Killeen mosque: McKinley and Dao, "Fort Hood Gunman Gave Signals Before His Rampage."

79 Hasan asked Danquah what advice: "Remarks Worried Muslim Leader," Associated Press, November 7, 2009.

79 deployment to Afghanistan was imminent: Anita Porterfield and John Porterfield, *Death on Base: The Fort Hood Massacre* (Denton, TX: University of North Texas Press, 2015), p. 74.

79 he stopped, as usual, at a 7-Eleven: Octavia Nasr, Tracy Sabo, and Kevin Bohn, "Fort Hood Suspect Nidal Hasan Seemed 'Cool, Calm, Religious,'" CNN.com, Nov. 7, 2009.

79 identifying himself as a "Soldier of Allah": Associated Press, "Hasan Called Himself 'Soldier of Allah' on Business Cards," Nov. 12, 2009.

79 rented a spartan one-bedroom for three hundred dollars a month . . . returned to the mosque: Maria Newman and Michael Brick, "Neighbor Says Hasan Gave Belongings Away Before Attack," *New York Times,* Nov. 6, 2009.

80 at 1:15 p.m. . . . drew his semiautomatic pistol . . . "Allahu Akbar!": *United States of America v. Nidal Hasan,* USCA Misc. Dkt. No. 12-8029/AR [hereafter *U.S. v. Hasan*], Sanity Board Report (U.S. Army Trial Judiciary, Third Judicial Circuit, Jan. 13, 2011), p. 27.

80 private Francheska Velez: Manny Fernandez, "Witnesses Relive Horror of Fort Hood Attacks," *New York Times,* Aug. 10, 2013.

80 Specialist Jason Hunt, twenty-two: Philip Jankowski, "Prosecution Can't Use Hasan Documents," *Killeen Daily Herald,* Aug. 15, 2013.

80 physician's assistant, Michael Cahill: Josh Rubin, Matt Smith, and Chelsea J. Carter, "Nidal Hasan Hopes for Death in Fort Hood Killings, Lawyers Say," CNN.com, Aug. 7, 2013.

81 more than two hundred rounds: Josh Rubin, "FBI agent Lays Out 'Gruesome,' 'Chaotic' Fort Hood Scene," CNN.com, Aug. 14, 2013.

81 so much gun smoke in Building 42003: *U.S. v. Hasan,* Sanity Board Report, p. 27.

81 shot Specialist Matthew Cooke: McKinley and Dao, "Fort Hood Gunman Gave Signals Before His Rampage."

81 Looking for more targets . . . The first two police officers: *U.S. v. Hasan,* Sanity Board Report, pp. 27–28.

81 "When I walked in there" . . . 270 bullet holes . . . 146 shell casings: Rubin, "FBI Agent Lays Out 'Gruesome,' 'Chaotic' Fort Hood Scene."

82 Nader was finishing a round of golf: Nader Hasan interview.

82 "You know who that is?": Lieberman Report, p. 39.

82 for calling his cousin "a good American": Nader Hasan, live interview by Shepard Smith, *Fox Report,* Nov. 5, 2009, http://www.huffingtonpost.com/2009/11/05/nidal-hasan-cousin-of-mal_n_347850.html.

82 issuing a statement: Associated Press, "Fort Hood Suspect Said Methodical Goodbyes," Nov. 6, 2009, http://abclocal.go.com/story?section=news/national_world&id=7104336.

82 Nader received hostile e-mails: Nader Hasan interview.

82 wished he had died during his assault: *U.S. v. Hasan,* Sanity Board Report, p. 28.

83 he identified with Carlos Bledsoe: *U.S. v. Hasan,* Panel Selection (July 9–16, 2013).

83 Hasan wrote a note: Nidal Hasan, letter to Fox News, Oct. 18, 2012; Catherine Herridge and Pamela Browne, "Hasan Sends Writings to Fox News Ahead of Fort Hood Shooting Trial," Fox News, Aug. 1, 2013, http://www.foxnews.com/politics/2013/08/01/hasan-sends-writings-ahead-fort-hood-shooting-trial/.

83 "defense of others": *U.S. v. Hasan,* Memorandum of Law for Proposed Defense: Defense of Others (June 10, 2013).

83 "The two biggest gaps": Louise Richardson, *What Terrorists Want: Understanding the Enemy, Containing the Threat* (New York: Random House, 2006), p. 43.

83 to protect someone in immediate danger: Manny Fernandez, "Fort Hood Suspect Says Rampage Was to Defend Afghan Taliban Leaders," *New York Times,* June 4, 2013.

84 **Nidal had nothing to live for:** Nader Hasan interview.

84 **garnered comment from Awlaki:** Middle East Media Research Institute, "Maj. Nidal Hasan, Fort Hood Shooter and Lone-Wolf Jihadi, Celebrated and Lionized by Terror Groups and Leaders," The Cyber and Jihad Lab, Aug. 15, 2013, http://cjlab.memri.org/uncategorized/maj-nidal-hasan-fort-hood-shooter-and -lone-wolf-jihadi-celebrated-and-lionized-by-terror-groups-and-leaders-al-qaeda-aqap-taliban-imu-and-more-as-well-as-top-online-jihadi-f/.

84 **the judge did not allow Hasan to plead guilty:** Mark Memmott, "Why the Fort Hood Suspect Couldn't Plead Guilty to Murder," NPR, July 2, 2013, http://www.npr.org/sections/thetwo-way/2013/07/02/197964034/why-the-fort-hood-suspect-cant-plead-guilty-to-murder; see "Pleas of the Accused," 10 U.S.C. § 845, Art. 45, Uniform Code of Military Justice [hereafter U.C.M.J.].

84 **found guilty and sentenced to death:** Billy Kenber, "Nidal Hasan Sentenced to Death for Fort Hood Shooting Rampage," *Washington Post,* Aug. 28, 2013.

84 **not to prosecute Hasan as a terrorist:** Susan Crabtree, "Pentagon Will Not Label Fort Hood Shootings as Terrorist Attack," *Washington Times,* Oct. 22, 2012.

84 **medical and other benefits:** After much discussion in Congress, in early 2015 a bill was passed to expand Purple Heart eligibility to the victims of perpetrators who had been in contact with a foreign terrorist organization prior to an attack. The medals were finally awarded five years after the attack.

84 **complex discussions:** If the Pentagon had declared Hasan to be a terrorist, this could have been used by his defense team as an example of undue "command influence" that interfered with the chances of Major Hasan receiving a fair trial.

84 **does not have a category for terrorism offenses:** 10 U.S.C. §§ 877–934, U.C.M.J., subchapter X.

84 **The last time the army carried out an execution:** Richard Serrano, "Last Solider to Die at Leavenworth Hanged in an April Storm," *Los Angeles Times,* July 12, 1994.

CHAPTER 5: PRE-CRIME

85 **Steven Spielberg's *Minority Report*:** *Minority Report,* directed by Steven Spielberg (Century City, CA: Twentieth Century Fox, 2002).

86 **radicalization "indicators":** Silber and Bhatt, *Radicalization in the West,* pp. 31, 33.

86 **"sweeping generalizations":** Al Baker, "New York City Police Report Explores Homegrown Terrorism," *New York Times,* Aug. 16, 2007.

86 **"It plays right into extremists' plans":** "NYPD Warns of Homegrown Terrorism Threat," NBCNews.com, Aug. 15, 2007.

86 **"lines between mainstream Muslims"** . . . **"imminent security threats"** . . . **"freedom of association concerns"** . . . **"If taken in its entirety":** Ibid., p. 12; "CountertERRORism Policy: MACLC's Critique of the NYPD's Report on Homegrown Radicalism," Muslim American Civil Liberties Coalition, 2008,

p. 9, pdf at ttps://www.brennancenter.org/sites/default/files/legacy/Justice/20081024.CountertERRORism.Policy.pdf.

86 **Demographics Unit . . . "ancestries of interest":** Matt Apuzzo, "New York Drops Unit That Spied on Muslims," *New York Times,* April 15, 2004.

87 **"level of rhetoric":** Matt Apuzzo, "Inside the Demographics Unit, the CIA Spy Team the NYPD Says Doesn't Exist," *Huffington Post,* Aug. 31, 2011.

87 **"Locations of Concern":** "Albanian Location of Concern Report," NYPD Intelligence Division, Demographics Unit, pdf at http://hosted.ap.org/specials/interactives/documents/nypd/nypd-albania.pdf.

87 **outside the NYPD's jurisdiction:** Apuzzo, "New York Drops Unit That Spied on Muslims."

87 **"militant paintball trips":** Chris Hawley and Matt Apuzzo, "NYPD Infiltration of Colleges Raises Privacy Fears," Associated Press, Oct. 11, 2011.

87 **the NYPD was looking on "college campuses":** Michael A. Sheehan, *Crush the Cell: How to Defeat Terrorism Without Terrorizing Ourselves* (New York: Three Rivers Press, 2008), p. 159.

87 **Imam Hamid Raza, a Brooklyn-based cleric . . . visits from strangers . . . became fearful of new worshippers . . . strange man appeared who seemed nervous . . . wanted to become a Muslim:** See *Hamid Hassan Raza et al. v. City of New York,* Case No. 13-cv-03448-PKC-JMA, Complaint (Eastern District of New York, June 18, 2013).

88 **defended its surveillance of Raza's mosque:** Adam Klasfeld, "Ugly Fight Ahead Over NYC Muslim Surveillance," Courthouse News Service, Sept. 12, 2013, http://www.courthousenews.com/2013/09/12/61093.htm.

88 **eleven plaintiffs in New Jersey:** *Syed Farhaj Hassan et al. v. City of New York,* Case No. 2:12-cv-03401-WJM-MF, Opinion (District of New Jersey, Feb. 20, 2014).

88 **reversed that decision:** *Hassan v. City of New York,* No. 14-1688, Opinion (Third Circuit, October 13, 2015), http://pdfserver.amlaw.com/nlj/HASSAN_ca3_20151013.pdf.

89 **sixteen serious plots:** NYPD, "Terrorist Plots Targeting NYC," NYC.gov, http://www.nyc.gov/html/nypd/html/pr/plots_targeting_nyc.shtml.

89 **bring down the Brooklyn bridge . . . NYPD counted it:** Benjamin Weiser, "A Bridge Under Scrutiny, by Plotters and the Police," *New York Times,* April 26, 2011.

89 **"plot" never more than a vague idea:** Phil Hirschkorn, "Homegrown Terrorist Bryant Neal Vinas Shows His Face in Brooklyn," CBS News, April 25, 2012, http://www.cbsnews.com/news/homegrown-terrorist-bryant-neal-vinas-shows-his-face-in-brooklyn/.

90 **computer consultant Steve Llaneza . . . Matthew's court date:** Author interview with Steve Llaneza, June 20, 2014. Llaneza's discussion of his son in this section is from this interview.

94 **sentenced for the illegal possession:** Tracy Seipel, "San Jose Neighbors Stunned by Alleged Terrorist Living in Their Midst," *San Jose Mercury News,* Feb. 9, 2013.

94 effectively became his home caregiver . . . plumbing company: Llaneza interview.

94 An FBI informant at the plumbing company . . . "unable to operate complex machinery": *United States of America v. Matthew Aaron Llaneza*, Case No. 4:13-cr-00145-YGR [hereafter *U.S. v. Llaneza*], Plaintiff's Sentencing Memorandum (Northern District of California, Feb. 24, 2014), p. 6.

94 didn't "really talk much": *U.S .v. Llaneza*, Defense's Sentencing Memorandum, Exhibit E.

94 stay away from weapons . . . shooting range: *U.S. v. Llaneza*, Plaintiff's Sentencing Memorandum, p. 10.

95 convert back to Christianity: *U.S .v. Llaneza*, Defense's Sentencing Memorandum, Exhibit F.

95 "harmless": *U.S. v. Llaneza*, Plaintiff's Sentencing Memorandum, p. 11.

95 "build a career for himself" . . . hire Matthew: *U.S .v. Llaneza*, Defense's Sentencing Memorandum, Exhibit F.

95 informant's positive reports . . . jihad in the States: *U.S. v. Llaneza*, Criminal Complaint, Affidavit of Christopher T. Monika (Feb. 7, 2013), pp. 1–2.

95 attending a vocational school: *U.S. v. Llaneza*, Defense's Sentencing Memorandum, pp. 7–8 and Exhibit F.

95 map out a plan . . . antigovernment militias . . . "avoid unintended casualties" . . . January 2013 the friends met again: *U.S. v. Llaneza*, Plaintiff's Sentencing Memorandum, p. 3.

96 Matthew offered to travel to Afghanistan . . . travel to Pakistan by ship . . . two cell phones: *U.S. v. Llaneza*, Criminal Complaint, pp. 3-4.

96 "I have jihad in my heart" . . . On the evening of February 7, 2013: *U.S. v. Llaneza*, Plaintiff's Sentencing Memorandum, p. 4.

96 asked him if he still wanted to proceed . . . In the early morning hours . . . his waiting friend nearby . . . attempted to detonate the bomb: *U.S. v. Llaneza*, Plaintiff's Sentencing Memorandum, pp. 4–5.

97 mounted six terrorist plots . . . The FBI has been responsible for thirty: "Homegrown Extremism 2001–2015."

97 more than a thousand Muslim men were detained: Dan Eggen, "Interrogations to Begin Soon for Illegal Mideastern Aliens," *Washington Post*, Feb. 8, 2002.

97 "no-fly" list: Ann David, "Why a 'No Fly List' Aimed at Terrorists Delays Others," *Wall Street Journal*, April 22, 2003.

97 fifteen thousand informants: Trevor Aaronson, "The Informants," *Mother Jones*, Sept. 2011.

98 secret internal FBI report: "Secret FBI Report Questions Al Qaeda Capabilities," ABC News, March 9, 2005, http://abcnews.go.com/WNT/Investigation/story?id=566425.

98 informants committed: U.S. Department of Justice, "Federal Bureau of Investigation Annual Otherwise Illegal Activity Report," Jan. 31, 2012, pdf at http://www.documentcloud.org/documents/742049-fbi-oia-report.html.

98 Shahed Hussain, a Pakistani-born con artist . . . relocated to the town of

Newburgh: Peter Finn, "Documents Provide Rare Insight into FBI's Terrorism Stings," *Washington Post,* April 13, 2012.

99 **violence worse than that of the Bronx:** According to FBI crime statistics, Newburgh has 54.67 crimes per 1,000 residents, whereas the Bronx has 32.12 crimes per 1,000 residents. See website Neighborhood Scout for "Crime Rates for Newburgh, NY," http://www.neighborhoodscout.com/ny/newburgh/crime/, and "Crime Rates for Bronx, NY," http://www.neighborhoodscout.com/ny/bronx/crime/.

99 **he befriended James Cromitie:** Finn, "Documents Provide Rare Insight into FBI's Terrorism Stings."

99 **a preposterous plot:** Javier C. Hernandez and Sewell Chan, "N.Y. Bomb Plot Suspects Acted Alone, Police Say," *New York Times,* May 21, 2009.

99 **at one point promised Cromitie:** Finn, "Documents Provide Rare Insight into FBI's Terrorism Stings."

99 **the "Newburgh Four" left bags:** Hernandez and Chan, "N.Y. Bomb Plot Suspects Acted Alone, Police Say."

99 **At Cromitie's sentencing:** Benjamin Weiser, "3 Men Draw 25-Year Terms in Synagogue Bomb Plot," *New York Times,* June 29, 2011.

99 **An appeals judge wrote:** Anahad O'Connor, "Judge Upholds Verdicts in Synagogue Bomb Plot," *New York Times,* May 3, 2011.

100 **2006 in Liberty City:** "5 Convicted in 'Liberty City' Terror Trial," CNN.com, May 12, 2009, http://www.cnn.com/2009/CRIME/05/12/liberty.seven/.

100 **Alberto Gonzales commented:** Abby Goodnough, "Trial Starts for Men in Plot to Destroy Sears Tower," *New York Times,* Oct. 3, 2007.

100 **on trial three times:** Aaronson, *The Terror Factory,* pp. 85–86.

100 **two of only four acquittals:** "Homegrown Extremism 2001–2015."

100 **North Carolina group led by Daniel Patrick Boyd . . . weapons training in rural North Carolina:** See *United States of America v. Jeff Boyd et al.,* Case No. 5:09-CR-216-1-FL [hereafter *U.S. v. Boyd*], Superseding Indictment (Eastern District of North Carolina, Sept. 24, 2009).

100 **Boyd was convicted:** FBI, "North Carolina Resident Daniel Patrick Boyd Sentenced for Terrorism Violations," press release, Aug. 24, 2012, https://www.fbi.gov/charlotte/press-releases/2012/north-carolina-resident-daniel-patrick-boyd-sentenced-for-terrorism-violations.

101 **Council on American-Islamic Relations:** Council on American-Islamic Relations, "The FBI's Use of Informants, Recruitment and Intimidation Within Muslim Communities," March 1, 2009, http://ca.cair.com/download.php?f=/downloads/CAIR_FBI_Abuses_Annotated_Source_List—Articles_and_Cases.pdf.

101 **Art Cummings met with Muslim American leaders . . . "Tell me you're joking":** Cummings interview.

101 **investigate the issue of radicalization:** Raymond Hernandez, "Muslim 'Radicalization' Is Focus of Planned Inquiry," *New York Times,* Dec. 16, 2010.

101 **tips from the local community:** "Homegrown Extremism 2001–2015."

102 **The night Matthew Llaneza was arrested . . . qualified for disability payments**: Llaneza interview.

102 **an entrapment defense**: See "Homegrown Extremism 2001–2015."

102 **in a memo to the judge**: *U.S. v. Llaneza*, Defense's Sentencing Memorandum, p. 3.

103 **four jihadist defendants have been acquitted**: See "Homegrown Extremism 2001–2015."

103 **attend the sentencing hearing**: Llaneza interview.

103 **an effort to fit in**: Associated Press, "15-Year Sentence for Man Who Wanted to Bomb Bank," Feb. 28, 2014.

103 **"This case, like many others"**: Robert Salonga, "San Jose Man Gets 15 Years in Prison for Oakland Bank Bombing Plot," *San Jose Mercury News*, Feb. 27, 2014.

103 **The U.S. Attorney's Office argued**: *U.S. v. Llaneza*, Plaintiff's Sentencing Memorandum, p. 6.

103 **Matthew pleaded guilty**: *U.S. v. Llaneza*, Judgment in a Criminal Case (Feb. 24, 2014).

103 **the only family member . . . The judge expressed disappointment**: Llaneza interview.

104 **fifteen years**: *U.S. v. Llaneza*, Judgment in a Criminal Case.

104 **"If nine-eleven hadn't happened"**: Llaneza interview.

CHAPTER 6: LEADER-LED JIHAD

106 **"a fundamental misreading of the al-Qaeda threat"**: Bruce Hoffman, "The Myth of Grass-Roots Terrorism," *Foreign Affairs*, May/June 2008.

106 *New York Times* **even ran a story about the debate**: Elaine Sciolino and Eric Schmitt, "A Not Very Private Feud Over Terrorism," *New York Times*, June 8, 2008.

106 **"Maybe he's mad that I'm the go-to guy now"**: Previous three paragraphs draw on Bergen, *Longest War*, pp. 201–2.

107 **the son of Alhaji Umaru Mutallab**: BBC, "Profile: Umar Farouk Abdulmutallab," Oct. 12, 2011, http://www.bbc.com/news/world-us-canada-11545509.

107 **a solemn loner in his teens**: Farouk1986, "I Think I Feel Lonely," online posting, Jan. 28, 2005, Islamic Forum Counselling Room, July 13, 2015, http://www.gawaher.com/topic/7544-i-think-i-feel-lonely/.

107 **worshipping at the mosque that was built by his father**: "Umar Farouq Abdulmutallab: One Boy's Journey into Jihad," *Sunday Times* (London), Jan. 3, 2010.

107 **study engineering at the academically rigorous University College, London**: Eric Lipton and Scott Shane, "Questions on Why Suspect Wasn't Stopped," *New York Times*, Dec. 27, 2009.

107 **"accepting martyrdom as a possibility"**: *United States of America v. Umar Farouk Abdulmutallab*, Case No. 2:10-cr-20005 [hereafter *U.S. v. Abdulmutallab*], Memorandum for the Court Prepared by Dr. Simon Perry (Eastern District of Michigan, Southern Division, Feb. 10, 2012).

108 **Living alone in a three-bedroom:** "Umar Farouq Abdulmutallab: One Boy's Journey into Jihad."

108 **presided over a "War on Terror Week":** Adam Nossiter, "Lonely Trek to Radicalism for Terror Suspect," *New York Times,* Jan. 16, 2010.

108 **seek out Awlaki in the mountains and deserts of Yemen:** *U.S. v. Abdulmutallab,* Government's Sentencing Memorandum (Feb. 2, 2012).

108 **"why he wanted to become involved in jihad":** Scott Lewis, "Exclusive: FBI Agents Reveal Underwear Bomber Abdulmutallab Wore Explosive Underwear for Three Weeks," WXYZ, Sept. 27, 2012, http://www.wxyz.com/news/local-news/investigations/fbi-agents-underwear-bomber-abdulmutallab-wore-underwear-for-3-weeks.

108 **"Oh mother":** *U.S. v. Abdulmutallab,* Memorandum for the Court Prepared by Dr. Simon Perry (Feb. 10, 2012).

108 **He sent a text also to his father:** "Umar Farouq Abdulmutallab: One Boy's Journey into Jihad."

108 **Around the same time:** Anwar Awlaki, "Could Yemen Be the Next Surprise of the Season?" PureIslam, http://www.pureislam.co.za/index.php?option=com_content&view=article&id=191:could-yemen-be-the-next-surprise-of-the-season&catid=100&Itemid=478.

108 **Alarmed by the text from his son:** Office of the Press Secretary, "White House Review Summary Regarding 12/25/2009 Attempted Terrorist Attack," White House Statement, January 7, 2010, Washington, DC.

109 **NCTC analysts made no effort:** Mark Hosenball, "Islamic Radicalization: Umar Farouk Abdulmutallab," *Newsweek,* Jan. 1, 2010.

109 **Asiri had recently sent his younger brother:** "Al-Qaeda Names Saudi Arabia Bomber," Al Jazeera, Aug. 30, 2009, http://www.aljazeera.com/news/middleeast/2009/08/200983091051611545.html.

109 **Asiri showed Abdulmutallab:** *U.S. v. Abdulmutallab,* Government's Sentencing Memorandum (Feb. 2, 2012).

109 **In early December:** *U.S. v. Abdulmutallab,* Memorandum for the Court Prepared by Dr. Simon Perry (Feb. 10, 2012).

109 **a black al-Qaeda flag with white Arabic lettering:** Video of Umar Farouk Abdulmutallab training in Yemen, on YouTube at http://www.youtube.com/watch?v=zenEMePcmko.

109 **The young Nigerian:** *U.S. v. Abdulmutallab,* Memorandum for the Court Prepared by Dr. Simon Perry (Feb. 10, 2012).

110 **On December 16:** Dana Hughes and Kirit Radia, " 'Underwear Bomber's' Alarming Last Phone Call," ABCNews, Dec. 31, 2009, http://abcnews.go.com/WN/bombers-phone-call-father/story?id=9457361.

110 **He chose Detroit:** *U.S. v. Abdulmutallab,* Memorandum for the Court Prepared by Dr. Simon Perry (Feb. 10, 2012).

110 **Secreted on his person . . . There were 290 passengers:** *U.S. v. Abdulmutallab,* Government's Opening Statement (Nov. 4, 2011).

110 **The bomb, stitched:** *U.S. v. Abdulmutallab,* Government's Sentencing Memorandum (Feb. 2, 2012).

110 **During the flight, Abdulmutallab was fasting:** *U.S. v. Abdulmutallab*, Government's Opening Statement (Nov. 4, 2011).

110 **He spent around twenty minutes washing his face:** *U.S. v. Abdulmutallab*, Memorandum for the Court Prepared by Dr. Simon Perry (Feb. 10, 2012).

110 **Telling his seatmates that his stomach was upset:** Lewis, "Exclusive: FBI Agents Reveal Underwear Bomber Abdulmutallab Wore Explosive Underwear for Three Weeks"; and *U.S. v. Abdulmutallab*, Government's Opening Statement (Nov. 4, 2011).

110 **After making his final prayers . . . a popping sound, like a very loud firecracker . . . "Your pants are on fire" . . . Abdulmutallab remained motionless . . . The aircrew used blankets and fire extinguishers:** *U.S. v. Abdulmutallab*, Government's Opening Statement (Nov. 4, 2011).

111 **The smell of Abdulmutallab's burned flesh permeated the cabin:** Ryan Corsaro, "Inside the 'Underwear Bomber' Sentencing," CBSNews, Feb. 16, 2012, http://www.cbsnews.com/news/inside-the-underwear-bomber-sentencing/.

111 **Customs and Border Protection agents detained:** *U.S. v. Abdulmutallab*, Government's Opening Statement (Nov. 4, 2011).

111 **Christmas dinner was in the oven:** Cummings interview.

111 **SIGINT . . . "based on everything we have":** Leiter interview.

112 **"I don't want to hear you guys arrested him":** Cummings interview.

112 **Two of the FBI agents who had escorted Abdulmutallab:** *U.S. v. Abdulmutallab*, Memorandum for the Court Prepared by Dr. Simon Perry (Feb. 10, 2012).

112 **Abdulmutallab was lucid and answered the agents' questions:** *U.S. v. Abdulmutallab*, Opinion and Order Denying Defendant's Motion to Suppress Statements Made at the University of Michigan Hospital (Sept. 16, 2011).

112 **after an hour of discussion:** Jo Becker and Scott Shane, "Secret 'Kill List' Proves a Test of Obama's Principles and Will," *New York Times*, May 29, 2012.

112 **On December 28:** "Al-Qaeda Wing Claims Christmas Day US Flight Bomb Plot," BBC, Dec. 28, 2009, http://news.bbc.co.uk/2/hi/middle_east/8433151.stm.

113 **six bottles of Clairoxide hair bleach . . . "had a lot of girlfriends":** Peter Bergen, "The Front," *The New Republic*, Oct. 19, 2009.

114 **They installed a commercial-grade refrigerator:** Christopher Dickey, *Securing the City: Inside America's Best Counter-Terrorism Force—The NYPD* (New York: Simon and Schuster, 2009), p. 212.

114 **Matthew Rugo and Curtis Jetton:** Cindy George, "Survivor Pleads Guilty in Fatal Bomb Blast," *Chron*, Dec. 21, 2007.

114 **Five years after his birth:** Michael Wilson, "From Smiling Coffee Vendor to Terror Suspect," *New York Times*, Sept. 25, 2009.

115 **prayed with this more radical contingent:** Matt Apuzzo and Adam Goldman, *Enemies Within: Inside the NYPD's Secret Spying Unit and Bin Laden's Final Plot Against America* (New York: Touchstone, 2013), p. 99.

115 **Zazi stopped wearing jeans:** Michael Wilson, "From Smiling Coffee Vendor to Terror Suspect," *New York Times*, Sept. 25, 2009.

115 **"dishonest" to Islam:** Samantha Gross, David Caruso, and Michael Rubinkam,

"Terror Suspect Zazi Surrounded by Radical Influences," NBC New York, Oct. 3, 2009.

115 **increasingly angered by the U.S.-led war in Afghanistan:** *U.S. v. Najibullah Zazi,* Transcript of Criminal Cause for Pleading (Feb. 22, 2010).

115 **He began listening:** Tamer El-Ghobashy, "Recordings Inspired Terrorist," *Wall Street Journal,* April 17, 2012.

115 **In August 2008:** *United States v. Mohammed Wali Zazi,* 1:10-cr-00060, [hereafter *U.S. v. Mohammed Zazi*] (Eastern District of New York, Aug. 18, 2011).

116 **Medunjanin harbored a vision:** Mitchell D. Silber, *The Al Qaeda Factor: Plots Against the West* (Philadelphia: University of Pennsylvania Press, 2012), p. 159.

116 **In Peshawar . . . someone who could speak to Zazi:** *U.S. v. Mohammed Wali Zazi* (Aug. 18, 2011).

116 **from camp dishwasher . . . Shukrijumah sold used cars:** Susan Candiotti and Ross Levitt, "From Dishwasher to al Qaeda Leadership: Who Is Adnan Shukrijumah?" CNN.com, Aug. 6, 2010.

116 **Shukrijumah told his mother:** Associated Press, "Report: New Al Qaeda Leader Knows U.S. Well," Fox News, Aug. 6, 2010.

116 **"Did you hear what happened?" . . . His mother advised:** Candiotti and Levitt, "From Dishwasher to al Qaeda Leadership."

116 **It was Shukrijumah . . . potential targets:** *U.S. v. Adis Medunjanin et al.,* 1:10cr19, Superseding Indictment (S-3) (Eastern District of New York, July 7, 2010).

117 **five days of training on building hydrogen peroxide . . . e-mailed to himself before leaving Pakistan:** *U.S. v. Najibullah Zazi* (Feb. 22, 2010).

117 **Vinas had traveled to Pakistan's tribal areas:** *United States of America v. Bryant Neal Vinas,* Case No. 08-CR-823 [hereafter *U.S. v. Vinas*], Guilty Plea Hearing (Eastern District of New York, taken Jan. 29, 2009, unsealed July 23, 2009).

118 **Vinas had bounced around in Pakistan for months:** Vinas traveled to Pakistan in the fall of 2007, but he was involved in an al-Qaeda attack, on an American base, only in September 2008. *U.S. v. Vinas,* Guilty Plea Hearing (taken Jan. 29, 2009, unsealed July 23, 2009), and author interview with Don Borelli, Manhattan, Oct. 1, 2014.

118 **the three al-Qaeda recruits met on a basketball court:** Silber interview.

118 **"to make America weak" . . . "people would have a lot of fear":** Associated Press, "3rd Day of Testimony for Subway Plot Mastermind," ABC News, April 19, 2012.

118 **checked into the HomeStead Studio Suites motel:** Apuzzo and Goldman, *Enemies Within,* p. 267.

118 **On the night of September 6 . . . "the marriage is ready":** *U.S. v. Mohammed Wali Zazi* (Aug. 18, 2011).

119 **The leaders of al-Qaeda typically used dozens:** Senior FBI official, interview by author.

119 **The e-mail address Zazi used to touch base with:** *U.S. v. Mohammed Wali Zazi* (Aug. 18, 2011).

119 **the Brits tipped off American officials . . . On September 6, as Zazi repeatedly**

pinged: Cahall, Sterman, Schneider, and Bergen, "Do NSA's Bulk Surveillance Programs Stop Terrorists?"

120 **The FBI found . . . "Don't make any mistakes":** Cummings interview.

120 **In the trunk of his car he had secreted:** *U.S. v. Najibullah Zazi,* Memorandum of Law in Support of the Government's Motion for a Permanent Order of Detention (Eastern District of New York, Sept. 24, 2009).

120 **"Serious case":** Author interview with Philip Mudd, Alexandria, VA, May 10, 2014.

121 **worried about Zazi . . . one of their informants:** Cohen interview.

121 **"I thought the Bureau was regularly on the wrong side":** Mudd interview.

121 **went ballistic . . . "We did what we were asked to do":** Cohen interview.

121 **"colossal screwup" . . . "We got lucky":** Senior FBI official, interview by author, Washington, DC, 2015.

122 **officials came up with a plan:** Cohen interview.

122 **gave Port Authority officials a description:** Apuzzo and Goldman, *Enemies Within,* pp. 60–61.

122 **looked like they were targeting Zazi:** Cohen interview.

122 **officers' bomb-sniffing . . . a bomb tech earlier in his career:** Cummings interview.

122 **"We are done":** Phil Hirschkorn, "Would-Be Subway Suicide Bomber Najibullah Zazi Speaks," CBS News, April 19, 2012, http://www.cbsnews.com/news/would-be-subway-suicide-bomber-najibullah-zazi-speaks/.

123 **They found an electronic scale of a type:** *U.S. v. Najibullah Zazi,* Memorandum of Law in Support of the Government's Motion for a Permanent Order of Detention (Eastern District of New York, Sept. 24, 2009).

123 **multiple brand-new backpacks:** Cummings interview.

123 **Zazi flew back to Colorado:** *U.S. v. Najibullah Zazi,* Memorandum of Law in Support of the Government's Motion for a Permanent Order of Detention.

123 **"We love death more than you love life" . . . After hanging up he crashed his car:** *U.S. v. Medunjanin* (May 20, 2014).

123 **"Soon we will launch an attack in Washington":** Associated Press, "Taliban Leader Vows to Attack D.C. 'Soon,'" CBS News, March 31, 2009, http://www.cbsnews.com/news/taliban-leader-vows-to-attack-dc-soon/.

124 **Jordanian doctor, released a lengthy interview:** An interview with Shaheed Abu Dujaanah al Khorshani (Humam Khalil Abu-Mulal al-Balawi)," Feb. 28, 2010, NEFA Foundation.

124 **Hakimullah Mehsud, also appeared alongside Balawi:** Stephen Farrell, "Video Links Taliban in Pakistan to C.I.A. Attack," *New York Times,* Jan. 9, 2010.

124 **Shahzad was the youngest of four children:** James Barron and Sabrina Tavernise, "Money Woes, Long Silences and a Zeal for Islam," *New York Times,* May 5, 2010.

124 **In 1999, Shahzad went to college in the States . . . "personable, a nice guy, but unremarkable":** "Profile: Faisal Shahzad," BBC.com, Oct. 5, 2010, http://www.bbc.com/news/world-us-canada-11475789.

124 **On weekends . . . "had it coming" . . . By 2002 . . . snazzy black Mercedes:** Andrea Elliott, Sabrina Tavernise, and Anne Barnard, "For Times Sq. Suspect, Long Roots of Discontent," *New York Times,* May 15, 2010.

125 **conversant in four languages:** Josh Barbanel, Andrew Grossman, and Sumathi Reddy "From New Citizen to Suspect in a Year," *Wall Street Journal,* May 5, 2010.

125 *Friends* and *Everybody Loves Raymond* . . . **"fashion, shoes, bags, SHOP-PING!!":** Kealan Oliver, "Huma Mian: Profile of Wife of Faisal Shahzad, Times Square Bomb Suspect," CBS News, May 5, 2010, http://www.cbsnews.com/news/huma-mian-profile-of-wife-of-faisal-shahzad-times-square-bomb-suspect.

125 **"Im a Muslim & Im Proud!" and "I LOVE ALLAH":** "Times Square Suspect's Wife Born and Raised in Colo.," ABC affiliate Denver, May 5, 2010, http://www.thedenverchannel.com/news/times-square-suspect-s-wife-born-and-raised-in-colo-.

125 **Faisal was granted a green card in early 2006:** Nina Bernstein, "Bombing Suspect's Route to Citizenship Reveals Limitations," *New York Times,* May 7, 2010.

125 **earning seventy thousand dollars . . . "Everyone knows" . . . "clashing with":** Elliott, Tavernise, and Barnard, "For Times Sq. Suspect, Long Roots of Discontent."

125 **"By now Shahzad was listening to:** Scott Shane and Mark Mazzetti, "Times Sq. Bomb Suspect Is Linked to Militant Cleric," *New York Times,* May 6, 2010.

126 **In the Pakistani capital of Islamabad:** Andrea Elliott, "Militant's Path from Pakistan to Times Square," *New York Times,* June 22, 2010.

126 **Shahzad asked permission from his father:** James Barron and Sabrina Tavernise, "Money Woes, Long Silences and a Zeal for Islam," *New York Times,* May 5, 2010.

126 **"sheikhs are in the field" . . . On April 17:** Elliott, Tavernise, and Barnard, "For Times Sq. Suspect, Long Roots of Discontent."

126 **He took out a $65,000 equity loan:** Amy Haimerl, "Faisal Shahzad's $65,000 Home Equity Piggy Bank," CNNMoney.com, May 6, 2010.

126 **pressure his wife . . . On June 2 . . . crash course in bomb making:** Elliott, Tavernise, and Barnard, "For Times Sq. Suspect, Long Roots of Discontent."

127 **who gave him five thousand dollars:** *United States of America v. Faisal Shahzad,* Case No. 10CR541 [hereafter *U.S. v. Shahzad*], "Government's Memorandum in Connection with the Sentencing of Faisal Shahzad" (U.S. District Court Southern District of New York, Sept. 29, 2010).

127 **"And . . . uh . . . jihad . . . the importance that it has":** Taliban video of Faisal Shahzad, Sept. 30, 2010, available at http://www.nytimes.com/video/nyregion/1248069111343/taliban-video-of-faisal-shahzad.html.

127 **the bank had foreclosed:** Elliott, Tavernise, and Barnard, "For Times Sq. Suspect, Long Roots of Discontent"; John Christoffersen, "Times Square Bomb Investigation: FBI Searches Bridgeport Home of Faisal Shahzad," Associated Press, July 4, 2010.

127 **He began accumulating the supplies for his bomb:** Government's Memorandum in Connection with the Sentencing of Faisal Shahzad, *U.S. v. Shahzad* (Sept. 29, 2010).

127 **He received five thousand dollars:** U.S. Department of Justice, Office of Public Affairs, "Faisal Shahzad Pleads Guilty in Manhattan Federal Court to 10 Federal Crimes Arising from Attempted Car Bombing in Times Square," Justice News, June 21, 2010, http://www.justice.gov/opa/pr/faisal-shahzad-pleads -guilty-manhattan-federal-court-10-federal-crimes-arising-attempted-car.

128 **a 1993 Nissan Pathfinder he found through Craigslist:** William K. Rashbaum, Mark Mazzetti, and Peter Baker, "Arrest Made in Times Square Bomb Case," *New York Times,* May 3, 2010.

128 **9-millimeter Kel-Tec semiautomatic rifle:** U.S. Department of Justice, Office of Public Affairs, "Faisal Shahzad Pleads Guilty in Manhattan Federal Court to 10 Federal Crimes Arising from Attempted Car Bombing in Times Square."

128 **the precaution of practicing his shooting at a gun range . . . spent the past three months . . . if all went to plan:** Government's Memorandum in Connection with the Sentencing of Faisal Shahzad, *U.S. v. Shahzad* (Sept. 29, 2010).

128 **Shahzad parked the SUV at the corner . . . three propane gas tanks:** Criminal Complaint, *U.S. v. Shahzad* (May 4, 2010).

128 **planned to do another bombing in two weeks:** Government's Memorandum in Connection with the Sentencing of Faisal Shahzad, *U.S. v. Shahzad* (Sept. 29, 2010).

128 **Street vendor:** Ray Kelly, *Vigilance: My Life Serving America and Protecting Its Empire City* (New York: Hachette Books, 2015), pp. 243–244.

128 **The officer began evacuating the area:** *U.S. v. Shahzad,* Criminal Complaint (May 4, 2010).

128 **Illegal fireworks could have been up to one thousand times more powerful:** David Falchek and Steve McConnell, "Investigators Say Times Square Bomb Suspect Bought Fireworks in Matamoras," *Times Tribune,* May 6, 2010.

129 **"That plot was only thwarted through chemistry and physics":** Borelli interview.

129 **for the blast of the bomb detonating . . . he sent a message to his Taliban contact:** Government's Memorandum in Connection with the Sentencing of Faisal Shahzad, *U.S. v. Shahzad* (Sept. 29, 2010).

129 **That night, NYPD intelligence officials:** Cohen interview.

129 **found its unique vehicle identification number:** *U.S. v. Shahzad,* Criminal Complaint (May 4, 2010).

129 **"I don't know, but he called me back the next" . . . a savvy Customs and Border Protection agent:** Cohen interview.

129 **Worried by TV coverage:** Borelli interview.

130 **He made a last-minute reservation:** Mark Mazzetti, Sabrina Tavernise, and Jack Healy, "Suspect, Charged, Said to Admit to Role in Plot," *New York Times,* May 4, 2010.

130 **just been added to the no-fly list . . . jet's doors closed:** Scott Shane, "Lapses Allowed Suspect to Board Plane," *New York Times,* May 4, 2010.

130 **"I was expecting you"**: Pierre Thomas, "Exclusive: The Moment When Federal Dragnet Closed on Bomb Suspect," ABC News, May 6, 2010, http://abcnews.go.com/WN/Blotter/customs-agent-arrested-faisal-shahzad-talks-exclusively-abc/story?id=10574411.

130 **most likely in a suicide bombing**: Cohen interview.

130 **"I'm going to plead guilty one hundred times forward"**: Plea, *U.S. v. Shahzad* (June 21, 2010).

CHAPTER 7: JIHADINAMERICA.COM

131 **greatest desire was to be a U.S. Army general**: Zachary Chesser, letter to author, May 27, 2014.

131 **grandfather was career army . . . they were married**: Author interview with Barbara Chesser, Virginia, May 24, 2014.

131 **PhD at the University of Virginia . . . taught at the University of Missouri**: *United States of America v. Zachary Adam Chesser*, Case No. 1:10-cr-395 [hereafter *U.S. v. Chesser*], Exhibit 1 (Eastern District of Virginia, Feb. 18, 2011).

131 **Fairfax County**: Barbara Chesser interview.

132 **economist for the Department of Transportation**: *U.S. v. Chesser*, Exhibit 1 (Feb. 18, 2011).

132 **prosecutor for the DC government . . . marriage was unraveling**: Barbara Chesser interview.

132 **songs about torturing and killing Osama bin Laden**: Zachary Chesser, letter to author, May 27, 2014.

132 **"America will stand proud and tall"**: Author's personal collection.

132 **reading at a sixth-grade level by age six**: Barbara Chesser interview.

132 **obsessional interests**: *U.S. v. Chesser*, Defendant's Position (Feb. 18, 2011).

132 **cruelty to animals . . . boycotting Nike**: Zachary Chesser, letter to author, May 27, 2014.

132 **a longhaired, vocal pacifist**: *U.S. v. Chesser*, Defendant's Position (Feb. 18, 2011).

132 **dabbled in Buddhism . . . draw well and played the guitar**: *U.S. v. Chesser*, Exhibit 1 (Feb. 18, 2011).

132 **Japanese for four years**: *U.S. v. Chesser*, Defendant's Position (Feb. 18, 2011).

132 **"He had a tendency"**: Barbara Chesser interview.

133 **the animated series *South Park***: *U.S. v. Chesser*, Exhibit 2 (Feb. 18, 2011).

133 **"ginormous" fan**: Barbara Chesser interview.

133 **Standing six foot one**: *U.S. v. Chesser*, Exhibit 1 (Feb. 18, 2011).

133 **break-dancing**: *U.S. v. Chesser*, Defendant's Position (Feb. 18, 2011).

133 **sports and calculus equally manageable**: Zachary Chesser, letter to the author, May 27, 2014.

133 **daughter of Somali immigrants**: *U.S. v. Chesser*, Defendant's Position (Feb. 18, 2011).

133 **didn't approve of his daughter dating**: Barbara Chesser interview.

133 **"I became Muslim after reading"**: Zachary Chesser, interview with Aaron Y. Zelin, June 29, 2010.

133 **playing on a football team:** Zachary Chesser, letter to the author, May 27, 2014; Senate Committee on Homeland Security and Governmental Affairs, "Zachary Chesser: A Case Study in Online Islamist Radicalization and Its Meaning for the Threat of Homegrown Terrorism," Feb. 2012.

133 **the summer of 2008:** *U.S. v. Chesser,* Affidavit (July 21, 2010).

133 **"I had very little exposure":** *U.S. v. Chesser,* Statement of Responsibility (Feb. 18, 2011).

133 **After three months of practicing . . . "Islam does not allow paramours":** Senate Committee on Homeland Security and Governmental Affairs, "Zachary Chesser: A Case Study in Online Islamist Radicalization and Its Meaning for the Threat of Homegrown Terrorism," Feb. 2012.

133 **not use toilet paper:** *U.S. v. Chesser,* Exhibit 2 (Feb. 18, 2011).

133 **couldn't even vote:** *U.S. v. Chesser,* Defendant's Position (Feb. 18, 2011).

134 **prevented him from having health insurance . . . "That imam, he doesn't know":** Barbara Chesser interview.

134 **robes worn by men in the Gulf States:** *U.S. v. Chesser,* Defendant's Position (Feb. 18, 2011).

134 **pant legs well above his shoes:** *U.S. v. Chesser,* Exhibit 1 (Feb. 18, 2011).

134 **odd, slightly foreign accent:** Barbara Chesser interview.

134 **quit his job at Blockbuster:** Zachary Chesser, letter to author, May 27, 2014.

134 **stopped going out to dance clubs:** *U.S. v. Chesser,* Exhibit 1 (Feb. 18, 2011); Zachary Chesser, letter to author, May 27, 2014.

134 **could no longer be around her partner . . . "My religion precludes me":** Barbara Chesser interview.

134 **rants delivered by Hitler . . . "I don't believe in violence":** *U.S. v. Chesser,* Exhibit 1 and 2 (Feb. 18, 2011).

134 **Muslim Student Association . . . very exciting:** Zachary Chesser, letter to author, May 27, 2014.

134 **referring to him as "Jesus":** *U.S. v. Chesser,* Defendant's Position (Feb. 18, 2011).

134 **during the spring of 2010 . . . Zac assured her:** Barbara Chesser interview.

135 **long available only in Arabic . . . "Internet led to a rapid rise":** Zachary Chesser, letter to author, May 27, 2014.

136 **"medium of communication" . . . "The upside is that you can try":** Silber interview.

136 **"hands down the most influential" . . . "44 Ways to Support Jihad":** Zachary Chesser, letter to the author, May 27, 2014.

136 **Khan eventually rivaled, and aided . . . From his home in suburban Charlotte:** Jason Leopold, "The FBI Discussed an 'End-Game' for a US Citizen Killed in a Drone Strike," *Vice News,* June 8, 2015, https://news.vice.com/article/the-fbi-discussed-an-end-game-for-a-us-citizen-killed-in-a-drone-strike.

137 **born in Saudi Arabia . . . moved to Queens when he was seven:** Michael Moss, "An Internet Jihad Aims at U.S. Viewers," *New York Times,* Oct. 15, 2007.

137 **later settled in suburban Long Island . . . wrote for the school newspaper:**

Timothy Bolger, "Slain al-Qaeda Mouthpiece Samir Khan's Westbury Roots," *Long Island Press,* Oct. 6, 2011.

137 **Muslim summer camp . . . stopped listening to hip-hop . . . baggy pants:** Moss, "An Internet Jihad Aims at U.S. Viewers."

137 **In the tenth grade . . . refused to cite:** Matthew Chayes et al., "Samir Khan, al-Qaida Figure, Grew Up on Long Island," *Newsday,* Oct. 6, 2011.

137 **"Before 9/11 people saw this change":** Ibid. Samir Khan's family did not respond to detailed questions from the author submitted to them through their lawyer, Jameel Jaffer.

137 **U.S. foreign policy was to blame . . . Islamic Thinkers Society:** Chayes et al., "Samir Khan, al-Qaida Figure, Grew Up on Long Island."

137 **"Death to All Juice":** Robert Spencer, " 'Death to All Juice': Calling for Genocide with Plausible Deniability?" JihadWatch, Dec. 31, 2008, http://www .jihadwatch.org/2008/12/death-to-all-juice-calling-for-genocide-with-plausible -deniability.

137 **The group later evolved into an even more militant arm:** From an unpublished law enforcement assessment of the Islamic Thinkers Society and Revolution Islam.

138 **"Many of our hard working brothers":** "Jihad Recollections Issue 1 Rabi' al-Thani," April 2009.

138 **Khan's family moved:** Moss, "An Internet Jihad Aims at U.S. Viewers."

138 **subdivision of Charlotte:** Dina Temple-Raston, "American Editor Brings U.S. Savvy to Jihad Outreach," NPR, Oct. 12, 2010.

138 **He wrote about:** Samir Khan, "The US Cannot Ban Alcohol Without Purifying the Nation," *Inshallahshaheed* (blog), Sept. 11, 2005, http://inshallahsha-heed.blogspot.com/2005_09_01_archive.html.

138 **praised attacks . . . dead American soldiers in Iraq . . . consulted with a local lawyer:** Temple-Raston, "American Editor Brings U.S. Savvy to Jihad Outreach."

138 **FBI had begun paying attention . . . "wussies":** Leopold, "The FBI Discussed an 'End-Game' for a US Citizen Killed in a Drone Strike."

138 **never allowed to speak at the mosque again:** Author interview with Jibril Hough, Charlotte, NC, Nov. 7, 2013.

139 **"an ideal arena":** Gabriel Weimann, *Terror on the Internet: The New Arena, the New Challenges* (Washington, DC: United States Institute of Peace, 2006), p. 29.

139 *New York Times* **ran a story . . . "very carefully" . . . dreamt of meeting bin Laden:** Moss, "An Internet Jihad Aims at U.S. Viewers."

139 **"When I saw that video":** "The Internet Jihadi," *New York Times,* online video, Oct. 14, 2007, http://www.nytimes.com/video/world/1194817096243/the -internet-jihadi.html.

139 **a well-known leader:** Temple-Raston, "American Editor Brings U.S. Savvy to Jihad Outreach."

139 **"We need to talk to Samir" . . . Khan soon lost his job:** Hough interview.

140 **In secret memos, agents noted that his "pro-jihad blog":** Franco Ordoñez and Marisa Taylor, "Record: FBI Plotted Samir Khan Arrest, but Dropped Plan," McClatchy DC, March 8, 2015, http://www.mcclatchydc.com/news/nation-world/national/national-security/article24781111.html.

141 **"flimsy excuse" . . . English teacher . . . "global superpowers":** Samir Khan, "I Am Proud to Be a Traitor to America," *Inspire,* Fall 2010.

141 **young Samir would prove valuable:** Author interview with U.S. official working in Yemen at the time.

143 **"not to contribute":** Author interview with Nicholas Rasmussen, MacLean, VA, May 6, 2014.

144 **getting in touch with him via encrypted e-mail:** *Inspire,* Fall 2010.

144 **"my beloved Shaykh":** Khan, "I Am Proud to Be a Traitor to America."

144 **harebrained scheme to equip a pickup truck:** Yahya Ibrahim, "The Ultimate Mowing Machine," *Inspire,* Fall 2010, https://azelin.files.wordpress.com/2010/10/inspire-magazine-2.pdf.

144 **bin Laden wrote in a memo:** Joby Warrick, "Bin Laden's Last Stand: In Final Months, Terrorist Leader Worried About His Legacy," *Washington Post,* April 30, 2012.

144 **"the *Vanity Fair* of jihadist publications":** "Inspire Reactions," *Inspire,* Spring 2011, https://azelin.files.wordpress.com/2011/03/inspire-magazine-5.pdf.

144 **not to take the risk of traveling:** Al Malahem, "Interview with Shaykh Abu Sufyan," *Inspire,* Fall 2010, https://azelin.files.wordpress.com/2010/10/inspire-magazine-2.pdf.

144 **"We used to say":** Cummings interview.

145 **"There had to be a person, a radical imam or the old guy":** George Piro interview by author, Miami, Florida, May 11, 2015.

145 **"If someone is an apostate":** Zachary Chesser, "A New Year: Reality and Aspirations," comment on an online posting on Anwar al-Aulaqi website, Jan. 9, 2009.

145 **"Destroying the West":** *U.S. v. Chesser,* 1:10-CR-395, Defendant's Position with Regard to Sentencing Factors (Eastern District of Virginia, February 18, 2011).

145 **"Open Source Jihad":** Zachary Chesser, letter to the author, May 27, 2014.

145 **security-screening manual:** U.S. Attorney's Office, "Leader of 'Revolution Muslim' Sentenced to 138 Months for Using Internet to Solicit Murder, Encourage Violent Extremism," June 22, 2012, http://www.justice.gov/archive/usao/vae/news/2012/06/20120622mortonnr.html.

145 **easy country to enter:** Zachary Chesser, letter to the author, May 27, 2014.

145 **most anarchic countries in the world:** Jeffrey Gettleman, "The Most Dangerous Place in the World," *Foreign Policy,* Sept. 30, 2009.

146 **attract the attention of law enforcement:** Zachary Chesser, letter to the author, May 27, 2014.

146 **He posted a query:** Zachary Chesser, "Lies of the Telegraph," comment on an online posting on Anwar al-Aulaqi website, Dec. 28, 2008.

146 **corresponding through Awlaki's blog:** Senate Committee on Homeland Secu-

rity and Governmental Affairs, "Zachary Chesser: A Case Study in Online Islamist Radicalization and Its Meaning for the Threat of Homegrown Terrorism."

146 **inability to find a wife:** Zachary Chesser, comment on post entitled, "44 Ways to Support Jihad," Jan. 10, 2009.

146 **had grown up a devout Catholic:** *U.S. v. Chesser,* Defendant's Position (Feb. 18, 2011).

146 **e-mail saying he was soon to be married . . . father reluctantly attended:** *U.S. v. Chesser,* Exhibit 1 (Feb. 18, 2011).

147 **extremist hallmarks:** Exceptions to this were David Headley, who generally presented himself as a typical, secular American, a pose that he needed to maintain for his cover as an American businessman while he was scoping out the 2008 Mumbai attacks and planning the attack on the *Jyllands-Posten* newspaper in Denmark. The younger Tsarnaev brother, Jahar, also did not exhibit any of the religiosity his brother did.

147 **now attracting the attention of the FBI . . . sent the cleric several e-mail messages . . . "LearnTeachFightDie" . . . "had wanted to travel overseas to fight in a jihad":** *U.S. v. Chesser,* Affidavit (July 21, 2010).

147 **dropped out of George Mason . . . Shirley Gate Mosque:** Zachary Chesser, letter to the author, May 27, 2014.

147 **slept on the concrete floor:** Barbara Chesser interview.

147 **texts from the mosque's library . . . Unbeknownst to his family:** *U.S. v. Chesser,* Exhibit 1 (Feb. 18, 2011).

148 **travel to Somalia:** *U.S. v. Chesser,* Criminal Information (Oct. 20, 2010).

148 **Unaware that no airline would allow:** Zachary Chesser, letter to the author, May 27, 2014.

148 **made by speedboat:** *U.S. v. Chesser,* Affidavit (June 21, 2010).

148 **hidden her daughter's passport:** *U.S. v. Chesser,* Criminal Information (Oct. 20, 2010).

148 **he tried "just about everything":** *U.S. v. Chesser,* Affidavit (June 21, 2010).

148 **December 2009:** *U.S. v. Chesser,* Criminal Complaint (Oct. 20, 2010).

148 **"website dedicated to those":** Ibid.

148 **mission statement:** *U.S. v. Chesser,* Affidavit (July 21, 2010).

148 **January 2010:** *U.S. v. Chesser,* Criminal Complaint (Oct. 20, 2010).

148 **decided to start posting on the popular militant website:** Chesser e-mailed Morton offering his services: *United States of America v. Jesse Curtis Morton,* CR No. 1:12cr35, [hereafter *U.S. v. Morton*], Criminal Complaint (Eastern District of Virginia, June 14, 2012).

148 **videos of Awlaki and longer papers about militant Islam:** *U.S. v. Morton,* Criminal Complaint (June 14, 2012).

148 **access to administer and update:** *U.S. v. Morton,* Affidavit (May 13, 2011).

149 **"I have above average artistic" . . . the "real world":** Senate Committee on Homeland Security and Governmental Affairs, "Zachary Chesser: A Case Study in Online Islamist Radicalization and Its Meaning for the Threat of Homegrown Terrorism."

149 **he and Morton once attended a protest:** Zachary Chesser, letter to the author, May 27, 2014.

149 **"The role of AQC":** Zachary Chesser, reply to "Quoted in Metro Article about Jihad Jane, Etc," Jarretbrachman.net, March 19, 2010, http://jarretbrachman.net/?p=580.

149 **did "not know anybody else":** Zachary Chesser, letter to the author, May 27, 2014.

149 **"enormous influence":** Ibid.

149 **boasted on Brachman's website:** Zachary Chesser, reply to "Quoted in Metro Article about Jihad Jane, Etc."

150 **a cofounder of Revolution Muslim . . . a New York City cabdriver with four kids:** Bilal Haye, "Yousef Al-Khattab, Man Behind Virulent Islamic Website, Grew Up Jewish," *The Brooklyn Ink,* April 23, 2010, http://thebrooklynink.com/2010/04/23/11041-yousef-al-khattab-man-behind-virulent-islamic-website-grew-up-jewish/.

150 **"I love him more than I love myself":** Drew Griffin, "Revolution Muslim Leader Changes Tune," CNN.com, Dec. 9, 2010.

150 **"inside job":** "U.S. Based Revolution Muslim Website Spreading Messages of Hate," Fox News, March 26, 2008.

150 **"speak in front of their homes" . . . gave the addresses of synagogues:** *United States of America v. Yousef Al-Khattab,* CR. No. 1:13cr418, [hereafter *U.S. v. Al-Khattab,*] Criminal Information (Eastern District of Virginia, Oct. 30, 2013).

150 **included a link to *The Anarchist Cookbook*:** FBI, Washington Field Office, "Leader of Muslim Revolution Sentenced for Using Internet to Threaten Jewish Organizations," April 25, 2014, https://www.fbi.gov/washingtondc/press-releases/2014/leader-of-revolution-muslim-websites-sentenced-for-using-internet-to-threaten-jewish-organizations.

150 **accused Chabad of funding terrorism:** *U.S. v. Al-Khattab,* Criminal Complaint (Oct. 30, 2013).

150 **high school dropout from Pennsylvania:** Carrie Johnson and Alice Crites, " 'Jihad Jane' Suspect Dropped Out Before High School, Married at 16," *Washington Post,* March 11, 2010.

150 **traveled to Europe in the summer of 2009:** Charlie Savage, "Pennsylvania Woman Tied to Plot on Cartoonist," *New York Times,* March 9, 2010.

151 **provocative interview to CNN:** Drew Griffin and Kathleen Johnston, "Peaceful Preaching Inside, Violent Message Outside a New York Mosque," CNN.com, Nov. 5, 2009.

151 **"[CNN] suggested that we justify":** Younus Abdullah Muhammad, "CNN Homegrown Psy-Ops Continue: Attempting to Extinguish the Light of Indigenous Resistance to the Empire," *IslamPolicy,* May 24, 2011, http://www.islampolicy.com/2010/12/cnn-homegrown-psy-ops-continue.html.

151 **"even though they seem":** Silber interview.

151 **eighteen other contributors:** "Homegrown Extremism 2001–2015."

151 **Zachary Chesser's onetime favorite show:** Barbara Chesser interview.

152 **its two hundredth episode:** "Security Brief: Radical Islamic Website Takes on 'South Park,'" CNN.com, April 19, 2010.

152 **dressed in a bear costume . . .** "That's right, friends": "200," *South Park*, season 14, episode 5, broadcast April 14, 2010, Comedy Central.

152 **1989 fatwa by Ayatollah:** *U.S. v. Chesser*, Criminal Information (Oct. 20, 2010).

152 **"media enticing post":** Zachary Chesser, letter to the author, May 27, 2014.

152 **"outright insulted" the Prophet "by showing him in a bear suit" . . .** "We have to warn Matt and Trey": *U.S. v. Chesser*, Criminal Complaint (Oct. 20, 2010).

152 **photograph showing van Gogh lying dead:** *U.S. v. Morton*, Criminal Complaint (June 14, 2012).

152 **address of *South Park*'s network . . . and provided a link . . . "pay them a visit":** *U.S. v. Chesser*, Criminal Complaint (Oct. 20, 2010).

153 **attacked at his home in early 2010:** Marie Louise Sjolie, "The Danish Cartoonist Who Survived an Axe Attack," *Guardian*, Jan. 4, 2010.

153 **"They're going to be basically on a list":** *U.S. v. Chesser*, Criminal Complaint (Oct. 20, 2010).

153 **uploaded audio clips:** *U.S. v. Morton*, Criminal Complaint (June 14, 2012).

153 **urged the assassination of anyone who "defamed" . . .** "Harming Allah and his Messenger": *U.S. v. Chesser*, Criminal Complaint (Oct. 20, 2010).

153 **"The kuffar are starting to really pick up":** *Washington Post*, "An American Terrorist: Zachary Chesser Timeline," *Washington Post*, April 20, 2010.

153 **He felt he deserved the spotlight:** Zachary Chesser, letter to the author, May 27, 2014.

153 **deleted the clause:** *U.S. v. Morton*, Criminal Complaint (June 14, 2012).

153 **"scare the kuffar":** U.S. Attorney's Office, "Leader of 'Revolution Muslim' Sentenced to 138 Months for Using Internet to Solicit Murder, Encourage Violent Extremism," June 22, 2012, http://www.justice.gov/archive/usao/vae/news/2012/06/20120622mortonnr.html.

153 **"By placing the Prophet Muhammad":** Jesse Morton and Zachary Chesser, "Clarifying the South Park Response and Calling on Others to Join in the Defense of the Prophet Muhammad," RevolutionMuslim, www.revolutionmuslim.blogspot.com, April 22, 2010.

153 **threats to various members of the Chesser family:** *U.S. v. Chesser*, Defendant's Position (Feb. 18, 2011).

154 **an irrevocable break with her son . . . "I thought you had grown up":** Barbara Chesser interview.

154 **The Muhammad story line continued:** "201," *South Park*, season 14, episode 6, broadcast April 21, 2010, Comedy Central.

154 **"worked phenomenally" . . . the imam defending Revolution Muslim . . . "CNN forgot about the rest of the world":** Zachary Chesser, letter to the author, May 27, 2014.

154 **slippery slope to more censorship . . . "If artists have to be afraid":** Joshua Rhett Miller, "'Everybody Draw Mohammed Day' Unleashes Facebook Fracas," Fox News, May 19, 2010.

154 **May 20, 2010 as "Everybody Draw Mohammed Day" . . . she drew a poster:** Steve Almasy, "After Four Years, American Cartoonist Molly Norris Still in Hiding After Drawing Prophet Muhammed," CNN.com, Jan. 14, 2015.

154 **water down the pool of potential targets:** *U.S. v. Chesser,* Criminal Complaint (Oct. 20, 2010).

155 **tens of thousands of members:** *U.S. v. Morton,* Criminal Complaint (June 14, 2012).

155 **temporarily shut down:** Richard Allen Greene, "Pakistan Shuts Down Facebook Over 'Draw Mohammed Day,'" CNN.com, May 19, 2010, http://www .cnn.com/2010/TECH/05/19/pakistani.facebook.shutdown/.

155 **a teenager in Mississippi and a man from Texas:** *U.S. v. Chesser,* Criminal Complaint (Oct. 20, 2010).

155 **KIRO radio interviewed Norris:** "Dave Ross Interviews Molly Norris," April 23, 2010, http://kiroradio.com/listen/16801/.

155 **"I am a coward":** Michael Cavna, "Post 'South Park': Cartoonist Retreats from 'Everybody Draw Mohammed Day,'" *Washington Post,* April 25, 2010.

155 **"should be taken as a prime target":** Almasy, "After Four Years, American Cartoonist Molly Norris Still in Hiding After Drawing Prophet Muhammed."

155 **"Desensitizing Federal Agents":** *U.S. v. Chesser,* Criminal Complaint (Oct. 20, 2010).

155 **"Boom! No more kuffar":** U.S. Attorney's Office, "Leader of 'Revolution Muslim' Sentenced to 138 Months for Using Internet to Solicit Murder, Encourage Violent Extremism."

156 **"Actually Leaving for Jihad":** *U.S. v. Chesser,* Affidavit (July 21, 2010).

156 **pick up her birth certificate:** *U.S. v. Zachary Adam Chesser,* Defendant's Position (Feb. 18, 2011).

156 **would arrange for his travel:** Zachary Chesser, letter to the author, May 27, 2014.

156 **July 9, 2010 . . . flight with service to Uganda:** *U.S. v. Chesser,* Criminal Complaint (July 21, 2010).

156 **walk into Kenya and then on into Somalia . . . no-fly list:** *U.S. v. Chesser,* Defendant's Position (Feb. 18, 2011).

156 **bombs went off in Kampala:** Xan Rice, "Uganda Bomb Blast Kills at Least 74," *Guardian,* July 12, 2010.

156 **planning to attend a camp in Somalia . . . foreign fighters were highly respected:** *U.S. v. Chesser,* Affidavit (July 21, 2010).

156 **July 21, 2010:** U.S. Attorney's Office, "Fairfax County Man Accused of Providing Material Support to Terrorists," July 21, 2010.

156 **"real world" . . . In his own mind . . . "One will find that I have a surprising footprint":** Zachary Chesser, letter to the author, May 27, 2014.

157 **pleaded guilty before his trial started . . . Chesser's wife was charged:** *U.S. v. Chesser,* Plea Agreement (Feb. 18, 2011).

157 **pleaded guilty and was deported:** Carol Cratty, "Wife of Terrorism Convict Pleads Guilty; Will Have to Leave U.S.," CNN.com, Nov. 8, 2010, http://www .cnn.com/2010/CRIME/11/08/us.guilty.plea/.

157 **sentenced to two and a half years:** FBI, Washington Field Office, "Leader of Muslim Revolution Sentenced for Using Internet to Threaten Jewish Organizations," April 25, 2014, https://www.fbi.gov/washingtondc/press-releases/2014/leader-of-revolution-muslim-websites-sentenced-for-using-internet-to-threaten-jewish-organizations.

157 **more than ten years in prison:** U.S. Attorney's Office, "Leader of 'Revolution Muslim' Sentenced to 138 Months for Using Internet to Solicit Murder, Encourage Violent Extremism."

157 **assaulting a fellow prisoner:** Zachary Chesser, letter to the author, May 27, 2014.

157 **home to a who's who of terrorists:** Mark Binelli, "Inside America's Toughest Federal Prison," *New York Times,* March 26, 2015.

158 **Morton then uploaded:** *U.S. v. Morton,* Criminal Complaint (June 14, 2012).

158 **"You may have noticed":** Mark D. Fefer, "On the Advice of the FBI, Cartoonist Molly Norris Disappears from View," *Seattle Weekly,* Sept. 14, 2010.

158 **"I think all the social media":** Author interview with senior FBI official, Washington, D.C., 2015.

159 **"reviewed" Molly Norris's statement:** Zachary Chesser, letter to the author, Feb. 6, 2015.

159 **"As philosopher Karl Popper wrote":** *U.S. v. Morton,* Prosecution Sentencing Memorandum (June 14, 2012).

159 **has not been heard from:** Almasy, "After Four Years, American Cartoonist Molly Norris Still in Hiding After Drawing Prophet Muhammed."

CHAPTER 8: EXPORTING JIHAD: AMERICANS ABROAD

160 **"The only reason we are staying here":** Andrea Elliot, "The Jihadist Next Door," *New York Times,* Jan. 27, 2010.

160 **"just been shot in neck":** abu m, @abumamerican, Twitter, April 25, 2013: 10:45 a.m., https://twitter.com/abumamerican/status/327478460891156480.

160 **"sitting in tea place":** abu m, @abumamerican, Twitter, April 25, 2013: 10:52 a.m., https://twitter.com/abumamerican/status/327480320641339392.

161 **"no windpipe or artery":** abu m, @abuamerican, Twitter, April 25, 2013: 11:09 a.m., https://twitter.com/abumamerican/status/327484574651265024.

161 **photo of himself:** Jason Straziuso, "'Just Been Shot in the Neck by Shabab Assassin': American Jihadi in Somalia Tweets Attempt on His Life," Associated Press, April 26, 2013 [original tweet unavailable].

161 **"they are sending forces from multiple directions":** abu m, @abuamerican, Twitter, April 25, 2013: 9:03 p.m., https://twitter.com/abumamerican/status/327633960245014528.

161 **"After the failed assassination":** abu m, @abuamerican, Twitter, April 29, 2013: 9:01 a.m., https://twitter.com/abumamerican/status/328901740730658816.

161 **recruited more Americans:** U.S. House of Representatives, Committee on Homeland Security, "Al Shabaab: Recruitment and Radicalization within the Muslim American Community and the Threat to the Homeland," July 27, 2011, p. 1,

http://homeland.house.gov/sites/homeland.house.gov/files/Investigative%2
report.pdf.

161 **Shafik Hammami, was born . . . Sunday school:** Author interview with Shafik Hammami, Daphne, AL, Nov. 13, 2013.

163 **Omar was baptized . . . ten dollars . . . his heritage:** Andrea Elliot, "The Jihadist Next Door," *New York Times,* Jan. 27, 2010.

163 **Shafik taught his children:** Shafik Hammami interview.

163 **childhood pursuits . . . *Tom Sawyer* . . . "pointless and stupid":** Elliot, "The Jihadist Next Door."

163 **shifted to the gifted program:** Shafik Hammami interview.

163 ***1984 . . . The Catcher in the Rye* . . . "social butterfly":** Elliot, "The Jihadist Next Door."

163 **questioning the tenets:** Shafik Hammami interview.

163 **"How can God" . . . barbecuing him on a large grill:** Omar Hammami, *The Story of An American Jihaadi* (published online by author, May 16, 2012), pp. 12–13, https://azelin.files.wordpress.com/2012/05/omar-hammami -abc5ab-mane1b9a3c5abr-al-amrc4abkc4ab-22the-story-of-an-american -jihc481dc4ab-part-122.pdf.

164 **trip Omar made . . . first time in his life:** Shafik Hammami interview; Omar Hammami, *The Story of An American Jihaadi.*

164 **Western one consisted of drugs . . . started performing:** Elliot, "The Jihadist Next Door."

164 **"Bin Laden is awesome":** Author interview with Bernie Culveyhouse, December 27, 2013.

164 **trying to convert:** Elliot, "The Jihadist Next Door."

164 **"We can't do this":** Culveyhouse interview.

164 **His next conversion:** Elliot, "The Jihadist Next Door."

164 **practice of witchcraft . . . "I had a fucked-up":** Culveyhouse interview.

165 **"cognitive opening":** Silber and Bhatt, *Radicalization in the West,* p. 6.

165 **"It's just simple monotheism" . . . "God doesn't have a son":** Culveyhouse interview.

165 **Omar charged and started to strangle him:** Elliot, "The Jihadist Next Door."

165 **"We kill people for making fun":** Culveyhouse interview.

165 **took the ACTs:** Elliot, "The Jihadist Next Door."

166 **early admission on a scholarship:** Shafik Hammami interview.

166 **"big breath of fresh air":** Culveyhouse interview.

166 **"real hatred for America" . . . "Why did this happen?" . . . "Allahu Akbar!":** Omar Hammami, *The Story of An American Jihaadi,* p. 21.

166 **news came in . . . "Why are these people" . . . "Maybe it's because":** Culveyhouse interview.

166 **ordered him to leave the house:** Shafik Hammami interview.

166 **slept in a storage locker . . . "Fuck you, too!" . . . cleaning the Mobile mosque . . . took telemarketing jobs:** Culveyhouse interview.

167 **as educated as the average citizen:** The 360 militants examined for this book are on average as educated as the typical American. A little under half (45 per-

cent) had more than a high school education, meaning they either had some college education, were college graduates, or had some graduate study or had earned a graduate degree, compared to the little over half of all Americans who have an education beyond high school. Ten percent of the militants had some graduate study or a graduate degree, compared to 10 percent for the general public.

167 **only a third were known to have jobs:** "Homegrown Extremism 2001–2015."

167 **5 percent:** U.S. Department of Labor, Bureau of Labor Statistics, http://data .bls.gov/pdq/SurveyOutputServlet.

167 **religious conference** . . . **"How 'bout that hockey"** . . . **job delivering milk** . . . **working as a delivery boy** . . . **Culveyhouse married Ayan** . . . **"fuck up the world"** . . . **Hammami began writing:** Bernie Culveyhouse interview.

168 **with about a third traveling or attempting to travel to Afghanistan** . . . **a fifth volunteered to fight in Somalia** . . . **quarter were drawn to the Syrian war:** "Homegrown Extremism 2001–2015."

169 **Culveyhouse found a documentary** . . . **was crying** . . . **teach a circle of students in Mecca** . . . **decided to go with him** . . . **mother, wife, and daughter** . . . **Sadiyo, Hammami's wife, was pregnant** . . . **serious respiratory problems:** Culveyhouse interview.

170 **"The bureaucracy of Egypt":** Omar Hammami, *The Story of An American Jihaadi.*

170 **named her Taymiyya:** Culveyhouse interview.

170 **Debra and Shafik flew:** Shafik Hammani interview.

170 **"You should actually"** . . . **"going to medical school"** . . . **"become a doctor"** . . . **Culveyhouse's family obligations** . . . **"You're not a true Muslim"** . . . **"Dude, you're my best friend"** . . . **joined Islamic Networking:** Culveyhouse interview.

172 **"crusader" army:** Omar Hammami, *The Story of An American Jihaadi,* p. 110.

172 **"an obligation":** Elliot, "The Jihadist Next Door."

172 **"Brother, I'm done with studying"** . . . **Hammami told his family:** Culveryhouse interview.

172 **"the only white man"** . . . **chatting with a Somali woman:** Omar Hammami, *The Story of An American Jihaadi,* p. 39.

172 **"How did you let my son":** Culveyhouse interview.

172 **had invaded** . . . **contacting his local congressman:** Shafik Hammami interview.

172 **decided to leave** . . . **Daniel Maldonado:** Culveyhouse interview.

173 **port city of Kismayo** . . . **issued an AK-47** . . . **"the dream of any Muslim"** . . . **gave Hammami diarrhea** . . . **He took courses** . . . **strange slime in their stools** . . . **no one understood any of his jokes** . . . **she told him she was going to divorce him** . . . **"Abu Mansoor al-Amriki":** Omar Hammami, *The Story of An American Jihaadi,* pp. 2–44.

174 **a news item aired about an American:** Shafik Hammami interview.

174 **"All Muslims of America":** "The Alabama Jihadist, Hammami's Debut as Al-Amriki," *New York Times,* Jan. 27, 2010.

174 **Shafik recognized his son:** Shafik Hammami interview.

174 **some forty Americans:** U.S. House of Representatives, Committee on Homeland Security, "Al Shabaab: Recruitment and Radicalization within the Muslim American Community and the Threat to the Homeland."

174 **Nineteen Minnesota residents:** "Homegrown Extremism 2001–2015."

174 **less than fifteen thousand dollars a year . . . unemployment rate was 17 percent:** Minneapolis Community Planning and Economic Development, with data from the 1999 U.S. Census of Population and Housing (SF3), "Cedar-Riverside/Minneapolis: Median Household Income (in 1999 Dollars)," http://www.ci.minneapolis.mn.us/neighborhoods/cedar-riverside/neighborhoods_cedarriverside_income.

175 **"We don't typically have Muslim ghettos":** Mudd interview.

175 **"true brotherhood" of jihad:** Andrea Elliot, "Charges Detail Road to Terror for 20 in U.S.," *New York Times,* Nov. 23, 2009.

175 **One of the seven:** "Joining the Fight in Somalia," *New York Times,* Oct. 30, 2011.

175 **worked at the Minneapolis airport:** Andrea Elliot, "A Call to Jihad, Answered in America," *New York Times,* July 11, 2009.

175 **counsel drunken Somali kids:** "Joining the Fight in Somalia."

175 **Ahmed left Minneapolis:** *United States of America v. Ahmed Ali Omar et al.,* CR No. 09-50 [hereafter *U.S. v. Omar et al.*], Indictment (U.S. District Court District of Minnesota, Aug. 20, 2009).

175 **drove a truck loaded with explosives:** U.S. Attorney's Office, "Terror Charges Unsealed in Minnesota Against Eight Defendants, Justice Department Announces," Nov. 23, 2009, https://www.fbi.gov/minneapolis/press-releases/2009/mp112309.htm.

176 **finger inside the truck:** Dina Temple-Raston, "Missing-Somali Case Gives Recruitment Clues to FBI," NPR, Nov. 24, 2009, http://www.npr.org/templates/story/story.php?storyId=120757628.

176 **suicide bombing at a jazz club:** Testimony of Peter Bergen before the Subcommittee on Intelligence, Information Sharing, and Terrorism Risk Assessment, "Reassessing the Evolving Al-Qaeda Threat to the Homeland," Nov. 19, 2009, pdf at http://www.gpo.gov/fdsys/pkg/CHRG-111hhrg55595/html/CHRG-111hhrg55595.htm.

176 **State Department designated al-Shabaab:** U.S. Department of State, Office of the Coordinator for Counterterrorism, "Designation of al-Shabaab as a Foreign Terrorist Organization," Feb. 26, 2008, http://www.state.gov/j/ct/rls/other/des/102446.htm.

176 **Codenamed Operation Rhino:** Michael Taxay, *Terrorist Financing* (Columbia, SC: Executive Office for U.S. Attorneys, Office of Legal Education, 2014), p. 8.

176 **Boelter went on local Somali radio:** Author interview with Ralph Boelter, Washington, DC, Oct. 10, 2014.

176 **fifteen Americans died while fighting:** Committee on Homeland Security, Majority Investigative Report, "Al Shabaab: Recruitment and Radicalization Within the Muslim American Community and the Threat to the Homeland,"

July 27, 2011, https://homeland.house.gov/hearing/al-shabaab-recruitment-and
-radicalization-within-muslim-american-community-and-threat/, p. 278.

176 **Ahmed Hussein Mahamud:** *United States of America v. Ahmed Hussein Mahamud,* CR No. 11-191 [hereafter *U.S. v. Mahamud*], Indictment (District of Minnesota, June 7, 2011).

176 **Mohamud Abdi Yusuf:** *United States of America v. Mohamud Abdi Yusuf,* Case No. 4:10-cr-00547-HEA. Change of Plea (District of Minnesota, Nov. 3, 2011).

176 **in 2013, Basaaly Saeed Moalin:** *United States of America v. Ahmed Nasir Taalil Mohamud et al.,* Case No. 10-CR-4246 JM. Judgement (Southern District of California, Jan. 1, 2014).

177 **Ruben Shumpert:** Jason Ryan, "License to Kill? Intelligence Chief Says U.S. Can Take Out American Terrorists," ABC News, Feb. 3, 2010, http://abc-news.go.com/Politics/license-kill-intelligence-chief-us-american-terrorist/story?id=9740491.

177 **U.S. soldier, Craig Baxam:** U.S. Attorney's Office, "Former U.S. Soldier Who Sought to Join Terrorist Group Convicted and Sentenced to Seven Years in Prison," Jan. 13, 2014, https://www.fbi.gov/baltimore/press-releases/2014/former-u.s.-soldier-who-sought-to-join-terrorist-group-convicted-and-sentenced-to-seven-years-in-prison.

177 **killing more than seventy:** Sudarsan Raghavan, "Arrests Made in Bomb Attacks on World Cup Fans in Uganda," *Washington Post,* July 13, 2010.

177 **twenty-eight-year-old Somali man armed . . . Danish intelligence officials:** John F. Burns, "Cartoonist in Denmark Calls Attack 'Really Close,'" *New York Times,* Jan. 2, 2010.

177 **Osama bin Laden scolded:** Combating Terrorism Center, "Letter from Usama bin Laden to Mukhtar Abu al-Zubayr," Aug. 7, 2010, https://www.ctc.usma.edu/posts/letter-from-usama-bin-laden-to-mukhtar-abu-al-zubayr-original-language-2.

177 **defeated al-Shabaab units in Mogadishu:** David Smith, "Al-Shabaab Rebuilds Forces in Somalia as African Union Campaign Stalls," *Guardian,* Oct. 28, 2013.

177 **he revealed his face:** "The Alabama Jihadist, Propaganda Video: Amriki Unmasked," *New York Times,* Jan. 27, 2010.

178 **"Send Me a Cruise [Missile]," "Make Jihad with Me," and "Blow by Blow":** Adam Rawnsley, "American Terrorist Proves He Still Can't Rap," *Wired,* April 11, 2011, http://webcache.googleusercontent.com/search?q=cache:8oBbHD_8v2oJ:www.wired.com/2011/04/american-terrorist-proves-he-still-cant-rap/+&cd=1&hl=en&ct=clnk&gl=us.

178 **"How dare you" . . . "daycare centers and maternity wards":** "The Alabama Jihadist, Propaganda Video: A Rebuttal to Obama," *New York Times,* Jan. 27, 2010, http://www.nytimes.com/interactive/2010/01/27/magazine/20100127_OMAR_TIMELINE.html.

178 **"What scared us . . . message counterresonate?":** Liepman interview.

179 **November 27, 2007:** FBI Special Agent Jessica Foran, "Omar Shafik Hammami Added to the FBI's Most Wanted Terrorists List," FBI, Nov. 14, 2012, https://

www.fbi.gov/mobile/press-releases/2012/omar-shafik-hammami-added-to-the
-fbis-most-wanted-terrorists-list

179 **Omar Hammami was indicted . . . military tactician:** *United States of America v. Omar Shafik Hammami,* CR No. 07-00384-KD [hereafter *U.S. v. Hammami*], Indictment (Southern District of Alabama, Sept. 24, 2009).

179 **oversee al-Shabaab's foreign fighters:** "Somalia's al-Shabaab Kills US Fighter," Al Jazeera, Sept. 12, 2013, http://www.aljazeera.com/news/africa/2013/09/201391293315761506.html.

179 **job in computer programming . . . transformational moment for him . . . "This is not a righteous war" . . . When he listened to Hammami's response:** Culveyhouse interview.

180 **Abu Musab al-Suri:** Omar Hammami, *The Story of An American Jihaadi,* p. 2.

180 **fifty-page strategy paper:** Abu Jihad Al-Shami, *The Vision of the Jihaadi Movement and the Strategy for the Current Stage,* pdf at https://azelin.files.wordpress.com/2010/11/abu-jihad-al-shami-the-vision-of-the-jihad-movement-the-strategy-for-the-current-stage.pdf.

180 **autobiography . . . other wives . . . "all the hugs" . . . Alabama visit:** Omar Hammami, *The Story of An American Jihaadi.*

180 **"These brothers":** abu m, @abuamerican, Twitter, April 19, 2013.

180 **"boston proves" . . . "Fact they managed":** abu m, @abuamerican, Twitter, April 20, 2013.

181 **"homie":** abu m, @abuamerican, Twitter, April 8, 2013.

181 **"pass the barf bag":** abu m, @abuamerican, Twitter, Jan. 27, 2013.

181 **references to Tupac, Kid Rock:** abu m, @abuamerican, Twitter, Feb. 20, 2013.

181 **baby back ribs:** abu m, @abuamerican, Twitter, Feb. 3, 2013.

181 **"War booty":** abu m, @abuamerican, Twitter, Jan. 5, 2013.

181 **"usurping king":** abu m, @abuamerican, Twitter, Jan. 29, 2013.

181 **released a short video:** Omar Hammami, "Video: Urgent Message," March 16, 2012, http://jihadology.net/2012/03/16/new-video-message-from-omar-hammami-abu-manṣur-al-amriki-urgent-message/.

181 **Hammami was not at risk:** William Maclean, "U.S. Fighter in Somalia Says Threatened by Fellow Militants," Reuters, March 17, 2012, http://www.reuters.com/article/2012/03/17/us-somalia-conflict-alshabaab-idUSBRE82G0CG20120317.

182 **al-Shabaab's leaders simply didn't like Hammami:** Author interview with senior FBI official.

182 **ran a feature about him:** Spencer Ackerman, "'There's No Turning Back': My Interview with a Hunted American Jihadist," *Wired,* April 4, 2013, http://www.wired.com/2013/04/omar-hammami/.

182 **released a lengthy pamphlet:** Aaron Y. Zelin, "New Statement from Harakat al-Shabab al-Mujahidin: 'Abu Mansur al-Amriki: A Candid Clarification,'" *Jihadology,* Dec. 17, 2012, http://jihadology.net/2012/12/17/new-statement-from-%E1%B8%A5arakat-al-shabab-al-mujahidin-abu-man%E1%B9%A3ur-al-amriki-a-candid-clarification/.

182 **vicious takedown . . . "paralyzed" . . . "So long, the American!":** Abu Hamza

Al-Muhajir, *Turning Away from the Truth Won't Make It Disappear,* Feb. 2012, pdf at http://selectedwisdom.com/wp-content/uploads/2013/02/Turning _Away_From_the_Truth.pdf.

182 **"Yeah, I'm definitely a terrorist":** "'American al-Shabab' Disavows Militant Group, al-Qaida'," Voice of America, Sept. 5, 2013, http://www.voanews.com/content/american-alshabab-disavows-militant-group-alqaida/1743983.html.

182 **"Regardless of the fact":** abu m, @abuamerican, Twitter, Sept. 5, 2013: 6:19 p.m.

183 **shot and killed him:** "U.S.-born 'Jihadist Rapper' Omar Hammami Reportedly Killed in Somalia," *Guardian,* Sept. 12, 2013.

183 **"We confirm the martyrdom":** abu m, @abuamerican, Twitter, Sept. 15, 2013: 8:11 p.m.

183 **"Shafik, rest assured":** abu m, @abuamerican, Twitter, Sept. 28, 2013: 9:44 p.m.

183 **"Please keep me abreast":** Shafik Hammami, @ShafikHammami, Twitter, Sept. 28, 2013: 11:03 a.m.

183 **"Although the West":** Shafik Hammami interview.

183 **"To me it's just":** Culveyhouse interview.

184 **"Darlin', we have been":** Gena Somra, "Parents Despair for 'Most Wanted' Terrorist Son," CNN.com, June 7, 2013, http://www.cnn.com/2013/06/07/us/us-somalia-family-despair/.

184 **"Turn on your TV":** *United States of America v. Tahawwur Rana,* Case No. 09 CR 830 [hereafter *U.S. v. Rana*], Government's Santiago Proffer (U.S. District Court, Northern District of Illinois, Eastern Division, April 11, 2011) [hereafter "Government's Santiago Proffer," *U.S. v. Rana*].

184 **Headley switched on the television:** David Coleman Headley's testimony in *U.S. v. Rana* [hereafter "Headley's testimony," *U.S. v. Rana*], Volume 2-A, Transcript of Trial, "Headley Direct" (May 24, 2011), p. 74.

184 **Ever since a stray bomb had:** Ibid. (May 23, 2011).

184 **a socialite from Philadelphia's Main Line:** Ginger Thompson, "A Terror Suspect with Feet in the East and West," *New York Times,* Nov. 21, 2009.

184 **prominent Pakistani TV anchor:** "Terror Suspect Has Roots in Pakistan, U.S.," CNN.com, Dec. 9, 2009.

184 **a Lashkar team of ten . . . forced to navigate:** Metropolitan Transit Authority (MTA), *Mumbai Terrorist Attacks,* Nov. 26–29, 2008, pdf at http://fas.org/irp/eprint/mumbai.pdf.

185 **Five nautical miles offshore of Mumbai:** "FINAL FORM/REPORT (Under Section 173 Cr.P.C.)," Court of Addl. CH. M.M. 37 Court, Esplanade; MTA, *Mumbai Terrorist Attacks.*

185 **made their way to the taxi:** Government's Santiago Proffer, *U.S. v. Rana,* p. 32.

185 **One of the gunmen:** "FINAL FORM/REPORT."

185 **arrived at Café Leopold:** MTA, *Mumbai Terrorist Attacks.*

185 **emptied their AK-47s . . . central railway . . . Oberoi Hotel:** "FINAL FORM/REPORT.

185 **Alan Scherr . . . diners screamed:** "Forgive Mumbai Attackers, Victims' Relative Says," CNN.com, Dec. 4, 2008.

185 **Alan was trying desperately:** *United States of America v. David Coleman Headley*, Case No. 09-CR-830 [hereafter *U.S. v. Headley*], Government's Position Paper as to Sentencing Factors (Northern District of Illinois, Eastern Division, Jan. 22, 2013).

185 **Thirty-six guests and hotel staff . . . landmark Taj Hotel:** "FINAL FORM/ REPORT."

185 **assaulted the Mumbai branch of Chabad:** Ibid.; Liz Robbins and Jack Healy, "Brooklyn Couple Killed in Attacks," *New York Times*, Nov. 28, 2008.

185 **The Holtzbergs' two-year old son:** Robbins and Healy, "Brooklyn Couple Killed in Attacks."

186 **as Lashkar's planners had intended:** MTA, *Mumbai Terrorist Attacks.*

186 **When the attacks were finally over, 166 people were dead:** "FINAL FORM/ REPORT."

186 **the most spectacular terrorist operation:** But not the most deadly, which were the Madrid bombings in 2004, which killed 191 people.

186 **the American passport, the Western-sounding name:** During the trial of Tahawwur Rana, Headley recounted his surveillance activity and the importance that his Lashkar handlers placed on his ability to blend in, due to his Western roots and appearance. Headley's testimony in *U.S. v. Rana*, 1:09-cr-00830, Volume 1-B Transcript of Trial "Headley Direct" (May 23, 2011).

186 **Watching the TV coverage with Headley:** Cathy Scott-Clark and Adrian Levy, *The Siege: 68 Hours Inside the Taj Hotel* (New York: Penguin, 2013), p. 127.

186 **She knew enough about her husband's work with Lashkar:** Faiza Outalha, interview by Rahul Kanwal, for *Headlines Today, India Today,* aired October 11, 2011.

186 **"My God, police will come to me" . . . Headley laughed it off:** "Warned US About Impending Terrorist Attack: Headley's Wife," YouTube video of interview for ABP News, aired June 27, 2012, at https://www.youtube.com/watch?v=ignSO8J0_OA.

186 **he became concerned:** Headley's testimony in *U.S. v. Rana*, Volume 2-A (May 24, 2011), p. 74.

186 **"I have been watching these cartoons":** National Investigation Agency, "Interrogation Report of David Coleman Headley," June 3–9, 2010, Government of India, http://www.investigativeproject.org/documents/case_docs/1602.pdf.

187 **He was multilingual:** Ibid., p. 2.

187 **spied for the Drug Enforcement Administration:** Headley's testimony in *U.S. v. Rana*, Volume 1-A (May 23, 2011), p. 35.

187 **partied in Mumbai:** See generally S. Hussain Zaidi with Rahul Bhatt, *Headley and I* (India: HarperCollins, 2012).

187 **life of international intrigue a lot more entertaining:** Headley's testimony in *U.S. v. Rana*, Volume 1-A (May 23, 2011), p.63.

187 **began in Washington:** Thompson, "A Terror Suspect with Feet in the East and West."

187 **born in Washington on June 30, 1960:** Zaidi and Bhatt, *Headley and I*, p. 17.

187 **Anglicize his name:** National Investigation Agency, "Interrogation Report of

David Coleman Headley," pp. 32, 40; "In the Matter of Petition for Change of Name of Daood Gilani Decree for Change of Name," First Judicial District of Pennsylvania Court of Common Pleas of Philadelphia County Trial Division—Civil, Nov. 2005.

188 **donned a sari and learned the language and how to cook . . . the shine was off:** Sarah Jacob, "Full Transcript Of David Headley's Uncle's Interview," NDTV, May 4, 2010, http://www.ndtv.com/india-news/full-transcript-of-david-headleys-uncles-interview-416769.

188 **When David was ten:** Joe Barrett, Douglas Belkin, Peter Loftus, and Eric Bellman, "For Terror Suspect, a Life of Contradictions," *Wall Street Journal,* Dec. 12, 2009.

188 **David went to school in Karachi . . . At age seventeen:** Headley's testimony in *U.S. v. Rana,* Volume 1-A (May 23, 2011), pp. 58–61.

188 **stepmother was not to Headley's liking . . . new life as a barkeep:** Rotella, "The American Behind India's 9/11."

188 **featuring Pakistani decorations:** Sally A. Downey, "A. Serrill Headley, 68; Owned Phila.'s Khyber Pass Pub," *Philadelphia Inquirer,* Jan. 25, 2008.

188 **"the Prince":** Rotella, "The American Behind India's 9/11."

188 **Headley married . . . Like many women . . . call him an infidel . . . divorced . . . work as a mule:** Joseph Tanfani, John Shiffman, and Kathleen Brady Shea, "Terror Suspect Was Drug Dealer, Then Informant David Headley, Who Has Local Roots, Grew Up in Two Worlds. He Is Charged in the Mumbai Killings," *Philadelphia Inquirer,* Dec. 13, 2009.

188 **He was first arrested . . . agreed to cooperate . . . sentence cut . . . Three years after his release:** Rotella, "The American Behind India's 9/11."

189 **In 1997 he was convicted again:** Headley's testimony in *U.S. v. Rana,* Volume 1A (May 23, 2011), pp. 62–63.

189 **fifteen months:** Tanfani, Shiffman, and Shea, "Terror Suspect Was Drug Dealer."

189 **He finally set himself up:** Thompson, "A Terror Suspect with Feet in the East and West"; National Investigation Agency, "Interrogation Report of David Coleman Headley."

189 **began cultivating an interest in his father's:** Jason M. Breslow, "The Memoir of an 'American Terrorist,'" *Frontline,* PBS.org, April 21, 2015, http://www.pbs.org/wgbh/pages/frontline/foreign-affairs-defense/american-terrorist/the-memoir-of-an-american-terrorist/.

189 **encountered members of the jihadist group . . . "One second spent" . . . The sermon made a deep impression:** Headley's testimony in *U.S. v. Rana,* Volume 1-A (May 23, 2011), p. 69

189 **watched the news coverage obsessively:** Rotella, "The American Behind India's 9/11."

189 **"America got what it deserved" . . . girlfriend recounted:** "A Perfect Terrorist," documentary transcript, *Frontline,* PBS.org, 2011, http://www.pbs.org/wgbh/pages/frontline/afghanistan-pakistan/david-headley/transcript-13/.

189 **happy to overlook the incident:** Ginger Thompson, Eric Schmitt, and Souad

Mekhennet, "D.E.A. Deployed Mumbai Plotter Despite Warning," *New York Times,* Nov. 7, 2010.

189 **Four months after 9/11, Headley went back:** Headley's testimony in *U.S. v. Rana,* Volume 1-A (May 23, 2011), pp. 72–72; National Investigation Agency, "Interrogation Report of David Coleman Headley," p. 21.

190 **In February 2002 he attended an initial course . . . In 2003, for three months, he attended . . . Later that year he trained as a Lashkar spy:** Headley's testimony, *U.S. v. Rana,* Volume 1A (May 23, 2011), pp. 71–78.

190 **Headley's mother expressed . . . In August 2005 he had an altercation . . . soon she was telling official . . . In June 2006 . . . applied for a green card . . . she explained that Headley had received:** Rotella, "The American Behind India's 9/11."

190 **Headley officially changed his name:** "In the Matter of Petition for Change of Name of Daood Gilani Decree for Change of Name."

190 **Headley also moved his Pakistan-based wife:** Thompson, "A Terror Suspect with Feet in the East and West."

190 **a friend's house in Lahore . . . spend their honeymoon:** Faiza Outalha interview by Kanwal.

190 **The couple stayed . . . plenty of videos . . . These would be shared:** National Investigation Agency, "Interrogation Report of David Headley," pp. 51–52.

191 **honeymoon ended acrimoniously:** Rotella, "The American Behind India's 9/11."

191 **December 2007, Faiza had an altercation . . . filed a criminal case:** Faiza Outalha interview by Kanwal; "Interrogation Report of David Coleman Headley," National Investigation Agency, p. 82.

191 **told American officials:** Faiza Outalha interview by Kanwal.

191 **Headley "is a criminal":** "Warned US About Impending Terrorist Attack: Headley's Wife."

191 **visited the embassy three times:** James Glanz, Sebastian Rotella, and David E. Sanger, "In 2008 Mumbai Attacks, Piles of Spy Data, but an Uncompleted Puzzle," *New York Times,* Dec. 22, 2014.

191 **"made some of the things that were being alleged":** Author interview with senior FBI official.

191 **Somehow Headley and Faiza managed to reconcile:** Rotella, "The American Behind India's 9/11."

191 **gave him twenty-five thousand dollars:** "Government's Santiago Proffer," *U.S. v. Rana;* Headley's testimony, *U.S. v. Rana,* Volume 1B (May 23, 2011), p. 141.

192 **He set up an office:** "Opening Statements by Government, *U.S. v. Rana,* Volume 1-A (May 23, 2011), p. 6.

192 **he made several trips to Mumbai:** *U.S. v. Headley,* "Government's Position Paper as to Sentencing Factors" (Jan. 22, 2013).

192 **struck up a friendship with Rahul Bhatt . . . Armani suits, Rolex Submariner watch:** S. Hussain Zaidi and Rahul Bhatt, *Headley and I* (India: HarperCollins, 2012), p. 112.

192 **He even befriended . . . His handlers encouraged:** Headley's testimony, *U.S. v. Rana*, Volume 2-A (May 24, 2011), p. 249.

192 **he loved being the perfect terrorist:** S. Hussain Zaidi and Rahul Bhatt, *Headley and I*.

192 **He appears to have had a classic case:** Author e-mail interview with forensic psychiatrist Marc Sageman, who testified at the trial of Headley's friend Rana, by e-mail, July 13, 2015.

192 **antisocial personality disorder:** "Anti-Social Personality Disorder: Symptoms," Diseases and Conditions, MayoClinic.org, April 12, 2013, http://www.may clinic.org/diseases-conditions/antisocial-personality-disorder/basics/symptoms/con-20027920.

193 **Mumbai operation had been postponed or even canceled:** Headley's testimony, *U.S. v. Rana*, Volume 1-B (May 23, 2011), p. 208.

193 **Lashkar felt it needed:** National Investigation Agency, "Interrogation of David Headley."

193 **Headley met with a frogman:** Headley's testimony, *U.S. v. Rana*, Volume 1-B (May 23, 2011), pp. 209–10.

193 **A month later:** Ibid., p. 216.

193 **He eventually decided . . . he took more boat trips:** "Interrogation of David Headley," National Investigation Agency Government of India.

193 **red string bracelets:** Headley's testimony, *U.S. v. Rana*, Volume 2-A (May 24, 2011), p. 293.

193 **Lashkar had by now found ten recruits . . . end with a "stronghold" option . . . kept in isolation in a Karachi safe house:** MTA, *Mumbai Terrorist Attacks*.

193 **They reviewed Headley's surveillance videotapes:** Scott-Clark and Levy, *The Siege: 68 Hours Inside the Taj Hotel*, p. 121.

193 **The gunmen were all given Indian ID cards . . . They were outfitted with:** "FINAL FORM/REPORT."

194 **One of them dropped a GPS . . . The Indians were impressed:** Cummings interview.

194 **The FBI still had no idea:** Robert Holley of the FBI, quoted in "American Terrorist," *Frontline*, April 21, 2015, PBS, transcript at http://www.pbs.org/wgbh/pages/frontline/foreign-affairs-defense/american-terrorist/transcript-80/.

194 **Headley started brainstorming another terror spectacle:** "Second Superseding Indictment," *U.S. v. Rana* (July 2010).

194 **"Call me old fashioned" . . . In January 2009 . . . Headley traveled to Copenhagen . . . "Mickey Mouse project" . . . On one of his e-mail accounts, he listed:** Criminal Complaint, *U.S. v. Headley* (Oct. 11, 2009).

194 **using tactics similar to those . . . The plan involved beheading:** Headley's testimony, *U.S. v. Rana*, Volume 2-B (May 24, 2011), p. 435.

194 **Headley picked up some hats:** "Cross-Examination by Mr. Blegen," Headley's testimony, *U.S. v. Rana*, Volume 4-B (May 26, 2011), p. 939.

195 **On March 3, 2009 . . . "I would like my sons":** E-mail from David Headley to Tahawwur Rana, March 3, 2009, Government Exhibit, March 3, 2009, DH/TR.

195 **put the Copenhagen attack on hold:** "Second Superseding Indictment," *U.S. v. Rana* (July 2010).

195 **Headley had a dream:** "Headley Cross—Resumed by Mr. Swift," Headley's testimony in *U.S. v. Rana*, Volume 4-A (May 26, 2011), p. 832; "Headley Direct—Resumed," Headley's testimony in *U.S. v. Rana*, Volume 3-A (May 25, 2011), p. 486.

195 **He made contact with Ilyas Kashmiri:** Ibid.

195 **Osama bin Laden publicly denounced:** Inal Ersan, "Bin Laden Warns EU over Prophet Cartoons," Reuters, March 20, 2008, http://www.reuters.com/article/2008/03/20/us-security-binladen-idUSN1933824120080320.

195 **Three months later:** Jane Perlez and Pir Zubair Shah, "Embassy Attack in Pakistan Kills at Least 6," *New York Times*, June 3, 2008.

195 **Headley met with Kashmiri:** "Second Superseding Indictment," *U.S. v. Rana* (Feb. 2, 2010).

195 **Kashmiri congratulated him:** "Government's Santiago Proffer," *U.S. v. Rana;* Plea Agreement, *U.S. v. Headley* (March 18, 2010).

195 **deploying a truck bomb . . . Headley said the building's design would render . . . Kashmiri told Headley that he knew men:** Headley's testimony, *U.S. v. Rana*, Volume 2-B (May 24, 2011), p. 404.

196 **the British tipped off the FBI:** Glanz, Rotella, and Sanger, "In 2008 Mumbai Attacks, Piles of Spy Data, but an Uncompleted Puzzle."

196 **Now under surveillance:** Rotella, "The American Behind India's 9/11; "Headley Direct—Resumed," Headley's testimony in *U.S. v. Rana*, Volume 3-A (May 25, 2011), p. 474.

196 **come up with only two thousand:** Ibid.

196 **When Headley returned:** "Criminal Complaint," *U.S. v. Headley;* Robert Holley of the FBI, quoted in "American Terrorist," *Frontline.*

196 **"The two questions are":** Mudd interview.

196 **FBI officials decided to follow:** Author interview with senior FBI official, Washington, DC, 2015.

196 **Agents examined . . . Mudd and his colleagues:** Mudd interview.

196 **a married schoolteacher with no criminal record . . . Khan would go on to lead:** Bergen, *Longest War*, p. 198.

196 **the right question was . . . "enterprise investigation" . . . good takedown:** Mudd, interview.

197 **particularly concerned . . . a vulnerability . . . "Do we have to identify":** Liepman interview.

197 **arrested at O'Hare Airport on October 3, 2009:** "Government's Santiago Proffer," *U.S. v. Rana.*

197 **He soon told investigators:** "Criminal Complaint," *U.S. v. Headley.*

197 **involvement in the Mumbai attacks:** Robert Holley of the FBI, quoted in "American Terrorist," *Frontline.*

197 **Rana was arrested fifteen days later . . . known of the Copenhagen operation:** U.S. Department of Justice, Office of Public Affairs, "Two Chicago Men Charged in Connection with Alleged Roles in Foreign Terror Plot That Focused

on Targets in Denmark," Justice News, Oct. 27, 2009, http://www.justice.gov/opa/pr/two-chicago-men-charged-connection-alleged-roles-foreign-terror-plot-focused-targets-denmark.

197 **six Americans had been murdered:** Government's Position Paper as to Sentencing Factors, *U.S. v. Headley* (Jan. 22, 2013).

198 **instead was sentenced to thirty-five years:** U.S. Department of Justice, Office of Public Affairs, "David Coleman Headley Sentenced to 35 Years in Prison for Role in India and Denmark Terror Plots," Justice News, Jan. 24, 2013, http://www.justice.gov/opa/pr/david-coleman-headley-sentenced-35-years-prison-role-india-and-denmark-terror-plots.

198 **Rana was sentenced to fourteen:** U.S. Department of Justice, Office of Public Affairs, "Tahawwur Rana Sentenced to 14 Years in Prison for Supporting Pakistani Terror Group and Terror Plot in Denmark," Jan. 17, 2013, FBI.gov, https://www.fbi.gov/chicago/press-releases/2013/tahawwur-rana-sentenced-to-14-years-in-prison-for-supporting-pakistani-terror-group-and-terror-plot-in-denmark.

198 **out of the country:** See "Homegrown Extremism 2001–2015."

198 **indicted Omar Hammami in 2007:** "Indictment," *U.S. v. Hammami.*

CHAPTER 9: TRACKING THE TERRORISTS

199 **Awlaki's star was rising so fast . . . request a "detailed" résumé . . . instructed both men to provide written accounts:** Osama bin Laden, "Letter to Shaykh Mahmud dated 27 Aug. 2010," Combating Terrorism Center, SOCOM-2012-0000003-HT, pdf at https://www.ctc.usma.edu/v2/wp-content/uploads/2012/05/SOCOM-2012-0000003-Trans.pdf.

199 **delivered the speech . . . "America is not":** See "Text: Obama's Speech in Cairo," *New York Times,* June 4, 2009.

200 **the first prizewinner . . . "I face the world as it is":** See Office of the Press Secretary, White House, "Remarks by the President at the Acceptance of the Nobel Peace Prize," Dec. 10, 2009, Washington, DC, https://www.whitehouse.gov/the-press-office/remarks-president-acceptance-nobel-peace-prize.

201 **mandated a troop surge:** Luis Martinez, "US Military in Afghanistan by the Numbers: 2,184 Dead, 19,600 Wounded," ABC News, May 27, 2014, http://abcnews.go.com/blogs/politics/2014/05/u-s-military-in-afghanistan-by-the-numbers-2184-dead-19600-wounded/.

201 **ramped up the CIA drone program:** "Drone Wars Pakistan: Analysis," New America, http://securitydata.newamerica.net/drones/pakistan-analysis.html; "Drone War Yemen: Analysis," New America, http://securitydata.newamerica.net/drones/yemen-analysis.html.

201 **authorize the assassination:** Mark Mazzetti, Charlie Savage, and Scott Shane, "How a U.S. Citizen Came to Be in America's Cross Hairs," *New York Times,* March 9, 2013.

201 **The Obamas were singing carols:** Peter Baker, "Obama's War Over Terror," *New York Times,* Jan. 4, 2010.

201 **taking walks on the beach:** Daniel Klaidman, *Kill or Capture: The War on Terror and the Soul of the Obama Presidency* (New York: Houghton Mifflin Harcourt, 2012), pp. 175–176.

201 **Ben Rhodes, an adviser on national security:** Author interview with Ben Rhodes, Washington, DC, May 8, 2014.

202 **Obama interrupted his vacation:** Office of the Press Secretary, White House, "Statement by the President on the Attempted Attack on Christmas Day and Recent Violence in Iran," Dec. 28, 2009, Washington, DC, https://www.white house.gov/the-press-office/statement-president-attempted-attack-christmas -day-and-recent-violence-iran.

202 **"A systemic failure has occurred":** Klaidman, *Kill or Capture,* p. 177.

202 **Michael Leiter of the NCTC thought:** Leiter interview.

202 **the White House's subsequent investigation . . . Yet the intelligence community:** Office of the Press Secretary, White House, "Summary of the White House Review of the December 25, 2009 Attempted Terrorist Attack," Jan. 7, 2010, Washington, DC, https://www.whitehouse.gov/the-press-office/white -house-review-summary-regarding-12252009-attempted-terrorist-attack.

202 **Brennan had been personally briefed:** Author interview with senior Saudi official, Washington, DC, Oct. 2009.

202 **When Obama returned to the White House:** Jake Tapper, Karen Travers, and Huma Khan, "Obama: System Failed in a 'Potentially Disastrous Way,'" ABC News, Jan. 5, 2010, http://abcnews.go.com/print?id=9484260.

202 **officials around the table . . . candid and apologetic . . . national security community was committed:** Leiter interview.

203 **"I want these things fixed":** Interview with senior U.S. official.

203 **terrorism had been one issue . . . explained to his national security team:** Rhodes interview.

203 **American drone attack in Pakistan . . . first two years of the Obama presidency:** Peter Bergen, "Warrior in Chief," *New York Times,* April 28, 2012.

203 **vastly accelerated the campaign in Yemen:** "Drone Wars Yemen: Analysis," New America, http://securitydata.newamerica.net/drones/yemen-analysis.html.

203 **Just one U.S. drone strike:** Ibid.

203 **120 drone and cruise missile strikes:** Ibid. As of Aug. 8, 2014, there had been 129 strikes in Yemen.

203 **use in Pakistan's tribal regions:** Adam Entous, Siobhan Gorman, and Julian E. Barnes,"U.S. Tightens Drone Rules," *Wall Street Journal,* Nov. 4, 2011.

204 **in Yemen a year later . . . governed by stricter rules:** Becker and Shane, "Secret 'Kill List' Proves a Test of Obama's Principles and Will."

204 **According to conservative estimates . . . More liberal estimates:** "Drone Wars Yemen: Analysis," New America; "Drone Wars Pakistan: Analysis," New America.

204 **Obama remarked drily to his aides:** Peter Hamby, "10 More Secrets from Campaign 2012," CNN.com, Nov. 4, 2013.

204 **Abdulmutallab's FBI interrogations:** Charlie Savage, "Christmas Day Bomb Plot Detailed in Court Filings," *New York Times,* Feb. 10, 2012.

204 **a fiery interview posted to YouTube:** Middle East Media Research Institute,

"Yemeni-American Jihadi Cleric Anwar Al-Awlaki in First Interview with Al-Qaeda Media Calls on Muslim U.S. Servicemen to Kill Fellow Soldiers," May 23, 2010, http://www.memri.org/report/en/0/0/0/0/0/0/4202.htm.

204 **he claimed Major Hasan:** Savage, "Christmas Day Bomb Plot Detailed in Court Filings."

205 **Awlaki brushed aside criticism . . . invoked a common Binladenist theme:** Middle East Media Research Institute, "Yemeni-American Jihadi Cleric Anwar Al-Awlaki in First Interview with Al-Qaeda Media Calls on Muslim U.S. Servicemen to Kill Fellow Soldiers."

205 **as more of a threat:** Larry Shaughnessy, "U.S. Official: Al Qaeda in Yemen Bigger Threat Than in Pakistan," CNN.com, Dec. 17, 2010.

205 **tribal disputes are often settled with artillery:** Peter L. Bergen, *Holy War, Inc.: Inside the Secret World of Osama bin Laden* (New York: Free Press, 2001), pp. 167–94.

205 **White House officials began debating:** Author interview with senior White House official.

205 **verbal approval to target Awlaki:** Klaidman, *Kill or Capture,* p. 264.

205 **the president had agonized:** Author interview with senior Obama administration official.

205 **the decision to kill Awlaki:** Ibid.

206 **Awlaki was on a JSOC kill/capture list:** Dana Priest, "U.S. Military Teams, Intelligence Deeply Involved in Aiding Yemen on Strikes," *Washington Post,* Jan. 27, 2010.

206 **two lawyers at the Justice Department . . . Merely being an American citizen . . . "imminent" threat of violent attack . . . hiding in a remote area of Yemen . . . comport with the "law of war":** *New York Times v. United States Department of Justice,* Case No. 13-422-cv [hereafter *New York Times v. U.S. Dept. of Justice*], Memorandum for the Attorney General, pp. 67–97 (2d Circuit, June 23, 2014), http://www.nytimes.com/interactive/2014/06/23/us/23awlaki-memo.html.

206 **A confidential Justice Department memo . . . no longer required the "United States to have clear evidence" . . . "recently" involved in "activities":** U.S. Department of Justice, "Lawfulness of a Lethal Operation Directed Against a U.S. Citizen Who Is a Senior Operational Leader of Al-Qa'ida or an Associated Force," White Paper, Nov. 8, 2011, pp. 7–8, pdf at https://www.documentcloud.org/documents/602342-draft-white-paper.html.

206 **monitoring Awlaki's e-mail account:** Peter Bergen, "Target an American with Drones?" CNN.com, Feb. 11, 2014.

206 **Vicki Divoll:** Vicki Divoll, "U.S. Targets an American Abroad," *Los Angeles Times,* April 23, 2010.

206 **Koh, a rumpled, combative academic:** Klaidman, *Kill or Capture,* p. 6.

207 **the only Obama official to acknowledge publicly:** Tara McKelvey, "Interview with Harold Koh, Obama's Defender of Drone Strikes," *Daily Beast,* April 8, 2012, http://www.thedailybeast.com/articles/2012/04/08/interview-with-harold-koh-obama-s-defender-of-drone-strikes.html.

207 **Koh gave a speech:** U.S. Department of State, Speech by Harold Koh, Annual Meeting of the American Society of International Law, March 25, 2010, transcript at http://www.state.gov/s/l/releases/remarks/139119.htm.

207 **something bothered Koh . . . secure facility at the State Department . . . Awlaki's plots, many of which involved . . . Awlaki was "satanic":** Klaidman, *Kill or Capture*, pp. 215–16.

207 **the third issue of *Inspire*:** *Inspire* No. 3, Nov. 2010, https://azelin.files.word press.com/2010/11/inspire-magazine-3.pdf.

207 **Awlaki had played a lead role:** Eric Holder, Memo to Patrick J. Leahy, May 22, 2013, pdf at http://www.justice.gov/slideshow/AG-letter-5-22-13.pdf.

207 **AQAP mailed two packages . . . mobile phone circuit boards served as detonators . . . With grim humor . . . brought down a UPS flight:** *Inspire* No. 3.

208 **both were discovered:** Eric Schmitt and Scott Shane, "Saudis Warned U.S. of Attack Before Parcel Bomb Plot," *New York Times,* Nov. 5, 2010.

208 **Saudi counterterrorism official:** Mark Mazzetti and Robert F. Worth, "U.S. Sees Complexity of Bombs as Link to Al Qaeda," *New York Times,* Oct. 30, 2010.

208 **$4,200 that AQAP had spent:** *Inspire* No. 3.

208 **"Terror Tuesdays":** Klaidman, *Kill or Capture*, p. 256.

208 **Awlaki posed a greater threat:** Ibid., p. 261.

208 **"Bring it to me":** Ibid., pp. 263–64.

208 **Obama received word:** Interview with senior U.S. official.

208 **JSOC initially took the lead:** Interview with U.S. official familiar with the operation.

208 **launching strikes:** Interview with senior U.S. official.

208 **Drones tracking Awlaki:** Klaidman, *Kill or Capture*, p. 262.

209 **Important leads on Awlaki's whereabouts:** Ibid., pp. 237, 263. On December 21, 2011, Ahmed Warsame gave his age as twenty-five at a court hearing in the case against him.

209 **Al-Qaeda in Yemen's key go-between:** Ibid., pp. 237, 251.

209 **tracked Warsame:** Ibid., p. 238.

209 **the USS *Boxer*:** Ibid., pp. 238–39; Charlie Savage, "U.S. Tests New Approach to Terrorism Cases on Somali Suspect," *New York Times,* July 6, 2011.

209 **interrogated Warsame:** Klaidman, *Kill or Capture*, p. 250.

209 **educated in the United Kingdom:** Ibid., pp. 251–52. Warsame also spoke fluent English at the court hearing on December 21, 2011.

209 **a detailed account:** Ibid., pp. 251–52, 262–63.

209 **As the interrogation wore on:** Interview with a U.S. official familiar with the operation.

209 **Warsame's disclosures:** Martha Raddatz, "U.S. Missiles Missed Awlaki by Inches in Yemen," ABC News, July 19, 2011.

209 **special operations planners:** Ibid.

209 **pushing hard to "remove him":** David Nakamura, "Obama on 'Tonight Show' with Jay Leno: Full Video and Transcript," *Washington Post,* Oct. 26, 2011, http://www.washingtonpost.com/blogs/44/post/obama-on-tonight-show-with -jay-leno-full-video-and-transcript/2011/10/26/gIQAHXJjIM_blog.html.

209 **truck was driving fast . . . JSOC plane fired . . . Awlaki summoned:** Raddatz, "U.S. Missiles Missed Awlaki by Inches in Yemen."

210 **"We only blew his bumper off":** Interview with a U.S. official in Yemen at the time.

210 **Harrier jets . . . survived the attack:** Raddatz, "U.S. Missiles Missed Awlaki by Inches in Yemen."

210 **men gave their lives . . . Awlaki witnessed:** Johnsen, *Last Refuge,* p. 276.

210 **"It was one of the worst nights of my life" . . . JSOC's botched attack:** Interview with a U.S. official in Yemen at the time.

210 **remained in a house:** David S. Cloud, Jeffrey Fleishman, and Brian Bennett, "Anwar Awlaki Killed by U.S. Drone in Yemen," *Los Angeles Times,* Oct. 1, 2011.

210 **A number of children were in the house:** Peter Bergen, "The American Who Inspires Terror from Paris to the U.S.," CNN.com, Jan. 12, 2015.

210 **the CIA was in charge:** Cloud, Fleishman, and Bennett, "Anwar Awlaki Killed by U.S. Drone in Yemen."

210 **On the morning of Friday, September 30, 2011 . . . at 9:55 a.m.:** Bergen, "The American Who Inspires Terror from Paris to the U.S."

210 **announced that Awlaki had been killed:** "Remarks at the Change of Command Ceremony for the Chairman of the Joint Chiefs of Staff at Fort Myer, Virginia," White House, Sept. 30, 2011, transcript at http://www.gpo.gov/fdsys/pkg/DCPD-201100695/html/DCPD-201100695.htm.

211 **the Islamic community leader . . . called Samir's father . . . "I always felt":** Hough interview.

211 **family issued a statement . . . killed by his own government . . . statement asked:** Victor Manuel Ramos, "Khan's Parents Speak Out over Yemen Death," *Newsday Long Island,* Oct. 6, 2011.

211 **Khan was never the intended target:** Mark Mazzetti, Eric Schmitt, and Robert F. Worth, "Two-Year Manhunt Led to Killing of Awlaki in Yemen," *New York Times,* Sept. 30, 2011; interview with senior U.S. administration official.

211 **Colorado-born Abdulrahman . . . drone strike . . . Only sixteen:** Nasser al-Awlaki, "The Drone That Killed My Grandson," *New York Times,* July 17, 2013.

211 **strike had been "sloppy":** Rhodes interview.

211 **Presidential Policy Guidance on drone strikes:** See White House, "U.S. Policy Standards and Procedures for the Use of Force in Counterterrorism Operations Outside the United States and Areas of Active Hostilities," pdf at https://www.whitehouse.gov/sites/default/files/uploads/2013.05.23_fact_sheet_on_ppg.pdf.

212 **only with "near-certainty":** Office of the Press Secretary, White House, "Remarks by the President at the National Defense University, May 23, 2013, Fort McNair, Washington, DC, https://www.whitehouse.gov/the-press-office/2013/05/23/remarks-president-national-defense-university.

212 **more than three dozen militants indicted or convicted:** "Homegrown Extremism 2001–2015," as of Sept. 1, 2015.

212 **massive ramp-up of the CIA drone campaign . . . decimated al-Qaeda's core:** See "Drone Wars Pakistan: Analysis," New America.

212 **in a trove of documents:** See Office of the Director of National Intelligence, "Bin Ladin's Bookshelf," http://www.dni.gov/index.php/resources/bin-laden -bookshelf?start=1.

212 **forty-eight-page memo . . . "I am leaning toward":** Letter to Shaykh Mahmud, dated Oct. 21, 2010, SOCOM-2012-0000015-HT, pdf http://assets.national journal.com/pdf/OBL13.pdf.

212 **"the killing of many jihadi cadres" . . . suggested that operatives travel:** Peter Bergen, "Secrets of the bin Laden Treasure-Trove," CNN, May 20, 2015.

212 **"the Americans have great accumulated expertise of photography":** Peter Bergen, "Bin Laden: Seized Documents Show Delusional Leader and Micromanager," CNN.com, April 30, 2012.

213 **short on cash . . . "killing and fighting the American people" . . . advised jihadist militants in North Africa . . . offered similar advice to AQAP . . . bin Laden's advice either didn't make it:** Bergen, "Secrets of the bin Laden Treasure-Trove."

213 **145 to 168 civilians have been killed:** "Drone Wars Pakistan: Analysis," New America, as of Aug. 7, 2015.

213 **drove approval ratings for the United States:** Andrew Dugan and Mohamed Younis, "Pakistani Disapproval of U.S. Leadership Soars in 2012," Gallup, Feb. 14, 2013, http://www.gallup.com/poll/160439/2012-pakistani-disapproval -leadership-soars.aspx.

213 **one of his chief motivations:** Plea, *U.S. v. Shahzad* (June 21, 2010), pp. 8, 29.

213 **Pew poll conducted in forty-four countries:** "Global Opposition to U.S. Surveillance and Drones, but Limited Harm to America's Image," Pew Research Center, July 14, 2014, http://www.pewglobal.org/2014/07/14/global-opposition-to-u-s -surveillance-and-drones-but-limited-harm-to-americas-image/.

213 **consider the program illegal:** See Jessica Elgot, "'Illegal' Drone Strikes Condemned in Landslide Vote by European Politicians," *Huffington Post United Kingdom,* Feb. 27, 2014, http://www.huffingtonpost.co.uk/2014/02/27/europe -meps-vote-against-drone-strikes_n_4866217.html.

214 **"we need to tighten up here":** Rhodes interview.

214 **the *Guardian* broke:** Glenn Greenwald, "NSA Collecting Phone Records of Millions of Verizon Customers Daily," *Guardian,* June 6, 2013.

214 **"We know of at least fifty threats":** Jackie Calmes, "Obama Says Surveillance Helped in Case in Germany," *New York Times,* June 19, 2013.

214 **General Keith Alexander, the director of the NSA, testified:** Testimony of director of the National Security Agency General Keith Alexander before the House Permanent Select Committee on Intelligence, "Hearing on Disclosure of National Security Agency Surveillance Programs," June 18, 2013 [hereafter "Testimony by General Keith Alexander"], p. 10, pdf at http://fas.org:8080/irp/ congress/2013_hr/disclosure.pdf.

214 **A typical NSA talking point was:** National Security Agency, "Media Leaks One Card," released to Al Jazeera, Oct. 17, 2013, response to FOIA request in pdf at https://s3.amazonaws.com/s3.documentcloud.org/documents/813055/nsa- talking-points.pdf.

215 **October 29, 2013, House Intelligence Committee hearing:** Andrea Peterson, "Here's Why NSA Officials Never Seem to Stop Talking About 9/11," *Washington Post,* Oct. 30, 2013.

215 **Bob Schieffer said on** *Face the Nation*: Bob Schieffer, interview on *Face the Nation,* "Rogers, Udall, and the Latest from Egypt," aired July 28, 2013, CBS.

215 **The single plot the government publicly cited . . . series of conversations with Aden Hashi Ayro . . . "time to finance the jihad" . . . Moalin transferred thousands of dollars:** Ibid.; Ellen Nakashima, "NSA Cites Case as Success of Phone Data-Collection Program," *Washington Post,* Aug. 8, 2013.

216 **ruled on December 16, 2013:** *Klayman et al. v. Obama et al.,* Case No. 13-0851, Memorandum Opinion (District Court of DC, Dec. 16, 2013), pp. 56–64.

216 **"utter lack of evidence":** Ibid., p. 62.

216 **A White House review panel:** President's Review Group on Intelligence and Communications Technologies, "Liberty and Security in a Changing World: Report and Recommendations of the President's Review Group on Intelligence and Communications Technologies," Washington, DC, 2013, p. 104, pdf at https://www.whitehouse.gov/sites/default/files/docs/2013-12-12_rg_final_report.pdf.

216 **"We found none" . . . far more useful:** Michael Isikoff, "NSA Program Stopped No Terror Attacks, Says White House Panel Member," NBC News, Dec. 20, 2013.

216 **A HuffPost/YouGov poll:** Peter Moore, "NSA Surveillance an 'Unnecessary Intrusion,'" YouGov, July 10, 2014, https://today.yougov.com/news/2014/07/10/nsa-surveillance/.

216 **announced that it would reform surveillance:** Office of the Press Secretary, White House, "FACT SHEET: The Administration's Proposal for Ending the Section 215 Bulk Telephony Metadata Program," March 27, 2014, Washington, DC, https://www.whitehouse.gov/the-press-office/2014/03/27/fact-sheet-administration-s-proposal-ending-section-215-bulk-telephony-m.

216 **this proposal became law:** Jeremy Diamond, "NSA Surveillance Bill Passes After Weeks-Long Showdown," CNN, June 2, 2015.

216 **Thomas Galati, a senior official in the Intelligence Division:** *Handschu v. Special Services Division,* Case No. 71-civ-2203, Deposition of Thomas Galati (Southern District of New York, June 28, 2012), p. 124, http://www.ap.org/Images/Pages-from-Galati-EBT-6-28-12_tcm28-8694.pdf; Adam Goldman and Matt Apuzzo, "NYPD: Muslim Spying Led to No Leads, Terror Cases," Associated Press, Aug. 21, 2012, http://www.ap.org/Content/AP-In-The-News/2012/NYPD-Muslim-spying-led-to-no-leads-terror-cases.

217 **the Demographics Unit was disbanded:** Apuzzo and Goldstein, "New York Drops Unit That Spied on Muslims."

217 **These cases argue . . . tip from the local Muslim American community or a family member:** "Homegrown Extremism 2001–2015."

218 **sixteen people on the U.S. no-fly list:** Steve Kroft, "Unlikely Terrorists on No Fly List," CBS News, Oct. 5, 2006, http://www.cbsnews.com/news/unlikely-terrorists-on-no-fly-list/.

218 **more than forty thousand:** Eileen Sullivan, "No-Fly List Rules Get Changes," Associated Press, Aug. 20, 2014, http://www.businessinsider.com/us-changing -no-fly-list-rules-2014-8.

218 **thirty-two Joint Terrorism Task Force "fusion centers":** Federal Bureau of Investigation, "Protecting America from Terrorist Attack: Our Joint Terrorism Task Forces," FBI.gov, http://www.fbi.gov/about-us/investigate/terrorism/ terrorism_jttfs.

218 **the "shoe bomber," Richard Reid:** "Shoe Bomber: Tale of Another Failed Terrorist Attack," CNN.com, Dec. 25, 2009.

219 **suspicious SUV parked in Times Square:** Al Baker and William K. Rashbaum, "Police Find Car Bomb in Times Square," *New York Times*, May 1, 2010.

219 **$72 billion . . . Before 9/11, the budget:** Intelligence Resource Program, "Intelligence Budget Data," Federation of American Scientists, http://fas.org/irp/ budget/.

219 **a speech at National Defense University:** "Remarks by the President at the National Defense University."

220 **he assured David Remnick . . . "a jayvee team":** David Remnick, "Going the Distance," *The New Yorker,* Jan. 27, 2014.

CHAPTER 10: THE BOSTON BOMBERS

221 **following an intense firefight with the police:** Registry Division of the City of Boston, "The Commonwealth of Massachusetts Medical Examiner's Certificate of Death Registry of Vital Records and Statistics," May 10, 2013, pdf at http:// cache.boston.com/multimedia/2013/05/10tsarnaev/death_certificate.pdf.

221 **multiple gunshot wounds, the most severe of which:** *United States of America v. Dzokhar Tsarnaev,* Case No. 13-MJ-2106-MBB [hereafter *U.S. v. Tsarnaev*], Sealed Transcript (U.S. District Court District of Massachusetts, April 22, 2013), p. 4.

221 **Other shots had:** Ibid.; *United States of America v. Robel Phillipos,* Case No. 13-MJ-2102-MBB [hereafter *U.S. v. Phillipos*], Criminal Complaint (U.S. District Court, District of Massachusetts, May 1, 2013).

221 **"The U.S. government is killing":** *U.S. v. Tsarnaev,* Case No. 1:13-cr-10200-GAO, Government's Opposition to Tsarnaev's Motion to Vacate Special Administrative Measures ("SAMS") (U.S. District Court, District of Massachusetts, Oct. 21, 2013).

222 **in which some twenty-three thousand runners:** "2013 Boston Marathon Statistics," Boston Athletics Association, http://registration.baa.org/2013/cf/Public/ iframe_Statistics.htm.

222 **carrying large backpacks:** Criminal Complaint, *U.S. v. Tsarnaev* (April 21, 2013), pp. 4–5.

222 **Tamerlan was wearing:** Ibid.; FBI Boston, "Remarks of Special Agent in Charge Richard DesLauriers at Press Conference on Bombing Investigation," April 18, 2013, https://www.fbi.gov/boston/press-releases/2013/remarks-of

-special-agent-in-charge-richard-deslauriers-at-press-conference-on-bombing
-investigation-1.

222 **hundreds of thousands of other spectators:** According to Thomas Grilk, the Executive Director of the Boston Athletics Association, on a good day, the association estimates five hundred thousand people line the course. "Jury Trial—Day Twenty-Seven Testimony of Thomas Grilk," *U.S. v. Tsarnaev* (March 26, 2015).

222 **The two men dropped:** *After Action Report for the Response to the 2013 Boston Marathon Bombings,* Dec. 2014 [hereafter *After Action Report*], pdf at http://www.mass.gov/eopss/docs/mema/after-action-report-for-the-response-to-the-2013-boston-marathon-bombings.pdf.

222 **At 2:49 p.m. the first bomb went off:** Indictment, *U.S. v. Tsarnaev* (June 27, 2013), pp. 8–9.

222 **thirteen seconds later:** *After Action Report.*

222 **The bombs were filled with:** Criminal Complaint, *U.S. v. Tsarnaev* (April 21, 2013); Indictment, *U.S. v. Tsarnaev* (June 27, 2013).

222 **More than 170 other people were wounded:** "The Boston Victims," *New York Times,* April 20, 2013.

222 **Martin Richard's seven-year-old sister lost a leg:** David Abel, "For Richard Family, Loss and Love," *Boston Globe,* April 13, 2014.

222 **Twenty minutes after he deposited:** "Exhibit 456: Dzhokhar Tsarnaev Buys Milk at Whole Foods After Marathon Bombing," *Masslive,* March 11, 2015, http://videos.masslive.com/republican/2015/03/exhibit_456_dzhokhar_tsarnaev.html; Excerpt Jury Trial—Day Twenty-Seven, Opening Statement by Mr. Weinreb, *U.S. v. Tsarnaev* (March 4, 2015), p. 8.

222 **he sent a text . . . Baudy replied . . . Jahar wrote back:** Kathy Curran, "Dzhokhar Tsarnaev Sent Text Messages After Boston Marathon Bombings," WCVB, May 9, 2013, http://www.wcvb.com/investigative/dzhokhar-tsarnaev-sent-text-messages-after-boston-marathon-bombings/20071568.

222 **Monaco had been in her new job . . . on the secure phone:** Author interview with Lisa Monaco, Washington, DC, June 15, 2015.

223 **Monaco was a native of the Boston suburbs and had attended Harvard:** Matt Viser, "Newton Native in Key Counterterrorism Job," *Boston Globe,* April 19, 2013.

223 **Her oldest brother had raced . . . and her twin brother was among the spectators:** Monaco interview.

223 **longest-serving chief of staff to FBI director Robert Mueller:** Shane Harris, "Obama Taps Lisa Monaco as Next White House Counterterrorism Adviser," *Washingtonian,* Jan. 25, 2013.

223 **basement office . . . Within twenty minutes . . . Monaco's immediate questions:** Monaco interview.

223 **In the days after:** Excerpt of Jury Trial—Day Twenty-Seven Opening Statement by Mr. Weinreb, *U.S. v. Tsarnaev* (March 4, 2015), p. 9; Sarah Coffey, Patricia Wen, and Matt Carroll, "Bombing Suspect Spent Wednesday as Typical Student," *Boston Globe,* April 19, 2013.

223 **Jahar went to pick up his car:** Molly Hennessy-Fiske, "Owner: Bombing Suspect Demanded His Car Back from Shop on Tuesday," *Los Angeles Times,* April 19, 2013.

223 **working out . . . he had a meal:** Michael Wines and Ian Lovett, "The Dark Side, Carefully Masked," *New York Times,* May 4, 2013.

224 **After carefully reviewing a deluge:** FBI, "Video and Photos Released in Bombings Case," in "Updates on Investigation into Multiple Explosions in Boston," FBI.gov, April 18, 2013, https://www.fbi.gov/news/updates-on-investigation -into-multiple-explosions-in-boston.

224 **Jahar texted one of his buddies:** *United States of America v. Diaz Kadyrbayev and Azamat Tazhayakov,* 13CR10238, Indictment (U.S. District Court District of Massachusetts, Aug. 8, 2013).

224 **At around 10:00 p.m. the Tsarnaev brothers . . . They drove a Honda Civic to the campus of MIT:** Indictment, *U.S. v. Tsarnaev* (June 27, 2013).

224 **An hour later they carjacked . . . With pride, he added . . . stopped to get gas:** Jury Trial—Day Thirty-Two Testimony of Dun Meng, *U.S. v. Tsarnaev* (March 12, 2015).

224 **As they careened . . . Tamerlan fired at the cops:** Indictment, *U.S. v. Tsarnaev* (June 27, 2013); Excerpt of Jury Trial—Day Twenty-Seven Opening Statement by Mr. Weinreb, *U.S. v. Tsarnaev* (March 4, 2015).

224 **Jahar fled on foot . . . smashed his two cell phones:** Indictment, *U.S. v. Tsarnaev* (June 27, 2013).

224 **Hours later:** *United States of America v. Dias Kadyrbayev, Azamat Tazhayakov, Robel Kidane Phillipos,* Case No. 13cr10238DPW, Superseding Indictment (U.S. District Court District of Massachusetts, Aug. 29, 2013).

224 **That afternoon:** Christian Caryl, "The Bombers' World," *New York Review of Books,* June 6, 2013.

225 **born in Kyrgyzstan following the 1944 mass deportation:** Leila Saralayeva, "Boston Suspects' Chechen Family Traveled Long Road," Associated Press, April 20, 2013.

225 **Anzor married . . . their oldest child . . . For murky reasons:** Sally Jacobs, David Filipov, and Patricia Wen, "The Fall of the House of Tsarnaev," *Boston Globe,* Dec. 15, 2013.

225 **On 9/11 they were living:** Peter Foster and Tom Parfitt, "Boston Bomber Arrested: Tamerlan Tsarnaev's Hateful Rage Behind American Dream," *Telegraph,* April 20, 2013.

225 **Over the course of 2002 and 2003:** Inspectors General of the Intelligence Community, Central Intelligence Agency, Department of Justice, and Department of Homeland Security, "Unclassified Summary of Information Handling and Sharing Prior to the April 15, 2013 Boston Marathon Bombings," April 10, 2014.

225 **They settled in a third-floor apartment:** Masha Gessen, *The Brothers: The Road to an American Tragedy* (New York: Riverhead Books, 2015), pp. 67–70.

225 **Zubeidat, a cosmetologist . . . less far-fetched . . . Jahar captained:** Jacobs, Filipov, and Wen, "The Fall of the House of Tsarnaev."

225 **upon graduation he won scholarships:** Janet Reitman, "Jahar's World," *Rolling Stone,* July 17, 2013.

225 **easygoing, party-loving skateboarder:** Peter Finn, Carol Leonnig, and Will Englund, "Tamerlan Tsarnaev and Dzhokhar Tsarnaev Were Refugees from Brutal Chechen Conflict," *Washington Post,* April 19, 2013.

226 **Tamerlan was the star:** Jacobs, Filipov, and Wen, "The Fall of the House of Tsarnaev."

226 **His mother adored . . . family laughed at his jokes:** Caryl, "The Bombers' World."

226 **drove around town in a white Mercedes:** Jacobs, Filipov, and Wen, "The Fall of the House of Tsarnaev."

226 **dressed in the style:** Gessen, *The Brothers,* p. 79; Marc Fisher et al., "The Tsarnaev Family: A Faded Portrait of an Immigrant's American Dream," *Washington Post,* April 27, 2013; Jacobs, Filipov, and Wen, "The Fall of the House of Tsarnaev."

226 **worked as a pizza delivery man:** Gessen, *The Brothers,* p. 81.

226 **leisure time drinking and smoking . . . Worried about this:** Jacobs, Filipov, and Wen, "The Fall of the House of Tsarnaev."

226 **he felt alienated . . . He added, however:** Johannes Hirn, "Will Box for Passport," *the comment,* 2010, pdf at http://www.bu.edu/com/comment/library/downloads/2010_comment.pdf.

226 **This was a prerequisite . . . filed for divorce:** Jacobs, Filipov, and Wen, "The Fall of the House of Tsarnaev."

227 **In 2012 she was accused:** Danielle Horn, "Arrests: $1,600 in Clothes Stolen," Natick Patch, June 14, 2012, http://patch.com/massachusetts/natick/arrests-1-600-in-clothes-stolen.

227 **moved out of the family home . . . arrested . . . heard a "voice" in his head . . . married Katherine Russell:** Jacobs, Filipov, and Wen, "The Fall of the House of Tsarnaev."

227 **They had met . . . The match did not thrill:** Jury Trial—Day Fifty, Witnesses for the Defense Judith Russell, *U.S. v. Tsarnaev* (April 27, 2015).

227 **Both Katherine's grandfather and her father:** Michael Cooper, Serge F. Kovaleski, Richard A. Oppel Jr., and John Eligon, "Path from 'Social Butterfly' to Boston Suspect's Widow," *New York Times,* May 3, 2013; Monica Hesse, "Katherine Russell: Boston Bombing Suspect Widow's Enigmatic Life Journey," *Washington Post,* May 5, 2013.

227 **The couple soon had a baby girl:** Ibid.

227 **Tamerlan and Katherine lived on welfare payments:** Evan Allen, "Family of Suspected Bombers Received Welfare, Food Stamps," *Boston Globe,* April 26, 2013.

227 **Katherine started working:** Patricia Wen, "Tsarnaev's Family So Far Absent from Trial," *Boston Globe,* April 17, 2015; Jacobs, Filipov, and Wen, "The Fall of the House of Tsarnaev."

227 **quit boxing entirely and traded:** Fisher et al., "The Tsarnaev Family."

228 **converted to Islam:** Cooper, Kovaleski, Oppel, and Elligon, "Path from 'Social Butterfly' to Boston Suspect's Widow."

228 "His brother pressured [Jahar] a lot" . . . "His brother would": Caryl, "The Bombers' World."

228 Jahar's wrestling team traditionally asked: Wines and Lovett, "The Dark Side, Carefully Masked."

228 The Russians told the FBI: Inspectors General of the Intelligence Community, Central Intelligence Agency, Department of Justice, and Department of Homeland Security, "Unclassified Summary of Information Handling and Sharing Prior to the April 15, 2013 Boston Marathon Bombings," April 10, 2014 [hereafter Inspectors General et al., "Unclassified Summary"].

228 opened an "assessment": Ibid.

228 run Tamerlan's phone number: Author interview with senior FBI official.

228 The file on Tamerlan was closed: Inspectors General et al., "Unclassified Summary."

228 When Russian officials went: Ibid.; Mark Hosenball, "Boston Bomb Suspect's Name Was on Classified Government Watch Lists," Reuters, April 24, 2013, http://www.reuters.com/article/2013/04/24/us-usa-explosions-boston-suspect-idUSBRE93N06720130424.

229 On September 11, 2011 . . . Investigators reported . . . no sign of forced entry: Susan Zalkind, "The Murders Before the Marathon," *Boston Magazine*, March 2014.

229 in 2009, after he hit: Cambridge Police Department, Cambridge MA, "Incident Report," Aug. 12, 2009, pdf at http://a.abcnews.go.com/images/Blotter/tamerlan_tsarvaev_police_report.pdf.

229 in January 2012, Tamerlan told his family that he had decided to return: Gessen, *The Brothers,* p. 101.

229 became close to Magomed Kartashov: Ibid.; Jacobs, David, and Wen, "The Fall of the House of Tsarnaev."

229 Russian security officials have claimed: American investigators never unearthed any evidence that supported this claim. For more, see Majority Staff of the Committee on Homeland Security, "The Road to Boston: Counterterrorism Challenges and Lessons from the Marathon Bombings," U.S. House of Representatives Committee on Homeland Security, March 2014, pdf at http://fas.org/irp/congress/2014_rpt/boston.pdf.

229 In mid-July 2012, Tamerlan returned: Inspectors General et al., "Unclassified Summary."

229 his full beard: Fisher et al., "The Tsarnaev Family."

229 In November he confronted: Jury Trial—Day Fifty Witnesses for the Defense Abderrazak Razak, *U.S. v. Tsarnaev* (April 27, 2015).

229 "Why are you pushing Muslims to celebrate this holiday": Alan Cullison et al., "Turn to Religion Split Suspects' Home," *Wall Street Journal,* April 22, 2013.

229 When a preacher: Islamic Society of Boston, "Boston Mosque Details Transparent Interactions with Suspect," April 22, 2013, pdf at http://msnbcmedia.msn.com/i/msnbc/sections/news/Islamic_Society_Statement.pdf.

230 Salafists do not celebrate birthdays: The Permanent Committee for Scholarly Research and Ifta', "The First and Second Questions of Fatwa No. 16419," King-

dom of Saudi Arabia: Portal of the General Presidency of Scholarly Research and Ifta', http://alifta.net/Fatawa/FatawaChapters.aspx?languagename=en&View =Page&PageID=10776&PageNo=1&BookID=7.

230 **Two months later . . . Later, several elders:** Islamic Society of Boston, "Boston Mosque Details Transparent Interactions with Suspect."

230 **At the Cambridge mosque . . . Tamerlan started recommending:** Sally Jacobs, "Tsarnaev Friend Tells of Beliefs in Conspiracies," *Boston Globe,* Aug. 8, 2013.

230 **Both Tamerlan and Jahar came to share:** Jacobs, Filipov, and Wen, "The Fall of the House of Tsarnaev."

230 **Tamerlan maintained a YouTube account:** Will Englund and Peter Finn, "Bombing Suspect's YouTube Account Mirrored Jihadist Conflicts in Caucasus," *Washington Post,* April 20, 2013.

230 **The video showed al-Qaeda fighters:** Adam Serwer, "Did Boston Bombing Suspect Post Al Qaeda Prophecy on YouTube?" *Mother Jones,* April 19, 2013.

231 **downloaded an issue of *Inspire*:** The *Inspire* article, "Make a Bomb in the Kitchen of Your Mom," appears to have influenced the brothers' bomb design, but an analysis by the FBI's Terrorist Explosive Device Analytical Center found that the brothers' bombs had a "much more sophisticated design" than was featured in the article, making it likely that the Tsarnaevs found additional bomb-making manuals online. For more detail, see Richard Esposito, "Exclusive: Government Doc Shows How Closely Boston Marathon Bombers Followed al Qaeda Plans," NBC, April 26, 2013.

231 **Tamerlan bought forty-eight firework mortars:** Indictment, *U.S. v. Tsarnaev* (June 27, 2013).

231 **Six weeks later:** Indictment, *U.S. v. Tsarnaev* (June 27, 2013); Exhibit No. 1165, "Manchester Firing Range Surveillance Video," *U.S. v. Tsarnaev,* accessed via *Boston Globe,* http://www.bostonglobe.com/metro/2015/03/03/boston -marathon-bombing-trial-witnesses-and-exhibits/TNLn7fn2CJ5GbC7jx EMBwM/story.html#e425_Manchesterfiringrangesurveillancevideo.

231 **During this period:** Indictment, *U.S. v. Tsarnaev* (June 27, 2013).

231 **created a second Twitter account:** Excerpt of Jury Trial—Day Twenty-Nine, Testimony of Steven Kimball, *U.S. v. Tsarnaev* (March 9, 2015), p. 6.

231 **a month before the bombing:** Criminal Complaint, *U.S. v. Phillipos* (May 1, 2013), p. 11n1.

231 **He even discussed "martyrdom":** Denise Lavoie, "Tsarnaev Told Friend Martyrs Go to Heaven, Prosecutor Says," WBUR, July 7, 2014, http://www.wbur .org/2014/07/07/azamat-tazhayakov-trial-opening-statements.

232 **A resident of Watertown discovered Jahar:** David Abel, "Boat Owner Seeks to Clarify Record on Tsarnaev Capture," *Boston Globe,* Oct. 16, 2013.

232 **where he lay unconscious:** Scott Helman and Jenna Russell, *Long Mile Home: Boston Under Attack, the City's Courageous Recovery, and the Epic Hunt for Justice* (New York: Dutton, 2014), p. 244; "Motion to Suppress Statements," *U.S. v. Tsarnaev* (May 7, 2014).

232 **Members of the FBI's:** Helman and Russell, *Long Mile Home,* p. 244.

232 **forgo reading him his Miranda rights:** Ethan Bronner and Michael Schmidt,

"In Questions at First, No Miranda for Suspect," *New York Times*, April 22, 2013.

232 **Jahar, still seriously wounded:** "Motion to Suppress Statements," *U.S. v. Tsarnaev* (May 7, 2014); Schwartapfel, "Tending to Tsarnaev."

232 **He described freely . . . Because they managed:** Eric Schmitt, Mark Mazzetti, Michael Schmidt, and Scott Shane, "Boston Plotters Said to Initially Target July 4 for Attack," *New York Times*, May 2, 2013.

232 **He told investigators:** Helman and Russell, *Long Mile Home*, p. 244.

233 **The BAU is split:** Author interview with FBI behavioral analysts, Quantico, VA, 2015.

233 **focused largely on the outward manifestations:** Silber and Bhatt, *Radicalization in the West*, pp. 23–57.

233 **FBI behavioral analysts use a different framework . . . "pathway to violence" . . . is useful for analyzing any individual:** Author interview with FBI behavioral analyst, Quantico, VA, 2015.

233 **published a classic text:** Reid J. Meloy, *The Psychopathic Mind: Origins, Dynamics, and Treatment* (Lanham, MD: Jason Aronson, 1988).

234 **"If you're in a bar":** FBI behavioral analyst interview.

234 **Calhoun entered the field in a circuitous manner . . . professional historian:** Author interview with Frederick Calhoun, Washington, DC, July 24, 2015.

234 **U.S. Marshals . . . asked him to write:** Ibid. See Frederick Calhoun, *The Lawmen: United States Marshals and Their Deputies* (Washington, DC: Smithsonian Press, 1989).

234 **Calhoun heard that the Marshals . . . could focus on other behaviors:** Calhoun interview.

235 **starts with Gavin de Becker . . . roster of clients:** Beverly Beyette, "High-Tech Methods: He Stars as Protector of Celebrities," *Los Angeles Times*, March 10, 1989.

235 **profiled more than five thousand:** Ibid.

235 **From this vast array . . . He called the system MOSAIC . . . more important to understand this *process*:** Gavin de Becker, *The Gift of Fear: And Other Survival Signals That Protect Us from Violence* (New York: Dell, 1997), pp. 19, 92–104.

235 **MOSAIC program was so effective . . . Stephen Weston, who had commanded:** Calhoun interview.

235 **synthesized their work . . . a six-stage process . . . neither psychological nor sociological . . . "no pretense of understanding":** Frederick S. Calhoun and Stephen W. Weston, *Threat Assessment and Management Strategies: Identifying the Howlers and Hunters* (Boca Raton, FL: CRC Press, 2009), pp. 43–44.

236 **helped shape the thinking:** Interview with FBI behavioral analyst. All quotes in the following discussion are from this interview.

237 **Calhoun and Weston published another book . . . they lay out a series of "inhibitors" . . . "topple like dominoes":** Frederick S. Calhoun and Stephen W. Weston, *Concepts and Case Studies in Threat Management* (Boca Raton, FL: CRC Press, 2013), pp. 5, 101.

237 **One analyst explained . . . "leakage":** FBI behavioral analyst interview.

238 **Leakage was identified:** Calhoun and Weston, *Threat Assessment and Management Strategies,* p. 182.

240 **forensic psychologist Reid Meloy:** J. Reid Meloy and Jessica Yakeley, "The Violent True Believer as a 'Lone Wolf'—Psychoanalytic Perspectives on Terrorism," *Behavioral Sciences and the Law* 32, no. 3 (2014).

240 **worked as a consultant . . . "moral outrage" . . . "framed by an ideology":** J. Reid Meloy, "The Lone Terrorist in the Workplace," *Psychology Today,* Dec. 16, 2014.

242 **hundreds of news articles:** An especially good series was Jacobs, Filipov, and Wen's "The Fall of the House of Tsarnaev."

242 **"Why each hunter acts":** Calhoun and Weston, *Threat Assessment and Management Strategies,* p. 44.

242 **Jahar sat through his months-long trial:** "Jury Finds That Bomber Showed No Remorse," Associated Press, May 16, 2015.

242 **On May 15, 2015:** Department of Justice, Office of Public Affairs, "Statement by Attorney General Lynch on the Sentencing of Dzhokhar Tsarnaev," May 15, 2015, http://www.justice.gov/opa/pr/statement-attorney-general-lynch-sentencing-dzhokhar-tsarnaev.

242 **"I am sorry for the lives that":** Milton Valencia and Patricia Wen, "Tsarnaev Apologizes for Attack; Judge Sentences Him to Death," *Boston Globe,* June 24, 2015.

242 **O'Toole told Jahar . . . invoking Verdi's opera *Otello*:** Milton J. Valencia, "Judge Excoriates Tsarnaev Before Imposing Death Sentence," *Boston Globe,* June 24, 2015.

CHAPTER 11: FUTURE JIHAD

244 **Seconds before he detonated:** Peter Bergen, "The All-American al Qaeda Suicide Bomber," CNN.com, July 31, 2014, http://www.cnn.com/2014/07/31/opinion/bergen-american-al-qaeda-suicide-bomber-syria/.

244 **al-Qaeda's Syrian affiliate tweeted:** @abusulayman321 (account suspended), Twitter, May 27, 2014, http://www.thegatewaypundit.com/wp-content/uploads/2014/05/abu-ameriki.png.

244 **Abusalha's family learned their:** Greg Miller, Adam Goldman, and Nicole Rodriguez, "American Suicide Bomber in Syria Raises Fears for U.S.," *Washington Post,* June 2, 2014.

244 **the first American suicide attacker:** Bergen, "The All-American al Qaeda Suicide Bomber."

244 **In the martyrdom video . . . paints a grim picture:** Mona El-Naggar and Quynhanh Do, "Video Released of U.S. Bomber in Syria," *New York Times,* July 31, 2014.

245 **Over footage of a woman . . . "a thousand men" . . . Paradise of martyrdom:** Bergen, "The All-American al Qaeda Suicide Bomber."

245 **"You think you are safe" . . . addresses his family:** El-Naggar and Do, "Video Released of U.S. Bomber in Syria."

245 **a truck decorated with the distinctive . . . carefully honed recruiting :** Bergen, "The All-American al Qaeda Suicide Bomber."

246 **this author posted a piece:** "Al Qaeda Responds to Fareed, Peter Bergen and CNN," *Fareed Zakaria GPS,* March 31, 2011, http://globalpublicsquare.blogs .cnn.com/2011/03/31/al-qaeda-responds-to-fareed-peter-bergen-and-cnn/.

246 **the trove of documents recovered:** See "Bin Ladin's Bookshelf," Director of National Intelligence, http://www.dni.gov/index.php/resources/bin-laden -bookshelf?start=1.

246 **"the information technology revolution":** Bergen, "Secrets of the bin Laden Treasure-Trove."

246 **In an essay titled "The Tsunami" . . . Awlaki then turned . . . In other words:** Ken Dilania and Eileen Sullivan, "AP Enterprise: al-Qaida's Syrian Cell Alarms US," Associated Press, Sept. 13, 2014, http://bigstory.ap.org/article/ap -enterprise-al-qaidas-syrian-cell-alarms-us.

247 **enabling ISIS to recruit some thirty thousand:** Eric Schmitt and Somini Sengupta, "Thousands Enter Syria to Join ISIS Despite Global Efforts," *New York Times,* Sept. 26, 2015.

247 **only two hundred members:** See "Intelligence Report, Interrogation of KSM, Dec. 3, 2003," in *9/11 Commission Report.*

248 **at least forty-six thousand Twitter accounts:** J. M. Berger and Jonathon Morgan, *The ISIS Twitter Census: Defining and Describing the Population of ISIS Supporters on Twitter* (Washington, DC: Brookings Institution, 2015), pdf at http://www.brookings.edu/~/media/research/files/papers/2015/03/isis-twitter -census-berger-morgan/isis_twitter_census_berger_morgan.pdf.

248 **Obama's chief counterterrorism adviser, Lisa Monaco:** Monaco interview.

248 **Assad was a secular dictator . . . This trifecta:** Bergen, "The All-American al Qaeda Suicide Bomber."

248 **Syria had been the entry point:** Richard A. Oppel Jr., "Foreign Fighters in Iraq Are Tied to Allies of U.S.," *New York Times,* Nov. 22, 2007.

248 **before the American invasion in 2003 . . . pledging allegiance:** National Counterterrorism Center, "Al-Qa'ida in Iraq (AQI)," http://www.nctc.gov/site/ groups/aqi.html.

249 **al-Qaeda's number two . . . an end to Zarqawi's televised executions:** Ayman al-Zawahiri, letter to Abu Musab al-Zarqawi, July 9, 2005, http://www.cfr.org/ iraq/letter-ayman-al-zawahiri-abu-musab-al-zarqawi/p9862.

249 **the schism became official:** Liz Sly, "Al-Qaeda Disavows Any Ties with Radical Islamist ISIS Group in Syria, Iraq," *Washington Post,* Feb. 3, 2014.

249 **a merger with al-Nusra . . . fed up . . . alliance building:** Peter Bergen, "A Terror Group Too Brutal for Al Qaeda?" CNN.com, Feb. 5, 2014.

250 **perhaps the most well-funded terrorist:** Scott Bronstein and Drew Griffin, "Self-Funded and Deep-Rooted: How ISIS Makes Its Millions," CNN.com, Oct. 7, 2014.

250 **more than thirty terrorist groups:** "Islamic State's 35 Global Affiliates Interactive World Map," IntelCenter, 2015, http://intelcenter.com/maps/is-affiliates

-map.html. As of May 19, 2015, thirty-five jihadi groups had pledged allegiance to or support for ISIS.

251 **Most worrying were:** Peter Bergen, "ISIS Goes Global," CNN.com, March 8, 2015.

251 **Terrorist groups in Afghanistan:** "Islamic State's 35 Global Affiliates Interactive World Map."

251 **The Libyan branch . . . on January 27, 2015 . . . ISIS released a video:** Bergen, "ISIS Goes Global."

251 **celebrated in granular detail:** Author interview with a U.S. government official.

251 **links to ISIS central:** For an analysis of Libya's links to militant groups in Iraq, see the Sinjar documents, Combating Terrorism Center, "Al-Qa'ida's Foreign Fighters in Iraq: A First Look at the Sinjar Records," Jan. 2, 2007, https://www.ctc.usma.edu/posts/al-qaidas-foreign-fighters-in-iraq-a-first-look-at-the-sinjar-records.

251 **a revered figure in ISIS propaganda:** See *Dabiq*, Issue 6, http://media.clarionproject.org/files/islamic-state/isis-isil-islamic-state-magazine-issue-6-al-qaeda-of-waziristan.pdf.

251 **"all Syria, all the time":** Author interview with senior U.S. counterterrorism officials, Washington, DC, 2014.

251 **Abusalha was one of about:** Bergen, "The All-American al Qaeda Suicide Bomber."

251 **some 250 Americans:** Barbara Starr, " 'A Few Dozen Americans' in ISIS Ranks," CNN.com, July 15, 2015, http://www.cnn.com/2015/07/15/politics/isis-american-recruits/.

252 **a handy fifty-page booklet . . . bringing a sleeping bag . . . ISIS recruits were advised to say "tourism" . . . an idealized yet accessible picture of life:** "Hijrah to the Islamic State," pdf at https://thejihadproject.files.wordpress.com/2015/05/hijrah-to-the-islamic-state.pdf.

253 **showing "services for Muslims":** "The Failed Crusade," *Dabiq*, Issue 4, pp. 27–29, http://media.clarionproject.org/files/islamic-state/islamic-state-isis-magazine-Issue-4-the-failed-crusade.pdf.

253 **a sort of classified ad:** "The Return of Khilafah," *Dabiq*, Issue 1, p. 11, http://media.clarionproject.org/files/09-2014/isis-isil-islamic-state-magazine-Issue-the-return-of-khilafah.pdf.

253 **A video showed smiling kids:** "Jihad 2.0: Social Media in the Next Evolution of Terrorist Recruitment," Testimony of Peter Bergen before the Senate Committee on Homeland Security and Governmental Affairs, May 7, 2015, http://www.hsgac.senate.gov/download/?id=b8d3c492-dc32-45d9-9306-c1d0b75cbcee.

254 **a Malaysian doctor:** Atika Shubert, "The Women of ISIS: Who Are They?" CNN.com, May 29, 2015, http://www.cnn.com/2015/05/29/middleeast/who-are-the-women-of-isis/.

254 **in one of her frequent posts:** "10 Marriage Facts from the Islamic State," *Ansarukhilafah*, Feb. 28, 2015, https://ansarukhilafah.wordpress.com/2015/02/28/10-marriage-facts-from-the-islamic-state/.

254 **Another 2015 ISIS publication:** "The Islamic State," 2015. It is no longer available online. Excerpts were taken from author's copy.

255 **bulldozer breaking down the great sand berm:** Ian Black, "Isis Breach of Iraq-Syria Border Merges Two Wars into One 'Nightmarish Reality,'" *Guardian,* June 18, 2014.

255 **controlled large swaths of the Middle East:** "What Is 'Islamic State'?" BBC .com, June 29, 2015.

255 **"When people see":** Osama bin Laden, Dec. 13, 2001. Translation by the Department of Defense.

255 **propaganda video . . . An ISIS fighter from South Africa:** ISIS video, "Ɨ d Greetings From the Land of the Caliphate," Aug. 2014, http://jihadology .net/2014/08/02/al-ḥayat-media-center-presents-a-new-video-message-from-the -islamic-state-id-greetings-from-the-land-of-the-caliphate/.

255 **"You can still survive":** "10 Facts from the Islamic State That You Should Know," *Ansarukhilafah,* Feb. 28, 2015, https://ansarukhilafah.wordpress .com/2015/02/28/10-facts-from-the-islamic-state-that-you-should-know/.

255 **more than ninety countries . . . total number of Westerners:** Starr, "'A Few Dozen Americans' in ISIS Ranks."

255 **fighters had traveled to Syria from:** Peter Bergen, "The British Connection to ISIS Beheadings," CNN.com, Sept. 16, 2014, http://www.cnn.com/2014/09/14/ opinion/bergen-british-connection-isis-beheadings/.

256 **Not every fighter had joined ISIS:** A New America report "ISIS in the West" released on November 15, 2015, on Western foreign fighters, based on data on more than 450 Western foreign fighters, has found that over half joined ISIS and only 10 percent joined the al-Nusra Front.

256 **more than four dozen American citizens:** "Americans Linked to ISIS," CNN. com, April 23, 2015, http://www.cnn.com/interactive/2015/04/us/americans -isis/.

256 **Joshua Van Haften:** "Homegrown Extremists, 2014 Joshua Van Haften," New America, http://securitydata.newamerica.net/extremists/terror-plot .html?id=636388087.

256 **Tairod Pugh:** "Homegrown Extremists, 2015 Tairod Pugh," New America, http://securitydata.newamerica.net/extremists/terror-plot.html?id=564752175.

256 **Ariel Bradley:** Joy Lukachick Smith, "Chattanooga Woman Marries ISIS Fighter, Cheers For Marines Shooter," *Chattanooga Times Free Press,* July 26, 2015.

256 **investigating cases in all fifty states:** Jesse Byrnes, "FBI Investigating ISIS Suspects in All 50 States," *The Hill,* Feb. 25, 2015, http://thehill.com/blogs/blog -briefing-room/233832-fbi-investigating-isis-suspects-in-all-50-states.

256 **"The challenge that we faced":** Monaco interview.

257 **One in five were teenagers . . . One in five . . . On average . . . Women were present rarely:** Peter Bergen and David Sterman, "Who Are ISIS' American Recruits?," CNN.com, May 6, 2015.

257 **Hoda Muthana . . . "mother of jihad" . . . told her parents . . . From Syria she tweeted . . . married an Australian:** Ellie Hall, "Gone Girl: An Interview with

an American in ISIS," *BuzzFeed,* April 17, 2015, http://www.buzzfeed.com/ellie vhall/gone-girl-an-interview-with-an-american-in-isis.

257 **she tweeted . . . "chillin in the Khilafa":** Middle East Media Research Institute, "American ISIS Member Joins Women's Clique in Syria," April 22, 2015, http://www.memrijttm.org/content/view_print/blog/8383.

258 **the average insurgency:** Ben Connable and Martin C. Libicki, *How Insurgencies End* (Washington, DC: RAND Corporation, 2010).

258 **deeply worried Obama administration:** Carrie Johnson, "FBI Director: Radicalization of Westerners in Syria Is of Great Concern," NPR, May 2, 2014.

258 **little interest in investigating:** J. M. Berger, *Jihad Joe: Americans Who Go to War in the Name of Islam* (Washington, DC: Potomac Books, 2011), pp. 30–32.

258 **FBI director James Comey:** Sari Horwitz and Adam Goldman, "FBI Director: Number of Americans Traveling to Fight in Syria Increasing," *Washington Post,* May 2, 2014.

259 **shooting at the Jewish Museum in Brussels:** "Brussels Jewish Museum Murders: Nemmouche to be Extradited," BBC.com, June 26, 2014, http://www.bbc.com/news/world-europe-28033608.

260 **"Visa Waiver" countries:** Rebecca Kaplan, "French Terror Attacks Bring New Scrutiny to Visa Waiver Program in U.S.," CBS News, Jan. 12, 2015.

260 **a one-way ticket:** See "Homegrown Extremism 2001–2015."

260 **Nicole Mansfield:** Peter Bergen and Tim Maurer, "Rapping for al Qaeda in Syria," CNN.com, Nov. 18, 2013.

260 **scant evidence:** Bergen and Sterman, "Who Are ISIS' American Recruits?"

260 **The only case in which a returned fighter:** Tracy Connor, "Abdirahman Sheik Mohamud, Ohio Terror Suspect, a 'Normal Kid': Lawyer," NBC News, April 17, 2015.

261 **Representative Peter King . . . warned about the Americans:** Committee on Homeland Security, "King Opens Third Committee on Homeland Security Hearing on Radicalization, Focusing on al Shabaab," July 17, 2011, https://homeland.house.gov/press-release/king-opens-third-committee-homeland-security-hearing-radicalization-focusing-al.

261 **those Americans who returned from the Somali jihad:** Peter Bergen and David Sterman, "ISIS Threat to U.S. Mostly Hype," CNN.com, Sept. 5, 2014. Kamal Said Hassan, for instance, a twenty-eight-year-old Minneapolis man who traveled to Somalia and attended an al-Shabaab training camp before returning to the United States, was arrested and, in 2009, pleaded guilty to supporting al-Shabaab.

261 **none of the successful terrorist attacks:** Peter Bergen and David Sterman, "Is the U.S. at Risk of a Paris-like Attack?," CNN.com, Jan. 16, 2015.

261 **As James Comey noted:** Brent Kendall and Jay Solomon, "FBI Cites Online Terror Recruiting, Training, Damps Subway-Plot Claim," *Wall Street Journal,* Sept. 25, 2014.

262 **Nine out of ten . . . Americans drawn to join:** Bergen and Sterman, "Who Are ISIS' American Recruits?"

262 **"Unabomber," Ted Kaczynski:** Alston Chase, "Harvard and the Making of the Unabomber," *The Atlantic,* June 2000.

262 **virtually, instantly find thousands:** Credit to Jason Burke, *The New Threat: The Past, Present, and Future of Islamic Militancy* (New York: New Press, 2015) for this important insight.

262 **Gustave Le Bon . . . rich with insights . . . "collective mind":** Gustave le Bon, *The Crowd: A Study of the Popular Mind* (1895; repr. New York: Dover, 2002).

263 **Alex, a twenty-three-year-old . . . even sending her gifts:** Rukmini Callimachi, "ISIS and the Lonely Young American," *New York Times,* June 27, 2015.

263 **virtual pack:** This excellent phrase is from Gabriel Weimann's *Terrorism in Cyberspace: The Next Generation* (Washington, DC: Woodrow Wilson Center, 2015).

263 **geared more toward:** All the issues of *Dabiq* are made available online by the Clarion Project. See "The Islamic State's (ISIS, ISIL) Magazine," http://www .clarionproject.org/news/islamic-state-isis-isil-propaganda-magazine-dabiq.

263 **in the third issue of *Dabiq*:** "A Call to Hijrah," *Dabiq,* Issue 3, p. 31, pdf at http://media.clarionproject.org/files/09-2014/isis-isil-islamic-state-magazine -Issue-3-the-call-to-hijrah.pdf.

263 **Issue seven:** "From Hypocrisy to Apostasy," *Dabiq,* Issue 7, pp. 50–51, pdf at http://media.clarionproject.org/files/islamic-state/islamic-state-dabiq-magazine -issue-7-from-hypocrisy-to-apostasy.pdf.

263 **Coulibaly had released a video:** Julian Borger, "Paris Gunman Amedy Coulibaly Declared Allegiance to Isis," *Guardian,* Jan. 11, 2015.

263 **seventy-one-page booklet . . . Tips included . . . instructions on how:** "How to Survive in the West: A Mujahid Guide," 2015, pdf at http://www.blazingcatfur .ca/wp-content/uploads/2015/04/ISIS-How-to-survive-in-the-west.pdf.

264 **discussion on social media:** Rukmini Callimachi, "Clues on Twitter Show Ties Between Texas Gunman and ISIS Network," *New York Times,* May 11, 2015.

264 **Simpson, a thirty-year-old Illinois native:** Adam Goldman and Mark Berman, "FBI Had Known About Suspected Texas Shooter for Years," *Washington Post,* May 4, 2015.

264 **using the hashtag "texasattack" . . . He also tweeted:** Catherine Shoichet and Michael Pearson, "Garland, Texas, Shooting Suspect Linked Himself to ISIS in Tweets," CNN.com, May 4, 2015.

264 **was a spectacular flop:** Kevin Conlon and Kristina Sgueglia, "Two Shot Dead After They Open Fire at Mohammed Cartoon Event in Texas," CNN.com, May 4, 2015.

264 **claiming Simpson and Soofi:** Holly Yan, "ISIS Claims Responsibility for Texas Shooting but Offers No Proof," CNN.com, May 5, 2015, http://www .cnn.com/2015/05/05/us/garland-texas-prophet-mohammed-contest-shooting/ index.html.

264 **Christopher Lee Cornell . . . posted material supportive:** *U.S. v. Cornell,* Case No. 1:15-mj-00024, Criminal Complaint (Southern District of Ohio, Jan. 14, 2015).

264 **Cornell told a local news station:** Leslie Tripp Holland and Kim Hutcherson, "TV Station Wins Fight to Air Interview with Terror Plot Suspect," CNN.com, March 9, 2015.

264 **charged three Brooklyn men:** *U.S. v. Juraboev,* Case No. 1:15-m-00172, Complaint and Affidavit in Support of Arrest Warrant (Eastern District of New York, Feb. 24, 2015).

265 **charged John Booker:** U.S. Attorney's Office, "Second Topeka Man Charged in Connection with Car Bomb Plot," press release, April 10, 2015, http://www.fbi.gov/kansascity/press-releases/2015/second-topeka-man-charged-in-connection-with-car-bomb-plot.

265 **two New York City women:** U.S. Attorney's Office, "Two Queens Residents Charged with Conspiracy to Use a Weapon of Mass Destruction," press release, FBI.gov, April 2, 2015, http://www.fbi.gov/newyork/press-releases/2015/two-queens-residents-charged-with-conspiracy-to-use-a-weapon-of-mass-destruction; *United States of America v. Noelle Velentzas,* Case No. 1:15-mj-00303-VVP [hereafter *U.S. v. Velentzas*], Complaint and Affidavit in Support of Arrest Warrants (Eastern District of New York, April 1, 2015).

265 **Siddiqui had contact:** Complaint and Affidavit in Support of Arrest Warrants, *U.S. v. Velentzas,* pp. 11–12.

265 **seized multiple propane tanks:** Letter to Judge Pohorelsky, *U.S. v. Velentzas* (April 1, 2015), p. 2.

265 **11 a.m. on December 2, 2015 . . . killing fourteen people:** Adam Nagourney, Ian Lovett, and Richard Perez-Pena, "San Bernardino Shooting Kills at Least 14; Two Suspects Are Dead," *New York Times,* Dec. 2, 2015.

265 **The men and women killed ranged in age:** Sarah Parvini, "San Bernardino Shooting Victims: Who They Were," *Los Angeles Times,* Dec. 6, 2015.

266 **in a post on Facebook:** Michael S. Schmidt and Richard Perez-Pena, "F.B.I. Treating San Bernardino Attack as Terrorism Case," *New York Times,* Dec. 4, 2015.

266 **constructed nineteen pipe bombs . . . would take a larger magazine:** Ibid.

266 **hide their tracks:** Pierre Thomas and Jack Date, "San Bernardino Shooters Tried to Destroy Phones, Hard Drives, Sources Say," ABC News, Dec. 3, 2015.

266 **an ISIS radio station:** Bill Chappell, "ISIS Praises San Bernardino Attackers; 'We Will Not Be Terrorized,' Obama Says," NPR, Dec. 5, 2015.

266 **botched Garland, Texas, operation:** Scott Shane, "Texas Attacker Left Trail of Extremist Ideas on Twitter," *New York Times,* May 5, 2015.

266 **more than $70,000 a year:** Julie Turkewitz and Benjamin Mueller, "Couple Kept Tight Lid on Plans for San Bernardino Shooting," *Boston Globe,* Dec. 3, 2015.

266 **two-story townhouse:** Laura J. Nelson, Rong-Gong Lin II, and Jack Dolan, "Suspects Dropped Off Baby Before San Bernardino Shooting Rampage," *Los Angeles Times,* Dec. 3, 2015.

267 **Farook was born . . . Cal State in San Bernardino:** Soumaya Karlamangla, Paloma Esquivel, and Laura J. Nelson, "Rampage Killers Led Secret Life, Hiding Plans and Weapons," *Los Angeles Times,* Dec. 3, 2015.

267 **Malik was born in Pakistan and moved:** Declan Walsh, "Tashfeen Malik Was a 'Saudi Girl' Who Stood Out at a Pakistani University," *New York Times,* Dec. 6, 2015.

267 **The couple met through a site:** Christopher Goffard, "They Met Online, Built

a Life in San Bernardino—and Silently Planned a Massacre," *Los Angeles Times,* Dec. 5, 2015.

267 **Malik arrived . . . permanent resident:** Julia Preston, "Smooth Visa Process for Woman in Attack Is Focus of Inquiry," *New York Times,* Dec. 4, 2015.

267 **Malik became increasingly religious . . . graduation picture:** Tim Craig, Abby Phillip, and Joel Achenbach, "From Pharmacy Student to Suspected San Bernardino Terrorist: The Baffling Journey of Tashfeen Malik," *Washington Post,* Dec. 5, 2015.

267 **become more devout:** Associated Press, "The Latest: California County to Close Most Offices for Week," Dec. 3, 2015.

267 **remained fully veiled:** Goffard, "They Met Online, Built a Life in San Bernardino—and Silently Planned a Massacre."

267 **refused to drive:** Craig, Phillip, and Achenbach, "From Pharmacy Student to Suspected San Bernardino Terrorist: The Baffling Journey of Tashfeen Malik."

267 **trying to reach out:** Christine Hauser, "The Investigation: What We Know," *New York Times,* Dec. 4, 2015.

267 **475 Western recruits to ISIS:** Peter Bergen, Courtney Schuster, and David Sterman, "ISIS in the West: The New Faces of Extremism," New America, Nov. 2015.

268 **nine hundred investigations into militants:** Kevin Johnson, "Comey: Feds Have Roughly 900 Domestic Probes About Islamic State Operatives, Other Extremists," *USA Today,* Oct. 23, 2015.

268 **refugees had played no role:** Peter Bergen, "Syrian Refugees Are Not a Threat to U.S." CNN.com, Nov. 21, 2015.

268 **Pamela Geller, long the most visible:** Shoichet and Pearson, "Garland, Texas, Shooting Suspect Linked Himself to ISIS in Tweets."

268 **grew up in Long Island:** Anne Barnard and Alan Feuer, "Outraged, and Outrageous," *New York Times,* Oct. 8, 2010.

268 **a fifth column of "Islamofascists":** Pamela Geller, "Democrats, Dhimmicrats: The Fifth Column," PamelaGeller.com, http://pamelageller.com/category/democrats-dhimmicrats-the-fifth-column/.

269 **but an Islamic community center:** See the Muslim Community Center in Lower Manhattan (Park51) section of the *New York Times,* http://topics.nytimes.com/top/reference/timestopics/organizations/p/park51/index.html.

269 **a *60 Minutes* profile:** Scott Pelley, "The Heated Debate over New York's Islamic Center," CBS News, Sept. 24, 2010.

269 **denied entry to the United Kingdom:** "US Bloggers Banned from Entering UK," BBC.com, June 26, 2013, http://www.bbc.com/news/uk-23064355.

269 **a "special class" that Americans:** Manny Fernandez, Richard Perez Pena, and Fernanda Santos, "Gunman in Texas Shooting Was F.B.I. Suspect in Jihad Inquiry," *New York Times,* May 4, 2015.

269 **"the paranoid style in American politics" . . . "The central image is that of":** Richard Hofstadter, *The Paranoid Style in American Politics* (New York: Vintage, 2008), pp. 3–40.

269 **Frank Gaffney:** Frank Gaffney, *The Muslim Brotherhood in the Obama Administration* (Sherman Oaks, CA: David Horowitz Freedom Center, 2012).

269 **former federal prosecutor Andrew McCarthy:** Andrew C. McCarthy, *How Obama Embraces Islam's Sharia Agenda* (New York: Encounter Broadside, 2010).

269 **Robert Spencer wrote the book:** Robert Spencer, *Stealth Jihad: How Radical Islam Is Subverting America without Guns or Bombs* (Washington, DC: Regnery Publishing, 2008).

269 **journalist Paul Sperry:** Paul Sperry, *Infiltration: How Muslim Spies and Subversives Have Penetrated Washington* (Nashville: Nelson Current, 2005).

269 **Muslims make up:** Embassy of the United States of America–Baghdad, Iraq, "Muslims in American—A Statistical Portrait," http://iraq.usembassy.gov/resources/information/current/american/statistical.html.

270 **former Speaker of the House Newt Gingrich:** Scott Shane, "In Islamic Law, Gingrich Sees a Moral Threat to U.S.," *New York Times,* Dec. 21, 2011.

270 **James Woolsey:** "Shariah: The Threat to America," Center for Security Policy, October 2010, https://www.centerforsecuritypolicy.org/upload/wysiwyg/article%20pdfs/Shariah%20-%20The%20Threat%20to%20America%20%28Team%20B%20Report%29%20Web%20Version%2009302010.pdf.

270 **state legislatures had introduced bills:** Kimberly Railey, "More States Move to Ban Foreign Law in Court," *USA Today,* Aug. 4, 2013.

270 **Since 9/11, extremists:** "Homegrown Extremism 2001–2015." On April 3, 2014, for instance, a man shot and killed a fourteen-year-old boy and his grandfather at the Jewish Community Center of Greater Kansas City and then drove to a nearby Jewish retirement community, where he shot and killed a third person. Police arrested a suspect, Frazier Glenn Cross, who shouted, "Heil Hitler!" after he was taken into custody. Cross was a well-known right-wing extremist who had founded the Carolina Knights of the Ku Klux Klan.

270 **antigovernment militants:** See "Homegrown Extremism 2001–2015."

270 **On June 17, 2015, Dylann Roof . . . "to start a race war":** Ralph Ellis, Greg Botelho, and Ed Payne, "Charleston Church Shooter Hears Victim's Kin Say, 'I Forgive You,'" CNN.com, June 19, 2015.

271 **poll found that:** "Americans Terror Fears Rise After Paris Attacks—*Washington Post*/ABC News Poll," *Washington Post,* Jan. 12–15, 2015, poll at http://www.washingtonpost.com/politics/polling/americans-terror-fears-rise-paris-attacks/2015/01/22/9cf5dc2e-9f19-11e4-91fc-7dff95a14458_page.html.

271 **golden age of terrorism:** Peter Bergen, "The Golden Age of Terrorism," CNN.com, July 28, 2015.

271 **45 bombings:** "Weather Underground," Global Terrorism Database, http://apps.start.umd.edu/gtd/search/Results.aspx?expanded=no&casualties_type=b&casualties_max=&dtp2=all&success=yes&perpetrator=1231&ob=GTDID&od=desc&page=1&count=100#results-table.

271 **Black Panthers:** "Black Panthers," Global Terrorism Database, http://www.start.umd.edu/gtd/search/Results.aspx?start_yearonly=1970&end_yearonly=1979&start_year=&start_month=&start_day=&end_year=&end

_month=&end_day=&asmSelect0=&perpetrator=4659&dtp2=all&success
=yes &casualties_type=b&casualties_max=.

271 **Fuerzas Armadas de Liberación Nacional:** "Fuerzas Armadas de Liberación
Nacional, Global Terrorism Database, http://apps.start.umd.edu/gtd/search/
Results.aspx?expanded=no&casualties_type=b&casualties_max=&start _year
only=1970&end_yearonly=1979&dtp2=all&success=yes&country=217&
perpetrator=2874&ob=GTDID&od=desc&page=1&count=100#results-table.

271 **an astonishing 112 hijackings:** Office of the Assistant Secretary for Research
and Technology, Bureau of Transportation Statistics, "Figure 7-13 Hijacking
Worldwide: 1970–98," http://www.rita.dot.gov/bts/sites/rita.dot.gov.bts/files/
publications/the_changing_face_of_transportation/html/figure_07_13.html.

271 **killed 184 people and injured more than 600 . . . decade and a half since:** Bergen, "The Golden Age of Terrorism."

271 **"Experts view risk" . . . "the voluntariness of exposure":** Clinton M. Jenkin,
"Risk Perception and Terrorism: Applying the Psychometric Paradigm," *Homeland Security Affairs* 2, Article 6 (July 2006).

272 **twelve thousand times more likely:** Plumer cites the probability of death by
terrorist attack as 1 in 20 million; Brad Plumer, "Eight Facts About Terrorism in the United States," *Washington Post,* April 16, 2013; *The Economist* cites
probability of death by car accident as 1 in 1,656 in any given year: "Danger of
Death!" *The Economist,* Feb. 14, 2013.

272 **fifteenth leading cause of death:** Kenneth D. Kochanek, Sherry L. Murphy, and
Jiaquan Xu, "Deaths: Final Data for 2011," *National Vital Statistics Reports* 63,
no. 3 (July 27, 2015), http://www.cdc.gov/nchs/data/nvsr/nvsr63/nvsr63_03.
pdf, p. 9.

272 **some eighty-eight thousand Americans died:** United Nations Office on Drugs
and Crime, "Global Study on Homicide—Homicide Counts and Rates, Time
Series 2000–2012," http://www.unodc.org/gsh/en/data.html.

272 **around *five thousand* times more likely:** Peter Bergen, "Gun Violence Is a National Security Issue," CNN.com, Dec. 19, 2012.

272 **had forty-one gun murders:** Kevin Smith, Sarah Osborne, Ivy Lau, and Andrew Britton, "Homicides, Firearm Offences and Intimate Violence, 2010/11,"
Home Office Statistical Bulletin, Suppl. 2 (Jan. 2012), https://www.gov.uk/
government/uploads/system/uploads/attachment_data/file/116483/hosb0212.
pdf, p. 55.

272 **States had around *eleven thousand*:** National Vital Statistics System, National
Center for Health Statistics, CDC, "10 Leading Causes of Injury Death by Age
Group Highlighting Violence-Related Injury Deaths, United States," 2010, pdf
at http://www.cdc.gov/injury/wisqars/pdf/10LCID_Violence_Related_Injury
_Deaths_2010-a.pdf.

273 **"Subjects have expressed doubt":** FBI behavioral analyst interview.

273 **All Dulles Area Muslim Society . . . On the night of 9/11 . . . Magid is outraged:** Author interview with Imam Magid and Rizwan Jaka, Sterling, VA,
July 14, 2015.

274 **a densely argued, eighteen-page critique . . . meaning of *jihad*:** "Open Letter to

Dr. Ibrahim Awwad Al-Badri, Alias 'Abu Bakr Al-Baghdadi,' and to the Fighters and Followers of the Self-Declared 'Islamic State," Sept. 19, 2014, http://www .lettertobaghdadi.com/pdf/Booklet-English.pdf, pp. 9–10.

274 created "doubt" . . . Four years earlier . . . "There's no justification" . . . "If nonviolence does not work" . . . being ensnared by ISIS . . . "Do you have any doubts" . . . constantly in touch: Imam Magid interview.

276 Amir, a twenty-two-year-old: Laurie Goodstein, "U.S. Muslims Take on ISIS' Recruiting Machine," *New York Times,* Feb. 19, 2015.

276 the end of 2015: Chuck Goudie, "19-Year-Old Bolingbrook ISIS suspect Considers Plea Deal," ABC7Chicago, June 25, 2015, http://abc7chicago.com/ news/19-year-old-bolingbrook-isis-suspect-considers-plea-deal/805768/.

276 Kerry Cahill: Hancock, "The Survivors."

276 received a frantic call: Tom Spencer, "Fort Hood Tragedy Forms Unexpected Friendship," *Austin American Statesman,* Jan. 18, 2013.

276 Joleen's husband, Michael . . . 11:15 that night: Hancock, "The Survivors."

277 "The sun of our solar system": Spencer, "Fort Hood Tragedy Forms Unexpected Friendship."

277 photograph of Major Nidal Hasan: Hancock, "The Survivors."

277 Kerry went on a crusade . . . father was awarded a posthumous . . . landed a role in the HBO show . . . traveled to Washington for . . . correspondence with Awlaki . . . government report: Author interview with Kerry Cahill, New Orleans, Jan. 4, 2015.

277 Nader Hasan had little idea . . . few Muslim leaders: Hancock, "The Survivors."

277 driven home by a conversation . . . "Your community is against this" . . . "As a Muslim American . . . created the Nawal Foundation: Nader Hasan interview.

278 "The Nawal Foundation was born": "An Unimaginable Alliance," *Emel,* Issue 96, Sept. 2012.

278 "I ask every Muslim": Nader Hasan interview.

278 Pew poll: "Muslim Americans: No Signs of Growth in Alienation or Support for Extremism," Pew Research Center, Aug. 30, 2011, http://www.people -press.org/2011/08/30/muslim-americans-no-signs-of-growth-in-alienation-or -support-for-extremism/

278 interviewed on ABC News: Hancock, "The Survivors."

278 message would be . . . Kerry Cahill was watching: Nader Hasan interview.

279 wrote an e-mail . . . "How are you doing?": Spencer, "Fort Hood Tragedy Forms Unexpected Friendship."

279 Kerry felt that: Kerry Cahill interview.

279 led to a meeting: Nader Hasan interview.

279 Nader picked up Kerry: Kerry Cahill interview.

279 he pointed out George W. Bush's: Hancock, "The Survivors."

279 American flag flying . . . homemade baklava: Nader Hasan interview.

279 gave it to Nader: Hancock, "The Survivors."

279 "I'll answer anything": Nader Hasan interview.

279 "I'm now angrier . . . foster mutual respect . . . "We have to move": Kerry Cahill interview.

EPILOGUE: AN ORDINARY AMERICAN TERRORIST

281 **"In the name . . . I did the shootings"**: FBI Tampa, "Investigative Update Regarding Pulse Nightclub Shooting," June 20, 2016, https://www.fbi. gov/contact-us/field-offices/tampa/news/press-releases/investigative-update-regarding-pulse-nightclub-shooting.

281 **"My name is . . . Islamic State."**: Ibid.

281 **legally purchased**: Bureau for Alcohol, Tobacco, Firearms, and Explosives, Text of official tweet: "BREAKING: ATF Orlando 'We have completed urgent traces on firearms involved in #Orlando shooting. Firearms purchased legally,'" June 12, 2016, https://twitter.com/ATFHQ/status/742075110161588224?ref_src=twsrc^tfw.

281 **military assault rifle**: "The gun the Orlando shooter used was a Sig Sauer MCX, not an AR-15. That doesn't change much," *Washington Post,* June 14, 2016.

281 **"Latin Night"**: "All people come out and dance on Latin night," New York Times, June 12, 2016, http://www.nytimes.com/live/orlando-nightclub-shooting-live-updates/all-people-come-out-and-dance-on-latin-night/.

281 **Mateen was laughing**: "Witness: Orlando shooter laughed during rampage," CNN.com, June 14, 2016.

282 **deadliest mass shooting**: "Was Orlando the Deadliest Mass Shooting in U.S. History?" The Atlantic, June 15, 2016, http://www.theatlantic.com/news/archive/2016/06/orlando-deadliest-mass-shooting/487058/.

282 **American citizen born in . . .**: "Omar Mateen Posted to Facebook Amid Orlando Attack, Lawmaker Says," *New York Times,* June 16, 2016.

282 **married and had a three-year-old**: "Marriage certificate shows Orlando shooter married wife months after divorce," *Sun Sentinel,* June 16, 2016.

282 **employed as a security guard**: "Orlando shooter last worked as security guard at PGA Village in Port St. Lucie," *TCPalm,* June 14, 2016.

282 **the twelve perpetrators**: Peter Bergen, "Jihadist Terrorism 15 Years After 9/11: A Threat Assessment," New America, September 2016, https://na-production.s3.amazonaws.com/documents/jihadist_terrorism_after_911_FINAL.pdf.

283 **called a local TV station**: "'I'm the shooter. It's me': Gunman called local TV station during attack, station says," *Washington Post,* June 15, 2016.

283 **pledged his allegiance**: "Orlando shooter posted messages on Facebook pledging allegiance to the leader of ISIS and vowing more attacks," *Washington Post,* June 15, 2016.

283 **expelled from high school**: "Troubled. Quiet. Macho. Angry. The volatile life of the Orlando shooter." *Washington Post,* June 17, 2016.

283 **no evidence Mateen had had a gay relationship**: "Orlando shooting investigators can't substantiate claim Omar Mateen was gay." CBS/AP, June 24, 2016, http://www.cbsnews.com/news/orlando-shooting-investigation-omar-mateen-gay/.

283 **he was dismissed**: "Why Orlando shooter was kicked out of corrections officer training," *Miami Herald,* June 18, 2016.

284 **He was turned down:** "Omar Mateen failed multiple times to start career in law enforcement, state records show," *Sun Sentinel,* June 16, 2016.

284 **ISIS publicly urged:** "ISIS calls for more attacks on West during Ramadan," CNN.com, May 22, 2016.

284 **"soldiers of the caliphate in America":** "ISIS Claims Responsibility for Orlando Attack in Radio Statement," *New York Times,* June 13, 2016.

284 **acquaintance of Moner Abu Salha:** "Orlando gunmen Omar Mateen investigated twice by FBI," CBS12, June 12, 2016, http://cbs12.com/news/local/fbi-omar-mateen-investigated-for-ties-to-fort-pierce-suicide-bomber.

284 **stabbed his brother:** Naftali Bendavid and Tamara Audi, "Ahmad Khan Rahami Took Long Path to Radicalization," *Wall Street Journal,* September 23, 2016.

285 **Rahami traveled to Afghanistan and neighboring Pakistan:** Jon Boone, "Ahmad Khan Rahami spent time at Pakistan seminary tied to Taliban," *Guardian,* September 23, 2016.

285 **watching extremist videos obsessively:** Ibid.

285 **The bomb device that Rahami detonated:** Antonio Planas and Matt Stout, "Attack had eerie resemblance to Boston Marathon bombings," *Boston Herald,* September 20, 2016.

285 **first successful jihadist terrorist attack:** Peter Bergen, "An ordinary American terrorist," CNN.com, September 20, 2016.

285 **It's telling that in the notebook that Rahami kept:** Marc Santora, Rukmini Callimachi and Adam Goldman, "Flagged Two Times in 2014, Ahmad Rahami Passed Scrutiny," *New York Times,* September 21, 2016.

286 **Lost in the intense coverage of the ISIS-inspired threat:** Peter Bergen, "Jihadist Terrorism 15 Years After 9/11: A Threat Assessment," New America, September 2015, https://na-production.s3.amazonaws.com/documents/jihadist_terrorism_after_911_FINAL.pdf.

286 **"I will suspend . . . our allies":** "Trump: Suspend immigration from areas with 'proven history of terrorism,'" *The Hill,* June 13, 2016, http://thehill.com/blogs/ballot-box/presidential-races/283299-trump-suspend-immigration-from-areas-with-proven-history.

BIBLIOGRAPHY

BOOKS

Aaronson, Trevor. *The Terror Factory: Inside the FBI's Manufactured War on Terrorism*. Brooklyn, NY: Ig Publishing, 2013.

Allison, Graham. *Nuclear Terrorism: The Ultimate Preventable Catastrophe*. New York: Times Books, 2004.

Atwan, Abdel Bari. *Islamic State: The Digital Caliphate*. Oakland: University of California Press, 2015.

Bergen, Peter. *Holy War, Inc.: Inside the Secret World of Osama bin Laden*. New York: Free Press, 2001.

———. *The Longest War: The Enduring Conflict between America and al-Qaeda*. New York: Free Press, 2011.

———. *Manhunt: The Ten-Year Search for bin Laden from 9/11 to Abbottabad*. New York: Crown, 2012.

———. *The Osama bin Laden I Know: An Oral History of al Qaeda's Leader*. New York: Free Press, 2006.

Berger, J. M. *Jihad Joe: Americans Who Go to War in the Name of Islam*. Washington, DC: Potomac Books, 2011.

Burke, Jason. *The New Threat: The Past, Present, and Future of Islamic Militancy*. New York: New Press, 2015.

Buruma, Ian. *Murder in Amsterdam: The Death of Theo van Gogh and the Limits of Tolerance*. New York: Penguin Press, 2006.

Burt, Andrew. *American Hysteria: The Untold Story of Mass Political Extremism in the United States*. Guilford, CT: LP, 2015.

Bush, George W. *Decision Points.* New York: Crown, 2010.

Calhoun, Frederick S., and Stephen W. Weston. *Concepts and Case Studies in Threat Management*. Boca Raton, FL: CRC Press, 2013.

———. *Threat Assessment and Management Strategies: Identifying the Howlers and Hunters*. Boca Raton, FL: CRC Press, 2009.

Combating Terrorism Center. *The Osama bin Laden Files: Letters and Documents Discovered by SEAL Team Six During Their Raid on bin Laden's Compound*. New York: Skyhorse Publishing, 2012.

de Becker, Gavin. *The Gift of Fear: And Other Survival Signals That Protect Us from Violence*. New York: Dell Trade, 1997.

Gaffney, Frank. *The Muslim Brotherhood in the Obama Administration*. Sherman Oaks, CA: David Horowitz Freedom Center, 2012.

Gartenstein-Ross, Daveed, and Laura Grossman. *Homegrown Terrorists in the U.S. and U.K.: An Empirical Examination of the Radicalization Process*. Washington, DC: FDD Press, 2009.

Geller, Pamela. *Stop the Islamization of America: A Practical Guide to the Resistance.* Washington, DC: WND Books, 2011.

Gessen, Masha. *The Brothers: The Road to an American Tragedy.* New York: Riverhead Books, 2015.

Helman, Scott, and Jenna Russell. *Long Mile Home: Boston Under Attack, the City's Courageous Recovery, and the Epic Hunt for Justice.* New York: Dutton, 2014.

Herridge, Catherine. *The Next Wave: On the Hunt for Al Qaeda's American Recruits.* New York: Crown Forum, 2011.

Hoffer, Eric. *The True Believer: Thoughts on the Nature of Mass Movements.* New York: Harper Perennial, 1951.

Hofstadter, Richard. *The Paranoid Style in American Politics.* New York: Vintage, 2008.

Horgan, John. *The Psychology of Terrorism.* New York: Routledge, 2005.

Hudson, Rex A. *Who Becomes a Terrorist and Why: The 1999 Government Report on Profiling Terrorists.* Gilford, CT: Lyons Press, 1999.

Johnsen, Gregory D. *The Last Refuge: Yemen, Al-Qaeda, and America's War in Arabia.* New York: W. W. Norton, 2013.

Kelly, Ray. *Vigilance: My Life Serving America and Protecting Its Empire City.* New York: Hachette Books, 2015.

Kessler, Ronald. *The Secrets of the FBI.* New York: Broadway Paperbacks, 2012.

Kilcullen, David. *Blood Year: Terror and the Islamic State.* Collingwood, Australia: Quarterly Essay, 2015.

Klaidman, Daniel. *Kill or Capture: The War on Terror and the Soul of the Obama Presidency.* New York: Houghton Mifflin Harcourt, 2012.

Kowalski, Dean A., ed. *Steven Spielberg and Philosophy: We're Gonna Need a Bigger Book.* Lexington: University Press of Kentucky, 2008.

Krueger, Alan B. *What Makes a Terrorist: Economics and the Roots of Terrorism.* Princeton: Princeton University Press, 2007.

Kukis, Mark. *"My Heart Became Attached": The Strange Odyssey of John Walker Lindh.* Washington, DC: Brassey's, Inc., 2003.

Lacey, Jim, ed. *A Terrorist's Call to Global Jihad: Deciphering Abu-Mus'ab al-Suri's Islamic Jihad Manifesto.* Annapolis, MD: Naval Institute Press, 2008.

Le Bon, Gustave. *The Crowd: A Study of the Popular Mind.* 1895; repr. New York: Dover, 2002.

Lia, Brynjar. *Architect of Global Jihad: The Life of Al-Qaeda Strategist Abu Mus'ab Al-Suri.* New York: Columbia University Press, 2008.

McCarthy, Andrew C. *How Obama Embraces Islam's Sharia Agenda.* New York: Encounter Broadside, 2010.

Meloy, J. Reid. *The Psychopathic Mind: Origins, Dynamics, and Treatment.* Lanham, MD: Jason Aronson, 1988.

———. *Violence Risk and Threat Assessment: A Practical Guide for Mental Health and Criminal Justice Professionals.* San Diego: Specialized Training Services, 2000.

———, and Jens Hoffmann, eds., *International Handbook of Threat Assessment.* New York: Oxford University Press, 2014.

Morell, Michael, with Bill Harlow. *The Great War of Our Time: The CIA's Fight Against Terrorism—from al Qa'ida to ISIS.* New York: Twelve, 2015.

Mudd, Philip. *Takedown: Inside the Hunt for Al Qaeda.* Philadelphia: University of Pennsylvania Press, 2013.

Noble, Kerry. *Tabernacle of Hate: Why They Bombed Oklahoma City.* Quebec: Voyageur Publishing, 1998.

Panetta, Leon, with Jim Newton. *Worthy Fights: A Memoir of Leadership in War and Peace.* New York: Penguin Press, 2014.

Sageman, Marc. *Leaderless Jihad: Terror Networks in the Twenty-First Century.* Philadelphia: University of Pennsylvania Press, 2008.

———. *Understanding Terror Networks.* Philadelphia: University of Pennsylvania Press, 2004.

Scahill, Jeremy. *Dirty Wars: The World Is a Battlefield.* New York: Nation Books, 2013.

Schuster, Henry, with Charles Stone. *Hunting Eric Rudolph: An Insider's Account of the Five-Year Search for the Olympic Bombing Suspect.* New York: Berkley Books, 2005.

Scott-Clark, Cathy, and Adrian Levy. *The Siege: 68 Hours Inside the Taj Hotel.* New York: Penguin, 2013.

Shane, Scott. *Objective Troy: A Terrorist, a President, and the Rise of the Drone.* New York: Tim Duggan Books, 2015.

Sheehan, Michael A. *Crush the Cell: How to Defeat Terrorism Without Terrorizing Ourselves.* New York: Three Rivers Press, 2008.

Silber, Mitchell D. *The Al Qaeda Factor: Plots Against the West.* Philadelphia: University of Pennsylvania Press, 2012.

Spellberg, Denise A. *Thomas Jefferson's Qur'an: Islam and the Founders.* New York: Knopf, 2013.

Sperry, Paul. *Infiltration: How Muslim Spies and Subversives Have Penetrated Washington.* Nashville: Nelson Current, 2005.

Stern, Jessica, and J. M. Berger. *ISIS: The State of Terror.* New York: Ecco, 2015.

Tankel, Stephen. *Storming the World Stage: The Story of Lashkar-e-Taiba.* New York: Columbia University Press, 2011.

Weimann, Gabriel. *Terror on the Internet: The New Arena, the New Challenges.* Washington, DC: United States Institute of Peace, 2006.

———. *Terrorism in Cyberspace: The Next Generation.* Washington, DC: Woodrow Wilson Center, 2015.

Weiss, Michael, and Hassan Hassan. *ISIS: Inside the Army of Terror.* New York: Regan Arts, 2015.

Wexler, Stuart. *America's Secret Jihad: The Hidden History of Religious Terrorism in the United States.* Berkeley, CA: Counterpoint Press, 2015.

Wiktorowicz, Quintan. *Radical Islam Rising: Muslim Extremism in the West.* Washington, DC: Rowman & Littlefield, 2005.

Wright, Lawrence. *The Looming Tower: Al-Qaeda and the Road to 9/11.* New York: Knopf, 2006.

Zaidi, S. Hussain, with Rahul Bhatt. *Headley and I.* New Delhi: HarperCollins, 2012.

DOCUMENTARIES

Americans for Peace and Tolerance, *Losing Our Sons* (2012).
HBO, *Terror in Mumbai* (2009).
PBS, *Frontline,* "American Terrorist" (2015).
PBS, *Frontline,* "Canada: The Cell Next Door" (2007).
PBS, *Frontline,* "A Perfect Terrorist" (2011).

A NOTE ON INTERVIEWS

This book would not have been possible without the interviews with American militants and their families and lawyers, federal and local law enforcement officials, leading U.S. counterterrorism officials and analysts, prominent Islamic clerics, and those who lost family members to jihadist attacks in the United States. Those whom I can name are listed here. Thanks to them and also to the many other officials at the White House, FBI, and National Counterterrorism Center who spoke to me but who cannot be named because of their present jobs.

J. M. Berger
Melvin Bledsoe
Monica Holley Bledsoe
Ralph Boelter
Don Borelli
Frederick Calhoun
Kerry Cahill
Barbara Chesser
Zachary Chesser
David Cohen
Bernie Culveyhouse
Art Cummings
Thomas Durkin
Daveed Gartenstein-Ross
Shafik Hammami
Nader Hasan
Bruce Hoffman

Jameel Jaffer
Rizwan Jaka
Shafi Khan
Zarine Khan
Andy Liepman
Michael Leiter
Steve Llaneza
Imam Mohamed Magid
Lisa Monaco
Philip Mudd
Matt Olsen
George Piro
Nicholas Rasmussen
Ben Rhodes
Marc Sageman
Mitch Silber
Abu Musab al-Suri

A NOTE ON SOURCES

Key to constructing the histories of the militants profiled in this book were the many thousands of pages of court documents that exist for most of their cases. Those documents are listed on pages 365–368. To create the database of 360 militants also examined for the book, the research team, led by David Sterman, examined tens of thousands of additional court documents, details of which are accessible at this website: http://securitydata.newamerica.net/extremists/analysis.html.

COURT DOCUMENTS

State v. Muhammad [Carlos Bledsoe], Case No. 60CR-09-2626, Arrest Report (Arkansas 6th Circuit, June 1, 2009).

State v. Muhammad [Carlos Bledsoe], Case No. 60CR-09-2626, Forensic Report (Arkansas 6th Circuit, July 19, 2010).

State v. Muhammad [Carlos Bledsoe], Case No. 60CR-09-2626, Hudson Interrogation (Arkansas 6th Circuit, June 1, 2009).

State v. Muhammad [Carlos Bledsoe], Case No. 60CR-09-2626, Search Warrant Affidavit (Arkansas 6th Circuit, June 1, 2009).

State v. Muhammad [Carlos Bledsoe], Case No. 60CR-09-2626, Search Warrant Inventory (Arkansas 6th Circuit, June 2, 2009).

U.S. v. Abdulmutallab, CR No. 2:10-20005, Government's Opening Statement (Eastern District of Michigan, November 4, 2011).

U.S. v. Abdulmutallab, CR No. 2:10-20005, Government's Sentencing Memorandum (Eastern District of Michigan, February 2, 2012).

U.S. v. Abdulmutallab, CR No. 2:10-20005, Memorandum for the Court Prepared by Dr. Simon Perry (Eastern District of Michigan, February 10, 2012).

U.S. v. Abdulmutallab, CR No. 2:10-20005, Opinion and Order Denying Defendant's Motion to Suppress Statements Made at the University of Michigan Hospital (Eastern District of Michigan, September 16, 2011).

U.S. v. Al-Khattab, Case No. 1:13-cr-418, Criminal Information (Eastern District of Virginia, October 30, 2013).

U.S. v. al-Marri, CR No. 09-10030, Plea Agreement (District Court for the Central District of Illinois, April 3, 2009).

U.S. v. Chesser, Case No. 1:10-cr-395, Affidavit (Eastern District of Virginia, July 21, 2010).

U.S. v. Chesser, Case No. 1:10-cr-395, Criminal Information (Eastern District of Virginia, October 20, 2010).

U.S. v. Chesser, Case No. 1:10-cr-395, Defendant's Position (Eastern District of Virginia, February 18, 2011).

U.S. v. Chesser, Case No. 1:10-cr-395, Plea Agreement (Eastern District of Virginia, February 18, 2011).

U.S. v. Cornell, Case No. 1:15-mj-00024, Criminal Complaint (Southern District of Ohio, January 14, 2015).

U.S. v. Dutschke, Case No. 3:13MJ20-SAA, Criminal Complaint (Northern District of Mississippi, April 26, 2013).

U.S. v. Hammami, CR No. 07-00384-KD, Indictment (Southern District of Alabama, September 24, 2009).

U.S. v. Hasan, USCA Misc. Dkt. No. 12-8029/AR, Memorandum of Law for

Proposed Defense: Defense of Others (United States Army Trial Judiciary, Third Judicial Circuit, June 10, 2013).

U.S. v. Hasan, USCA Misc. Dkt. No. 12-8029/AR, Panel Selection (United States Army Trial Judiciary, Third Judicial Circuit, July 9-16, 2013).

U.S. v. Hasan, USCA Misc. Dkt. No. 12-8029/AR, Sanity Board Report (United States Army Trial Judiciary, Third Judicial Circuit, January 13, 2011).

U.S. v. Headley, Case No. 09-CR-830, Criminal Complaint (Northern District of Illinois, October 11, 2009).

U.S. v. Headley, Case No. 09-CR-830, Government's Position Paper as to Sentencing Factors (Northern District of Illinois, January 22, 2013).

U.S. v. James et al., CR No. 8:05-00214-CJC, Plea Agreement for Defendant Kevin James (Central District of California, December 14, 2007).

U.S. v. Juraboev, Case No. 1:15-m-00172, Complaint and Affidavit in Support of Arrest Warrant (Eastern District of New York, February 24, 2015).

U.S. v. Kadyrbayev, Case No. 13-CR-10238, Indictment (District of Massachusetts, August 8, 2013).

U.S. v. Kadyrbayev et al., Case No. 13-CR-10238DPW, Superseding Indictment (District of Massachusetts, August 29, 2013).

U.S. v. Kashmiri et al., Case No. 09-cr-830, Second Superseding Indictment (Northern District of Illinois, July 2010).

U.S. v. Khan, CR No. 14-564, Criminal Complaint (Northern District of Illinois, October 6, 2014).

U.S. v. Khan, CR No. 14-564, Defense Memorandum of Law in Support of Motion to Suppress Statements (Northern District of Illinois, April 17, 2015).

U.S. v. Khan, CR No. 14-564, Indictment (Northern District of Illinois, January 9, 2015).

U.S. v. Khan, CR No. 14-564, Transcript of Proceedings (Northern District of Illinois, November 17, 2014).

U.S. v. Llaneza, Case No. 4:13-cr-00145-YGR, Criminal Complaint, Affidavit of Christopher T. Monika (Northern District of California, February 7, 2013).

U.S. v. Llaneza, Case No. 4:13-cr-00145-YGR, Defense's Sentencing Memorandum (Northern District of California, February 24, 2014).

U.S. v. Llaneza, Case No. 4:13-cr-00145-YGR, Judgment in a Criminal Case (Northern District of California, February 24, 2014).

U.S. v. Llaneza, Case No. 4:13-cr-00145-YGR, Plaintiff's Sentencing Memorandum (Northern District of California, February 24, 2014).

U.S. v. Lindh, CR No. 02-37-A, Plea Agreement (Eastern District of Virginia, July 15, 2002).

U.S. v. Mahamud, CR No. 11-191, Indictment (District of Minnesota, June 7, 2011).

U.S. v. Medunjanin, Case No. 12-4724, Appeal (Court of Appeals for the Second Circuit, May 20, 2014).

U.S. v. Medunjanin et al., Case No. 1-10-cr-0019, Superseding Indictment S-3 (Eastern District of New York, July 7, 2010).

U.S. v. Mohamud et al., Case No. 10-CR-4246 JM, Judgment (Southern District of California, January 1, 2014).

U.S. v. Morton, Case No. 1:12cr35, Affidavit (Eastern District of Virginia, May 13, 2011).

U.S. v. Morton, Case No. 1:12cr35, Criminal Complaint (Eastern District of Virginia, June 14, 2012).

U.S. v. Morton, Case No. 1:12cr35, Prosecution Sentencing Memorandum (Eastern District of Virginia, June 14, 2012).

U.S. v. Moussaoui, Case No. 01-455-A, Defense Exhibit 950 (Eastern District of Virginia, March 6, 2006).

U.S. v. Omar et al., Cr. No. 09-50, Indictment (District of Minnesota, August 20, 2009).

U.S. v. Rana, Case No. 1:09-cr-00830, Government's Santiago Proffer (Northern District of Illinois, April 11, 2011).

U.S. v. Rana, Case No. 1:09-cr-00830, Transcript of Trial (Northern District of Illinois, May 23, 2011).

U.S. v. Shahzad, Case No. 10-cr-541, Criminal Complaint (Southern District of New York, May 4, 2010).

U.S. v. Shahzad, Case No. 10-cr-541, Government's Memorandum in Connection with the Sentencing of Faisal Shahzad (Southern District of New York, September 29, 2010).

U.S. v. Shahzad, Case No. 10-cr-541, Plea (Southern District of New York, June 21, 2010).

U.S. v. Shnewer, Case No. 1:07-mj-02045-JS, Criminal Complaint (District of New Jersey, May 7, 2007).

U.S. v. Tsarnaev, Case No. 1:13-2106-HBB, Criminal Complaint (District of Massachusetts, April 21, 2013).

U.S. v. Tsarnaev, Case No. 1:13-cr-10200-GAO, Government's Opposition to Tsarnaev's Motion to Vacate Special Administrative Measures ("SAMs") (District of Massachusetts, October 21, 2013).

U.S. v. Tsarnaev, Case No. 1:13-cr-10200, Indictment (District of Massachusetts, June 27, 2013).

U.S. v. Tsarnaev, Case No. 1:13-10200-GAO, Jury Trial (District of Massachusetts, March 26, 2015).

U.S. v. Tsarnaev, Case No. 113-cr-10200-GAO, Motion to Suppress Statements (District of Massachusetts, May 7, 2014).

U.S. v. Tsarnaev, Case No. 13-MJ-2106-MBB, Sealed Transcript (District of Massachusetts, April 22, 2013).

U.S. v. Velentzas, Case No. 1:15-mj-00303-VVP, Complaint and Affidavit in Support of Arrest Warrants (Eastern District of New York, April 1, 2015).

U.S. v. Velentzas, Case No. 1:15-mj-00303-VVP, Letter to Judge Pohorelsky (Eastern District of New York, April 1, 2015).

U.S. v. Vinas, Case No. 08-CR-823, Guilty Plea Hearing (Eastern District of New York, January 29, 2009).

U.S. v. Wali Zazi, Case No. 1:10-cr-00060 (Eastern District of New York, August 18, 2011).

U.S. v. Yusuf, Case No. 4:10-cr-00547-HEA, Change of Plea (District of Minnesota, November 3, 2011).

U.S. v. Zazi, Case No. 09-cr-663, Memorandum of Law in Support of the Government's Motion for a Permanent Order of Detention (Eastern District of New York, September 24, 2009).

U.S. v. Zazi, Case No. 09-cr-663, Transcript of Criminal Cause for Pleading (Eastern District of New York, February 22, 2010).

ACKNOWLEDGMENTS

David Sterman is an invaluable colleague who worked on all phases of this book, performing and organizing research, overseeing the fact-checking, and finding photos. He also played the key role in assembling a database of the 360 U.S.-based jihadist militants examined for this project, which enabled all my statistical findings. Courtney Schuster, Emily Schneider, Bailey Cahall, Jennifer Rowland, and Andrew Lebovich also helped significantly with the research, and Alyssa Sims, Rebekah Ausbrook, Haley Peters, Daniel de Lisle, Jessica Yannette, and Robert Swestka helped with fact-checking. Lacy Hebert transcribed the many interviews. Thanks to you all.

All these very smart people work or have worked at New America, which has been my home for almost a decade and a half. I am especially lucky to work with our CEO and president, Anne-Marie Slaughter, whose smarts and generosity are well-known. Thanks also to the former president of New America Steve Coll, who was instrumental in launching the foundation's International Security Program, as well as to Lisa Hollingsworth, Lisa Watson, Grae Baxter, Meredith Hanley, Becky Shafer, Kirsten Berg, Fuzz Hogan, Konstantin Kakaes, Ian Wallace, Ryan Gerety, and Rachel White, all of whom have made New America such a congenial place to work over the years.

Thanks also to Michael Crow, the president of Arizona State University, who hired me as a professor, and to Jim O'Brien, his chief of staff. It has been a pleasure to launch under their guidance the Center on the Future of War, which has greatly supported this book. Thanks also to Christopher Callahan, the dean of the Walter Cronkite School of Journalism; Cameron Thies, the director of the School of Politics and Global Studies; and Pat Kenney, the dean of the College of Liberal Arts and Sciences.

A great deal of thanks is owed to my partner in the Future of War project, Daniel Rothenberg, who is simply the ideal colleague: highly organized and very thoughtful in every sense of that word. Daniel read the manuscript of this book, and his observations have measurably improved it. Richard Galant, who edits my stories at CNN.com, is one of the best editors in the business. A number of themes in this book were first developed under his guidance, and his smart ideas as a reader helped to sharpen them. The author Ken Ballen also read the manuscript carefully and made many valuable suggestions—the third of my books for which he has done this. Security expert Andrew Marshall, too, improved the manuscript with his suggestions, a favor he has done for every book I have written. Thanks to you all for your guidance and friendship. Thanks also to Keith Sinzinger, Tom Ricks, Frank Foer, and Lawrence Wright for looking at the manuscript.

At the FBI, a particular thanks to Susan McKee and Richard Quinn, who arranged multiple meetings and interviews with Bureau officials. At the National Counterterrorism Center, thanks to Tim Barrett and Joe Vealencis for arranging interviews. Thanks to Daveed Gartenstein-Ross for making available his archive of materials on Carlos Bledsoe.

I have worked at CNN in one capacity or another for two and half decades, and am grateful to continue to work there today with so many of its excellent reporters, executives, and producers. In particular: Wolf Blitzer, Amy Entelis, Brian Todd, Dugald McConnell, Gena Somra, Jill Chappell, Steven Page, Jay Shaylor, Jim Sciutto, Charlie Moore, Anderson Cooper, Kerry Rubin, Chuck Hadad, Poppy Harlow, Ken Shiffman, Rebecca Kutler, Richard Griffiths, Michael Smerconish, Rick Davis, Pat Wiedenkeller, Evan Perez, Tom Fuentes, Jamie Crawford, Barbara Starr, and Adam Levine.

Thanks also to the advisory council for New America's International Security Program—its cochairs, Chip Kaye and Fareed Zakaria, and members, Tom Freston, Fred Hassan, Bob Niehaus, Greg Craig, and Fran Townsend. We couldn't have done the research that went into this book without their invaluable support. And thanks to New America board member Kati Marton. Thanks also to the foundations and program officers who have supported our work, especially Marin Strmecki of the Smith Richardson Foundation, Lisa Magarrell at the Open Society Foundation, and Peter Rabley at Omidyar Network.

Thanks to the director Greg Barker, who optioned this book for the HBO documentary *Homegrown,* and to producers John Battsek and Julie Goldman, as well as cameraman Frank Lehmann. Thanks also to Sheila Nevins and Nancy Abraham at HBO. This is our second film working together as a team; it's wonderful to be reunited.

Thanks to Chris Clifford and Shannon Calabrese of Keppler Speakers, Matthew Jones and Erin Owenby of Leading Authorities, and Clark Forcey for your advice and help over the years. Thanks to Bruce Hoffman for involving me in the scholarly journal *Studies in Conflict and Terrorism.* Thanks to Karen Greenberg, Meena and Liaquat Ahamed, Chris and Holly Fussell, Colonel Joel Rayburn and Clare Lockhart, Henry and Sandra Schuster, Tom Carver and Katty Kay, Gavin and Odile Wilson, Vali and Darya Nasr, Kati Marton, and Gianni Koskinas for your friendship.

My agent, Tina Bennett of WME, is widely and justly regarded as the best nonfiction agent in the business, and I consider myself very lucky to be one of the authors she represents. Also at WME many thanks to Henry Reisch, Svetlana Katz, and Erin Conroy.

In particular I want to thank my mother-in-law, Albertha Mabile, who came to stay with us for six months after our daughter, Grace, was born and was indispensable. My father-in-law, Clebert Mabile, also stayed with us for long stretches and was a great help. So too did my sister-in-laws, Heidi Gould and Daphane Takacs. Thanks to you all. I'm lucky to be part of your family.

At Crown, thanks to the superb team of Molly Stern, Annsley Rosner, Rachel Rokicki, Dyana Messina, Sarah Pekdemir, Matthew Martin, Robert Siek, and Barbara Sturman. Copy editor Jenna Dolan made the book better and more accurate in innumerable small ways. And it's a joy to be working again with Carisa Hays, Crown's wonderful and effective director of publicity.

This book is my third with its formidable editor, Rachel Klayman. Rachel is widely recognized as one of the smartest editors in the country and she gets into the weeds of every aspect of the writing and publishing process, which makes every book she edits immeasurably better. Rachel is also a lot of fun to work with. Rachel brought into this project assistant editor Meghan Houser, who is also brilliant, and Meghan helped a great deal both with the overall conceptualization of the book and with improving pretty much every line in it.

Thanks also to all those who agreed to be interviewed for the book. Some of those interviewed are leading writers, scholars, and practitioners in the counterterrorism field whose work has been influential on mine. Their names can be found in the list on page 364.

Above all, thanks to my wife, Tresha Mabile. Tresha read many early drafts of the manuscript and gave invaluable feedback about what to cut and what to emphasize. She is the most wonderful wife, mother, and work partner, and it is to her and to our daughter, Grace, that this book is dedicated. (I apologize for all the missed weekends and vacations and promise to make it up to you both.) Tresha had the good idea of also dedicating the book to my mother, Sarah, who died just as this book was being finished. It is a great regret that she didn't get the chance to read this book, as she was the most stalwart and enthusiastic supporter of the work I have done that a son could imagine. We all miss her very much every day.

INDEX

ABOUT THE AUTHOR

Peter Bergen is vice president at New America in Washington, DC, as well as national security analyst for CNN, where he writes a weekly online column. He is also a professor and codirector of the Center on the Future of War at Arizona State University and has held teaching positions at the Kennedy School of Government at Harvard University and at the School of Advanced International Studies at Johns Hopkins University.

Bergen is the author of four previous books about terrorism, including three *New York Times* bestsellers and three *Washington Post* nonfiction books of the year. His books have been translated into twenty languages and made into four documentaries, and his writing has appeared in the *New York Times*, the *Washington Post*, the *Wall Street Journal*, *The Atlantic*, *Rolling Stone*, *Time*, *Foreign Affairs*, *Vanity Fair*, and elsewhere. In 1997, as a producer for CNN, Bergen produced Osama bin Laden's first television interview, in which bin Laden declared war against the United States for the first time to a Western audience.

He lives in Washington, DC, with his wife, documentary producer Tresha Mabile, and children, Pierre and Grace.